Credit Derivatives

For other titles in the Wiley Finance Series
please see www.wiley.com/finance

Credit Derivatives

Risk Management, Trading & Investing

Geoff Chaplin MA, DPhil, FFA

John Wiley & Sons, Ltd

Other Wiley Editorial Offices

John Wiley & Sons Inc., 111 River Street, Hoboken, NJ 07030, USA

Jossey-Bass, 989 Market Street, San Francisco, CA 94103-1741, USA

Wiley-VCH Verlag GmbH, Boschstr. 12, D-69469 Weinheim, Germany

John Wiley & Sons Australia Ltd, 33 Park Road, Milton, Queensland 4064, Australia

John Wiley & Sons (Asia) Pte Ltd, 2 Clementi Loop #02-01, Jin Xing Distripark, Singapore 129809

John Wiley & Sons Canada Ltd, 22 Worcester Road, Etobicoke, Ontario, Canada M9W 1L1

Wiley also publishes its books in a variety of electronic formats. Some content that appears
in print may not be available in electronic books.

Library of Congress Cataloging-in-Publication Data

Chaplin, Geoff.
    Credit derivatives : risk management, trading & investing / Geoff Chaplin.
        p.   cm. — (Wiley finance series)
    Includes bibliographical references and index.
    ISBN 13 978-0-470-02416-4 (cloth : alk. paper)
    ISBN 10 0-470-02416-X (cloth : alk. paper)
    1. Credit derivatives.   2. Risk management.   I. Title.   II. Series.
    HG6024.A3C4846 2005
    332.63′2—dc22   2005005801

British Library Cataloguing in Publication Data

A catalogue record for this book is available from the British Library

ISBN 10: 0-470-02416-X (HB)
ISBN 13: 978-0-470-02416-4 (HB)

Typeset in 10/12pt Times by TechBooks, New Delhi, India
Printed and bound in Great Britain by Antony Rowe Ltd, Chippenham, Wiltshire
This book is printed on acid-free paper responsibly manufactured from sustainable forestry
in which at least two trees are planted for each one used for paper production.

To: my parents, my partner and my children

Contents

Preface

This book arose out of several courses and training sessions given to finance professionals. Those courses, and this book, are intended for traders in the credit and other derivatives markets, quants wishing to develop some product knowledge in this area, risk managers and corporate treasurers, as well as investors and others requiring both product knowledge and a grasp of valuation and risk. The aim is to develop an understanding of the various credit derivative products. In order to achieve this it is necessary for the reader to have a certain amount of financial background – and a certain level of maturity when it comes to understanding structured products and the management of a portfolio of risks. I have tried to cover key credit background in Part I of the book. Readers with experience in this area can skip through most of the topics covered there – though generally the role of repo, and the difference between asset swap spreads and z-spreads, do not appear to be well understood, and the reader is advised to study these sections at least. Other areas that may be unfamiliar are the calibration of transition matrices to market data (spreads and volatilities), and the generation of correlated spread moves using the Normal 'Copula'.

The most common credit derivative product is the credit default swap (CDS), and this is covered along with other 'single name' credit derivatives in Part II. A relatively simple 'deterministic' pricing model is described, together with a general stochastic model, in section 9.4. A model is little use without data, and various data-related issues are discussed, together with detailed analysis of model shortcomings, potential improvements, and the setting of reserves. Chapters 10 to 12 analyse a variety of trades: credit curve trades, cross-currency hedges, spread and event risk, valuation and unwind of default swap positions, and a detailed breakdown of the basis between CDS premia and bond spreads. Non-vanilla default swaps, options, and total return swaps are also covered in Part II. Chapter 17 draws together many of the aspects of valuation, risk calculation and hedging with a discussion of book management applied to the single name credit risk book. Finally we end this section with a look at pricing single name default swaps via default time simulation. This introduces some of the techniques used in analysing portfolio products in the relatively simple context of default swaps.

Part III looks at nth-to-default products and CDOs. The latter form a very extensive topic in their own right: I have given a descriptive analysis of many of the different types of CDO structure, and product applications though, when it comes to using the pricing model, we concentrate on synthetic static CDOs (including standard CDO products such as iTraxx). Nevertheless the model described is appropriate to both the standardised products and the more complex waterfall structures seen in some cashflow CDOs. Examples are given to develop an intuitive understanding of the correlated 'default time' modelling approach, and of default time correlation. This part quotes valuation results extensively to illustrate important points. In addition software provided allows the user to reproduce quoted results and to experiment with different portfolios, structures and situations to learn more about both the product and the consequences of the modelling approach. Product risks and model deficiencies are discussed in detail, as is the question of reserves. A section is devoted to the correlation matrix. The preferred interpretation of the model is as an 'interpolation rule', driven by market prices – giving rise to 'implied correlation' – and then applied to non-traded products. Implied ('compound') correlation and 'base' correlations are covered here. Alternative Copulae are discussed and applied. This part concludes with a discussion of the management of a portfolio of 'correlation' products, and of high- and low-risk hedging techniques.

We revisit the topic of 'single' name credit default swaps in Part IV where we take account of counterparty risk. In addition, the topic of protection on counterparties is briefly covered.

In writing the book I have been conscious that CDO products, and methods of analysis, have been developing rapidly. Although the book is illustrated using some of these products, their precise form has changed in the past and will continue to change in the future. I have not been able to cover all aspects of credit derivatives – neither equity default swaps nor constant maturity default swaps have been discussed, and some model approaches have not been covered (for example, 'claim of market value' models and 'blended correlation'). I have chosen to concentrate on core products, general principles and features that are likely to continue to apply in the future. Nevertheless the book reflects the situation at the time of writing (late 2004): products, methodologies and interpretations will evolve.

Throughout this the book I have tried to illustrate ideas and principles using real world examples. In addition there are a variety of thought experiments and exercises to encourage the reader to test theories against real life, and to develop a deeper understanding of the various concepts through their application. A prerequisite to effective application and management of credit derivative positions is an understanding of the products, and an ability to discuss those products in a meaningful way. This book is intended to help in this process and is therefore not aimed solely at the trader, or the risk manager, or the investor, but is intended to be read by all. Consequently I have tried to separate the mathematics from product discussion and application. Of course a good understanding of one cannot be achieved without some understanding of the other. To this end I have used as simple a version of the theory as possible, yet one which is capable of capturing the key aspects of the problem. Generally simplifications amount to ignoring the details of premium payment (frequency and day-count conventions) and often using a constant hazard rate curve. I have also given many calculated results to illustrate points arising out of the theory, and provided software to allow the reader to examine further implications of the model.

Acknowledgements

It would not have been possible to write this book without the assistance and cooperation of many people and firms. In particular I would like to thank ABN AMRO, Bear Stearns, JPMorgan, Mizuho International and Morgan Stanley for access to research material, use of some of their material and other help. I would also like to thank several other institutions who have provided material and assistance – Bloomberg, the British Bankers' Association, the International Index Company, the International Swaps and Derivatives Association, Lombard Risk, Mark-it Partners, Mathsoft and Moody's Investors Service.

Many individuals have contributed to this book either directly or through my work or academic discussions. My thanks go to Richard Flavell who reviewed a plan and initial draft of some material for the book and made some very constructive and useful suggestions regarding the overall layout. I would also like to thank Phil Hunt, who was influential a few years ago in developing my understanding of some technical aspects, and also Charles Anderson for innumerable conversations on practical and risk issues. In addition, I specifically wish to thank Lee McGinty (JPMorgan) and Christopher Finger (RiskMetrics Group) for assistance and conversations over several points. Other practitioners and academics have contributed helpful advice, comments or useful discussions, in particular: Jim Aspinwall, Guillaume Blacher (BoA), Phelim Boyle (University of Waterloo), Declan Fitzmaurice (Nomura Securities), Con Keating, David Li (Salomon Smith Barney), Gerry Salkin (Imperial College London), Solon Saoulis, Darren Sherman (Mizuho International), Darren Smith (DKW), Jonathan Staples (Lombard Odie) and others. Also, several people – in particular Yuichi Katsura, Rafik Mrabat, Solene Sharpe and Maarten Wiersinga – were given the unenviable task of reading a draft of the book and I thank them for their assistance and comments. Finally I owe a deep debt of gratitude to Robert Reoch (Reoch Consulting) both for bringing me into the credit derivatives business and acting as my mentor, and for comments and suggestions on this book.

Any remaining errors are entirely my responsibility, and the views expressed are entirely my own.

Disclaimer and Software Instructions

DISCLAIMER

1. Use of company names in deal examples and illustrations in no way indicates the actual involvement of that company in the example deal or any similar deal. Use of such names is purely for a sense of realism.
2. Software is provided to illustrate certain points in the text only. It is in no way intended for commercial use and, indeed, commercial use of the software, examples, or underlying code in any form is strictly forbidden.

Most examples are in Excel (2002) spreadsheets, some requiring the dll.

A few applications are in Mathcad[1] sheets (and run under Mathcad 11 – an evaluation copy of which is provided). Sometimes the code and the application are in separate sheets. Mathcad users will need to copy these sheets to a single directory and re-establish the reference to the code sheet in the application sheet. For non-Mathcad users the sheets are also copied in rich text format to enable the code to be read.

INSTRUCTIONS FOR THE 'CDO PRICER' AND 'NDB PRICER'

- These spreadsheets require the 'Xlcall32.lib' and the 'bookdemo'xll' to be installed in the directory in which the spreadsheets are run.
- All other Excel applications should be closed down and calculation should be set to manual (with no 'recalculate on save'). Do not subsequently open up any other spreadsheets unless they are also set to manual calculation. Doing so can cause Excel to recalculate the CDO sheet and this will lead to a crash.
- Begin by opening the xll and enabling macros.
- Open the spreadsheet (either CDS or NDB) enabling macros, and go to the 'CDS calibration' sheet. Enter data in the yellow areas only – Name, Currency, Seniority, Notional Size, rating, CDS premium and recovery rate. Hit shift-F9 to recalculate the sheet. Implied default rates and survival probabilities are shown in AN-BF.

---

[1] Mathcad and Mathsoft are registered trademarks of Mathsoft Engineering and Education, Inc., http://www.mathsoft.com.

NDB Pricer

- Enter the NDB sheet.
- Set up the effective date and maturity date in C7 and D7. Enter cell E7 and recalculate that cell only.
- Enter the interest rate in cell F7 (either 0 or 4).
- Enter the number of names in the basket (2 or 3 only) in cell C11. Click the 'setup number of names' button.
- From the CDS calibration sheet copy the first 2 (or 3) names, currency, seniority and spreads and 'paste special/values' into cells B23–E24 (B23–E25).
- Cells C13 to C19 have been disabled.
- Choose the Copula required (cell C20).
  - Normal or Student's: enter a single correlation number in cell F15 and click 'set up parameters'. This creates a 2×2 (3×3) correlation matrix with a single non-trivial correlation. (Alternatively – for 3 names – a correlation matrix can be pasted into cells I23–K24).
  - Student's: enter the degrees of freedom in cell F17.
  - Clayton: enter the Clayton parameter in cell F15.
- Select the number of simulations required in cell B7. (A total of one million simulated defaults can give quite accurate pricing – 500 000 simulations for two names.)
- Click the 'Price'. DO NOT HIT SHIFT-F9.
- Cell E9 will produce identical sequences of random numbers if set to -1, different sequences if set to $+1$.
- Results appear in cells J8–O10 for the first, second (and third) to default.
  - Column J: contingent benefit = expected loss = non-refundable up-front premium (% notional in C18).
  - Column K: the value of a premium stream of 10 000 bp p.a. (% notional).
  - Column L: current fair value premium.
  - Column M: if column I contains the actual deal premium then column M gives the net value of the position (% notional, excluding accrued).
  - Column N: standard deviation of expected loss.
  - Column O: standard deviation of premium.

CDO Pricer

- Enter the CDO sheet.
- Set up the effective date and maturity date in C7 and D7. Enter cell E7 and recalculate that cell only.
- Enter the interest rate in cell F7 (either 0 or 4).
- Enter the number of names in the basket (100 only) in cell C11. Click the 'setup number of names' button.
- From the CDS calibration sheet copy the 100 names, currency, seniority, size and spreads and 'paste special/values' into cells B23–F122.
- Cells C13–C19 have been disabled.
- Choose the Copula required (cell C20).
  - Normal or Student's: enter a single correlation number in cell F15 and click 'set up parameters'. This creates a 100×100 correlation matrix with a single non-trivial correlation. (Alternatively a correlation matrix can be pasted into cells I23–DD122.)

– Student's: enter the degrees of freedom in cell F17.

– Clayton: enter the Clayton parameter in cell F15.

• Select the number of simulations required in cell B7. (A total of one million simulated defaults can give quite accurate pricing [depending on tranche] – 10 000 simulations for 100 names.)

• Define the tranche names and sizes in columns J and K. Choose waterfall 1 for column L. If the tranche premia are known, enter them into column M.

• Click the 'Price'. DO NOT HIT SHIFT-F9.

• Cell E9 will produce identical sequences of random numbers if set to −1, different sequences if set to +1.

• Results appear in cells N8–V17 for the tranches.

– Column N: contingent benefit = expected loss = non-refundable up-front premium (% notional in C18).

– Column O: the value of a premium stream of 10 000 bp p.a. (% notional).

– Column P: current fair value premium. For the equity piece the premium may be a mix of an up-front amount (e.g. 500 bp) – the net value then gives the up-front premium (as a percentage of notional).

– Column Q: if column M contains the actual deal premium then column Q gives the net value of the position (% notional, excluding accrued).

– Column R: standard deviation of new premium.

– If 'write output?' is set to 1 (cell I3) then simulated default times are written to 'C:\CDO intermediate output' (you will need to create this directory manually). This slows down run time.

APPLICATION RESTRICTIONS

The software is intended only to illustrate points made in the text. To restrict its possible commercial application the following limitations are imposed.

1. Only 0 or 4% flat interest rate curves.
2. Only flat hazard rate curves.
3. Only continuous CDS and portfolio product premia.
4. No IMM maturity dates.
5. The basket pricer will only handle two or three name baskets, and the CDO pricer will only handle 100 reference names.
6. The following are disabled:
   (a) Hedge calculations (except for the default event hedge of section 23.2).
   (b) VaR and tranche option calculations.
   (c) Semi-closed form pricing – crude Monte Carlo simulation only is used.

Table of Spreadsheet Examples and Software

Part	Section	Name	Topic	Type
I	2.3	Chapter 2.xls	Basic TM example adjusting for 'NR'	Excel
I	2.4	Chapter 2 and Chapter 15.xls	Use of TM to get spreads; modified TM to fit spreads and volatility	Excel
I	6.2	Chapter 6.xls	Random number to forward rating	Excel
I	6.3	Chapter 6 corr spreads.xls	Correlated forward spreads	Excel
II	8.5	Chapter 8.xls	Potential future exposure calculation	Excel
II	9.2, 9.3	Chapter 9.xls	Recovery modelling; simple CDS and bond calibration and sensitivities	Excel
II	9.1	Chapter 9 and Chapter 19 hedge theory.mcd	CDS, F2D sensitivity code and tests	Mathcad & rtf
II	10.1.1, 10.1.2	Chapter 10.xls	Approx. cross-currency CDS pm calculation; spread hedge calculation	Excel
II	11.5	Chapter 11.xls	Spread, LIBOR and bond yield volatility	Excel
II	12.1, 12.2, 12.3	Chapter 12.xls	Forward CDS; unwind/back-to-back/valn calcn	Excel

Continued

Part	Section	Name	Topic	Type
II	13.5	N2D CDO CLN price and hedge.mcd, and N2D CDO CLN pricing app.mcd	CLN pricing	Mathcad & rtf
II	13.6	Chapter 13.xls	Capital guaranteed note	Excel
II	15.2	Chapter 2 and Chapter 15.xls		Excel
II	15.2	Chapter 15 stochastic hazard rate.mcd	Hazard rate tree	Mathcad & rtf
II	18.2	Chapter 18.xls	Single name default time simulation; simulated correlated default times (two names)	Excel
III	19.3	Chapter 9 and Chapter 19 hedge theory.mcd	First- and second-to-default, zero and 100% correlation	Mathcad & rtf
III		CDO pricer.xls	CDO pricing tool	Excel & DLL
III		N2D pricer.xls	N2D pricing tool	Excel & DLL
III	21.1	Chapter 21.xls	F2D priced using modified TM	Excel
III	21.5	N2D CDO CLN price and hedge.mcd, and N2D CDO CLN pricing app.mcd	Basket, CDO and CLN pricing code and implementation	Mathcad & rtf
III	22.2	Chapter 22.xls	Demo CDO and base correlation	Excel
III	22.2	Chapter 22 charts.xls	Demo CDO and base correlation	Excel
III	Chapter 22	Chapter 22 Normal Copula closed form N2D pricing.mcd	Closed form pricing for correlated baskets	Mathcad
III	23.3	Chapter 23.xls	Correlated default times using the Clayton Copula	Excel
IV	25.1	Chapter 25.mcd	Uncorrelated and counterparty risk	Mathcad & rtf
IV	25.3	N2D CDO CLN price and hedge.mcd	Correlated counterparty risk pricing code (used by 'Chapter 25.mcd')	Mathcad & rtf
		Test data name spreads.xls	Data for Mathcad CDO pricing app	Excel

In addition, an evaluation copy of Mathcad is included.

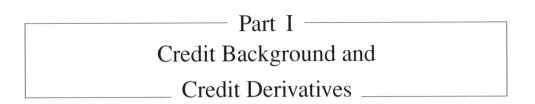

Part I
Credit Background and
Credit Derivatives

1
Credit Debt and Other Traditional Credit Instruments

The reader is assumed to be familiar with government bonds, with the LIBOR market and to have had some familiarity with traditional credit instruments (bonds and loans). The following sections briefly review these areas and develop some techniques for the analysis of credit risk – particularly in relation to credit portfolios.

1.1 BONDS AND LOANS; LIBOR RATES AND SWAPS; 'REPO' AND GENERAL COLLATERAL RATES

1.1.1 Bonds and Loans

A **bond** (Bloomberg definition) is a certificate of debt issued by a government or corporation with the promise to pay back the principal amount as well as interest by a specified future date.

A **loan** is a broader concept than a bond – it is a sum of money lent at interest. In practice bonds are usually traded instruments (at least in principle) whereas loans are usually private agreements between two or more parties (usually a corporate entity and a bank). There is a growing market in **secondary trading** of loans – where the cashflows under the loan agreement are **assigned** (sold) to a third party. For this to be possible the loan agreement has to allow this transfer to take place – such loans are **assignable loans**. Many loans – though this is becoming less common than historically – are non-assignable (the ownership of the cashflows cannot be transferred). Some loans are non-assignable except in default. (We see later that these variations have implications for the credit derivatives market – they potentially restrict the deliverability of some debt into default swap contracts.)

When we speak of a **credit bond** (or loan) we are explicitly recognising the risk that the payments promised by the borrower may not be received by the lender – an event we refer to as **default** (we discuss this further below).

1.1.2 BBA LIBOR and Swaps

According to the British Bankers' Association 'LIBOR stands for the London Interbank Offered Rate and is the rate of interest at which banks borrow funds from other banks, in marketable size, in the London interbank market'. BBA LIBOR rates are quoted for a number of currencies and terms up to one year, and are derived from rates contributed by at least eight banks active in the London market. (See http://www.bba.org.uk for more information.) LIBOR rates clearly refer to risky transactions – the lending of capital by one bank to another – albeit of low risk because of the short-term nature of the deal and also the high quality of the banks contributing to the survey.

An **interest rate swap** contract (Bloomberg) is 'a contract in which two parties agree to exchange periodic interest payments, especially when one payment is at a fixed rate and the other varies according to the performance of a reference rate, such as the prime rate'.

Typically, interest rate swaps are for periods of more than a year, and usually the reference rate is LIBOR. The swap itself is a risky deal although on day one the value of the fixed flows equals the value of the floating payments, so the risk is initially zero. Risk emerges as interest rate levels change, affecting the value of the floating and fixed payments differently. (Expected risk at a forward date will not be zero if the interest rate curve is not flat, though it will typically be small in relation to the value of one of the legs of the swap.) Swaps are low risk, although **swap rates themselves are risky rates largely because the reference floating rate (LIBOR) is a risky rate**.

1.1.3   Collateralised Lending and Repo

Banks often use listed securities as **collateral** (assets pledged as security) against cash they borrow to meet other needs. Such lending (of securities) and borrowing (of cash) is referred to as collateralised borrowing and the rate of interest applicable to generic collateral is the **general collateral (GC) rate**. Typically such collateralised lending agreements are for short terms (they may be on a rolling overnight basis) and the GC rate itself is usually a few (2–7) basis points below LIBOR rates.

The reader should note several things at this point.

1. Any structured product created by a bank can in principle be securitised and used as collateral to obtain the cash required to finance the transaction. General collateral rates are therefore key in determining the cost of any structured deal (including credit derivatives).
2. GC rates are not readily available – they are known by the repo trading desk but not made publicly available. Some US repo rates are published on Reuters. The European Banking Federation sponsors the publication of EUREPO, a set of GC repo rates relating to European government bonds. However LIBOR rates are very easy to obtain and are also close to GC.
3. Investment banks typically mark their positions to market by discounting off the LIBOR and swap curve (because LIBOR is the financing cost, and for arbitrage reasons – see, for example, Chapter 9).

LIBOR (and swap) rates are therefore essential to the development of the pricing of credit derivatives.

We shall look at the deal underlying collateralised lending (a 'repo') in detail since an understanding of it is required later. A **repo** or **repurchase agreement** is a contract giving the seller of an asset the right, and the obligation, to buy it back at a predetermined price on a predetermined date. The borrower of cash ('lender' of the asset) sells the asset to a counterparty under the repo contract and receives cash (equal to the market value of the asset[1]). Prior to termination of the deal, any cashflows generated by the asset are passed on to the original owner of the asset, and the borrower of cash pays interest at a rate specific to that asset – the **repo rate**. On the termination of the deal the borrower of cash repays the loan and receives the asset back. In the event of default of the asset, the end date of the repo would be accelerated – the asset passes back to the original owner and the debt is repaid. See Figures 1.1–1.3.

We can see that, although legal ownership of the asset passes from the original owner, **economic ownership** remains with the original owner (i.e. the original owner of the asset receives all the cashflows from the asset in any eventuality as if he owned that asset).

---

[1] Poor quality collateral may be subject to a 'haircut' where the cash lent is less than the current market value – usually by 5% or so.

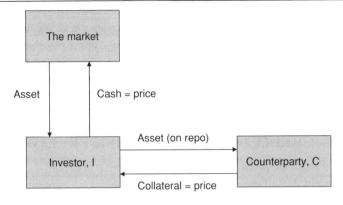

Figure 1.1   Repo deal – initial, ongoing and final flows

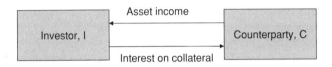

Figure 1.2   Repo deal – ongoing cashflows

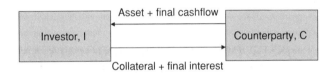

Figure 1.3   Repo deal – final capital and asset flows

Typically repo deals are short term – from overnight to a few months.

GC rates are tiered according to the class of asset. There are different GC rates for government bonds depending on the country of issue; GC rates for corporate bonds are determined by the rating. However a particular asset – for example, a certain bond – may go **special** on repo. An institution may need to borrow a particular asset (for example, it may have sold the asset short) and may be prepared to 'pay' in order to receive that asset. Under the repo deal the institution pledges (lends) cash against the asset it borrows and, if the asset were not special, would receive interest at the GC rate. But if the asset goes special the repo rate for that asset falls *below* the GC rate – and may fall to zero or even become negative. ('Special' repo rates have an impact on the basis between bonds and default swaps (Part II).) The borrower of the bond lends cash and therefore receives a sub-LIBOR return on that cash.

1.1.4   Repo as a Credit Derivative

A repo is not traditionally regarded as a credit derivative even if the collateral is a credit risky asset, although it is almost identical to a 'Total Return Swap' (Part II) which *is* usually classed as a credit derivative. Furthermore, there is a significant and complex embedded credit risk if there is a correlation between the borrower of cash and the reference entity of the collateral (see Parts III and IV). A default of the borrower may cause a sudden drop in the value of the collateral in this case, so the lender of cash is taking on a non-trivial credit derivative risk. A similar risk exists in default swap contracts where the counterparty and the reference entity are correlated: indeed we can view a repo as an outright purchase of the collateral with a forward sale back to the original owner, plus a purchase of default protection on the reference entity from the borrower of cash. The question of the embedded counterparty credit risk is analysed in detail in Parts III and IV.

1.2   CREDIT DEBT VERSUS 'RISK-FREE' DEBT

We often talk of a **risk-free bond** – one where there is no risk of default – and usually identify this with government debt of certain countries issued in their own currency.[2] The yield curve associated with government debt is then often called the **risk-free curve**. This identification is in the first instance only approximate – any government can default on its own debt. The risk may be remote but it still exists in principle. The second problem with the identification of risk-free rates with the government curve is that trading in government debt is only a part of debt trading and special factors – such as a heavy issuance programme, a buy-back programme, or regulatory requirements on banks (for example) to hold government debt – can distort the price of government debt and separate the government yield curve from 'underlying' risk-free rates.

We shall see later (Part II) that, whatever 'risk-free' rates may be, they are irrelevant to the pricing of credit derivatives.

1.3   ISSUE DOCUMENTS, SENIORITY AND THE RECOVERY PROCESS

1.3.1   Issue Documents and Default

A bond is subject to a legally binding document (the 'issue document') which is usually substantial (100 pages or so) and describes the parties involved in the issue of the bond, the borrower, legal jurisdiction, etc., together with payment information such as the cashflow dates and amounts. Loans are subject to corresponding loan documentation.

One item defined in the documentation is the **grace period** or the number of **days of grace** for the bond cashflows. If a scheduled payment is not made on the due date, this does not constitute default – the borrower is allowed a period of time in which to make the payment. This is intended to cover administrative errors and omissions, and other events which might make payment impossible in the very short term.

The documentation also specifically covers what constitutes default, and what recourse the lender has in the event of a default event.

Typically **default** is defined as failure to pay a significant promised cashflow. Generally it is not just failure to pay a cashflow on that bond which causes default – failure of the borrowing entity to pay any significant loan cashflow usually triggers default on all bonds and loans issued by that entity (i.e. a **cross-default clause** usually applies).

---

[2] In contrast, debt issued by a country in a currency other than its own is typically identified as credit debt, e.g. Brazilian debt in US dollars.

1.3.2   Claim Amount

In the event of default the lender usually has the right to claim a sum of money from the borrower, and this sum of money is usually par plus accrued coupon up to the date of default. The amount that the lender can claim from the borrower is referred to as the **claim amount** or **claim value**, and in the above example the claim amount is 'par plus accrued' (usually this is just known as 'par' – the accrued is implicit).

The claim amount is a key element in the valuation of credit derivatives (including bonds) so we shall introduce some notation and capture the above in a formula. If we define $C(t)$ to be the claim amount at time t, then the above paragraph tells us that

$$C(t) = 1 + A(t) \tag{1.1}$$

where $A(t)$ is the accrued on the bond at time t. (We shall work in par amounts of 1 rather than 100 or 1000.)

Variations in the claim amount occur. For example, deep discount debt may have a claim amount that rises from the issue price to par at maturity, according to some formula or printed schedule. This is not necessarily the case – for example, convertible bonds usually have a low coupon but have a claim amount of par.

Some issue documents (usually only a few loan documents) say that the borrower can claim the promised cashflows in the event of default. Thus the future cashflows are not replaced by a single immediately payable sum. However, at the default date we can value these cashflows to get a financially equivalent amount. We refer to such a claim amount as 'treasury', meaning it is financially equivalent to the value of a series of bond cashflows.

An alternative claim model is sometimes useful for risk calculations (particularly for sovereign debt – see below) so we show the formula for this case and make a few further comments. It is notationally easier to work in continuous time[3] but in this case we shall show the formula both in continuous and discrete time. Of course, the continuous time formula can be made to reproduce the discrete time formula by giving the continuous cashflows a certain functional form (a sum of 'Dirac delta functions'[4]).

First, the continuous time version: let $c(t)$ be the rate of cashflow promised under the bond at time t for $t < T$ the bond maturity, and let $d(t)$ be the discount factor for a payment at time t.[5] Then the claim amount is given by

$$C(t) = \int_t^T c(x) \cdot d(x) \, dx \tag{1.2a}$$

Second, in the discrete time case let the cashflow at time t_i be c_i, where i is a counter over the payment dates. For a bond these cashflows are just the coupon payments at an ordinary coupon date, and the coupon payment plus maturity amount at the maturity date. Then we can express the claim amount as

$$C(t) = \sum_{i=1}^n c_i \cdot d(t_i) \tag{1.2b}$$

---

[3] Another reason we prefer a continuous time approach is that default can occur at any time – over a weekend, or overnight – so a continuous time model of the default event process seems more natural.

[4] A Dirac delta function is such that $\delta(x) = 0$ except at $x = X$, and $\int_{-\varepsilon}^{\varepsilon} \delta(x) \, dx = 1$. See, for example, Hoskins (1999).

[5] We understand that we are making a valuation 'now', at time $t = 0$. We could make the formulae more general (but unnecessarily so for our purposes at the moment) by making 'now' a variable too, which would allow us to write down a formula for forward claim amounts. This is necessary in an implementation of the above model for bond and CDS pricing, and is left as an exercise for the reader.

where n is the number of cashflows. In the typical case – claim amount of par (plus accrued) – on the default event all debt becomes an immediately due cash amount. Thus a bond with a one-year outstanding life and a bond with a 30-year outstanding life will both have exactly the same market value after default (assuming zero accrued for simplicity) – both have the same claim value (par), which is due immediately.

1.3.3   The Recovery Process and Recovery Amount

The issue document also covers the question of how a claim on one bond relates to claims on other debt. This is a complicated issue involving the law – usually requiring back taxes to be settled before anything else, and employees to get back pay before banks get repayment of debt, etc. Settlement of claims on debt will be described in the issue document which will usually (in the case of corporate and bank borrowers) refer to the **seniority** of debt, and the order in which different seniorities are to be recompensed. Some debt may be *secured on a specific asset* – for example, a property. In the event of default, settlement on this specific asset is related to the amount that the specific asset realises on sale. Typically, debt is generally secured on residual assets of the firm. Terminology varies, but debt commonly found in the market and in bank portfolios normally falls into one of three further levels of seniority: **loans**, **senior** secured, and **subordinated** (or **junior**) debt. It is often the case that 'loans' differ from bonds in that they are usually more senior, in addition to other points discussed in section 1.1.1.

Once a corporate entity defaults, the administrators of the company seek to realise maximum value from the assets of the company. When the value of these assets is realised then the cash is used in the prescribed order until it is used up. If cash is available after paying (in full) the most senior creditors (such as tax, accountant's fees, back pay, etc., and debt secured on specific assets) then claims on loans become the most senior debt. If this can be met in full, then the remaining cash is applied to senior unsecured bonds and, if these can be repaid in full, it moves on to junior debt. If, at any point, cash is insufficient to cover the claims of that seniority in full, then all claims receive the same proportion (the **recovery rate**) of the claim amount. The cash is then used up. Thus, in a corporate default where the cash is insufficient to cover all the claims, one seniority level will receive a partial recovery; more senior levels of debt receive 100% of the claim amount, and more junior levels receive zero. Any deviation from the legal framework and the legally binding issue documents can be challenged in the courts by the creditors.

Since these concepts will be used repeatedly, we shall summarise the above in a formula. Let s denote the seniority level we are looking at, where $s = 0$ denotes junior (subordinated) debt, $s = 1$ is senior bonds, $s = 2$ is loans. (We can, of course, introduce more seniority levels as appropriate, but these three are generally all that is required in practice.) Then the amount recovered is

$$R_s \cdot C(t) \qquad (1.3)$$

where

$$1 \geq R_2 \geq R_1 \geq R_0 \geq 0, \qquad (1.4a)$$

and if $1 > R_s > 0$ for some s, we have

$$R_p = 1 \text{ for } p > s \quad \text{and} \quad R_p = 0 \text{ for } p < s \qquad (1.4b)$$

(i.e. more senior debt gets full recovery and more junior debt gets zero recovery).

We state here that condition (1.4b) only applies when we are looking at the actual amounts finally recovered ('ultimate recovery – see Chapter 2). Recovery as applicable to credit derivative products is a different concept from the above (being the one-month post-default bond price) and conditions (1.4b) no longer apply – although (1.4a) remains: see Chapter 2 for further details.

The amount $1 - R_s$ is often referred to as the **loss given default** (LGD).

We shall address the question of how we estimate R prior to the default event in the following section. At present formula (1.3) and the following conditions apply to a specific defaulted entity – the recovery numbers for that entity are not the same as the recovery numbers for another entity.

1.3.4 Sovereign versus Corporate Debt

Issue documents for **sovereign debt** (e.g. Argentinean debt in USD) are very similar to those of corporates. Typically the claim amount is also par. Usually there is only one level of seniority for sovereigns. The major difference between corporate and risky government debt is in the recovery process itself. Firstly, there is no 'wind up' process via the courts as in the case of corporates. A 'defaulting' sovereign typically restructures its debt and investors lose value compared with their promised cashflows. The government may offer terms that are very different from the recovery levels one might expect from the issue document – typically long-dated debt recovers a smaller proportional of notional than short-dated debt. However, the lenders have no court to which they can go to seek a strict implementation of the process described in the issue document. In practice this means that recovery for sovereign debt is not at the same rate for all bonds[6] – instead it is typically high for short-dated debt and low for long-dated debt.

1.4   VALUATION, YIELD AND SPREAD

Bonds are bought and sold on the basis of a price. Often the price quoted is a clean price, and the consideration paid also takes into account the accrued interest. Given the market price of the debt, and the cashflow schedule, we can calculate the yield (internal rate of return) and the '**spread**'. There are various ways of measuring spread (see Chapter 5 for further discussion), but for the moment we shall define spread as the difference between the bond's yield and the interpolated yield off the LIBOR/swap curve (interpolated to the maturity date of the bond).

High-grade debt may trade close to swap rates – even sub-LIBOR for very high-grade borrowers which are perceived to be less risky than the banks that define the LIBOR rate. Typically **investment grade debt** (debt rated BBB or better by the rating agencies) trades up to 300 bp over the swap curve depending on the name and varying with time and the economic cycle, sentiment, etc. Sub-investment grade debt typically trades wider – to 10 000 bp or 100 000 bp above the swap curve.

For investment grade names the market will usually talk in terms of spread rather than price. The reason for this is that the price of a 5-year Unilever bond (for example) will change moment by moment as interest rate futures tick up or down. However, the spread on the

---

[6] There are often other complications such as 'Brady Bonds' where some of the cashflows (e.g. maturity amount) will be received in full (because they are guaranteed by the US government) while other cashflows (coupons) will not be received.

bond typically changes much more slowly and may even be static for continuous days or weeks.

For sub-investment grade debt the market usually talks in terms of price. Where spreads are high (and bond prices may be 50% below those of low-risk debt) the main determinant of price is the perceived default risk, not interest rate levels.

1.5 BUYING RISK

A buyer of a credit bond is taking on the default risk of the underlying entity – the investor is not only buying an asset but also **buying risk**. Imagine an insurance policy which insures the par value of the bond in the event of default of the underlying name. The buyer of the insurance policy is the **buyer of protection**, and the writer of the policy is the seller of protection. We can also talk in terms of risk – the seller of protection is taking on risk, similar to the buyer of the bond itself, while the buyer of protection is also the seller of risk.

In the credit derivative market both sets of terminology are used – buyer or seller of protection or of risk. The word 'buyer' on its own conveys nothing – the buyer of protection is the seller of risk and vice versa. It is essential to be clear whether one is talking about risk or protection. Often 'selling' means selling protection when talking about single name default swaps, but selling a tranche of a CDO usually means buying protection.

In this book we shall generally talk in terms of buying or selling protection when we refer to credit derivatives.

1.6 MARKING TO MARKET, MARKING TO MODEL AND RESERVES

When it is required to value a deal – whether for the purpose of calculating profit to date, for accounting, or for regulatory or other reasons – the best approach in principle is to obtain a bid for the asset held. This is easy for liquid bonds for example, and is called **marking to market**.

For many other assets – such as credit derivatives, structured products and many option contracts – this is not always practical. For example, consider a portfolio of equity call options of various maturities and strikes. Typically some maturities and strikes on each name trade sufficiently frequently that market prices for these maturities and strikes are easily available. We can obtain these prices and interpolate for other maturities and strikes on the same underlying asset. Usually this interpolation uses a pricing model – such as the Black–Scholes model – and an intermediate variable (volatility) is obtained. Interpolation on this variable is performed (perhaps involving a further model such as a volatility smile model) and the interpolated variable put back into the model in order to get an estimated market price for the asset. This is referred to as **marking to model**.

Reserves

Reserves are set against the value for products marked to model to give rise to a 'conservative' valuation of the portfolio in the institutions' accounts. Even when products are marked to market they may be marked to mid: in this case a 'bid–offer' reserve will usually be held against the value to reflect the realisation value achievable on an asset.

Example 1

Suppose we mark to mid (and mid-prices are easily available). Suppose we are long a unit of Asset 1, mark it to mid-price P_1, and S_1 is the estimate of (half) the offer–bid difference. Then the value in the books would appear as $P_1 - S_1$.

Exercises

1. If we sell Asset 1 to a market-maker, how many trades does the market maker do?

   Hint: The answer is 2.

2. Suppose we are long Asset 1 above and short Asset 2, which is a very good hedge for all the risks in Asset 1. Should we mark to $P_1 - S_1 - P_2 + S_2$?

3. If we sell the hedged position in exercise 2 to a market-maker, how many trades does the market-maker do?

   Hint: The answer is 1.

Generally if we have a hedged 'trade' (made up of several 'deals' – Asset 1 and Asset 2 in the above) the costs and the risks to the market-maker of taking on the position are less, so the bid–offer spread on the trade will be tighter than on a single unhedged asset. The trade in exercise 2 would generally be marked to a better overall price than the unhedged asset. Similar arguments apply to other reserves mentioned below and later in the book.

If deals are marked to model there are uncertainties involved in arriving at the mid-price. In the equity option example above uncertainties arise from

(i) The interpolation routine to interpolate for the maturity and the strike of the actual option held.

(ii) The uncertainty in the validity and accuracy of the model being used (other traders may use a different model). (This is not really an issue for the equity option example but might apply if we were pricing exotic options.)

Marking to model generally gives rise to additional reserves. These will depend on the product and model being used and there may also be a general 'model reserve'. We shall discuss these in the context of credit derivatives products in Parts II and III.

Traders' P&L

Reserves may also apply to the calculation of traders' P&L – though not necessarily the same figures. The institution may take a cautious view of its books for a variety of reasons. On the other hand, reserves may be set against traders' P&L in order to avoid a situation where a trader can take a large mark-to-market profit (and bonus) on day 1 then, subsequently, the deal turns out to be worth far less than anticipated.

Reserves have little impact on a portfolio with high turnover: a deal done on day 1 with high reserves, and take off on day 2 will release the reserves and the actual profit calculation can be based on the buy and sell prices. Typically a high turnover portfolio faces low reserves anyway. The case where reserves tend to be high is a buy-and-hold book. Faced with a certain level of reserves the trader may take the view that putting a deal on the level of reserves against that position may eat too far into the P&L accumulated so far, and the deal will not be done.

Another problem in setting reserves is that some sort of approximation is made. This may imply that the reserves are low on one version of the trade and high on another, with the result that the trader deals only on one type of trade (where the reserves are too low).

Institutions take a variety of views regarding traders' P&L: at one extreme the trader's and the institution's reserves are the same; at the other extreme the trader may face an estimated bid–offer reserve only, and the institution takes the risk on other valuation estimates (and on the trader).

2
Default and Recovery Data; Transition Matrices; Historical Pricing

2.1 RECOVERY: ULTIMATE AND MARKET VALUE BASED RECOVERY

2.1.1 Ultimate Recovery

In Chapter 1 we discussed recovery in the context of bonds and corporate default. The recovery described was that obtained on the ultimate wind-up of the company and distribution of residual assets. This is referred to as **ultimate recovery**.

Ultimate recovery occurs after the default event has taken place, after accountants have been appointed to wind up the company, and after assets have been sold. This process clearly takes a considerable amount of time. Table 2.1 shows how long this takes (for US defaults) and how much it varies, and Table 2.2 shows the mean and the standard deviation of ultimate recovery rates.

It should be noted that the standard deviation of recovery is very high. If we suppose that recovery is equally likely to have any value between 0 and 100% (a uniform distribution[1]), then the expected recovery level is 50% and the standard deviation will be about 29%. The observed historical average recovery rate (for senior unsecured notes) actually happens to be very close to that of a uniform distribution, but the standard deviation is even higher. Thus, suppose we have a large portfolio of debt, and suppose that 100 of these names default. Then based on historical ultimate recoveries we would expect to get a recovery of around 50% on average for the 100 names but, if we were to pick one of these names at random, then its recovery would more likely be closer to 0 or 100% than to the average of 50%.

The historical data gives only very coarse information about the likely recovery level on any one specific company. Of course defaults are very rare compared with the number of firms in existence. The historical default information we have gives only a very rough idea of what the recovery level for a particular firm might be. We shall see some more information in the following sections but, even then, we will find that we cannot make a very good guess at the recovery level for a particular firm and seniority of debt. This will be seen to have quite significant implications for the valuation and risk management of credit derivatives.

Who is Interested in Ultimate Recovery Data?

The manager of a book of non-assignable loans has a portfolio of buy-and-hold assets. If a name suffers a credit event then the manager has to follow the wind-up process up to ultimate recovery. Funds that invest in distressed or defaulted debt (**vulture funds**) are also interested in ultimate recovery.

---

[1] See any standard text on probability and statistics: e.g. Billingsley (1995).

Table 2.1 Length of time in bankruptcy (years)

Type	Count	Average	Median	Mini-mum	Maxi-mum	Standard deviation
Ch. 11	116	1.68	1.43	0.19	7.01	1.20
Prepackaged Ch. 11	53	0.29	0.18	0.09	1.76	0.29
All	159	1.30	1.15	0.09	7.01	1.20

Table 2.2 Ultimate recovery rates

	Observations	Expected recovery	Standard deviation
Senior Bank Debt	750	78.8%	29.7%
Senior Secured Notes	222	65.1%	32.4%
Senior Unsecured Notes	419	46.4%	36.3%
Senior Subordinated Notes	350	31.6%	32.6%
Subordinated Notes	343	29.4%	34.1%

Source: Altman *et al.* (2003)

2.1.2 Market Recovery

The rating agencies have another definition of recovery: the price of traded debt in the marketplace one month after the 'default' event. This is clearly a very different concept from that of ultimate recovery. We shall refer to this definition of recovery as **market recovery** or 'one month post-default recovery' or simply 'recovery'.

Data for market recovery will clearly differ from ultimate recovery – because they are different concepts (distribution amount versus market price of debt) and because the data refers to very different times in the company's wind-up process. The rating agencies also use a definition of the default event which is broader than that which causes a wind-up of the company. For example 'bankruptcy' constitutes default as far as the rating agencies are concerned, yet does not necessarily lead to a wind-up of the company. Failure to pay the coupon or maturity amount (perhaps because of an administrative error) is a default event in the rating agencies' eyes, but may not lead to a default event as far as bonds are concerned (payment may be made within the grace period). Thus data on ultimate and market recovery is based on non-identical sets of events.

Compared with ultimate recovery, market recovery data shows relationships of recoveries on different seniorities of debt. Ultimate recovery data will show only (at most) one seniority with a recovery different from 0 or 1. However, market prices of defaulted debt are estimates of what ultimate recovery rates will be. Instead of inequality (1.4a) subject to condition (1.4b), we find that (for a specific firm) higher seniorities have higher recoveries. In other words

$$1 \geq R_2 \geq R_1 \geq R_0 \geq 0 \tag{2.1}$$

is all we find. For example post-defaulted (assignable) loans might be trading at 80, bonds at 50 and junior debt at 20, while ultimate recovery might turn out to be 100, 65 and 0 respectively.

Table 2.3 shows market recovery rates for several seniorities of debt. Note that the standard deviation in market recovery rates is less than that of ultimate recovery data – and very substantially less for junior debt.

Table 2.3 Market recovery rates and seniority: Mean recovery rates on defaulted instruments by priority in capital, 1982–2003

Defaulted instrument	Value Weighted			Issuer Weighted		
	2003	2002	1982–2003	2003	2002	1982–2003
Baank loans						
Senior Secured	76.0	63.1	59.3	64.6	65.9	65.1
Senior Secured	80.0	99.1	41.3	80.0	99.0	44.7
All Bonds	39.7	31.7	33.8	40.2	36.7	35.4
Equipments Trust	NA	36.7	61.0	NA	32.5	62.1
Sr. Secured	54.1	56.8	50.3	60.3	49.8	51.6
Sr. Unsecured	44.4	30.9	32.9	41.2	31.9	36.1
Sr. Subordinated	29.2	20.7	29.0	36.6	25.3	32.5
Subordinated	12.0	29.0	27.1	12.3	27.9	31.1
Jr. Subordinated	39.7	NA	22.9	40.4	NA	24.5
Preferred Stock	1.1	31.7	6.5	1.1	9.0	15.3
All Instruments	39.8	31.7	31.9	39.4	35.0	33.9

2.1.3 Recovery Rates and Industry Sector

Altman and Kishore (1996) have produced research showing that recovery rates depend not only on seniority but there is also a significant industry-related effect. For example utilities tend to have very high recovery rates whereas telecoms tend to be low. Table 2.4 is an extract of some of the recent results found by Moody's.

Table 2.4 Recovery and industry: Average recovery rates by industry category

Industry	Issuer weighted mean recovery rate		
	2003	2002	1982–2003
Utility-Gas	48.0	54.6	51.5
Oil and Oil Services		44.1	44.5
Hospitality	64.5	60.0	42.5
Utility-Electric	5.3	39.8	41.4
Transport-Ocean	76.8	31.0	38.8
Media, Broadcasting and Cable	57.5	39.5	38.2
Transport-Surface		37.9	36.6
Finance and Banking	18.8	25.6	36.3
Industrial	33.4	34.3	35.4
Retail	57.9	58.2	34.4
Transport – Air	22.6	24.9	34.3
Automotive	39.0	39.5	33.4
Healthcare	52.2	47.0	32.7
Consumer Goods	54.0	22.8	32.5
Construction	22.5	23.0	31.9
Technology	9.4	36.7	29.5
Real Estate		5.0	28.8

Continued

Table 2.4 *Continued*

Industry	Issuer weighted mean recovery rate		
	2003	2002	1982-2003
Steel	31.8	28.5	27.4
Telecommunications	45.9	21.4	23.2
Miscellaneous	69.5	46.5	39.5

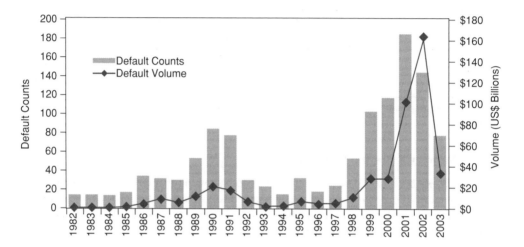

Figure 2.1 Default rates over time: Global corporate bond default counts and dollar volumes, 1983–2003

2.1.4 Recovery and Default Rates and the Economic Cycle

We would expect default rates to rise during recessions: there is also evidence that recovery rates drop during the lows of the economic cycle. Figures 2.1 and 2.2 show the history of default rates and average recovery rates on bonds and its relationship to the economic cycle.

2.1.5 Modelling Recovery Rates

Historical market recovery data shows the following features, which are potentially useful in modelling recovery when analysing bonds and credit derivatives:

1. A strong relationship between average recovery rate (averaged over a large number of defaulted names) and seniority of the defaulted debt.
2. A large standard deviation in the recovery rate (looking at a specific seniority across a large number of names).
3. Some relationship between industry and recovery rate.

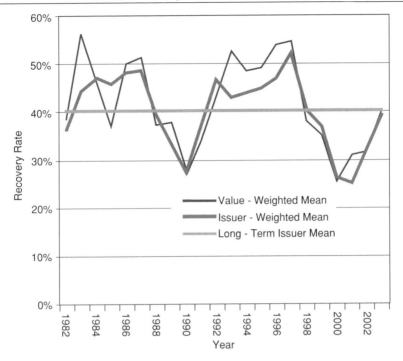

Figure 2.2 Recovery rates over time: Annual average senior unsecured bond recovery rates exhibit mean reversion

4. Some relationship between rating (investment grade versus high yield) and recovery rate (Figure 2.3).
5. A dependence on the economic cycle.

We need to have a model of the recovery rate for any bond issued by a specific entity – we need this not just to analyse that bond but also for credit derivatives related to that bond. The market typically uses the following simple model:

$$R(\text{seniority} = s, \text{referenceEntity}, \text{rating}) = \text{const}_{s,\text{IGHY}} \qquad (2.2)$$

In other words, the recovery rate assumed is dependent on the seniority of the debt, s, and whether the name has an investment grade or sub-investment grade rating (IGHY), but otherwise independent of the reference entity and generally not explicitly time dependent.

Actual values assumed in (2.2) vary from firm to firm, but typical figures might be 10%, 40%, 70% for subordinated debt (senior secured) bonds and loans respectively on investment grade names, and 0%, 25%, 50% for high-yield names. Generally assumptions are within 10% of these figures at the time of writing – though assumed recoveries are generally lower now than four or five years ago. This partly reflects recent poor experience in actual recoveries – and partly is a simple but crude way of implementing a time-dependent recovery assumption. Given that the impact of the economic cycle on recovery rates is slowly changing (Figure 2.1) then the assumed recovery represents an average over the life of deals we are valuing. As credit

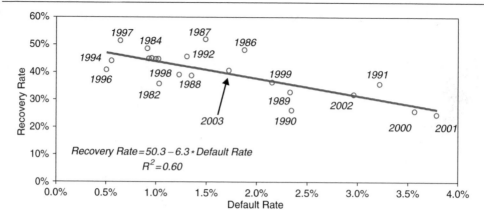

Figure 2.3 Recovery rate and rating (default rate): Correlation between annual issuer-weighted average recovery rates and issuer-weighted average default rates
© Moody's Investors Service, Inc. and/or its affiliates. Reprinted with permission. All rights reserved. Moody's default and recovery rates of corporate bond issuers. Moody's (January 2004)

derivative deals (on a mature book) may have a life of less than five years, the economic cycle has an impact on the recovery rate over the life of the deals, which may vary considerably over an economic cycle of 10 years or so.

The figures quoted above are used in the valuation of 'vanilla' credit derivatives. We shall see later that these instruments have relatively little sensitivity to the recovery assumption, so the recovery assumption is not important for these instruments. We shall return to this topic when we discuss book management, and 'digital' products.

There is no difficulty in principle in implementing a time-dependent recovery assumption though this is rarely done in practice, and also needs careful controls.[2]

2.2 DEFAULT RATES: RATING AND OTHER FACTORS

Rating agencies provide historical data on defaults. It should be borne in mind that this data relates to the agency's definition of default and is not necessarily directly relevant to either bond default risk (though the differences are likely to be small) or credit derivative trigger events.

Table 2.5 gives an example of historical default rates, and shows the key finding of the historical analysis, which is (as one would expect) that default risk increases as rating worsens.

Historical default rates tend to be used by rating agencies and investors in the analysis of portfolios and credit structures. The historical data gives much more information than just default and recovery rates, which we look at in the following section.

2.3 TRANSITION MATRICES

The change from being a non-defaulted firm to being in default is a 'change of state' and is described as a 'transition'. We can identify other changes of state – namely transitions from

---

[2] Time-dependent recovery assumptions can easily lead to negative implied default rates. The assumptions made need to be carefully controlled to avoid this and intuitively sensible recovery assumptions may not be consistent with the shape of credit spreads and the requirement to have non-negative implied default rates.

Table 2.5   Default risk and rating (Final column of Table 2.8)

Initial rating	Percent defaulted at year end
AAA	0.00
AA	0.01
A	0.05
BBB	0.28
BB	1.33
B	6.66
CCC	28.26

Table 2.6   Coarse transition matrix

	AAA	AA	A	BBB	BB	B	CCC	D	NR
AAA	89.54	5.91	0.43	0.09	0.03	0.00	0.00	0.00	4.00
AA	0.60	87.96	6.76	0.51	0.05	0.09	0.02	0.01	4.00
A	0.06	2.10	88.09	5.05	0.43	0.17	0.04	0.05	4.00
BBB	0.03	0.23	4.34	84.05	4.14	0.72	0.23	0.26	6.00
BB	0.02	0.06	0.41	5.78	76.33	7.08	1.09	1.22	8.00
B	0.00	0.08	0.27	0.35	4.80	74.58	3.92	5.99	10.00
CCC	0.11	0.00	0.22	0.68	1.46	9.00	51.66	24.87	12.00

one rating at the start of a period to another (possibly the same, and possibly default) at the end of the period. The probabilities associated with these changes of state are given in a **transition matrix** or TM. Tables 2.6 and 2.7 give examples of two such matrices – the former a 'coarse' matrix where only broad rating bands (e.g. AA, A, etc.[3]) are used, and the latter is a 'fine' matrix where individual notches are used (e.g. Aa1, Aa2, etc.).

For example, from Table 2.6 we see that there is an 84.05% chance that a BBB-rated name at the start of the year is also rated BBB at the end; a 6% chance that it moves to NR (not rated), and a 4.34% chance that it gets upgraded to A. The NR column refers to the chance that the name no longer has rated debt at the end of the year – for example, the only rated debt may have matured during the year. For convenience in subsequent calculations, we have included a row for defaulted names. We assume that once a name has defaulted, it is always in default.[4] Note that the sum of the figures in each row adds to 100% – every bond at the start of the year has to end up somewhere, either with some rating or in default or no longer rated. In contrast, the sum of the figures in the D column represents the chance that a defaulted name had defaulted the year before (and is therefore still in default) or came from some other rating – the sum is clearly greater than 100%. The sum of other columns is likewise less than 100% reflecting the general drift to default.

---

[3] Different rating agencies label their ratings in various ways – we shall use AA or Aa interchangeably, not necessarily implying one particular agency's approach to ratting. In addition, the particular numbers and matrices given are illustrative and not necessarily appropriate for real world applications.

[4] Of course this is not the case in reality – a company may go bankrupt (file for protection from creditors) and re-emerge from bankruptcy. But lacking information on how this re-emergence works, we assume that the company stays in default. This is not a bad assumption since – even if the company emerges with no missed payments on debt – in practice the associated recovery value (i.e. the post-default bond price) makes a reasoned guess on how that re-emergence (if any) might take place. Credit derivatives generally terminate on such events.

Table 2.7 Fine transition matrix: Exhibit 13 – Average one-year rating transition rates, 1983–2001

Rating From:	Rating to: Aaa	Aa1	Aa2	Aa3	A1	A2	A3	Baa1	Baa2	Baa3	Ba1	Ba2	Ba3	B1	B2	B3	Caa–C	Default	WR
Aaa	85.00	5.88	2.90	0.47	0.71	0.28	0.16	0.00	0.00	0.00	0.04	0.00	0.00	0.00	0.00	0.00	0.00	0.00	4.56
Aa1	2.54	76.02	7.87	6.58	2.31	0.32	0.05	0.18	0.00	0.00	0.09	0.00	0.00	0.00	0.00	0.00	0.00	0.00	4.04
Aa2	0.70	2.90	77.00	8.39	3.93	1.35	0.58	0.16	0.00	0.00	0.00	0.00	0.05	0.08	0.00	0.00	0.00	0.00	4.85
Aa3	0.08	0.61	3.36	77.88	8.89	3.14	0.85	0.24	0.21	0.16	0.00	0.04	0.09	0.00	0.00	0.00	0.00	0.08	4.38
A1	0.03	0.11	0.60	5.53	77.68	7.20	2.88	0.78	0.27	0.13	0.36	0.25	0.05	0.12	0.01	0.00	0.00	0.00	3.99
A2	0.05	0.06	0.29	0.77	5.34	77.47	7.18	2.87	0.80	0.39	0.28	0.10	0.11	0.03	0.07	0.00	0.03	0.02	4.13
A3	0.05	0.10	0.05	0.23	1.48	8.26	71.77	6.69	3.65	1.43	0.54	0.19	0.22	0.33	0.05	0.04	0.01	0.00	4.91
Baa1	0.08	0.02	0.13	0.18	0.20	2.71	7.67	71.19	7.37	3.14	1.04	0.46	0.35	0.55	0.09	0.00	0.02	0.08	4.73
Baa2	0.07	0.10	0.12	0.17	0.17	0.87	3.67	6.90	71.50	7.02	1.68	0.52	0.65	0.48	0.45	0.23	0.03	0.07	5.30
Baa3	0.03	0.00	0.03	0.07	0.18	0.57	0.65	3.22	9.33	67.03	6.38	2.59	1.90	0.80	0.31	0.18	0.16	0.43	6.15
Ba1	0.08	0.00	0.00	0.03	0.22	0.12	0.67	0.75	2.94	7.68	66.47	4.60	3.88	1.12	1.27	0.81	0.33	0.62	8.39
Ba2	0.00	0.00	0.00	0.03	0.04	0.15	0.13	0.35	0.70	2.30	8.35	63.96	6.20	1.67	3.70	1.35	0.53	0.65	9.88
Ba3	0.00	0.02	0.00	0.00	0.04	0.16	0.17	0.17	0.26	0.69	2.71	5.04	66.66	4.83	5.16	2.22	0.85	2.27	8.74
B1	0.02	0.00	0.00	0.00	0.06	0.09	0.15	0.07	0.24	0.30	0.42	2.52	5.70	66.89	5.22	4.58	1.78	3.71	8.23
B2	0.00	0.00	0.00	0.01	0.11	0.00	0.07	0.17	0.12	0.18	0.29	1.63	2.95	5.75	61.22	7.61	3.69	8.04	8.10
B3	0.00	0.00	0.06	0.00	0.02	0.04	0.06	0.11	0.12	0.20	0.18	0.35	1.17	4.02	3.36	62.05	6.84	12.50	8.91
Caa–C	0.00	0.00	0.00	0.00	0.00	0.00	0.00	0.00	0.48	0.48	0.64	0.00	1.36	1.85	1.23	2.87	54.21	26.54	10.36

Table 2.8   Coarse transition matrix adjusted for 'no longer rated' names

	AAA	AA	A	BBB	BB	B	CCC	D
	93.27	6.16	0.45	0.09	0.03	0.00	0.00	0.00
AA	0.62	91.63	7.04	0.53	0.05	0.09	0.02	0.01
A	0.06	2.19	91.76	5.26	0.45	0.18	0.04	0.05
BBB	0.03	0.24	4.62	89.42	4.40	0.77	0.24	0.28
BB	0.02	0.07	0.45	6.28	82.97	7.70	1.19	1.33
B	0.00	0.09	0.30	0.39	5.33	82.87	4.36	6.66
CCC	0.13	0.00	0.25	0.77	1.66	10.23	58.70	28.26
D	0.00	0.00	0.00	0.00	0.00	0.00	0.00	1.00

If we wish to use the transition matrix to calculate (for example) the price of a bond in order to give the buyer a fair compensation for historical default risk, then we need to make a reasoned estimate of what the transition matrix would look like if we knew how these NR names would behave if they had been rated. One reasonable assumption would be that, had they been rated, these names would have exactly the same experience as the other names in the sample. We shall use this assumption in what follows.[5]

Looking at the same row – debt rated BBB at the start of the year – we see that there is a 6% chance that the name no longer has a rating at the end of the year, and a 94% chance that the name is rated (including the possibility of default). We are assuming that these 94% of names are representative of the entire 100% of names, so we need to increase the transition probabilities by a factor of 100/94.0 for all those other states, and we can then ignore the NR names. Table 2.8 shows the results of making this adjustment to the matrix in Table 2.6. The spreadsheet 'Chapter 2.xls' contains the worked example.

2.4   'MEASURES' AND TRANSITION MATRIX-BASED PRICING

We introduce two concepts which are crucial to the understanding of subsequent analysis. The first is what we call the **natural measure** (also sometimes called **actuarial pricing** or (misleadingly) **historical pricing**). Suppose we want to know the 'worth' of a promise from a risky borrower to repay 1 EUR in a year's time. If the name were risk-free we would apply a discount factor (D) to the payment to get a current value. However, since the name is risky there is a chance (p, say) that the name defaults, in which case a recovery amount (R) is received (at the end of the year, say). In that case the promise is worth

$$W = [(1 - p) + p \cdot R] \cdot D \qquad (2.3)$$

since the promised amount is paid with probability $1 - p$, and the recovery amount is paid with probability p. We may use various analysis – for example, historical data or detailed company analysis – to make estimates of p and R. Such an approach is called the 'natural measure'. We do not necessarily use unadjusted historical data – we are trying to make our best estimates of the real chance of default, and the real recovery in the event of default. These estimates are not necessarily the historical rates – we may explicitly adjust for the state of the economy, known information regarding the company, the state of the property market or other asset markets, etc.

---

[5] Another argument might be that, since the bonds matured without default, the NR names would actually have had a much better experience than the sample as a whole, with far fewer defaults.

Table 2.9 Illustrative TM for pricing examples

Rating	A	B	D
A	0.98	0.01	0.01
B	0.01	0.96	0.03
D	0	0	1

The second concept is referred to as the **risk-neutral measure**. This is not appropriate use for calculating what the price of the contract 'should be', but instead works from market data to calculate the implied default probability and the implied recovery. Suppose the same borrower has also made a separate promise to pay 1 in a year, but nothing in the event of default. Suppose that both of these promises are trading actively in the marketplace and that we can observe market prices of P_1 for the contract governed by (2.3), and P_2 for this second contract, which obeys the formula

$$W = (1 - p) \cdot D \tag{2.4}$$

We can calculate p from P_2 ($p = 1 - P_2/D$) and hence R from P_1 [$R = (P_1 - P_2)/(D - P_2)$]. This is useful if there are other contracts with the same borrower of the same maturity that do not trade in the marketplace but we want to calculate a 'fair' value for them.

It should be noted that the use of transition matrices does not prejudge which measure we are going to use. In fact we shall use both natural and implied TMs in following work.

We illustrate the technique for pricing using a simplified matrix. Suppose we just have two ratings A and B, plus default. We suppose the 3 by 3 transition matrix is given by Table 2.9.

First, suppose we price 1-year zero coupon bonds (whose claim amount is par) issued by the same entity that is rated A,[6] but of two seniorities – senior bonds with an assumed recovery of 50%, and junior bonds with an assumed recovery of zero. For simplicity we shall assume that interest rates are zero (discount factor = 1). From (2.3) we see that the senior bond has an expected value of

$$P_{\text{sen}} = 0.99 + 0.01 \times 0.5 = 0.995 \quad \text{and} \quad P_{\text{jun}} = 0.99$$

Note incidentally that the senior bond gives a 0.5% – or approximately 50 bp – price appreciation over the year. The risk of default is 100 bp, and the loss given default $(1 - R)$ is 0.5 – so the rate of loss is 50 bp per annum, which equals the bond spread. Similarly the junior bonds gives 100 bp return, and the risk of default is 100 bp but the loss given default is $1 - R = 1$ since $R = 0$, and again the rate of loss is equal to the spread on the bond.

If we took a second entity rated B, then we would find prices of 0.985 (150 bp return = 3% × 0.5 LGD) for senior debt, and 0.97 (300 bp return = 3% × 1 LGD) for junior debt. Generally we find the spread on the bond is equal to the rate of default times the loss given default:

$$\text{spread} = \text{hazard rate} \times \text{loss given default (LGD)} \tag{2.5}$$

Now suppose we have a 2-year bond of the A issuer, and suppose the same transition matrix applies now and in the following year. At the end of year 1 the (senior debt of the) issuer may

---

[6] Actually debt is rated, not the entity. We assume that rating in the TM refers to the senior debt of the company. In this case the senior debt of the entity is rated A. The default probabilities and transition probabilities are given by this matrix and are now taken to refer to the company. The seniority of the debt we are pricing for that name only impacts the recovery assumptions we are using.

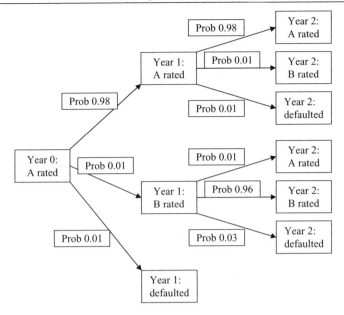

Figure 2.4 Two-year evolution 'tree' of A-rated name, and associated bond payoffs

still be rated A, or may be rated B, or the issuer may have gone into default. From each of the first two states there are similarly three possibilities – giving a total of nine outcomes in all each with an associated probability and payoff. Figure 2.4 summarises the possibilities, probabilities and payoffs.

We find that the value for 2-year senior debt is 0.9899 and junior debt is 0.9799.

Exercises

1. Repeat the above calculations for a B-rated 2-year bond.
2. Price a 5-year A-rated bond by the above method and 3×3 matrix.
3. Use the 'coarse' TM of Table 2.6 to price a 2-year BBB bond.
4. Use the 'fine' TM of Table 2.7 to price a 10-year Baa2 bond.
5. Is (2.5) still true for 2-year bonds?

The spreadsheet 'Chapter 2.xls' uses a coarse TM and a similar approach to calculate the fair spreads on par FRN bonds. Sheet 'TM data' contains, in rows 16–23, the 8×8 TM derived from historical data in the rows above. The user can replace this matrix by any other 8×8 transition matrix (subject to row sum $= 1$ and row 23 remaining unchanged) whether historically based or not. The sheet 'period TM probs' then calculates the probabilities of transition from each initial rating to each possible state at the end of year n. This is equivalent to calculating the probabilities of arriving at each node on the tree (see Figure 2.2). The 'Spreads' sheet takes assumed recovery (cell C3), initial rating data (B5) and maturity (B6) to calculate a fair market spread (B9). The table B15–G21 calculates the spreads up to five years for all initial ratings given the recovery assumption.

2.5   SPREAD JUMPS AND SPREAD VOLATILITY DERIVED FROM TRANSITION MATRICES

The transition matrix can be used to calculate more than just the historical fair-value spread given the TM. If we have a 5-year bond, then we can calculate the fair value spread (for example, if it's a BB bond with assumed recovery of 40%, then the 'Spreads' sheet gives 104 bp). In a year's time there is a 0.03% chance ('TM data' cell B20) that the name will have migrated to AAA (at which point the 4-year bond would have a spread of 1 bp ('Spreads' cell E15)). Similarly we could find the probabilities of the other transitions and the forward spreads, hence calculate the expected **forward spread**, and also the standard deviation (**volatility**) of the forward spread.

The sheet 'forward spreads and vol' performs similar calculations, but for constant maturity instruments (more useful for default swaps) and calculates the forward spreads (C6–C12 for the instrument described in 'Spreads' B3–B9) and standard deviation (E14) of the spread. Table B32–G38 performs the same calculations for all ratings and maturities with the recovery assumption of 'Spreads' B3 and expresses the volatility as a percentage of the initial spread.

Note that as rating changes, the spread jumps from one level to another. This is an important aspect of the credit market – spread movements in reality can be very large and very quick. Figure 21.5 illustrates this for some Telecoms 'spreads' (actually CDS premia).

The 'jump process' implied by the transition matrix approach models relatively realistically an important feature of the credit markets. Rating (or, more generally, perceived quality) is certainly a driving factor behind spreads and spread changes. However we often see spreads changing (on a daily basis or a secular change) where rating agencies are not changing the rating of individual names. We could say that the perceived quality is changing even though the rating is not, but 'perceived quality' has no measure other than spread. It is also very different from rating in that there are more than seven spread levels in the marketplace. Often the daily movements are small although there may be a long-term drift in spreads which is not reflected in rating changes. The spread volatility (cell E14) will not take into account volatility that arises from changing spreads when rating is constant, so E14 should be an underestimate of the spread volatility in absolute terms. Nevertheless modelling and analysing historical data based around rating is a useful tool and we can make adjustments to reflect the higher volatility we would expect to see in actual spreads compared with historically implied spreads.

2.6   ADJUSTING TRANSITION MATRICES

Suppose we wish to replicate spreads currently seen on 5-year maturity bonds (averaged across a given rating) rather than use the historical TM and get a different spread from actual market levels. One way to achieve this is to increase the default probability for a given rating and then multiply the non-default transition probabilities by a factor X so that the sum of the rows remains unity.[7] If $p(D)$ is the historical probability that the particular rating moves into default and $p(i)$ that it moves to rating i, then we have

$$\sum_i p(i) + p(D) = 1 \qquad (2.6)$$

---

[7] In section 2.6 we are following the general approach developed by Jarrow *et al.* (1997).

If we increase the default probability by an amount x to $pp(x)$, then we can multiply the other transition probabilities by X, where

$$X = \frac{1 - p(D) - x}{\sum_i p(i)} \tag{2.7}$$

X is the ratio of the new survival probability to the old survival probability. 'Modified TM data' implements this with desired changes in L20–L26, and the following sheets repeat the calculations of the sheets described above. By adjusting L20–L26 it is possible to get 'Modified spreads' F15–F21 to agree with current market spreads rather than historical spreads.

It is possible to further modify the matrix in 'modified TM data' by additionally increasing the chances of transition from the existing rating to other ratings (other than 'default'). This can be done in many ways, and one way would be to choose the amount by which you wish to reduce the probability that the rating remains unchanged and increase the probabilities of transition to other ratings collectively by the same amount, distributing the additional amount by increasing these other probabilities by multiplying by a factor. If we reduce the probability of the rating remaining unchanged from $pp(I)$ to $pp(I) - y$, where I is the initial rating, then we multiply the other (non-default) probabilities by Y, where

$$Y = \frac{1 - pp(D) - pp(I) + y}{\sum_{i \neq I} pp(i)} \tag{2.8}$$

Y is the ratio of the new probability that the name changes rating without defaulting, to the old one. 'Modified vols' calculates the new implied volatilities. Note that changes in default and in non-default transition probabilities are not independent, so a manual search for a solution is not easy.

Exercise
Implement the shift in transition probability described above. Find the shifts in default probabilities and the shifts in non-default transition probabilities required in order to generate the spreads given in the 'Modified spreads' sheet, and also to generate 100% spread volatility.

3
Asset Swaps and Asset Swap Spread;
z-Spread

Asset swap deals are of interest to us for two reasons. Firstly, the 'asset swap spread' is a widely used measure of credit risk in a general sense, and is also used as an alternative to talking about the price of a credit bond. Secondly, the asset swap contract itself is a derivative involving credit risk and, in some versions of the contract, embeds credit risk in a non-trivial way.

For further details of asset swap products the reader should consult Das (2004), or Flavell (2002).

3.1 'PAR–PAR' ASSET SWAP CONTRACTS

3.1.1 Contract Description and Hedging

The contract we describe is referred to as a **'par–par' asset swap**. The investor pays par to an asset swap desk to gain exposure to a par notional amount of a particular fixed coupon bond issued by a chosen reference name. The asset swap deal pays the investor floating payments (of LIBOR [or some other reference rate] plus the **asset swap spread**) until maturity or until the default of the reference name.

The investor receives the floating payments on pre-agreed dates – which may differ from the coupon payment dates and may be more frequent – and par at maturity. On default of the reference bond the investor receives a cash sum and the contract terminates. From the investor's point of view the asset swap deal converts a fixed coupon bond into an FRN initially costing par.

3.1.2 Hedging

The asset swap trading desk hedges the asset swap deal by entering two contracts. Firstly, the desk pays market price for the reference bond (sometimes buying the bond from the investor). Typically the price differs from par. Secondly, the desk enters into a contract with an interest rate swap desk where the asset swap desk pays

(a) (on day 1) the excess of par over the cost of the reference bond (which could be negative – i.e. a payment from the interest rate swap desk to the asset swap desk)
(b) (on bond coupon payment dates on the bond) the fixed coupons received on the bond

and, in return, receives from the interest rate swap desk

(c) (on asset swap coupon payment dates) the floating reference rate plus a fixed spread (the asset swap spread).

The asset swap deal and associated hedges are summarised in Figure 3.1.

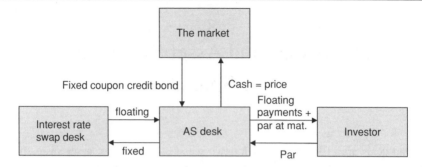

Figure 3.1   Asset swap contract and hedges

3.1.3   Default of the Reference Name

On default of the reference name the contract is unwound. The bond is sold for its post-default price (recovery), the interest rate swap is unwound – which may lead to a positive or negative cashflow depending on how interest rates have moved since inception – the net proceeds are returned to the investor, and the contract terminates.

The contract, as described above, is identical to an investment into par notional of the reference bond plus an interest rate swap, as described above. It should be noted that, in this form, the investor has full default risk exposure to the reference bond – and maintains economic ownership of the bond.

3.2   ASSET SWAP SPREAD

The asset swap spread is the number found from a calculation which balances the values of the fixed and floating streams in the interest rate swap. There is no simple short-cut to this calculation. Figure 3.2 shows screen images for the asset swap calculation function on Bloomberg for a 2007 Ford Motor Credit bond.

The key point to note is the following: the asset swap spread results from two deals – a purchase of a risky bond and an interest rate swap contract which includes a cashflow on day 1. The asset swap spread is one measure of the credit risk on an asset – we shall see alternative measures below (z and maturity spread) and in Part II (CDS premium).

3.3   MATURITY AND z-SPREAD

By **maturity spread** we mean the difference between the yield on the bond and the yield off the swap curve interpolated to the maturity date of the bond. This is a quick and easy calculation. Sometimes 'spread' is measured relative to a different reference curve or to a specific reference bond – for example, a government bond. Alternatives are commonly used in defining the terms of a spread option contract.

The maturity spread is intuitively a measure of the risk on a bond. The riskier a bond, the less the market will be prepared to pay for it, hence the lower the price, the higher the yield and the higher the spread.

Rather than maturity spread the z-**spread** is more commonly used – in practice the two numbers are very close and will be identical if the interest rate curve is flat. Consider a

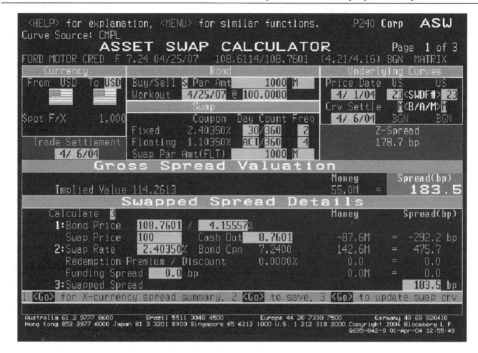

Figure 3.2   Asset swap calculation for Ford Motor Credit 2007 bond.
Source: Bloomberg L.P. Used with permission.

risky bond. If we discount the promised cashflows using discount factors (derived from the LIBOR/swap curve) then we arrive at a value V which is (usually) different from the market price P – typically $V > P$ unless the bond is less risky than the banks contributing to the LIBOR rates, in which case discounting off the LIBOR/swap curve will give $V < P$.

If, in the typical case, we need to discount off a more risky curve than the swap curve, we should do the following. The discount factors correspond to zero coupon rates. Increase all these zero coupon rates by an amount z, and calculate the new discount factor corresponding to the shifted zero coupon curve. Now discount the promised bond cashflows using these reduced discount factors – the more z increases, the more V reduces and we can find a z such that $V = P$.

The z-spread is the amount by which the zero coupon swap curve has to be shifted up so that the market price of the bond equals the discounted value of the promised payments off this shifted curve.

If the reference name is very low risk, the z-spread may be negative.

Note that only the bond transaction (purchase of the bond at the market price) contributes to the calculation of z-spread (or maturity spread). These are 'pure' measures of the underlying risk associated with the bond, whereas the asset swap spread is dependent on two transactions – the bond purchase and an interest rate swap deal.

Figure 3.2 shows not only the asset swap spread but also the z-spread. In the case of the Ford bond we note that the z-spread is below the asset swap spread. Also note that the bond price is above par, so the initial cashflow in the embedded interest rate deal in the asset swap contract is from the interest rate swap desk – money is being borrowed at LIBOR to invest in

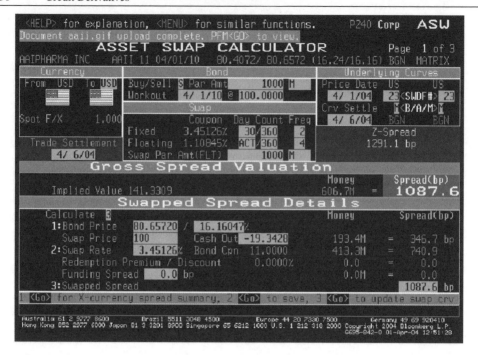

Figure 3.3   Asset swap and z-spread for Aipharma Inc.
Source: Bloomberg L.P. Used with permission.

a more risky asset. It should not be a surprise that the asset swap spread is above the z-spread in this case[1] since the asset swap is a geared investment in the reference bond.

Figure 3.3 is also an asset swap calculation, but now for a high-risk bond.

In this case the bond price is well below par – only part of the investor's cash is invested in a high-risk asset, the balance is invested in a low-risk interest rate swap. It should be no surprise that the asset swap spread is well below the z-spread as the asset swap is in this case a de-geared investment in the bond.

If we consider non-par asset swaps – those where the market price for the underlying bond is paid – then the spread on this contract will be much closer to the z-spread (and if the interest rate curve is flat, they should be equal).

3.4   CALLABLE ASSET SWAPS; 'PERFECT' ASSET SWAPS

Several variations of the par–par asset swap contract exist. We describe two and leave their analysis to the reader after Part II has been read.

3.4.1   Callable Asset Swaps

The asset swap desk buys a bond as a hedge against an asset swap deal. If the z-spread on this bond falls (because the bond is perceived as less risky) then the price rises above par (say)

---

[1] Where the price is 'close' to par, differences in timing of the fixed and floating cashflows and the shape of the interest rate curve can mean that the z-spread can be above or below the asset swap spread. The asset swap spread exceeds the z-spread if the bond is significantly above par, and is below the z-spread if the bond is significantly below par.

and the desk could sell the bond, unwind the interest rate swap, and make more than par on its hedge. If the desk has the right to unwind the asset swap at par then it can realise this profit. An asset swap with such an embedded option is called a **callable** asset swap.

The reader will see (after reading Part II) that a callable asset swap can be analysed as a bond purchase, an interest rate swap, and an option driven by the z-spread on the bond (changes in interest rate curve level are assumed to be exactly hedged by the interest rate swap).

3.4.2 'Perfect' Asset Swaps

One drawback of asset swaps from the investor's point of view is the contingent loss arising on default of the reference name. On this event unwinding, the embedded interest rate swap contract may lead to a loss because of adverse interest rate moves. This threat can be removed by changing the terms of the asset swap: either by the asset swap desk meeting the unwind cost (or taking the profit) of the interest rate swap, or by the asset swap desk retaining any unwind loss but passing on any unwind profit.

In the former case the expected cost is small – if the interest rate curve is flat then the expected unwind cost at any future date is zero and, over time, losses arising from adverse interest rate moves will be offset by profits from favourable ones. Note that the desk typically is a buyer of bonds (not of external asset swaps) so will have a considerable book of interest rate swaps where it is paying fixed, and will have a large contingent interest rate risk at any one time (interest rate moves have the same impact on the embedded interest rate swap deals on all the asset swap deals). It is hard to hedge this risk directly – there is an exposure to the reference name(s) but the size of that exposure depends on interest rate levels. 'Double trigger' default swaps (see Parts II and IV) can in principle be used to hedge this risk.

Where the interest rate curve is non-flat there is an expected future unwind cost at any date in the future, and the cost of this can be measured using the techniques of Part II.

In the latter product, variation expected value – even if the interest rate curve is flat – is not zero. The option can be seen as a swaption but contingent on the default of the reference name.

3.5 A BOND SPREAD MODEL

Investment grade credit debt is usually discussed in spread terms. This naturally leads to a 'spread model' of the bond's price. It is easiest to illustrate this model in terms of z-spread, z, and the zero coupon curve underlying the LIBOR/swap curve, $r(t)$.[2] The bond's price P is then given in terms of the cashflow $c(t)$ at time t by

$$P = \int_0^T c(t) \cdot \exp\{-[r(t) + z] \cdot t\} \, dt \qquad (3.1)$$

Typically the cashflow is concentrated on specific coupon payment and maturity dates. The above description in integral terms is general – it includes 'lumpy' cashflows if the cashflow function c is a sum of Dirac delta functions. The integral description is mathematically simple and allows us to concentrate on the underlying features of the model and its implications. In contrast, a valid implementation must take into account details such as

---

[2] Here we are quoting r and z on a continuous basis.

day count conventions, etc., and looks more like

$$P = \sum_{i=1}^{N} c_i \cdot \tilde{d}(t_i) + \tilde{d}(T) \tag{3.2}$$

where the $\tilde{d}$ are discount factors off the swap curve shifted by the z-spread, N is the number of coupon payments, coupons c_i are at time t_i, and maturity is at time T.

If we consider several bonds (of the same seniority) issued by the same entity, how are the z-spreads on these bonds related? Is there a term structure? Is there a coupon structure? How are z-spreads in different currencies related?

The model itself does not answer these questions. The description (3.1) relates the bond price to the promised cashflows, the discount curve and the z-spread for that bond. There is no explicit attempt to model default risk, or recovery risk (or 'loss given default'). The model is purely a translation of price into spread, and vice versa. There is no explicit attempt to model seniority differences. We would certainly expect senior and subordinated bonds (for example) to trade on different spreads but the model (3.1) has no insight to offer on how much this difference should be.

We might guess that the z-spread curve for various issues has a term structure but no coupon structure. One implication is that, if we are able to observe three bonds of the same maturity but having different coupons, then (directly from (3.2)) we see that price differences must be proportional to coupon differences. Typically the relative paucity of bullet bond issues, and idiosyncratic pricing in the bond market, make such implications difficult to test. It is difficult to find instances of several bonds from the same issuer with the same maturity date and same bond structure to test the above. However, when z-spreads become very high (the issuer is 'trading on a recovery basis'), the above implication can be disproved.

Intuitively, if we believe that an issuer is likely to achieve a 30% recovery, then a bond priced at 70 (because it has a low coupon) has much lower risk (($70 - 30)/70 = 56\%$ of notional) than a bond of similar maturity priced at 130 (because is has a high coupon) (where the risk is ($130 - 30)/130 = 77\%$ on notional). We would expect the higher priced bond to stand on a higher z-spread.

The spread 'model' (3.1) can be related to the model we develop in Part II, where we price bonds using a default and recovery model. We find that, if recovery is assumed to be zero, then the spread model is a theoretically valid description of bond pricing where the z-spread turns out to be the default rate (hazard rate) for the firm at time. Typically we would expect the default risk for a firm to be a function of time so, even though the basic form of the price model (3.1) is correct, we would wish to replace the constant z-spread by a function of time.

If recovery is, more realistically, anticipated to be above zero then the spread model for pricing bonds cannot be reconciled with a realistic default and recovery model.

4
Liquidity, the Credit Pyramid
and Market Data

4.1 BOND LIQUIDITY

We are used to looking at a government bond spread curve and seeing a sensible pattern – yields on bonds of different maturities follow a smooth curve (or surface) driven by maturity (and coupon, for example). A few bonds are special on repo and have yields that do not lie on the surface but are explained by this additional factor.

Credit bonds and loans generally do not trade in the same volumes as government bonds – they are less **liquid**. Figure 4.1 shows (maturity) spreads on Ford Motor Credit USD global issues – large and supposedly liquid issues on one of the most heavily traded credit names. Even here the pattern of spreads is not as smooth as we would expect and the deviations cannot be ascribed to repo, seniority or other independently measurable factors. Such differences are usually ascribed to **liquidity effects** or **illiquidity**.

The situation worsens if we move away from the major borrowers. Many companies only have one or two bonds in issue: one may trade regularly and the other may trade rarely. Even if the maturities are similar, an investor would prefer the bond that trades regularly because it is relatively easy to dispose of at a fair price, and there is also a transparent market that allows the valuation of this asset. How much cheaper (wider spread) should the other bond be? There is no straightforward answer to this question.

Bonds in issue are often more complex than the simple 'bullet' bond described above: one bond may be a convertible 5-year issue and may trade regularly; the other may be a 10-year callable issue and may trade rarely. Estimating a fair price for the callable given the convertible spread involves modelling (in some way) equity prices and volatility, interest rates and volatility, and default risk.

Suppose only one bond is in issue and rarely trades. Can we estimate the bullet spread, and how?

Looking at marks provided by credit traders may not give us the answer. Front book credit bond traders make markets in bonds and will attempt to make a market in illiquid issues and names. If possible they will attempt to match a seller with a buyer on such issues. If the desk has to hold an issue on its books it will take account of the capital required to finance this position, the length of time the issue may be on the books, the return on capital required, and factor this into the desk's bid price. Traders' mark-to-market levels are often driven by the last level at which an issue traded, and stale positions may not be repriced. Bond spread histories for such issues will usually show a 'step' graph pattern – periods of constant spreads with sudden jumps up or down when real deals occur.

4.2 THE CREDIT PYRAMID

The institutional asset portfolio of a commercial bank consists largely of bonds and loans. A large bank may have a portfolio of debt issued by 10 000 or more entities. This might

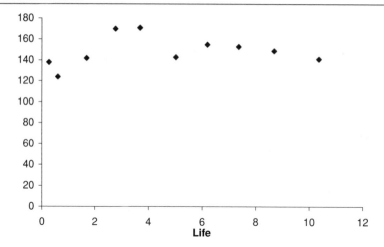

Figure 4.1   FMC USD 'global' bond spreads (2002 data)

consist of government debt issued by 20–50 countries, bonds and assignable loans issued by 2000 corporate (non-government) entities, and untraded debt issued by a further 8000 or more entities. Of the 2000 traded issues, perhaps 500 trade regularly in the bond market, perhaps another 500 trade irregularly in the bond and secondary loan market, and the other 1000 trade rarely. This pattern is illustrated in Figure 4.2.

Marking such a book to market would present considerable problems. Generally this is not a problem for 'buy and hold' investors such as commercial banks since they can report on a historic accounting basis (book value, or cost plus accruals). But suppose the bank wishes to clear the economic risk associated with a large part of its portfolio off its books by issuing a derivative related to the reference entities. Investors in the derivative (who are synthetically buying the underlying risks) will need to know the current spread associated with each of the names.

For 5% of the names we can look to an active market and get an accurate answer – at least in certain actively traded maturities. Other maturities present a problem. For the next 15% of the portfolio – the less actively traded names – there is no easy solution, but the following section outlines several approaches to broadening the active market and to the provision of spread estimates at maturities or on names that are rarely traded.

The bulk of the portfolio does not trade. Information that is available is accounting information for the company which, if there is traded equity on the company, can be used to estimate default risk and spread (as is done by MoodysKMV, and RiskMetric Group's CreditGrades™ (Finger, 2002), for example). Alternative approaches are to use the bank's internal rating for the entity, plus the bank's own history of borrowers' ratings, defaults and recoveries. Internal ratings could be mapped to rating agencies' ratings, and current average spreads per rating could be used as an estimate for the fair spread on the name (with some adjustment for seniority differences) – see section 4.4.

4.3   SURVEY AND ENGINEERED SPREAD DATA

Several products have been developed to try to improve the amount and quality of spread data for the less liquid credits and maturities. Generally this falls into either

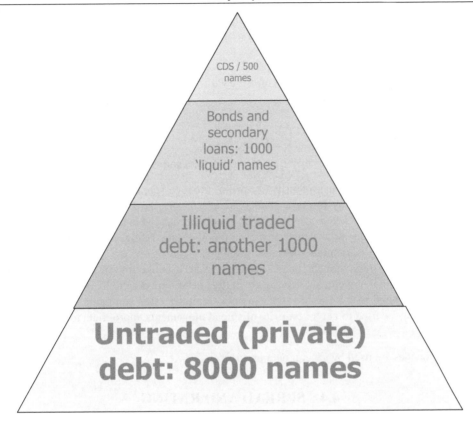

Figure 4.2   The Credit Pyramid

(1) 'survey data' where spreads are obtained as estimates rather than as actual trade or firm bid or offer prices from market participants, or
(2) 'engineered data' based on actual trades and quotes seen in the marketplace together with mathematical and statistical methods to fill the gaps in maturity or over time.

Some products combine both of these methods. The spreads estimated may be bond spread or default swap premium rates – the principles and methods used are nearly identical. We describe products for default swap data below.

4.3.1   Survey Data

Banks and other institutions are asked to contribute estimates of spreads for certain maturities on a range of names. The list of names expands as the participants feel confident in estimating the spreads for the name concerned and as the market demands more names. The contributing individuals are effectively acting as market-makers and are trying to come up with a spread (bid and offer) on which they would actually be prepared to deal. As such, a good market-maker will look at various sources of information – known deals, how the market has moved, how this company compares with other similar companies, ratings and changes, current company news, etc.

Two such products are Lombard Risk's ValuSpread, based on estimates from mid-office investment banking staff, and Mark-it Partners, based on feeds of daily mark-to-market curves direct from their contributors' books of record.

A criticism of the approach is that the spreads are only as good as the individuals' underlying estimates (although any sensible product offering will clean and rationalise the data it receives), and their methods are not transparent.

4.3.2   Engineered Data

This approach uses actual trade, firm quote, or other data and will try to do two things.

1. Given certain points on the maturity spectrum, produce spreads for all other maturities. Typically this is done by fitting a mathematical curve to the known data where several maturities (say 2- and 5-year) are known or, if only one spread is known, by looking at the curve appropriate to similar names (for example, the same rating, or similar spreads) and using that shape to extrapolate the missing spreads.
2. Given a historic spread for the name, estimate where it is likely to be trading now, given data on the general movement of spreads over the intervening period. In order to assess this, appropriate 'tags' may be used – for example, similarly rated companies from the same industry may be used to get an estimate of spread movements appropriate to the particular name.

Such approaches are used by several data providers.

4.4   SPREAD AND RATING

One method of estimating a fair spread for names that do not trade often, or at all, is to use rating information. Of course, where the name never trades it may not be rated by the public agencies, but a bank's internal rating – mapped to the equivalent rating agencies' rating – can be used.

The starting point is to collect data for traded names and calculate average spread and the standard deviation – see Table 4.1 for an example of such analysis (the results are purely illustrative and will vary over time).

It should be noted that spread is a very poor indicator of actual spread – a standard deviation of spreads within a single rating band of 60% being typical. Also there will be considerable

Table 4.1   Mean and standard deviation of 5-year spread by rating (results vary considerably over time)

Sector and rating	Mean (bp)	Standard deviation (%)
Bank AA	25	30
Bank A	50	20
Industrial AAA	15	80
Industrial AA	40	60
Industrial A	70	50
Industrial BBB	100	60
Industrial BB	200	60
Industrial B	300	50

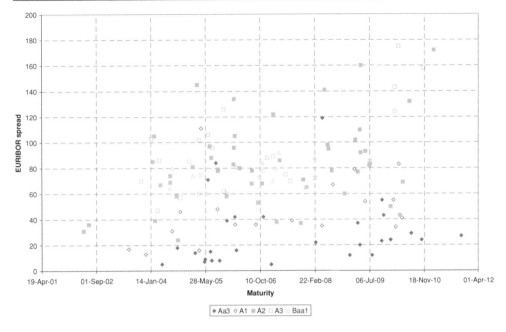

Figure 4.3   Bond spread by maturity and rating

overlap between spreads on one rating and those on adjacent ratings. Introducing further tags (such as country and industry) generally does not improve the situation significantly. The exception is banks and other regulated financial entities, where the standard deviation is substantially less (around 20%).

Such a process of estimation is only appropriate for derivatives based on large portfolios of names (e.g. where a commercial bank wishes to obtain default protection on a large portfolio of loans). Figure 4.3 shows spreads at a range of maturities for actively traded investment grade (by notch) names.

5
Traditional Counterparty
Risk Management

5.1 VETTING

Counterparty risk arises from interest rate swap trades, credit default swap trades and many other deals. The first counterparty risk control measure is to accept as a possible counterparty to a deal only those entities which are (for example)

(a) regulated by a central bank or insurance regulator
(b) rated A (or possibly BBB) or better
(c) domiciled in certain countries.

Counterparties which do not meet these criteria will generally not be accepted as counterparties without other conditions being met – for example, full collateral being posted or being accepted for certain types of trades or maturities only.

The intention of these restrictions is clearly to accept only 'low-risk' counterparties. Even once a counterparty has been deemed an acceptable risk, further measures described below are taken to control the risk on individual deals.

5.2 COLLATERALISATION AND NETTING

The second step (not always applied to all counterparties or to all products for a given counter-party) is to require that the counterparty **collateralises** deals and signs a 'netting' agreement.

Collateralisation means that each deal is marked-to-market (and both sides have to agree on what this value is) and any change in the value from one day to the next is matched by a cashflow from one counterparty to the other. Thus a mature deal – for example, an interest rate swap or default swap which had an initial value of zero – may have moved to being USD 2m positive value for party A and the opposite for party B. Under the collateralisation agreement party B will have paid party A USD 2m collateral (on which party B receives interest). If party B defaults, and the interest rate swap contract vanishes, then party A has 2m capital which it can use to replace the deal with another counterparty.

To be effective, collateralisation also requires a netting agreement – in the event of default by party B the net value of all the trades with party A (some of which have a positive mark to market, others have a negative mark-to-market) only is a claim of one on the other.

Note that collateralisation does not eliminate the counterparty risk for two reasons:

1. Overnight change on the day the counterparty defaults is not reflected in the collateral posted until the next day. This risk may be positive or negative. Also in practice the failure of a counterparty may take some time to establish. A counterparty may fail to post collateral one day because of an administrative error. If the counterparty is failing it will probably try to maintain trading relationships as long as possible – and make excuses why collateral has not been posted. In practice it takes between about 3 and 10 days to determine that a

counterparty has failed and to close a deal. A 10-day delay corresponds to roughly 20% of the underlying asset's annual volatility (being the square root of 10/260) and therefore represents a significant risk.
2. If the underlying contract is a credit derivative there may be a correlation between the counterparty and the reference name(s) in the credit derivative (which is commonly the case for portfolio credit derivatives). The default of the counterparty will be associated with a widening of the spread on the reference names and a substantial change in the value of the deal. The short-term move in the mark-to-market value may therefore be much more substantial than 20% of the annual volatility.

5.3   ADDITIONAL COUNTERPARTY REQUIREMENTS FOR CREDIT DERIVATIVE COUNTERPARTIES

Credit derivatives (and repo and asset swap deals) introduce a correlation risk between the counterparty and the reference name. Default of the counterparty may be related to a jump in the spread on the reference name(s), hence a step move in the value of the underlying deal when the counterparty defaults.

It is common to require that there is no correlation between the counterparty and the reference deal on credit derivatives, in addition to the other counterparty requirements described above. Assessing whether correlation exists between a reference entity and the counterparty is usually a subjective judgement and is typically based on some or all of

(a) region and industry overlaps
(b) direct and indirect business relationships
(c) equity correlation.

5.4   INTERNAL CAPITAL CHARGE

One way to control counterparty use is to assign a notional capital charge to the counterparty for each specific deal according to the perceived risk of both the counterparty and the deal. This initially requires the calculation of an appropriate measure of the risk on the deal – this might be the 'potential future exposure' (PFE) on the deal or the counterparty VaR for that deal. The more certain deals use up the allocated capital, the fewer such deals are done in favour of less counterparty capital-intensive deals. We shall see an example of PFE calculation for CDS in Part II.

6

Credit Portfolios and Portfolio Risk

In this section we introduce some further terminology applicable to credit risk measurement (VaR and CreditVaR), and we also look at some techniques used to assess the risk on credit portfolios. Detailed understanding of VaR approaches are not needed for this section – Jorion (2000) or Grayling (1997) provide much more detail.

6.1 VaR AND COUNTERPARTY VaR

Consider an asset. We can calculate a forward value of that asset but are interested in how far the value can fall below the expected value. More generally we are interested in the distribution of market values, and the low-value tail of this distribution. We shall refer to this concept as **VaR** – we shall suppose that we measure this as the deviation of value below the expected value corresponding to a certain percentile of the distribution of value. Our interest is in credit risky assets – the term **creditVaR** is sometimes used to refer to the risk to the value arising from changing credit spreads (or defaults).

A trade may have counterparty risk, for example, and interest rate swap or a credit default swap has exposure to a counterparty. We can calculate the expected exposure to the counterparty at a forward date. But, again, our interest may be in how great this exposure to the counterparty could be. In this case we are interested in the high-value tail of the distribution of the asset value at the forward date. We refer to this concept as **counterpartyVaR**. For both measures we need to be able to produce a distribution of forward values of the underlying asset.

Typically we are not interested in the VaR or counterpartyVaR numbers on a particular deal. We are much more interested in the VaR on the entire portfolio of assets, or the counterpartyVaR to a particular counterparty for all trades related to that counterparty. For example, let us suppose that we own a 5-year FMC bond priced at par. Then this will have a certain VaR – say X. Suppose we also own and insurance contract on this specific bond covering any loss in value arising from the default event. This will also have a VaR – say Y – and the sum of the two VaR figures is $X + Y$ (Y will only equal X if the distribution of values is symmetric.) If – when thinking about the two deals together – the bond falls in value, the insurance will rise in value since the combination of the two will always be worth par (see Part II). So in this case the VaR of the pair of deals is zero. We cannot add the VaR numbers for individual deals in order to get this: we have first to simulate forward values for the entire portfolio in a consistent way, calculate the portfolio value on each simulation, then look at the distribution of portfolio values to get the VaR.

6.2 DISTRIBUTION OF FORWARD VALUES OF A CREDIT BOND

The approach described here and in section 6.4 is used by RiskMetrics Group (Gupton *et al.*, 1997) and others for their CreditVaR calculations. The portfolio simulation approach is closely related to the Copula pricing model for CDO deals (Part III).

Suppose we need the distribution of values of a bond in one year's time. We shall replace the actual reference name by a 'generic name' – if the reference name's senior bond is rated A, we shall replace the name by a generic name referred to by the rating A. We can calculate the expected forward price of a bond of this name using the transition matrix as described in Sections 2.3 and 2.6. We shall do something extra here because we want to be able to price the bond in the presence of other reference entities whose transitions are correlated. For example, it might contain autos, telecoms, consumer good names, etc., and we would expect some significant relationship between how these names progress. We would expect autos to be subject to very similar economic influences and, if sales of autos drop significantly, all auto firms will be affected and all will tend to be downgraded and spreads to widen. Similarly, consumer goods and autos will show some correlation because of general economic factors, while utilities and brewing will be much less correlated. We therefore wish to build in the idea of correlated transitions.

First we shall create correlated transitions; then, once we have the forward rating for each entity, we use the forward rating and price the bond using the previous method. We have two fundamental choices – either to use the 'natural measure' (estimates of actual transition probabilities) or the risk-neutral measure (one that replicates the bond's actual spread and spread volatility). If we choose the latter, then the TMs are calibrated to replicate the average spread by rating the bonds in the actual portfolio held, rather than market average spreads. Once we have chosen the transition matrix we wish to use, we can simulate the forward prices of the bond as follows.

Pick a random number x from a normal distribution.[1] Calculate the cumulative probability $\Phi(x)$ associated with x. Compare this probability with the probability from the transition matrix that the A bond has migrated to

1. AAA
2. AA or better
3. A or better
4. etc.

For example, suppose the one-year transition probabilities from A to AAA, AA, . . . are 0.0009, 0.0225, 0.9043, 0.0548, 0.0073, 0.0026, 0.0001 and 0.0074. Then the probabilities that the A bond has migrated to AAA, AA or better, A or better, ... are 0.0009, 0.0234, 0.9277, 0.9826, 0.9899, 0.9925, 0.9926 and 1.0000. Suppose $x = 0$, then $\Phi(x) = 0.5$ and the name has migrated to A or better but not AA or better – in other words it remains A. If $x = -1.5$, then $\Phi(x) = 0.067$ and the name has migrated to AA; if $x = 1.5$, then $\Phi(x) = 0.933$ and the name has migrated to BBB; if $x = 2.5$, then $\Phi(x) = 0.994$ and the name has defaulted. Figure 6.1 summarises the procedure.

The spreadsheet 'Chapter 6.xls' sheet 'from random n to rating' gives an example of this approach. We can use this method to simulate the price of the bond at the end of the year (knowing the simulated rating and the forward life we can calculate the spread using the TM approach described in Chapter 2 and hence the price). Of course if we are using the natural measure then the prices themselves are unrealistic – but typically we are looking at the distribution of price changes and we apply those changes to the actual market price.

---

[1] There are a variety of ways of doing this. The method implemented in the spreadsheet 'Chapter 6 corr spreads.xls' follows 'Box-Muller' (Fishman, 1995; Press et al., 2004). Two random numbers from the uniform distribution are taken (a standard Excel function), one is converted to an exponential distribution, and then a simple transformation produces two independent numbers for the normal distribution. See the 'Normal Distribution' sheet.

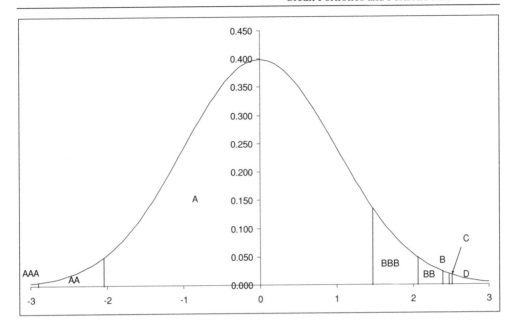

Figure 6.1   From random number to rating: Normal distribution and areas corresponding to rating transition probabilities

If we use the risk-neutral measure we not only incorporate accurate bond pricing but also a volatility measure for bond spreads based on (for example) actual spread volatility rather than just volatility arising from rating transitions.

We can now use this simulated forward bond price distribution for VaR calculation. Similar techniques can be used for credit derivatives – and we can also use this method to calculate the distribution of counterparty exposure on a credit default swap at a forward date.

If we need to simulate over an n-year period then we have two choices: either repeat the above method year by year or calculate the n-year transition matrix and apply the above method once. The latter approach is usually adopted because of speed.

6.3   CORRELATION AND THE MULTI-FACTOR NORMAL (GAUSSIAN) DISTRIBUTION

We wish somehow to correlate the transitions and defaults of the names in the portfolio. This is found to be trivial: if we can produce correlated numbers from the normal distribution, then following through the procedure in section 6.2 we get correlated transitions. How do we produce correlated normal random numbers? There are various ways: a common and simple method is to take the correlation matrix R and calculate the Cholesky decomposition L (Press et al., 2002). The Cholesky matrix is a triangular matrix with the following property:

$$R = L \cdot L^T \tag{6.1}$$

If x is a vector of uncorrelated uniform random numbers, then it turns out that Lx is a vector of random numbers with the correlations in R.

Example

Suppose we have two names in the portfolio, and suppose these have a 0.6 correlation. Then the above becomes

$$\begin{pmatrix} 1 & 0.6 \\ 0.6 & 1 \end{pmatrix} = \begin{pmatrix} 1 & 0 \\ a & b \end{pmatrix} \cdot \begin{pmatrix} 1 & a \\ 0 & b \end{pmatrix} = \begin{pmatrix} 1 & a \\ a & a^2 + b^2 \end{pmatrix}$$

so $a = 0.6$ and $b = \sqrt{(1 - 0.6^2)} = 0.8$. So, if we generate two independent uniform random numbers x_1 and x_2 then the two numbers x_1 and $0.6 \cdot x_1 + 0.8 \cdot x_2$ are normal random numbers with a 0.6 correlation. Generally if we take two (uncorrelated) random numbers x_1 and x_2 from a Normal distribution, then

$$\begin{pmatrix} 1 & 0 \\ \rho & \sqrt{(1 - \rho^2)} \end{pmatrix} \cdot \begin{pmatrix} x_1 \\ x_2 \end{pmatrix} = \begin{pmatrix} x_1 \\ \rho \cdot x_1 + \sqrt{(1 - \rho^2)} x_2 \end{pmatrix}$$

gives us two correlated Normal random numbers (with correlation ρ).

The spreadsheet 'Chapter 6 corr spreads.xls' sheet 'corr fwd spreads' implements this approach for two names. The extension to many names is mathematically trivial but is best handled in code rather than a spreadsheet. The process described above – generating correlated Normal random numbers using a correlation matrix and independent Normal random numbers – is referred to as the **Normal** or **Gaussian Copula** and is discusses in detail in Part III.

If we are looking at a very large portfolio (500 or more reference names) the procedure described above for correlating the transitions can be replaced by something more efficient using 'factor analysis' to simulate correlated spread movements and defaults (see Part III).

Note that not all symmetric matrices with unity on the diagonal, and off axis elements between -1 and $+1$, are correlation matrices. For example,

$$\begin{pmatrix} 1 & 0.99 & 0.99 \\ 0.99 & 1 & 0.5 \\ 0.99 & 0.5 & 1 \end{pmatrix}$$

is not a correlation matrix. Imaging that the random variables are three coins which may come up heads or tails. If A comes up heads then B is very likely to come up heads, and C is also very likely to come up heads. Likewise, if A comes up tails, B and C are both very likely to come up tails. So in most experiments all three coins come up with the same face showing. The correlation between B and C has to be high – it turns out that 0.5 is not possible. *The implication is that the correlation matrix cannot be set up arbitrarily, and cannot be stressed arbitrarily.*

6.4   CORRELATION AND THE CORRELATION MATRIX

As described in section 6.2, we replace names in the portfolio by generic names – the total number of names, N, is the same, we are just simplifying the pricing of each name. If we define an $N \times N$ correlation matrix, where there are N names in the portfolio, then we choose N correlated normal random numbers and use them to calculate the forward rating. Once we have the forward rating we calculate the forward price using the method of section 6.2.

The missing step so far is: 'How do we obtain the correlation matrix required in above, and what exactly does it mean?'

First think about the extreme case of 100% correlation – the x's we generate are identical for all names. Names that have the same rating at the start of the period will therefore have the same rating at the end. Names with different ratings at the start will not necessarily change ratings at the same time – the cumulative distribution profile of the transitions for a C name is quite different from that of a AAA name. If $x = 1$, then $\Phi(x) = 0.841$ and the AAA name stays as AAA but the C name moves into default. (See the cumulative probability table in 'modified TM data' of the spreadsheet mentioned above.)

Even for the simple case of 100% correlation is not intuitively clear what this correlation matrix means, or more generally how we can measure it directly. Observing the transitions of names over many years is not likely to lead to useful results since, in particular, default transitions are rare and a very large number of years would be required.

There are several approaches to correlation:

1. We could consider each name by name pair and calculate a correlation based on some data history. One approach commonly adopted is to use the equity price correlation matrix. The only justification for this is convenience – apart from those names that have no equity data; it is not clear that equity correlations have anything to do with correlated transitions.[2]

2. We introduced the idea in section 6.2 by describing the portfolio in terms of auto, consumer goods, and telecoms sectors. Here we are using industry as a **tag** to group companies together rather than considering a name-by-name correlation. A variety of tags are used in practice – for example 'industry' alone, or 'industry, country, and high-yield/investment-grade'. Tag correlation is related to 'factor analysis', discussed in more detail in Part III.

3. Another approach is to choose correlations arbitrarily (usually driven by tags – e.g. auto with auto in the same region, 0.3; telecom/consumer, same region, 0.2; etc.).

4. Yet another approach is to use some form of 'implied correlation' from market price data (see Part III).

In the context of VaR calculations it is common to use correlations derived from equity data. The process of derivation of those correlations is typically not pairwise but based on a factor approach. We shall revisit these topics in a different context in Part III.

---

[2] We shall discuss the Merton model and its relationship to this approach in Part III.

7

Introduction to Credit Derivatives

7.1 PRODUCTS AND USERS

Our purpose here is to give an outline of the credit derivative products traded, and to give some indication of how the market has developed. We shall define and examine these products in greater detail in Parts II–IV.

7.1.1 'Traditional' Credit Instruments

Fixed income derivative traders regard fixed income bonds as derivatives – they use the same techniques and models to value both cash and derivative instruments. Likewise we shall regard credit bonds and loans as credit derivatives. We shall present models which cover these instruments as well as the more obvious credit derivatives.

The traditional credit market covers many more instruments than simply bullet debt. Callable or puttable debt follows the same pattern as for the non-credit market. Such bonds require a model of interest rates and credit (spread and default risk). In addition, convertible debt gives an option to exchange the bonds for a certain number of shares. These add a third dimension to the model which also requires equity prices to be modelled.

Commercial banks have been offering a variety of derivatives of varying complexity for nearly as long as they have been granting loans. A 'guarantee' or 'letter of credit' is economically the same as insurance on a specific debt, and is similar to a single name credit default swap. A 'facility' or 'standby facility' is an agreement to lend a certain amount of money at a fixed spread (over LIBOR, for example) for a predetermined term and within a given timescale. It is economically the same as a spread option on a bond.

We shall define and analyse the modern versions of these products which trade in the investment banking and investment community generally. The commercial banking forms are often not priced in the same way, are generally not traded but held to maturity or expiry, and do not require a mark-to-market value – unlike the traded equivalents.

7.1.2 'Single Name' Credit Derivatives

A (single name) **credit default swap** (CDS) pays a pre-agreed sum of money on a trigger (credit) event in return for defaulted debt of the reference entity. It is similar to insurance on the debt of the company, with the main differences that it is not an insurance policy and there is usually a range of deliverable debt. The CDS forms the core of the credit derivative business in terms of numbers of deals done.

Spread options arise in a variety of forms. A typical example is the right to sell a bond at a certain spread over a reference rate at a certain time in the future. Instead of a bond the underlying instrument may be a default swap. Spread options rarely trade in naked form currently, however they regularly arise embedded in other products such as 'callable asset swaps' and 'callable default swaps'. Callability or puttability in bonds is usually more complicated, driven by both interest rate levels and spreads.

Total return swaps are also classed as credit derivatives, and typically arise when an investor (or bank) sells an asset to another investor (or bank) and simultaneously buys back all the cashflows and mark-to-market changes. Effectively the underlying traded asset is exchanged to an off-balance sheet asset, which is economically equivalent. A total return swap is very similar to a repo trade.

7.1.3   Credit-Linked Notes

A **credit-linked note** (CLN) is a structured product in the form of a bond typically created by a bank. The note may terminate early, and repay less than par, on a trigger (credit) event of a reference entity or entities. The simplest example is where a single name default swap is repackaged into a CLN, but the structure may be much more complicated than this, for example, being related to the risk on a mezzanine tranche of a CDO ('collateralised debt obligation').

7.1.4   Portfolio Credit Derivatives

A trivial example is a **basket** of CDSs. A single contract describes a collection of default swaps, but otherwise the two deals are identical. More often the deal is set up as an 'average basket' – subtly different from a collection of CDSs in the way the premiums reduce as defaults occur. An average basket is actually a single tranche CDO. Examples are the iTraxx and sub-index portfolio CDSs.

Nth to default baskets are quite different products. The market is mainly 'first to default' baskets. A payment is made (in return for defaulted debt) on a trigger event for any one of a pre-agreed list of reference names – usually between 3 and 10. The contract then terminates. The nth to default basket is becoming a vanilla product among portfolio credit derivatives.

We shall use the term **CDO** or **tranche of a CDO** to mean protection of losses on a reference portfolio for losses after the first $x\%$ up to $y\%$. The product often occurs when a commercial bank seeks protection on its portfolio of loans. It may retain the first few percent of losses but seek protection on the rest. Often the term 'CDO' is used to refer to the entire structure – a break reference portfolio (which may or may not exist as an actual portfolio) and tranches of protection which, in total, cover all the losses on the reference portfolio.

CDOs occur in many forms. A recent development has been the creation of standard reference portfolios of CDSs and standard 'tranching' of protection. An example is the iTraxx index – the successor to TRAC-X and iBoxx indices. The iTraxx Europe index relates to a standard portfolio of 125, and there are over 10 smaller indices (from 10 to 30 names) representing industry groups, sub and senior CDSs, high-yield and other sets of names. Market-makers trade standard portfolio structures based on this – generally a single tranche CDS (subject to premium which is close to the average CDS premium when the portfolio started). In addition they trade a standard indexing structure on the 125-name reference portfolio.

Portfolio spread options have also recently been introduced. The presence of actively traded tranches of standard CDOs has opened up the possibility of trading spread and spread volatility on a standard benchmark. The portfolio spread option gives the buyer the right to buy (or sell) the underlying CDO tranche at a predetermined tranche premium.

7.2   MARKET PARTICIPANTS AND MARKET GROWTH

The modern credit derivatives market started to develop in the 1990s and has seen rapid growth from the mid-1990s onwards. Figure 7.1 shows the historic and anticipated growth.

It should be borne in mind when looking at market data on credit derivatives that the underlying product is a structured product that is not traded through an exchange. There is no independent source of volume of transactions or size and type of deals, so data, particularly from the earlier years when the market was less transparent, has to be viewed with caution.

Table 7.1 shows that, although the CD market has grown dramatically, credit derivative trades are still a tiny fraction of the size of the interest rate swaps market – between 2% and 3%.

Figure 7.2 shows the breakdown of the market into products traded in terms of volume of transactions (notional traded): single name default swaps form approximately 50% of the market. These products form the core of the CD business, are the vanilla trading products, and form the core of the credit instruments that are used to hedge more complicated credit structures. Credit-linked notes are also largely embedded single name risks.

Other single name products – total return swaps and spread options – form a very small percentage of the trades (approximately 10%). Note that embedded credit derivatives, in particular spread options embedded in other products, are not captured by the survey.

Portfolio products form about 35% of the total. By numbers of trades these are almost entirely first-to-default baskets that have come to be seen as vanilla portfolio products. CDO deals and related structures form a tiny proportion of the deals by numbers, but tend to be deals in large notional sizes – and entire CDO (all tranches of protection) is typically USD/EUR 500m–1500m, and may be as large as USD/EUR 20bn.

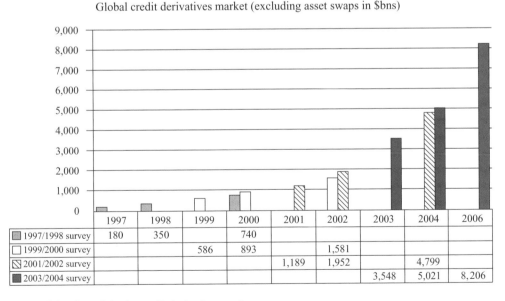

Global credit derivatives market (excluding asset swaps in $bns)

	1997	1998	1999	2000	2001	2002	2003	2004	2006
1997/1998 survey	180	350		740					
1999/2000 survey			586	893		1,581			
2001/2002 survey					1,189	1,952		4,799	
2003/2004 survey							3,548	5,021	8,206

Figure 7.1   Growth in the credit derivatives market
This extract, from the BBA Credit Derivatives Report 2003/2004, is reproduced with the permission of BBA Enterprises Ltd. All rights reserved. © BBA Enterprises Ltd. 2004

Table 7.1 The credit derivatives market compared to the swaps and equity options markets

ISDA Market Survey

Notional amounts outstanding, semiannual data, all surveyed contracts, 1987-present

Notional amounts in billions of US dollars

	Interest rate swaps		Cross-currency swaps		Interest rate options		Total IR and currency		Credit default swaps	Equity derivatives
	Activity	Outstanding	Activity	Outstanding	Activity	Outstanding	Activity	Outstanding	Outstanding	Outstanding
1H87	$ 181.50		$ 43.50				$ 225.00			
2H87	206.30	682.80	42.30	182.80			248.50			865.60
1H88	250.50		60.30				310.80			
2H88	317.60	1,010.20	62.30	316.80		327.30	379.90			1,654.30
1H89	389.20		77.60		186.80		653.60			
2H89	444.40	1,520.60	92.00	434.80	148.70	537.30	685.10			2,474.70
1H90	561.50		94.60		138.00		794.10			
2H90	702.80	2,311.50	118.10	577.50	154.30	561.30	975.20			3,450.30
1H91	762.10		161.30		198.80		1,122.20			
2H91	859.70	3,065.10	167.10	807.20	183.90	577.20	1,210.70			4,449.50
1H92	1,318.30		156.10		293.60		1,768.00			
2H92	1,504.30	3,850.80	145.80	860.40	298.80	634.50	1,948.90			5,345.70
1H93	1,938.40		156.80		509.70		2,604.90			
2H93	2,166.20	6,177.30	138.40	899.60	607.30	1,397.60	2,911.90			8,474.50
1H94	3,182.90		181.00		850.20		4,214.10			
2H94	3,058.00	8,815.60	198.30	914.80	663.00	1,572.80	3,919.30			11,303.20
1H95	3,428.90	10,817.00	153.80	1,039.70	675.80	2,066.20	4,258.50			13,922.90
2H95	5,269.90	12,810.70	301.30	1,197.40	1,339.60	3,704.50	6,910.80			17,712.60
1H96	6,520.30	15,584.20	374.00	1,294.70	1,415.70	4,190.10	8,310.00			21,068.90
2H96	7,157.90	19,170.90	385.10	1,559.60	1,921.50	4,722.60	9,464.50			25,453.10
1H97	10,792.20	22,115.40	463.10	1,584.80	2,566.60	5,033.10	13,821.90			28,733.30
2H97	6,274.90	22,291.30	672.30	1,823.60	1,411.80	4,920.10	8,359.00			29,035.00

1H98	36,974.00		
2H98	50,997.00		
1H99	52,710.50		
2H99	58,265.00		
1H00	60,366.00		
2H00	63,009.00		
1H01	57,305.00	631.50	
2H01	69,207.30	918.87	
1H02	82,737.03	1,563.48	2,312.13
2H02	101,318.49	2,191.57	2,455.29
1H03	123,899.63	2,687.91	2,784.25
2H03	142,306.92	3,583.55	3,444.08

Source: International Swaps and Derivatives Association (2004)

Credit derivatives products

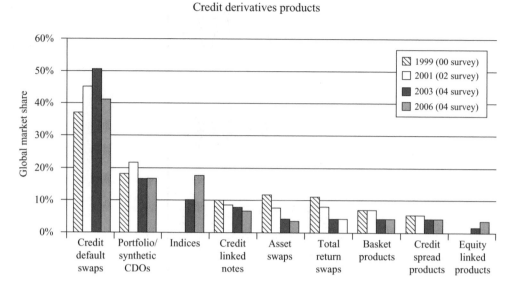

Figure 7.2   Market breakdown by product
This extract, from the BBA Credit Derivatives Report 2003/2004, is reproduced with the permission of BBA Enterprises Ltd. All rights reserved. © BBA Enterprises Ltd. 2004

By notional outstanding total return swaps assume a greater presence. This reflects the typically short life (three months or less) and the large notional size (often in billions) of the TRS deals.

Part II
Credit Default Swaps and Other Single Name Products

8
Credit Default Swaps; Product Description and Simple Applications

8.1 CDS PRODUCT DEFINITION

8.1.1 Contract Description and Example

A (single name) credit default swap (CDS) is a bilateral, off-balance-sheet agreement between two counterparties, in which one party ('the writer') offers the other party ('the buyer') protection against a credit event[1] by a third party ('the reference name') for a specified period of time, in return for premium payment.

The reference entity in the transaction may be a corporate (including banking entity) or a sovereign. In the case of a sovereign reference entity the default risk typically refers to obligations issued in a currency other than that of the sovereign.

The 'buyer' and 'writer' are both referred to as 'counterparties'. Note again that the 'buyer' and 'writer' are defined here in terms of protection rather than risk. Some traders and investors use the same terms to refer to buying or selling risk (the opposite position) – it is obviously important to be clear on the terminology you and your counterparties are using.

The 'buyer' and the 'writer' are often banks, insurance companies, or hedge funds, but can be any corporate or sovereign entity in principle. The quality of the counterparty to the deal has risk and pricing implications (but note the contents of section 8.1.2).

We can see, before looking at details of the contract, that the deal is a portfolio deal: it is dependent on three parties. We shall examine the pricing impactions of this later, and in most of this part we shall assume that both the writer and the buyer are risk free.

CDS Cashflows

1. The contract (typically) pays par in return for 100 nominal of debt if the reference entity suffers a credit event before the maturity of the deal. Deliverable obligations of the reference name are be specified in the documentation.
2. The buyer (typically) pays a premium quarterly in arrears (with a proportion up to the default date of the reference name in the event that default occurs before the maturity of the trade).

Example

On 2 January 2004, ABN AMRO Bank NV buys 5-year protection (terminating on 18 March 2009) on Ford Motor Credit from Deutsche Bank, on a notional amount of USD 10m, paying a premium of 200 bp p.a. (quarterly in arrears).

---

[1] For the moment think of a 'credit event' as 'default'. Section 8.3 defines the term more precisely – for typical CDS, other events such as 'bankruptcy' and 'restructuring' can trigger the CDS payment.

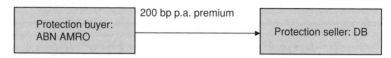

Figure 8.1   Vanilla CDS pre-default

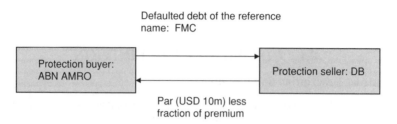

Figure 8.2   Vanilla CDS post-default

- *Pre-default* (Figure 8.1): ABN pays (usually on an actual/360 day count convention) a quarterly amount of (usually a little over) USD 50 000 to Deutsche Bank.
- *Post-default* (Figure 8.2): Approximately one month after a 'credit event' ABN delivers USD 10m worth (based on notional) of debt of FMC in return for USD 10m less the proportion of USD 200 000 from the previous dividend date to the default date. Note that delivered debt may be YEN, EUR or other currency debt, but the notional amount of debt is chosen to be the same as USD 10m, taking the current exchange rate (on the day that notice of the bond to be delivered is given).

Note that the reference entity – FMC – is not a party to the deal in any from, although it is the occurrence of a credit event on FMC that triggers the capital payment from DB to ABN.

The buyer of protection (ABN) usually has the choice of what debt to deliver – within constraints such as G7 currencies (USD, CAD, JPY, EUR and GBP) and the debt being less than 30 years maturity. This is called the **delivery option**, and was originally introduced to reduce the risk of a squeeze developing on a deliverable issue. In the former years of CDS trading there were examples of more protection being sold on a specific name and bond than there was deliverable debt to deliver into the contract. A credit event would cause that particular deliverable to rise to par. If the bond could be bought below par, the holders of protection with no debt to deliver could buy the bonds to deliver and obtain the capital gain on the CDS; holders of debt and CDSs would have no incentive to sell debt below par, and holders of bonds only would be bid up until the price reached par.

8.1.2   Market CDS Quotes

CDS quotes from brokers typically refer to inter-bank deals which are collateralised and where the counterparties are rated A or better, termed **professional counterparties**. Deals on a certain reference entity, to the same maturity, would not necessarily be done at the same price if one or other of the counterparties is of poorer quality (for example, an unrated corporate entity, such as a typical hedge fund) and/or if no collateral agreement is in place.

Market CDS quotes also refer to a **standard** CDS contract as follows:

(1) payoff of par;
(2) physical delivery with the delivery option (i.e. there is not a specified deliverable);

(3) premia paid quarterly in arrears with a proportion to the default date;

(4) various forms of restructuring are quoted and, although CDSs are normally on senior unsecured debt, subordinated CDSs are also quoted.

CDS premia are often referred to as **spreads**, which is misleading since they are not a spread to anything (the terminology arose because a CDS premium – expressed in basis points per 100 nominal – is of similar magnitude to a bond spread).

8.1.3 Related Products

We classify any product which is broadly economically identical to a CDS as a CDS for the purpose of later discussions. In particular, if a CDS is written under insurance company documentation rather than ISDA documentation and cashflow triggers are not materially different, then we regard this as a vanilla CDS.

Wrapped bonds have many of the features of a vanilla CDS contract. In the event of a credit event the writer (typically an insurance company) pays the promised cashflows on the bond rather than the original issuer. This is economically equivalent to paying the capital value of those cashflows at the time of default – a sum which will depend on interest rate levels at the time, as well as the life and coupon of the debt. Pricing and valuation are therefore different from a vanilla CDS, though the modifications required are straightforward.

Average baskets refer to a portfolio of names and are documented in a very similar way to a single name CDS. Each name may have a notional amount and premium rate associated with it. On a credit event on one name, the notional amount is paid in return for defaulted debt, the premium associated with that name ceases, and the basket continues with the remaining names. In this case an average basket is merely a portfolio of single name CDS contracts, the only difference being that a single piece of documentation is signed rather than many. Average baskets formed the predecessor to standardised portfolio credit derivatives – such as the products based on the iTraxx indices.

An alternative contract (a 'portfolio CDS') has a single premium rate which is reduced in proportion to the notional loss. In this case the basket is actually a single tranche CDO and behaves slightly differently from average baskets (see Part III). The iTraxx-based deals are mostly of this form.

Average baskets should not be confused with first-to-default baskets as both types are sometimes unhelpfully referred to as 'baskets'.

Bank guarantees are traditional contracts granted by commercial banks to certain customers. Economically they are similar in form to CDS contracts. Typically they exist on the banking books and are not marked-to-market (or even 'priced' when they are sold in a way that an investment banker would recognise).

8.2 DOCUMENTATION

8.2.1 ISDA Documentation and Insurance Contract Differences

CDS deals are structured over-the-counter products, as opposed to exchange-traded products, and as such are subject to their own documentation. This documentation specifies key items – maturity, premium, reference name, what constitutes a 'credit event', etc. – as well as technical details such as business calendars, legal jurisdiction or day-count convention. The banking community typically trades CDSs under an ISDA master agreement and ISDA standard documentation. This documentation represents a format that can be varied to a greater or lesser extent (and has changed over time – so many older contracts on the books of traders and investors have slightly different documentation). Again, the trading community prefers standardisation because it then avoids 'documentation risk' in hedging. The addendum to this section shows the format of the ISDA CDS documentation. Many of the terms in this document – including 'credit events' and 'restructuring' – are discussed in more detail below.

The general form of ISDA CDS documentation looks odd at first, since it closely resembles that of an interest rate swap (on which it is indeed based). Terms such as 'fixed rate payer' and 'floating rate payer' are not particularly helpful to an understanding of the product. The very name 'default "swap"' stems from the interest rate swap documentation that was 'borrowed' to document the first CDS deals, and from the analogy of paying a regular 'swap' premium (as opposed to a single up-front premium) in exchange for the protection on the reference entity's debt. At one time the term **default option** was used for deals where the CDS premium was paid up-front.

Insurance Contracts and Documentation

A CDS is economically very like an insurance contract on debt issued by a company. What are the differences between a CDS and an insurance policy? The key differences are as follows:

1. An insurance policy calls itself an 'insurance' policy or contract and is written by an insurance company; a CDS is typically written under ISDA documentation and does not call itself an insurance contract (the writer may be a bank, insurance company or other institution).
2. An insurance contract requires the owner of the insurance to own the insured risk at the time a claim is made.
3. In addition, insurance companies – the writers of insurance policies – are regulated by an insurance regulator; banks are regulated by a central bank; and other bodies may not have a regulator other than generally through accounting and legal requirements.

Insurance documentation may look very different from ISDA documentation. Materially different conditions may apply – for example, replacement clauses for reference entities may exist in certain circumstances (e.g. if the reference entity rating drops below a certain level it can be replaced with another reference entity). Often, however, insurance companies will now write CDS contracts under ISDA documentation. They are then not insurance contracts but simply a CDS where the counterparty is an insurance company.[2]

Exercise

What are the risk control implications of the following?

1. An insurance contract (written under ISDA) vs a banking contract. (Minimal – the counterparty is strictly regulated.)
2. A CDS written by a hedge fund vs a banking contract. (Unregulated counterparty, probably unrated.)
3. A CDS written by a corporate vs a banking contract. (As above, though large corporates typically have rated debt.)

How would you control the risk in the above?

---

[2] The insurance company may have to go through the process of setting up an SPV to write the CDS, and itself write some form of 'guarantee' or insurance on the SPV.

CDS Maturity, Premium, Trade and Effective Dates

Initially CDS deals were traded on a business day, with an effective date (the commencement of risk) several days later (now typically two days), and a maturity date at the business day anniversary of the effective date (say five years later). For example, a CDS traded on 5 February 2002 may have had an effective date of 12 February 2002 and a maturity date of 12 February 2007. This meant that a deal traded one day, and another offsetting 5-year deal (in the opposite direction) on the same name one day later, did not exactly match each other – there would be a day's unhedged exposure in five years' time (unless the second deal was deliberately done in a 'short' 5-year with a 12 February 2007 maturity). Dealers have now moved to an IMM style calendar – with set maturities on the 20th March/June/September/December, and coupon payments on the same dates. This means that a new 5-year deal will have anything from 5 to 5.25 years' life, and there is a 3-month window during which trading on the current 5-year contract will exactly match the maturity of other deals: a major benefit to the trading community and an improvement in liquidity. Deals under the old format, of course, persist on traders' and investors' books.

Payoff and Premium Variations

It is relatively common (around 5% of all trades) to see other premium schedules – semi-annual, annual, in-advance, without proportion (or refund). Single up-front (or at maturity) premia also occur. In these cases a proportion may or may not be refunded (paid) on early default.

Payoff may be 'par plus accrued' on the delivered asset. This only usually happens when the deliverable itself is specified (see below).

Deliverable Obligation

Occasionally one comes across a CDS where there is a specified deliverable – the buyer can deliver one and only one instrument. This is usually related to a commercial bank trade where the bank wants to get protection for a particular asset on its books. At one time regulatory treatment was unclear, and specifying the deliverable was an attempt to prove to an uncertain regulator that the protection did in fact cover the risky asset, and regulatory relief could then be obtained. It is rare to see specified deliverables currently (see also 'reference obligation' below).

We shall address the **fixed recovery** CDS under 'digital' CDS later.

Settlement: Cash or Physical

Cash settlement is an alternative possibility to physical settlement. On a credit event the writer pays par less the market value of defaulted debt of the reference name (less any accrued premium and subject to a minimum of zero). This typically involves a dealer poll to get independent valuations of defaulted debt of the appropriate seniority and taking an average price. The process has to be spelt out in detail in the CDS documentation, together with possible recourses for the other counterparty if they disagree. Usually the writer is the calculating agent.

Cash settlement is rare in a vanilla CDS contract. It is sometimes offered as an alternative if physical settlement is impossible for some reason (such as an inability to transfer debt because of a newly imposed legal restriction). It is more common in CLNs and portfolio CD products.

Convertibles

Convertibles may be delivered into a CDS contract if they meet the other criteria and are not explicitly excluded.

This was clarified[3] as a result of a case between Nomura and CSFB regarding Railtrack. Railtrack suffered a credit event (it was put into 'administration'). Bonds were not in default as no 'failure to pay' had occurred ('administration/Chapter 11' are credit events for a CDS but do not constitute default for bonds). It was perceived that Railtrack would continue to meet its obligations on its bonds – and most bonds were high coupon – so the debt continued to trade over par. Holders of such bonds and of CDS protection would not deliver notice that the CDS had been triggered because delivery of above par debt would result in a loss. On the other hand, writers of protection would deliver such a notice but typically the buyer would fail to deliver since this would result in a loss on bonds over par (the choice not to deliver is always available). However, Nomura owned some convertible debt trading at a price of around 60 (because it carried a low coupon). By delivering into the CDS contracts it owned, it could make a profit of 40.

This case does point out one additional risk of writing CDS protection rather than owning a bond. A 'technical' credit event (where a trigger event occurs but bonds are continuing to trade around par) allows the delivery of low coupon debt into the CDS for a loss to the writer of par minus the market price of the debt.

8.2.2 Reference Obligations and 'Mark-it RED'

Current documentation refers to a 'reference obligation'. The purpose of the reference obligation is to define the seniority of deliverable debt. If a credit event occurs then the buyer can deliver defaulted debt of the same seniority as the reference obligation or a higher seniority (for example, the CDS buyer could deliver transferable loans even if the CDS referenced senior unsecured debt). Some CDS deals written in the past under ISDA documentation do not have a reference obligation. In these cases the CDS refers to senior unsecured debt.

The aim of Mark-it RED[4] (reference entity database) is to define a standard list of reference obligations for each reference entity that trades in the credit markets.[5] The aim is to help to avoid confusion and simplify the process of choosing an appropriate reference obligation of the correct seniority at the time the CDS is written. Any error in the choice of reference obligation may make the CDS legally unclear or may change the seniority from what was intended. The use of standard identifiers – the 'RED CLIP codes' – helps to avoid such errors.

Quoted from Mark-it Partners summary[6]:

Mark-it RED provides confidence with market standard, scrubbed reference entity and obligation pairs.

- More than 2 000 scrubbed reference entity/obligation pairs.
- Audited, accurate legal reference entity names
- Proprietary, tried and tested reference data scrubbing process

---

[3] The uncertainty centred around the non-deliverability of 'contingent debt' under the ISDA documentation. It was not clear whether convertibles were contingent or not, and the court case clarified this.

[4] RED is operated by Mark-it Partners.

[5] In the process, RED also identifies the precise legal reference entity – the issuer, or the guarantor, of the debt. For example 'Ford Motor Credit Company' and 'Ford Motor Company' are different legal entities: both trade in the credit derivatives markets with very different risk profiles.

[6] Information provided courtesy of Mark-it Partners.

- Unique, six-digit alpha-numeric CLIPS to identify reference entities
- Unique, nine-digit alpha-numeric CLIPS to identify a reference entity/obligation pair
- Complete re-scrubs at least annually or within two months of a corporate event.

8.3 CREDIT TRIGGERS FOR CREDIT DERIVATIVES

8.3.1 Credit Events

Bonds are at risk to a 'default' event. What constitutes 'default' is specified in the issue document of the bond. Likewise CDS documentation must specify what constitutes a 'credit event' – the event that triggers the capital payoff on the CDS. Similar to most in the market we shall usually refer to a CDS credit event as 'default', although it is wider than bond default. The key credit events are

1. Failure to pay. This usually has to be of a certain amount of money – the failure to settle a telephone bill on time will not usually meet the requirement!
2. Bankruptcy – Chapter 11 (US), 'In Administration' (UK) and similar events. This may occur without a 'failure to pay' (default), and without an ultimate debt restructuring (e.g. Railtrack in the UK).
3. Restructuring (see below).

8.3.2 Restructuring

'Restructuring' refers to the event where the borrower rearranges the debt of the company, usually to the detriment of the lenders but usually with their permission (the alternative – not giving permission – being worse). This may involve lowering the coupon, lengthening the debt, reducing the nominal, reducing the seniority, or otherwise replacing the debt with something of lower value. Sovereign borrowers typically restructure, and it is far from uncommon for corporate entities to restructure. Until around 2001 when Conseco agreed a restructuring with its bankers, it was normal to trade CDSs with 'original restructuring'. CDSs currently trade with various types of restructuring clause.

1. No restructuring trigger (rare).
2. 'Original restructuring' (US until 2001, EU until 2003/2004).
3. 'Modified restructuring' (US 2001–2004).
4. 'Modified modified restructuring' (EU and US 2004–).

The detail of the following is not necessary for an understanding of the remainder of the book, but is described for completeness.

'Original restructuring' did not have a materiality clause but required the following:

1. A reduction in the rate or amount of interest or the amount of scheduled interest accruals.
2. A reduction in the amount of principal or premium payable at maturity or scheduled termination date.
3. A postponement or other deferral of a date or dates for (a) payment or accrual of interest, or (b) payment of principal or premium.
4. A change in the ranking in priority of payment of any obligation causing the subordination of that obligation.

5. Any change in the currency or composition of any payment of interest or principal where this results directly or indirectly from a deterioration in the financial condition of the reference entity.

The Conseco case caused US market participants to question the clause. Conseco and its banks agreed to a restructuring of certain loans, including an extension of maturities and a commitment to pay down those loans early from the proceeds of asset sales. Holders of long-dated bonds (trading at very depressed prices) and of CDS protection, delivered such debt into CDS protection under the above restructuring clause. Participants realised that the CDSs contained a significant 'cheapest to deliver option' triggered by restructuring, and this feature makes a CDS significantly different from a synthetic bond (the same is true of 'administration/Chapter 11' without a failure to pay, but this is much rarer than restructuring). NY dealers then started trading CDSs with no restructuring trigger, but this caused regulatory problems in some areas and led to the introduction of the 'mod R' clause.

Modified restructuring sought to limit the cases when a restructuring could trigger a CDS contract and introduce a 'restructuring maturity limitation'.

On the occurrence of a restructuring event only debt that has maturity on or before the earlier of

(a) 30 months after the restructuring date, and
(b) the latest maturity of the restructured debt,

is deliverable but subject to any debt being deliverable that has a life less than or equal to that of the CDS itself.

The above do not apply if the seller triggers the CDS.

Generally this results in deliverable debt being of a similar maturity to the CDS (if this is longer than 30 months), and results in the CDS being closer to a proxy bond.

Other conditions introduced at the same time were:

(c) restructured facilities must have at least four creditors and need at least a two-thirds majority to approve
(d) 'consent not-required debt' only is deliverable, or is generally transferable ('rule 144A, reg. S'),
(e) partial settlement is allowed.

Modified restructuring makes two changes to the above in a broadening of the scope of deliverable debt:

(a) *restructured* debt with up to 60 months' maturity is deliverable (other deliverable debt remains at 30 months), and
(b) the deliverable obligation must be *conditionally* transferable (consent may not be unreasonably withheld).

8.4   CDS APPLICATIONS AND ELEMENTARY STRATEGIES

The main application of a single name CDS is as a 'building block' for other more complex trades and as a liquid hedging tool. In the process, the vanilla CDS defines market levels. In this section we look at some basic applications of single name products in general terms, covering more detail (and more applications) in Chapters 10 to 15.

8.4.1 Single Names

Directional Trading/Relative Trades

If you take the view that spreads are going to narrow on General Motors, then you could buy GM debt. Alternatively, you could sell CDSs referencing GM – say 5-year at 200 bp. If you are right and spreads narrow to 150 bp then you could buy back the CDSs at 150 bp, making 50 bp per annum for 5 years – a profit of a little under 2.5% of notional (we look at an exact calculation in Chapter 12).

Using a CDS rather than a bond does not require capital but does require that you are a 'professional counterparty' so that the buyer of protection will trade with you on an unfunded basis.

Alternatively if you believe that GM will widen, a long protection position will make a similar profit if spreads subsequently widen to 250 bp and the protection could be sold for a 50 bp profit per annum. The alternative of shorting debt is difficult to achieve. To some extent the CDS market developed as an alternative to an open repo market in credit debt. CDSs are a simple practical means of taking a bearish position on credit debt.

Suppose, instead, your view is that GM looks more attractive than Ford. Selling protection on GM makes money if spreads narrow, but loses money if spreads widen. The opposite position in FMC – buying protection to the same maturity – will largely offset this if spreads move together. Money will be made if, as you expect, spreads widen on FMC relative to GM.

Exercise

Suppose 5-year GM is trading at 150 bp while FMC is 200 bp. Work through the example where

(a) spreads both widen by 50 bp
(b) where GM widens by 20 bp but FMC widens by 70 bp.

Debt Hedging

An owner of 5-year senior unsecured France Telecom bonds could hedge the risk (in a general sense) by buying CDS protection. In the occurrence of a credit event during the life of the CDS, the debt can be delivered into the CDS and par is received. The value of the bond (or its purchase price) may be 90, so this represents over-protection (equivalently, too much is being paid for the protection).

Prior to default, widening of the spread on FrTel bonds (leading to a fall in capital value) is likely to be accompanied by widening of the CDS spread (leading to a mark-to-market profit on the CDS). Therefore, there is some spread hedging between the two, and precisely how much depends on the 'delta hedge ratio' and the 'basis risk', both of which we examine in detail in Chapter 10. The CDS therefore protects not only against the default event risk but also against the mark-to-market change in value of the bond arising from spread change.

Suppose now that the FrTel asset is not a bond but a bank loan. It may be possible to arrange a CDS referencing loan at an appropriate cost but liquid CDS contracts usually cover risk on less senior debt and are more expensive. Even so, loans – being more senior than bonds – are in principle deliverable into standard CDS contracts. But on a credit event the owner of the loan may have a problem delivering the loan – it may be non-assignable. In this case the

CDS owner will have to buy defaulted debt to deliver to receive par and a profit of par less the recovery on bonds. The loan will remain on the books until 'ultimate recovery' is received – which will probably be more than the recovery price paid for the debt delivered into the CDS. The portfolio manager can therefore protect non-assignable loans using a vanilla CDS, albeit at a cost.

8.4.2　Sector/Portfolio Trades

Just as CDSs can be used to reflect a 'bullish' or 'bearish' view[7] on an individual name, they can also be used to reflect an absolute (spreads falling or rising) or relative view of one sector versus another – e.g. bullish of autos versus telecoms. Some index-based CDS products may be appropriate – for example, the iTraxx TMT (telecom, media and technology) and auto indices – but often the view has to be implemented by dealing in a portfolio of representative names.

If your view is that the motor industry looks attractive relative to telecoms, then again you could write protection on a portfolio of auto names and buy protection on a portfolio of telecom names in order to reduce exposure to any single name. The usual minimum trading size is 5m per name. If you think five names is the minimum number to get acceptable diversification, then a 100 bp move corresponds to a profit or loss of around 1.25m (25m × 5 year × 1%). Clearly how the view is implemented depends on how large an adverse move you are prepared to withstand, and the size of your risk limits.

> **Exercise**
> Suppose your risk appetite is 100k (i.e. you are prepared to risk a 100k loss on a deal before cutting it and licking your wounds). You set a stop at a 20bp adverse move. How many names could you incorporate in the 5-year mini-portfolio in order to implement the trade?
>
> *Hint*: On 5m nominal what loss does a 20 bp move correspond to?

An alternative approach would be to seek average basket deals each referencing 5–10 names with a total exposure on each of around 20m. The average basket allows more names but a smaller exposure per name, because a single piece of documentation (for each basket) is used. The disadvantage is the limitation on the possibilities for unwinds. Average baskets have less appeal than single name products and offsetting trades are harder to come by – liquidity is lower – often tying the buyer to go back to the original counterparty for an unwind.

Typically this style of trading is implemented by proprietary or hedge fund traders and as an overlay to the general hedging of positions by a trading book.

8.4.3　Income Generation

Certain funds sell options (for example, equity call options) as a means of enhancing return on a portfolio. Often this is done against positions actually held – a large rise in the share then results in a limited gain (on assets held) rather than an actual loss. CDSs can likewise be used to generate income by selling protection, but this would not normally have a natural hedge already in place. Such a trade often appeals to insurance companies or banks who are typically

---

[7] Interpreted with respect to bond prices – i.e. 'bullish' means bond prices are rising, bond spreads are falling and hence CDS premia are falling.

investors in risk. So far investors have not generally traded in this way, preferring to build a portfolio of credit bonds instead.

The question then is how best to reduce the risk on the portfolio (by diversification) and how to maximise a risk-adjusted return. This is generally handled by setting limits on individual exposures, country exposures, industry exposures, rating exposures, etc. Limits could be set in nominal terms, possibly by reference to risk-weighted exposure (nominal × default rate time life).

Exercise

The objective is to generate an income of 20m per annum subject to a 'risk' of the premium amount in any year. What portfolio make-up would you suggest?

Hint: The first problem is to clarify the question in the investor's mind. This is best done by working through an example. Suppose we have a portfolio with an average spread of 100 bp – and a 2bn size. If this is a *managed* portfolio of BBB names then the historical default rate may be 0.3% per annum (the one-year historical default rate even though it is a 5-year portfolio). If there are 100 names in the portfolio then we would expect 0.3 defaults, and probably[8] less than $0.3 + 2 \times 0.55 = 1.4$ defaults; so if recovery is 50% we would not anticipate a loss of more than 7m. Write a list of discussion points (e.g. spread and historical data; variability of rates over time; portfolios size and correlation; mark-to-market risk; . . .).

8.4.4 Regulatory Capital Reduction

This example illustrates some of the basic principles of using CDSs to reduce regulatory capital. The example is in the context of Basle 88 regulations – the same basic approach applies under Basle II but the capital percentages will be different. The example is not commonly implemented in this form – rather portfolio trades are done (these are covered in Chapter 10).

Suppose a bank owns a EUR 10m 5-year loan to a corporate entity generating 80 bp in spread. Currently the bank has to allocate 8% of notional as capital against this trade, which therefore generates a 10% return on capital.

The bank buys CDS protection on the reference entity at 60 bp – spreads may have narrowed since the loan was issued – for the same or slightly longer maturity than the loan (this is required in order to get any capital relief). The net income is now reduced to 20 bp. The regulatory capital depends on the counterparty to the CDS trade. If this counterparty is a G7 bank then the 8% requirement is reduced to 1.6%, so the return on capital is now increased to 12.5%. Capital which is released can be used to put in place new loans earning not just the spread but also fee income.

Economic Capital Reduction/Releasing Lines

The same deal could be done to reduce 'economic capital'. An institution has internal rules for assessing risk on any deal – loans and CDSs, etc. These rules may be rating and maturity dependent and will typically allocate an amount of capital to a deal which is used both to assess

---

[8] Think of the distribution of defaults in any year as a binomial distribution whose expected number of defaults is (number of names, n) × (default probability of a single name, q), with a standard deviation of $\sqrt{[n \times q \times (1 - q)]}$. (See any book on probability – for example, Billingsley, 1995.)

profitability – return on capital – and to restrict total risk. The regulatory capital example above applies equally to economic capital.

A commercial bank imposes limits on the exposure to a single client – a 'line'. Once a line is full no further lending can take place to that client. The option of selling existing loans to enable new loans to take place may not be attractive. The bank may require the consent of the borrower to sell these loans, which may jeopardise the client relationship. FMC may not be aware that a CDS deal referencing its debt has taken place – hence this offers the bank a chance to reduce the risk to FMC on its banking books *synthetically* without risking any banking relationship that may exist between the bank and FMC. The non-assignable loan stays on the books but, because CDS protection has been bought, the exposure (line) to FMC is reduced during the life of the CDS, and new lending can take place.

Other

We look in detail at examples of curve trading, recovery trading, and other applications from Chapter 10 onwards.

8.5   COUNTERPARTY RISK: PFE FOR CDS

The traditional approach to counterparty risk is covered in Part I, Chapter 5, together with the question of correlation risk for CDSs (and other deals).

Potential Future Exposure and Capital Allocation

A further step to prepare for counterparty risk is to reserve against it. Take a EUR 20m 5-year long CDS on a reference name subject to a contractual premium of 100 bp. The market spread yesterday was 200 bp and today it has moved to 210 bp. What is the current (approximate) M2M? What key factors affect the M2M in the future? At what time in the life of the deal does potential future exposure reach a maximum?

The current M2M is only the accrued premium if the premium on the deal is equal to the current 'fair' market premium. If spreads are static, then M2M remains zero, but if spreads are volatile it can become positive or negative. As life increases, the forward CDS spread becomes more uncertain but the life is shortening so the value of the premium difference is declining (see the spreadsheet 'Chapter 8.xls').

If the premium on the trade is other than the current fair market premium, then there is the initial mark-to-market value to add on. This may be positive or negative (e.g. in the above example the premium on the deal is 110 bp from today's market level, increasing the exposure to the counterparty.

How would you allocate capital? One approach is to take the maximum PFE × default risk of counterparty. If a cautious estimate of default risk is taken, this should reduce as the number of counterparties increases. A more sophisticated approach would be to look at counterparty VaR.

8.6   CDS TRADING DESK

8.6.1   Mechanics of Transacting a CDS Deal

As a structured product a CDS transaction requires the verification and exchange of contracts, involving the legal department. For vanilla deals this has been streamlined. Initially (circa

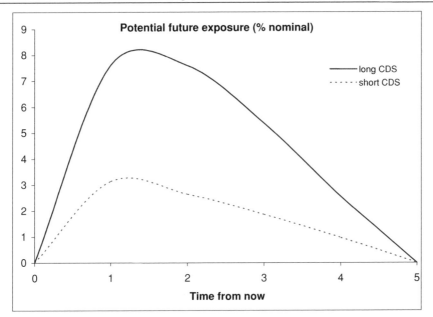

Figure 8.3   Potential future exposure on a 5-year CDS subject to 100 bp premium

mid-to late-1990s) 5–7 business days were allowed between agreeing the outline terms of the deal ('term-sheet') and signing the documentation ('confirmation'). This has been reduced and the term-sheet is now no longer used for vanilla deals between professional counterparties but a general form of contract is agreed between them before they begin dealing with each other. With that in place, the particular deal contract is usually signed within one day of dealing.

A second important item to check is the quality of the counterparty and the counterparty/ reference entity correlation risk assessment – tasks performed by the credit risk department.

On the trade date: General terms are agreed with the counterparty (possibly via a broker) – reference entity, maturity, premium, etc. A term sheet is produced for non-vanilla deals and passed to legal; the trade details are entered into risk management and reporting systems (as a 'pending' deal); credit risk approves lines for the counterparty and approves the correlation risk.

On the effective date (trade date + 1 day): The confirmation has been signed by both parties; the trade moves from 'pending' to 'live'. The writer goes on risk and premiums start to accrue.

8.6.2   Trade Monitoring, Credit Events, Unwinds

Trade monitoring includes the following processes:

1. Update of market data for risk assesment
2. Validation of and checks on market data against independent sources
3. Generation of risk reports, P&L and all other reports
4. Reconciliation of P&L changes with market moves
5. Updating counterparty risk exposures; posting of collateral
6. Monitoring for credit and rating events.

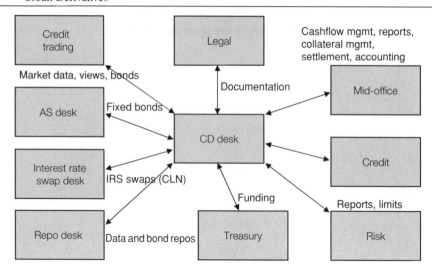

Figure 8.4   CDS dealing desk infrastructure

A credit event will spark a variety of actions. Deals will typically need to be rebooked, with updated deal information for credit event data: when the credit event occurred, what bond was delivered, notional amount and currency, which notices were given and by which party, the amount of accrued premium, final settlement amount (cash).

An 'unwind' will cause the original deal to stay on the books (to allow historical investigations) although the risk will be terminated. New data to be recorded includes the termination date, final payment, and calculation basis.

8.6.3   CDS Desk Interactions and Organisation

The desk interacts with credit, repo and asset swap trading desks, the sales desk, treasury and interest rate swap desk (particularly where CLN deals are concerned), and with risk and mid-office departments who monitor the deal and cashflows arising from the deal. The interactions are summarised in Figure 8.4.

The 'desk' itself may consist of geographically separate sections whose primary responsibility is for a region (typically North America, Europe or Asia). As one market closes responsibility for the book of that region passes to other desks – where there is limited trading in CDSs outside that desk's prime area of responsibility.

In addition, responsibility for investment grade reference entities and for 'high-yield' and 'emerging market' reference entities is usually split.

ADDENDUM: ISDA 2003 CDS CONFIRMATION

Reproduced by permission of International Swaps and Derivatives Association, Inc.

2003 MASTER CREDIT DERIVATIVES
CONFIRMATION AGREEMENT

This 2003 Master Credit Derivatives Confirmation Agreement ("Master Confirmation Agreement") is dated as of [_____] between [_____] ("Party A") and [_____] ("Party B").

The parties wish to facilitate the process of entering into and confirming Credit Derivative Transactions and accordingly agree as follows:

1. *Credit Derivatives Definitions.* This Master Confirmation Agreement hereby incorporates by reference the 2003 ISDA Credit Derivatives Definitions as supplemented by the May 2003 Supplement to the 2003 ISDA Credit Derivatives Definitions (together, the "Credit Derivatives Definitions"). Any capitalized term not otherwise defined herein shall have the meaning assigned to such term in the Credit Derivatives Definitions.

2. *Confirmation Process.* The parties intend to enter into separate Credit Derivative Transactions (each a "Transaction") with respect to each Reference Entity set out in a Transaction Supplement substantially in the form attached as Annex 1 (a "Transaction Supplement"). The confirmation applicable to each Transaction, which shall constitute a "Confirmation" for the purposes of, and will supplement, form a part of, and be subject to, the ISDA Master Agreement between Party A and Party B dated as of [_____], as amended and supplemented from time to time (the "Master Agreement"), shall consist of this Master Confirmation Agreement including the form of General Terms Confirmation attached as Exhibit A (the "General Terms Confirmation"), as supplemented by the trade details applicable to such Transaction as set forth in the Transaction Supplement.[9]

   In the event of any inconsistency between (i) this Master Confirmation Agreement, including the form of General Terms Confirmation and a Transaction Supplement and/or (ii) the Credit Derivatives Definitions and a Transaction Supplement, the Transaction Supplement shall govern for the purpose of the relevant Transaction. The Transaction Supplement shall set forth, at a minimum, all of the information set out in the applicable form of Transaction Supplement attached hereto as Annex 1.

3. *Non-Exclusive.* The parties acknowledge and agree that the execution of this Master Confirmation Agreement does not require them to document Transactions in accordance with this Master Confirmation Agreement.

4. *Preparation of Transaction Supplements.* The preparation of a Transaction Supplement shall be the responsibility of the Seller in respect of the Transaction to which the relevant Transaction Supplement relates.

---

[9] If the parties have not yet executed an ISDA Master Agreement, the following language shall be included: "The confirmation applicable to each Transaction shall consist of this Master Confirmation Agreement including the form of General Terms Confirmation attached as Exhibit A (the "General Terms Confirmation"), as supplemented by the trade details applicable to such Transaction as set forth in the Transaction Supplement and shall constitute a "Confirmation" as referred to in the ISDA Master Agreement specified below. The Confirmation applicable to each Transaction will evidence a complete and binding agreement between the parties as to the terms of the Transaction to which such Confirmation relates. In addition, the parties agree to use all reasonable efforts promptly to negotiate, execute and deliver an agreement in the form of an ISDA Master Agreement, with such modifications as the parties in good faith agree. Upon execution by the parties of such an agreement (the "Master Agreement"), each Confirmation already executed in connection with this Master Confirmation Agreement and all future Confirmations executed in connection with this Master Confirmation Agreement will supplement, form a part of, and be subject to, that Master Agreement. All provisions contained in or incorporated by reference in that Master Agreement upon its execution will govern each Confirmation except as expressly modified below. Until the parties execute and deliver that Master Agreement, each Confirmation confirming a Transaction entered into between the parties in connection with this Master Confirmation Agreement (notwithstanding anything to the contrary in a Confirmation), shall supplement, form a part of, and be subject to, an agreement in the form of the 2002 ISDA Master Agreement as if the parties had executed an agreement in such form (but without any Schedule except for the election of [New York Law] [English Law] as the governing law) on the Trade Date of the first such Transaction between the parties in connection with this Master Confirmation Agreement. In the event of any inconsistency between the provisions of that agreement and a Confirmation, the Confirmation will prevail for purposes of the relevant Transaction."

5. *Miscellaneous.*

    (a) *Entire Agreement.* This Master Confirmation Agreement constitutes the entire agreement and understanding of the parties with respect to its subject matter and supersedes all oral communication and prior writings with respect specifically thereto.

    (b) *Amendments.* An amendment, modification or waiver in respect of this Master Confirmation Agreement will only be effective if in writing (including a writing evidenced by a facsimile transmission) and executed by each of the parties or confirmed by an exchange of telexes or by an exchange of electronic messages on an electronic messaging system.

    (c) *Counterparts.* This Master Confirmation Agreement and each Transaction Supplement documented hereunder may be executed in counterparts, each of which will be deemed an original.

    (d) *Headings.* The headings used in this Master Confirmation Agreement are for convenience of reference only and shall not affect the construction of or be taken into consideration in interpreting this Master Confirmation Agreement.

    (e) *Governing Law.* This Master Confirmation Agreement and each Transaction confirmed by a Confirmation documented hereunder will be governed by and construed in accordance with the law specified in the Master Agreement.

IN WITNESS WHEREOF the parties have executed this document with effect from the date specified on the first page of this document.

[————]   [————]

By: ———————————   By: ———————————
Name: Name:
Title: Title:
Date: Date:

[Date]

Re:

General Terms Confirmation

Dear Sir or Madam,

The purpose of this General Terms Confirmation (this "General Terms Confirmation") is to confirm certain general terms and conditions of the Credit Derivative Transactions entered into between us under the 2003 Master Credit Derivatives Confirmation Agreement between us dated as of [_____] ("Master Confirmation Agreement").

This General Terms Confirmation hereby incorporates by reference the 2003 ISDA Credit Derivatives Definitions as supplemented by the May 2003 Supplement to the 2003 ISDA Credit Derivatives Definitions (together, the "Credit Derivatives Definitions"). In the event of any inconsistency between the Credit Derivatives Definitions and this General Terms Confirmation, this General Terms Confirmation will govern.

All provisions contained in the Master Agreement govern each Confirmation (each as defined in the Master Confirmation Agreement) except as expressly modified below.

The general terms of each Transaction to which this General Terms Confirmation relates are as follows, as supplemented by the Transaction Supplement related to such Transaction:

1. General Terms:

Trade Date:	As shown in the Transaction supplement
Effective Date:	As shown in the Transaction Supplement
Scheduled Termination Date:	As shown in the Transaction Supplement
Transaction Type:	As shown in the Transaction Supplement
Floating Rate Payer:	As shown in the Transaction Supplement (the "Seller")
Fixed Rate Payer:	As shown in the Transaction Supplement (the "Buyer")
Calculation Agent:	Seller
Calculation Agent City:	As shown in the Transaction Supplement
Business Day:	If the Transaction Type indicated in the Transaction Supplement is:
	Japan: New York, London and Tokyo (and TARGET Settlement Day if the Floating Rate Payer Calculation Amount is in EUR)
	Australia and New Zealand: If the Reference Entity indicated in the Transaction Supplement is: (i) an Australian Entity, New York, London[, Tokyo] and Sydney (and TARGET Settlement Day if the Floating Rate Payer Calculation Amount is in EUR); or (ii) a New Zealand Entity; New York, London[, Tokyo] and Auckland (and TARGET Settlement Day if the Floating Rate Payer Calculation Amount is in EUR)
	Asia: New York [and][,] London [and Tokyo] (and TARGET Settlement Day if the Floating Rate Payer Calculation Amount is in EUR)
	Singapore: New York, London[, Tokyo] and Singapore (and TARGET Settlement Day if the Floating Rate Payer Calculation Amount is in EUR)
Business Day Convention:	Following (which, subject to Sections 1.4 and 1.6 of the Credit Derivatives Definitions, shall apply to any date referred to in this General Terms Confirmation or in the related Transaction Supplement that falls on a day that is not a Business Day).

Reference Entity:	As shown in the Transaction Supplement
Reference Obligation(s):	As shown in the Transaction Supplement
Reference Price:	100%
All Guarantees:	Applicable

2. Fixed Payments:

Fixed Rate Payer Calculation Amount:	The Floating Rate Payer Calculation Amount
Fixed Rate Payer Payment Dates:	As shown in the Transaction Supplement
Fixed Rate:	As shown in the Transaction Supplement
Fixed Rate Day Count Fraction:	Actual/360

3. Floating Payment:

Floating Rate Payer
   Calculation Amount: As shown in the Transaction Supplement

Conditions to
   Settlement:

- Credit Event Notice

   Notifying Parties: Buyer or Seller

If the Transaction Type indicated in the Transaction Supplement is Japan, "Greenwich Mean Time" in Section 3.3 of the Credit Derivatives Definitions shall be replaced by "Tokyo time".

If the Transaction Type indicated in the Transaction Supplement is Japan, Section 3.9 of the Credit Derivatives Definitions shall not apply.

- Notice of Physical Settlement
- Notice of Publicly Available Information:

   Applicable

Credit Event: The following Credit Events shall apply to this Transaction:

Bankruptcy

Failure to Pay
   Grace Period Extension:
     Not Applicable
   Payment Requirement:
     If the Transaction Type indicated in the Transaction Supplement is Japan and the Floating Rate Payer Calculation Amount is in JPY, JPY 100 000 000 or its equivalent in the relevant Obligation Currency as of the occurrence of the relevant Failure to Pay

     In all other cases, USD 1 000 000 or its equivalent in the relevant Obligation Currency as of the occurrence of the relevant Failure to Pay

Restructuring: If indicated as applicable in the Transaction Supplement, the following terms shall apply:
   Restructuring Maturity Limitation and Fully Transferable Obligation:
     If the Transaction Type indicated in the Transaction Supplement is:
       Japan: Not Applicable
       Australia and New Zealand: Applicable
       Asia: Not Applicable
       Singapore: Not Applicable

Modified Restructuring Maturity Limitation and Conditionally
   Transferable Obligation:
   If the Transaction Type indicated in the Transaction Supplement is:
      Japan: Not Applicable
      Australia and New Zealand: Not Applicable
      Asia: Not Applicable
      Singapore: Not Applicable

Multiple Holder Obligation:
   If the Transaction Type indicated in the Transaction Supplement is:
      Japan: Not Applicable
      Australia and New Zealand: Applicable
      Asia: Applicable
      Singapore: Applicable

Default Requirement:
   If the Transaction Type indicated in the Transaction Supplement is
   Japan and the Floating Rate Payer Calculation Amount is in JPY,
   JPY 1 billion or its equivalent in the relevant Obligation Currency as
   of the occurrence of the relevant Credit Event.

In all other cases, USD 10 million or its equivalent in the relevant
   Obligation Currency as of the occurrence of the relevant Credit Event

Obligation(s):

For the purposes of the tables below:
"Yes" shall mean that the relevant selection is applicable; and
"No" shall mean that the relevant selection is not applicable.

1) If the Transaction Type indicated in the Transaction Supplement is Japan, the
following table shall apply for the purposes of the Transaction supplemented
by such Transaction Supplement:

	Obligation Categories: *(Select only one)*		Obligation Characteristics: *(Select all that apply)*
No	Payment	**Yes**	Not Subordinated
Yes	Borrowed Money	**No**	Specified Currency – Standard Specified Currencies
No	Reference Obligation(s) Only	**No**	Not Sovereign Lender
No	Bond	**No**	Not Domestic Currency
No	Loan	**No**	Not Domestic Law
No	Bond or Loan	**No**	Listed
		No	Not Domestic Issuance

2) If the Transaction Type indicated in the Transaction Supplement is Australia
and New Zealand, the following table shall apply for the purposes of the
Transaction supplemented by such Transaction Supplement:

	Obligation Categories: *(Select only one)*		Obligation Characteristics: *(Select all that apply)*
No	Payment	**No**	Not Subordinated
Yes	Borrowed Money	**No**	Specified Currency – Standard Specified Currencies

(Continued)

Obligation Categories: (Select only one)		Obligation Characteristics: (Select all that apply)	
No	Reference Obligation(s) Only	No	Not Sovereign Lender
No	Bond	No	Not Domestic Currency
No	Loan	No	Not Domestic Law
No	Bond or Loan	No	Listed
		No	Not Domestic Issuance

3) If the Transaction Type indicated in the Transaction Supplement is Asia, the following table shall apply for the purposes of the Transaction supplemented by such Transaction Supplement:

Obligation Categories: (Select only one)		Obligation Characteristics: (Select all that apply)	
No	Payment	Yes	Not Subordinated
No	Borrowed Money	No	Specified Currency – Standard Specified Currencies
No	Reference Obligation(s) Only	Yes	Not Sovereign Lender
No	Bond	Yes	Not Domestic Currency
No	Loan	Yes	Not Domestic Law
Yes	Bond or Loan	No	Listed
		Yes	Not Domestic Issuance

4) If the Transaction Type indicated in the Transaction Supplement is Singapore, the following table shall apply for the purposes of the Transaction supplemented by such Transaction Supplement:

Obligation Categories: (Select only one)		Obligation Characteristics: (Select all that apply)	
No	Payment	Yes	Not Subordinated
No	Borrowed Money	Yes	Specified Currency – Standard Specified Currencies **and Domestic Currency**
No	Reference Obligation(s) Only	Yes	Not Sovereign Lender
No	Bond	No	Not Domestic Currency
No	Loan	No	Not Domestic Law
Yes	Bond or Loan	No	Listed
		No	Not Domestic Issuance

4. Settlement Terms:

Settlement Method:	Physical Settlement
Settlement Currency:	The currency of denomination of the Floating Rate Payer Calculation Amount
Terms Relating to Physical Settlement:	
Physical Settlement Period:	Thirty (30) Business Days
Deliverable Obligations:	Exclude Accrued Interest
Deliverable Obligation Category and Characteristics:	

For the purposes of the tables below:

"**Yes**" shall mean that the relevant selection is applicable; and "**No**" shall mean that the relevant selection is not applicable.

1) If the Transaction Type indicated in the Transaction Supplement is Japan, the following table shall apply for the purposes of the Transaction supplemented by such Transaction Supplement:

Deliverable Obligation Categories: *(Select only one)*		Deliverable Obligation Characteristics: *(Select all that apply)*	
No	Payment	Yes	Not Subordinated
No	Borrowed Money	Yes	Specified Currency – Standard Specified Currencies
No	Reference Obligation(s) Only	No	Not Sovereign Lender
No	Bond	No	Not Domestic Currency
No	Loan	No	Not Domestic Law
Yes	Bond or Loan	No	Listed
		Yes	Not Contingent
		No	Not Domestic Issuance
		Yes	Assignable Loan
		Yes	Consent Required Loan
		No	Direct Loan Participation
		Yes	Transferable
		Yes – 30 years	Maximum Maturity
		No	Accelerated or Matured
		Yes	Not Bearer

2) If the Transaction Type indicated in the Transaction Supplement is Australia and New Zealand, the following table shall apply for the purposes of the Transaction supplemented by such Transaction Supplement:

Deliverable Obligation Categories: *(Select only one)*		Deliverable Obligation Characteristics: *(Select all that apply)*	
No	Payment	Yes	Not Subordinated
No	Borrowed Money	Yes	Specified Currency – Standard Specified Currencies **and Domestic Currency**

(Continued)

Deliverable Obligation Categories: (Select only one)		Deliverable Obligation Characteristics: (Select all that apply)	
No	Reference Obligation(s) Only	No	Not Sovereign Lender
No	Bond	No	Not Domestic Currency
No	Loan	No	Not Domestic Law
Yes	Bond or Loan	No	Listed
		Yes	Not Contingent
		No	Not Domestic Issuance
		Yes	Assignable Loan
		Yes	Consent Required Loan
		No	Direct Loan Participation
		Yes	Transferable
		Yes – 30 years	Maximum Maturity
		No	Accelerated or Matured
		Yes	Not Bearer

3) If the Transaction Type indicated in the Transaction Supplement is Asia, the following table shall apply for the purposes of the Transaction supplemented by such Transaction Supplement:

Deliverable Obligation Categories: (Select only one)		Deliverable Obligation Characteristics: (Select all that apply)	
No	Payment	Yes	Not Subordinated
No	Borrowed Money	Yes	Specified Currency – Standard Specified Currencies
No	Reference Obligation(s) Only	Yes	Not Sovereign Lender
No	Bond	No	Not Domestic Currency
No	Loan	Yes	Not Domestic Law
Yes	Bond or Loan	No	Listed
		Yes	Not Contingent
		Yes	Not Domestic Issuance
		Yes	Assignable Loan
		No	Consent Required Loan
		No	Direct Loan Participation
		Yes	Transferable
		Yes – 30 years	Maximum Maturity
		No	Accelerated or Matured
		Yes	Not Bearer

4) If the Transaction Type indicated in the Transaction Supplement is Singapore, the following table shall apply for the purposes of the Transaction supplemented by such Transaction Supplement:

Deliverable Obligation Categories: (Select only one)		Deliverable Obligation Characteristics: (Select all that apply)	
No	Payment	Yes	Not Subordinated
No	Borrowed Money	Yes	Specified Currency – Standard Specified Currencies and Domestic Currency
No	Reference Obligation(s) Only	Yes	Not Sovereign Lender
No	Bond	No	Not Domestic Currency
No	Loan	No	Not Domestic Law
Yes	Bond or Loan	No	Listed
		Yes	Not Contingent
		No	Not Domestic Issuance
		Yes	Assignable Loan
		No	Consent Required Loan
		No	Direct Loan Participation
		Yes	Transferable
		Yes – 30 years	Maximum Maturity
		No	Accelerated or Matured
		Yes	Not Bearer

Excluded Deliverable Obligations:	None
Partial Cash Settlement of Consent Required Loans:	Not Applicable
Partial Cash Settlement of Assignable Loans:	Not Applicable
Partial Cash Settlement of Participations:	Not Applicable
Escrow:	[Applicable] [Not Applicable]

5. Notice and Account Details:

Notice and Account
  Details for Party A:
Notice and Account
  Details for Party B:

[Buyer Contact Information:]
[Seller Contact Information:]

TRANSACTION SUPPLEMENT
Transaction Type: [Japan][Australia and New Zealand][Asia][Singapore]

This Transaction Supplement is entered into between the Buyer and Seller listed below on the Trade Date set forth below.

The purpose of this communication is to confirm the terms and conditions of the Credit Derivative Transaction entered into between us on the Trade Date specified below (the "Transaction"). This Transaction Supplement is entered into under the 2003 Master Credit Derivatives Confirmation Agreement dated as of [_____] and, together with the 2003 Master Credit Derivatives Confirmation Agreement and the General Terms Confirmation attached thereto, constitutes a "Confirmation" as referred to in the Master Agreement between the parties, as amended and supplemented from time to time.

The terms of the Transaction to which this Transaction Supplement relates are as follows:

Reference Entity:
[Reference Obligation,　　　　　　　　[The obligation[s] identified as follows:
If applicable:　　　　　　　　　　　　Primary Obligor: [   ]
　　　　　　　　　　　　　　　　　　Guarantor:　　　　　[   ]
　　　　　　　　　　　　　　　　　　Maturity:　　　　　　[   ]
　　　　　　　　　　　　　　　　　　Coupon:　　　　　　　[   ]
　　　　　　　　　　　　　　　　　　CUSIP/ISIN:　　　　　[   ]]]
Trade Date:
Effective Date:
Scheduled Termination Date:
Floating Rate Payer:　　　　　　　　　[   ] (the "Seller")
Fixed Rate Payer:　　　　　　　　　　[   ] (the "Buyer")
Calculation Agent City:　　　　　　　[   ]
Fixed Rate Payer Payment Dates:
Fixed Rate:　　　　　　　　　_____%
Floating Rate Payer Calculation Amount:　　　　[   ]
Restructuring Credit Event:　　　　　　　　　[Applicable] [Not Applicable]
[Additional Terms:　　　　　[   ]]

Please confirm your agreement to be bound by the terms of the foregoing by executing a copy of this Transaction Supplement and returning it to us [at the contact information listed above].

[_____]　　　　　　　　　　　　[_____]

By: _____　　　　　　　By: _____
Name:　　　　　　　　　　　　　　　　Name:
Title:　　　　　　　　　　　　　　　　Title:
Date:　　　　　　　　　　　　　　　　Date:

9

Valuation and Risk: Basic Concepts and the Default and Recovery Model

Sections 9.2 and 9.3 develop a mathematical framework for the modelling of credit risk aimed at the valuation of CDSs and bonds. The model presented is largely the industry standard among the banking community. Section 9.4 generalises this model and shows the circumstances in which the simpler model of 9.3 applies. We saw in Chapter 8 some of the major factors of relevance to the pricing of credit instruments. In this chapter we introduce a simple arbitrage model to help to identify the main driving factors in the valuation of CDSs, and to give a sound basis for the intuitive pricing of CDSs.

9.1 THE FUNDAMENTAL CREDIT ARBITRAGE – REPO COST

If FMC debt is trading at 7% and risk-free (government) rates are 4%, what is the correct CDS premium for Ford?

Suppose there is a 5-year FRN carrying a coupon (LIBOR plus a fixed spread S) such that the bond price is par. We shall also assume default risk is constant on FMC – so the bond will always be priced at par, or at the recovery level in the default event. Suppose we buy a CDS on FMC to the same maturity as the bond; into which the bond – and that bond only – is deliverable, and which pays par plus accrued interest on the bond. In order to have a zero cost (self-financing) position we can lend the bond out on repo, receive cash collateral equal to the price of the bond, and pay the repo rate on the FMC bond. We assume that the repo rate curve is flat (Figure 9.1).

Note that the position is insensitive to interest rate moves if the premium and interest payment dates coincide.

If default occurs, the bond is delivered into the CDS receiving par plus accrued, which is used to unwind the repo transaction. If the accrued coupon equals the accrued repo cost then there is no loss or gain, and therefore no risk on the deal.

As the deal is risk free then there should be no profit or loss: the net cashflow is LIBOR plus the spread, S, less the repo rate, less the CDS premium. If the cashflow is zero then *the CDS premium equals the spread on the (par FRN) bond plus the amount special on repo.*[1] Typical investment grade credit debt trades non-special, so generally the CDS premium equals the par FRN bond spread. In particular we see that 'risk-free' rates are irrelevant to the pricing of CDSs.

Generalising from constant default risk again has little impact if the spread curve is flat – we shall handle this fully later.

In reality (non-constant repo rate) there is a repo risk in the above. A term repo trade done at the outset has to be unwound on the default event at a cost which depends on the then repo rate. If the (theoretical) repo curve is flat, then the expected cost is zero, but if it is not flat then

---

[1] 'LIBOR less the repo rate' is referred to as 'the amount special (on repo)'.

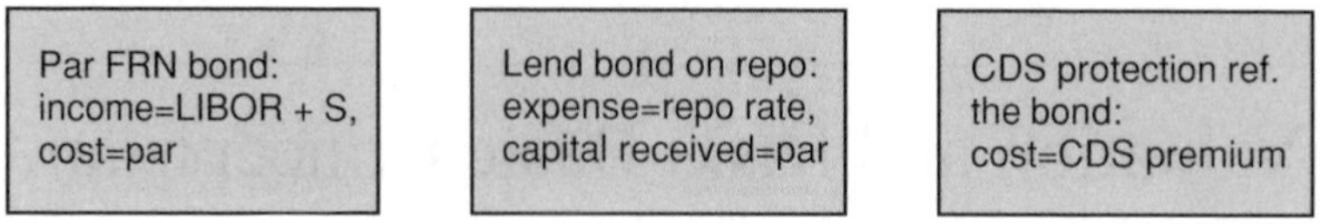

Par FRN bond: income=LIBOR + S, cost=par	Lend bond on repo: expense=repo rate, capital received=par	CDS protection ref. the bond: cost=CDS premium

Figure 9.1   The fundamental credit arbitrage

there will be a minor difference in the above equation arising from the expected unwind cost on the default event. This will increase as the repo curve steepens and as we look at names with higher and higher default risk. If, instead of a term repo trade, a rolling overnight repo is then done, the cost is uncertain. The expected cost can be calculated in principle from the repo curve.[2]

The repo curve pricing impact is actually minor in the context of other assumptions we have made – the key ones being no delivery option and non-standard payoff – and we shall see later that, in reality, bonds and CDS trade as separate markets with different but related spreads. The key point here is that the natural comparison is between the CDS premium and the (par FRN) bond spread to LIBOR. The argument applies more generally – the correct discounting curve for typical assets is the LIBOR curve (being the financing cost on repo-able assets).

We can set up a similar argument using fixed coupon par bonds instead of FRNs, and introduce a fixed/floating interest rate swap to eliminate interest rate risk. This gives the same result as if the interest rate curve is flat, but introduces expected unwind costs similar to that occurring if the interest rate curve is not flat.

9.2   DEFAULT AND RECOVERY MODEL; CLAIM AMOUNT

In this section we discuss the formal description of the default and recovery process.

9.2.1   Claim Amount

The 'claim amount' is the amount that can be claimed and becomes immediately payable on default. It is specified in the issue document of the debt. Ultimate recovery is based on the claim amount: if there are insufficient funds to pay the claim in full then a proportion of the claim amount is paid. In almost all cases of traded debt, the claim amount is par plus accrued interest (referred to as **claim amount of par**). For a few loan instruments the claim amount is the promised cashflows – economically equivalent to the capital value of those cashflows (and referred to as **claim amount of treasury**).

Claim of par plus accrued (in obvious notation):

$$C(t) = 1 + A(t) \tag{9.1}$$

Claim of treasury: let the cashflow at time t be $c(t)$ and let $d(t)$ be the discount factors off the government curve. Assume that cashflows are paid periodically with n payments due before and including maturity at time T. Then

$$C(t) = \sum_{i=1}^{n} c(t_i) \cdot d(t_i) \tag{9.2}$$

---

[2] Of course this is theoretical – the repo market is not liquid, term repo deals are hard to find and, in particular, there is not the repo curve data to allow these calculations to be performed in practice.

9.2.2   Recovery Modelling

For corporate entities in the USA, the UK and some other countries, the legal process is capable of enforcing equal recovery of the claim amount for all creditors with the same seniority of debt. In the event that the administrators or the company try to do something different, then creditors can take the company to court and enforce the distribution rules given in the documentation. For sovereigns no such process exists. In practice, although the documentation specifies what you can claim, there is no means of enforcing equal treatment of different claims. A good risk control measure would be to asses recovery on the basis of an alternative claim amount for sovereigns.

The simplest model is to assume that recovery is a fixed proportion of the claim amount for a given seniority of debt. Ultimate recovery is one of 100%, 0%, or some number between 0% and 100% for a particular seniority. But the settlement date of CDS contracts is long before ultimate recovery is known, and the debt trades at a price that reflects the anticipated recovery level for that seniority. So around one month post-default junior, senior and loans will trade at prices between 0 and 100 – typically with junior debt at a low price (but not 0), loans at a high price (but not 100), and senior debt in between. So our recovery model could be

$$R(\text{seniority}) = x(\text{seniority}) \tag{9.3}$$

where x is a constant for that seniority over all time (i.e. irrespective of whether default occurs in 2005 or 2015) and all reference entities. For example, we might – based on broad historic data – assume that junior debt recovers 20%, senior debt recovers 50% and loans recover 70%. This assumption might apply no matter what the company is – any industry, any rating of debt. This is the most common form of recovery model at the time of writing.

A more realistic implementation (but one that is rarely used) is to take account of industry group (for example, based on Altman and Kishore, 1996), and also investment grade/high-yield differences. This would make recovery a function of seniority, industry and rating. Our recovery model is then

$$R(\text{seniority}, \text{industry}) = x(\text{seniority}, \text{industry}) \tag{9.4}$$

where x is a constant for that seniority and industry, over all time and for reference entities within that industry group.

Recovery modelling can be made more realistic. An investor with access to good fundamental company research could also try to estimate recovery levels on the basis of company accounts and other information to come up with estimated recoveries specific to that company and seniority of debt. One could assume a time dependence of recovery – dependent on the economic cycle. This is rarely done in practice and rapidly leads to calibration problems – changing recovery over time has the effect of magnifying changes in the forward hazard rates and can rapidly lead to negative forward hazard rates. Also, time dependence of recovery (because of the economic cycle) would naturally be associated with time dependence of hazard rates. We shall see (in section 9.6) that this can lead to major complications over the modelling of CDSs if we want these dependencies to be reflected in a correlation of stochastic recoveries and hazard rates.

Recovery Uncertainty

Another way to make recovery modelling more realistic – which has little implication for CDS pricing but we shall see implications for portfolio products – is to reflect the uncertainty in our knowledge of the recovery rate for a specific company. For example, let us assume that the average recovery rate for senior debt is 40%. On a large portfolio of names with senior debt we would, over time, expect to see the average recovery rate for those that default to be 40%. But for any particular name the recovery may be anywhere between 0% and 100%, with a standard deviation (again an assumption based on historical data) of say 20%. We may need to investigate the impact of this uncertainty in our recovery knowledge. We can do this by performing only three sets of calculations. We can value the product with a low recovery assumption, with a high recovery assumption, and with an intermediate recovery assumption. Each of these recovery assumptions has an associated probability – the sum of these probabilities is 1; the expected recovery is 40%; and the standard deviation is 20%. We can choose the three recovery levels and then solve these equations to get the probabilities. In addition there are constraints to be satisfied – all the probabilities have to be between 0 and 1 – which acts as a constraint on our initial choice of recoveries.

Example 'Chapter 9.xls'

Suppose we take the three possible recovery levels to be 0% with probability p_0, 40% with probability p_M, and 80% with probability $1-p_0-p_M$. Then the expected probability (assumed to be 40%) is

$$0 \times p_0 + 40 \times p_M + 80 \times (1 - p_0 - p_M) = 40$$

so $p_0 = (1 - p_M)/2$, and the variance (assumed to be 20%) is

$$(0 - 40)^2 \times p_0 + (40 - 40)^2 \times p_M + (80 - 40)^2 \times (1 - p_0 - p_M) = 20^2$$

from which we find $p_M = 0.75$. Hence we find that the probability of a 40% recovery is 75%, and of 0% or 80% recovery is 12.5%. We can take a more realistic view of CDS valuation by taking these three separate recovery assumptions, calculating the implied probabilities, and then weighting the resulting values by the associated probabilities. Generally this is not done (the results are not significantly different from the base assumption). However, we shall use this model when we look at first-to-default products, and also CDSs when we include counterparty risk, where there are some interesting conclusions.

Exercise
Why do we not assume $R = 100\%$ as one of our three recovery assumptions?

9.2.3   Hazard (Default) Rate Model

A distinction is sometimes made between the **hazard rate** – the rate of default at any time assuming the entity has survived up to that point – and the **default rate** – the rate of default at a future time assuming only that the reference entity is alive now. We shall not make this distinction and use both these terms to mean hazard rate.

   We model the hazard rate process as a 'Poisson' process (Billingsley, 1995). This is a standard and widely used statistical model – it describes the rate of goals scored at a football game and the time until a goal is scored, the rate of clients joining a queue and, in our case, the rate at which a company defaults and the time to default. The model can be used to describe multiple events – e.g. goals – but our application is simpler: we are only interested in the first occurrence of default for a company.

There are only a few results we need to know about the Poisson process. Let's suppose for the moment that the hazard rate (the rate of default at any time) is a constant, h. The probability that a default occurs in the next moment of time Δt is $h \times \Delta t$. The probability that the name survives from now (time $= 0$) to time t is

$$S(t) = \exp(-h \cdot t) \tag{9.5}$$

and the probability that it survives from now up to that date, and then defaults in that interval (the 'default rate' as defined in the first paragraph)

$$prob(def\_in\_t\_to\_t + \Delta t | alive\_now) = \exp(-h \cdot t) \cdot h \cdot \Delta t.$$

Any practical implementation requires us to make the hazard rate a function of time. (This is referred to as a 'time-changed' Poisson process.[3]) The survival probability becomes

$$S(t) = \exp(-\int_0^t h(x)\,dx) \tag{9.6}$$

(when $h(t) = h$, a constant, then the above formula reduces to the previous one). Similarly, the probability of default in time t to $t + \Delta t$ is

$$\exp(-\int_0^t h(x)\,dx) \cdot h(t) \cdot \Delta t \tag{9.7}$$

We can also allow the hazard rate itself to be a stochastic process, and we do this in section 9.4.

Many of the practical pricing examples and illustrations in this book assume that the hazard rate is a constant. This is often sufficient to show the results we need – in many cases a hazard rate curve makes the sums more difficult but the point is unchanged. Any practical implementation will have to implement a non-constant hazard rate curve.

9.2.4 Choice of Hazard Rate Function/Interpolation Process

The hazard rate function turns out to be very similar both in interpretation and mathematically to the forward (spot) interest rate, with the survival probability corresponding to a discount factor. When we perform pure interest rate calculations we have to choose a form of interest rate function when we bootstrap the yield curve in order to interpolate discount factors. We should think of the spot rate (hazard rate) function as a complicated way of interpolating between discount factors (CDS levels) at different maturities. We have similar types of choices for the hazard rate function – for example, we often choose a piecewise linear function for interest rates, equivalent to using a piecewise linear function for hazard rates.

Most examples in the book assume that the hazard rate is a constant, purely for simplicity of exposition. In practice we have to use the more complex formula where the hazard rate is a function of time. When we do this it changes some very simple formulae into complex ones, and can have some serious implications for computing time. Any CDS calculation requires not only the evaluation of survival probabilities but also the evaluation of integrals of survival probabilities, discount factors and other functions (for example, see section 9.11 below). If we

---

[3] This corresponds to a change of variable in integration. In order to avoid our transformed time going backwards we clearly need the hazard rate to be positive at all times.

have to evaluate the survival probability numerically then we will have to perform numerical integrals which will slow down the implementation dramatically.

The following are some simple and flexible choices for the hazard rate function:

1. *Piecewise constant.* It turns out that the calculated CDS levels are also very nearly piecewise constant – simple but rather unrealistic, implying sudden jumps in the CDS premium as maturity changes.
2. *Piecewise linear.* This is intuitively sensible and the integral (the survival probability) is also easy to calculate in closed form. There are two criticisms. At the short and the long end extrapolation of the curve can lead to negative hazard rates or unrealistically high levels of hazard rate. The second objection is a purely practical one. Imagine we are calibrating our model to two CDS levels at two and five years. We have a linear curve – two unknowns and two simultaneous equations for the values of the CDSs, which is relatively slow to solve numerically.
3. *Piecewise linear with constant short and long stubs.* This is intuitively sensible in the range from the shortest to the longest CDS (or other instruments) we are calibrating to. It also has the advantage that
   (a) it eliminates the possibility of negative hazard rates at the short and long end and
   (b) at every stage of the calibrating process we only have to solve a single equation at a time – which is fast (whereas the piecewise linear approach requires us to solve a pair of non-linear equations in two unknowns for the first two maturities).
4. *Exponential form* (tending to a limit at high maturities). This can be useful when we want to perform a best fit (rather than exact fit) to data and want to avoid kinks in the curve which a low-level piecewise linear model would introduce.

There are other interpolation formulae (a Cox–Ingersol–Ross formula (Hull, 2002) is sometimes used). In practice, items 2 and 3 are the most common. For risk control purposes it may be useful to implement two interpolation functions in order to asses the impact of changing between them. For example, items 1 and 2 will show very substantially different values on individual CDS deals.

Exercise
Consider a name where the 2-year CDS is 100 bp and the 5-year CDS is 200 bp. What are the valuation implications of using a piecewise constant hazard rate (or CDS curve) rather than a linear rate?

9.3 DETERMINISTIC DEFAULT RATE MODEL

In this section we shall develop some simplified formulae for CDS valuation which are of the same form as those generally used by the market.[4] Section 9.4 will redevelop these in a much more general framework, and will show the assumptions under which the more complex formulae simplify to the approximation given here.

We also develop simplified formulae for bonds. These will be partially extended below and in section 9.4. In practice the form shown here is acceptable although the hazard rate parameter for bonds turns out to be different from the hazard rate parameter for CDSs.

---

[4] See Khuong-Huu (1999).

In this section we assume that the hazard rate process in the Poisson default model is a deterministic function of time. This may seem odd – anyone who has watched the credit markets knows that spreads and CDS premia change day by day, and often by large amounts. Take the simplest case where the deterministic hazard rate is assumed constant. This is saying that tomorrow's spread is going to be the same as today's spread but, of course, we know it will not be. Section 9.4 shows that, surprisingly, this does not matter for the purposes of valuation and risk calculations today. When we come in tomorrow and find the spread has changed, we simply need to recalibrate our curve to the new spread and revalue.

We also assume that the recovery rate is a known constant and, for the moment, assume that only one specific bond is deliverable into the CDS. Also for the moment we shall assume that counterparties are risk-free.

Notation

Time now	t
Hazard rate at time $s > t$	$\lambda(s)$
Survival probability	$S(s) = \exp(-\int_t^s \lambda(x)\, dx)$ (equation (9.6))
Recovery rate	R (equation (9.3))
Accrued on deliverable bond	$A(s)$
Discount factors	$D(s)$
Claim amount	$C(s)$ (given by equation (9.1))
CDS premium per annum	p
Maturity date of CDS deal	T

(Note that both the survival probability and the discount factor have a dependence on the time now, t, which we have suppressed for simplicity of notation.)

9.3.1 CDS valuation

In the event of default a physically settled CDSs pays par in exchange for defaulted debt. It is easier to assume cash settlement in the development of the formulae but this is economically equivalent to (and therefore the same formulae apply to the valuation of) physically settled CDSs since the delivered debt has a market price of the recovery. The value of this payoff, if it occurs at time s, is

$$[1 - R \cdot C(s)] \cdot D(s) = \{1 - R \cdot [1 + A(s)]\} \cdot D(s).$$

We see that this has a maximum value if $A(s)$ is zero, and a minimum amount just before the payment of the coupon.

The probability that the reference entity defaults in the interval s to $s + \Delta s$ is given by equation (9.7). Hence the probability weighted value of the payoff is

$$\{1 - R \cdot [1 + A(s)]\} \cdot D(s) \cdot S(s) \cdot \lambda(s) \cdot \Delta s.$$

Since t can be any moment between inception and maturity of the trade, the value of the contingent payoff (= 'expected loss') is

$$B(t) = \int_t^T \{1 - R \cdot [1 + A(s)]\} \cdot D(s) \cdot S(s) \cdot \lambda(s)\, dt \qquad (9.8)$$

Turning now to the premium stream, we shall develop formulae for two cases. Case (a), where premia are paid continuously – this leads to simple formulae which are easier to handle for theoretical analysis – and case (b), the standard situation, where the premium is paid quarterly in arrears with a proportion to the credit event date. Note that in both cases the total amount of premium paid is the same (whether default occurs or not). Also, if interest rates are zero then the value of the premium payments is identical. In fact, assuming continuous premia is a very good approximation to the standard case of quarterly in arrears with a proportion to the default date.

Take case (a) first. A premium payment due in the interval s to $s + \Delta s$ is $p \times \Delta s$, has a present value of $p \times \Delta s \times D(s)$ and will be paid if the name survives up to that time, so the probability weighted value is $p \times \Delta s \times D(s) \times S(s)$. This applies for all times up to maturity, so the value of the premium stream is

$$P(t) = p \int_t^T D(s) \cdot S(s) \, ds \tag{9.9}$$

Case (b) is notationally more difficult. Let the end quarter dates be at times s_i, and suppose there are n quarters up to the maturity date, so $i = 1$ up to n, and s_0 is the premium due date on or prior to t. The value of these quarterly payments is the premium amount $(s_i - s_{i-1}) \times p/360$ discounted back by $D(s)$ multiplied by the probability that the payment is made – the chance that the name survives up to time s_i, $S(s_i)$. So the value of the quarterly payments made on the scheduled dates is:

$$p \sum_{i=1}^{n} \frac{s_i - s_{i-1}}{360} \cdot D(s_i) \cdot S(s_i).$$

We now have to take into account the proportionate premium paid if default occurs in the interval s to $s + \Delta s$ and suppose s is in the ith period. The amount of premium is $(s - s_{i-1}) \times p/360$, and this is discounted back to get a value, and multiplied by the probability that default occurs in this interval. This can occur for any time up to expiry, so the value of the premium stream is given by

$$P(t) = p \sum_{i=1}^{n} \frac{s_i - s_{i-1}}{360} \cdot D(s_i) \cdot S(s_i) + \sum_{i=1}^{n} \int_{t_{i-1}}^{t_i} \frac{s - s_{i-1}}{360} \cdot D(s) \cdot S(s) \cdot \lambda(s) \, dt \tag{9.10}$$

Of course there are many variations in the premium payment (frequency, in advance/arrears, with/without a proportion to default, ...) giving rise to slightly different premium formulae, and potentially variations in day-count convention. We can see, comparing (9.10) and (9.11), that continuous premia are easier to handle notationally and we shall use formula (9.2) for theoretical work from now on. Practical implementations will look more like (9.11) and the variations thereon.

The net value of a long protection CDS position on the books is therefore given by

$$V(t) = \int_t^T \{1 - R \cdot [1 + A(s)]\} \cdot D(s) \cdot S(s) \cdot \lambda(s) \, ds - p \int_t^T D(s) \cdot S(s) \, ds \tag{9.11}$$

When the trade is fairly valued ($V = 0$) this gives a formula for the current fair-market premium, p_M. We can re-express (9.11) using this premium as

$$V(t) = (p_M - p) \int_t^T D(s) \cdot S(s) \, ds \tag{9.12}$$

The integral is the risky duration of the CDS. Periodic premia will also have an accrued premium to be accounted for.

We shall examine some further consequences of (9.11).

9.3.2 Accrued Interest and the Delivery Option

Formula (9.11) refers to a CDS where the bond to be delivered is known in advance. Let us now assume that we do not know which bond will be delivered. A worst case for the writer is that, at every date, there is a bond available which has zero accrued. This gives the highest value to the long-protection position, and gives rise to an offer side premium taking into account the value of the delivery option related to the choice of a bond with low accrued. The formula becomes

$$V(t) = \int_t^T (1 - R) \cdot D(s) \cdot S(s) \cdot \lambda(s)\,ds - p \int_t^T D(s) \cdot S(s)\,ds \tag{9.13}$$

Another extreme would be to assume that the only deliverable asset available at the time of default is a high coupon annual bond – with expected accrued (call it A) equal to half the annual coupon. In this case the payoff is $[1 - R(1 + A)]$ as against $(1 - R)$ in the case of zero accrued. Let us take some numerical examples: if $R = 0$ then the payoffs are the same; if $R = 1$ the payoffs are also the same (the CDS payoff has a cut-off at zero). If $R = 0.5$ and $A = 5\%$, the payoffs are $1 - 0.5 \times 1.05 = 0.475$ versus $1 - 0.5 = 0.5$, which is roughly a 5% difference. *So if we price a CDS assuming that a zero accrued bond is always available, then this may overestimate the value by up to around 5%.*

9.3.3 CDS under Constant Hazard Rate

Assume now that the hazard rate is constant, $\lambda(s) = \lambda$. Then equation (9.13) becomes

$$V(t) = \int_t^T (1 - R) \cdot \lambda \cdot D(s) \cdot S(s)\,ds - p \int_t^T D(s) \cdot S(s)\,ds$$

$$= [(1 - R) \cdot \lambda - p] \int_t^T D(s) \cdot S(s)\,ds \tag{9.14}$$

where the survival probability is now given by (9.5). The fair value premium for a CDS is when the inception value is zero, so

$$p = (1 - R)\lambda \tag{9.15}$$

This equation is generally regarded as an approximation to the CDS premium (or, conversely, to the hazard rate given the market premium and recovery rate). We can see that this result is exactly true at any level of CDS spread and under any interest rate environment as long as the hazard rate is a constant[5] (and premia are continuous). It is a very good approximation for normal premia.

---

[5] I am grateful to Charles Anderson for pointing this out to me.

9.3.4 Bond Valuation

The bond's 'dirty' price (including accrued) is the discounted value of probability weighted cashflows. These are in two parts: the promised cashflows, and the recovery in the event of default. We use the additional notation

Bond maturity date M
Number of promised cashflows m
Promised cashflow at times $c(s)$
Promised cashflow dates s_i

Following through a similar process to the above we see that the price of the bond is given by

$$BP(t) = \sum_{i=1}^{m} c(s_i) \cdot D(s_i) \cdot S(s_i) + \int_{t}^{M} R \cdot [1 + A(s)] \cdot D(s) \cdot S(s) \cdot \lambda(s)\,ds \qquad (9.16)$$

We examine some consequences of this formula.

9.3.5 Bond Price under a Constant Hazard Rate

Assume now that the hazard rate is constant, $\lambda(s) = \lambda$. Then equation (9.16) becomes

$$BP(t) = \sum_{i=1}^{m} c(s_i) \cdot D(s_i) \cdot \exp(-\lambda \cdot (s_i - t))$$

$$+ \int_{t}^{M} R \cdot [1 + A(s)] \cdot D(s) \cdot \exp[-\lambda \cdot (s - t)] \cdot \lambda\,ds \qquad (9.17)$$

The first term is the sum of the discounted promised cashflows, *discounted off the interest rate curve shifted by the hazard rate*. In particular, suppose that the forward interest rate is a constant r, so $D(s) = \exp[-r(s - t)]$. The first term is the sum of cashflows multiplied by $\exp[-(r + \lambda)(s - t)]$.

If recovery is zero, then the bond price is only the first term and the bond price is the sum of the cashflows discounted of the interest rate curve shifted by the CDS premium rate (from (9.15)). The formula reduces to the simple bond spread model of Part I, Chapter 3, equation (3.1), where the z-spread is the hazard rate.

Note that discounting of the interest rate curve shifted by 'the spread' (more correctly, the CDS premium) is only correct if recovery is zero. *Generally we must shift the interest rate curve by the hazard rate* and explicitly include a term for recovery.

9.3.6 Limiting Cases of the Bond Price

If the hazard rate is zero (the bond is risk-free) then the second term of (9.16) is zero. The survival probabilities are unity and the formula becomes the standard (risk-free) bond-pricing formula.

If the hazard rate becomes very large and $S(t)\lambda(t) \to \infty$ as $t \to 0$, then the survival probability to a future date becomes very low and the probability of default in the next moment of time approaches unity. In that case the recovery is paid imminently (and there are no other cashflows) so the bond price tends to the recovery. The bonds are said to be 'trading on a recovery basis'.

Note that, if the hazard rate declines from this extremely high level then default is almost certain within a finite interval but is deferred a little – so gets some discounting. Thus *as the hazard rate reduces from very high levels the bond price initially declines too.* Only as the hazard rate falls to levels where there is a significant survival probability does the bond price start to rise and pass the recovery rate. We see later in section 9.5.3 that we can get multiple implied hazard rates for a given recovery assumption, if we calibrate to bonds.

9.3.7 Risky Zero Coupon Bonds

If the claim amount is par (as assumed in the above formulae) note that the zero coupon bond price also tends to recovery level as the hazard rate rises to high levels. Zero and low-coupon bonds may have a claim amount given by a formula or a schedule of amounts rising from the issue price to par at maturity.

Exercise
Amend the above formulae for the case where the claim amount is, say, the discounted value of par, discounted at some fixed rate x.

Note that the ratio (risky zero coupon bond price)/(risk-free zero coupon bond price) does not have a simple form except when recovery is zero. Credit models which suppose the contrary will be at variance with the default and recovery model described here (and, more importantly, with market prices).

9.3.8 CDS and Bond Sensitivities

The valuation formulae allow us to calculate CDS and bond sensitivities to

(1) the default event
(2) the hazard rate curve or the calibrating data
(3) the interest rate curve.

We show some results for a couple of special cases.
First consider a CDS subject to a constant hazard rate and suppose that interest rates are also constant at r : the CDS value is given by

$$V(0) = [(1 - R) \cdot \lambda - p] \int_0^T D(s) \cdot S(s) \, ds = [(1 - R) \cdot \lambda - p] \int_0^T \exp[-(r + \lambda)s] \, ds$$

Evaluating the integral gives

$$V(t) = [(1 - R) \cdot \lambda - p] \frac{1 - \exp[-(r + \lambda)T]}{r + \lambda} \tag{9.18}$$

The interest rate sensitivity is the derivative of the above w.r.t. r, the hazard rate sensitivity is the derivative w.r.t. λ, and the default event risk can be deduced from first principles or as the $\lambda \to \infty$ limit of the above (in either case it is $1 - R$). In practice the former two sensitivities are often calculated by shifting the interest or hazard rate, recalculating and taking the difference. The spreadsheet 'Chapter 9.xls' – worksheets 'CDSsensitivity' and 'bond sensitivity' – shows some results.

Generally, interest rate sensitivities are small, and the hazard rate sensitivity is approximately

$$(1 - R) \cdot \frac{1 - \exp[-(r + \lambda)T]}{r + \lambda}$$

This can be interpreted as the loss given default times the *credit risky duration*. Note incidentally that the CDS hazard rate (and spread) sensitivity for different seniorities are in proportion to the loss given recoveries.

A bank will often wish to see sensitivity to a shift in the CDS curve of 1 bp. This will require recalibrating the implied hazard rate curve, then calculating the CDS values before and after the shift, taking the difference to get the CDS bp premium. The results will be very similar to the sensitivity to a shift of the hazard rate curve by $1/(1 - R)$ bp.

If we look at a risky bond and assume that coupons of g per annum are continuous for simplicity and the interest rate is r, then (9.16) becomes

$$BP(0) = \int_0^T g \cdot D(s) \cdot \exp(-\lambda \cdot s) \, ds + D(T) \cdot \exp(-\lambda \cdot T)$$
$$+ \int_0^M R \cdot D(s) \cdot \exp(-\lambda \cdot s) \cdot \lambda \, ds$$

Evaluating the integrals gives

$$BP(t) = \exp[-(r + \lambda)T] + (R\lambda + g)\frac{1 - \exp[-(r + \lambda)T]}{r + \lambda} \qquad (9.19)$$

Note that if the coupon is $r + \lambda(1 - R)$ then the bond price is unity.

Exercise
Relate the above result to equation (9.15) and section 9.1.

Sensitivities can be obtained as above by differentiation or by stressing. Generally the interest rate sensitivity is significant, and we can see that, if recovery is zero, the above equation is symmetrical in interest and hazard rates, so the sensitivities are equal.

Exercises

1. If the coupon is such that the bond price is par, show that the hazard rate sensitivity is equal and opposite to the CDS sensitivity.
2. Find the minimum bond price as a function of the hazard rate. Show that this price is below the recovery rate if the interest rate is positive.

9.4 STOCHASTIC DEFAULT RATE MODEL; HAZARD AND PSEUDO-HAZARD RATES[6]

The development of the pricing formulae in the previous section assumed, rather unrealistically, that the hazard rate was a deterministic function of time. We show how to resolve this problem in this section – at the cost of some rather more sophisticated mathematics although the treatment

---

[6] I am grateful to Phil Hunt for conversations relevant to this section. Any errors and misunderstandings are my own.

is kept as simple as possible. Knowledge of this section is not essential to the rest of the book, though some results from this section are quoted elsewhere.

The generalisation we make is that hazard rates, recovery rates and spot interest rates are all stochastic variables with unspecified distributions. We shall also introduce risky counterparties into the valuation formulae for the moment. We redefine and add to our notation:

Reference entity stochastic hazard rate
(and use h with a super-suffix for the
writer and buyer hazard rate) $h(s)$

Reference entity survival probability $S(s) = \exp[-\int_t^s h(x)\,dx]$ (revised (9.6))

Survival probability [writer] $S^w(s) = \exp[-\int_t^s h^w(x)\,dx]$

Survival probability [buyer] $S^b(s) = \exp[-\int_t^s h^b(x)\,dx]$

Reference entity stochastic recovery rate $R(s)$

Stochastic spot interest rate $r(s)$

Discount factors $D(s) = \exp[-\int_t^s r(x)\,dx]$

We assume that writer and buyer have zero recovery rate for claims on financial products.

We state that the value of a CDS deal is the expected value of the contingent payments. As in section 9.4, we obtain a very similar looking formula, bearing in mind that cashflows occur only if both counterparties to the deal survive:

$$V(t) = E\left\{ \int_t^T [1 - R(s)] \cdot D(s) \cdot h(s) \cdot S(s) \cdot S_b(s) \cdot S_w(s)\,ds \right.$$
$$\left. -p \int_t^T D(s) \cdot S(s) \cdot S_b(s) \cdot S_w(s)\,ds \right\} \tag{9.20}$$

where E denotes the expectation operator (and we have taken the accrued on the deliverable to be zero for simplicity).

We have not been explicit about the stochastic processes behind these variables: for the moment the formula is very general.[7] Our interest at present is how to simplify the above formula. First recall that the expectation is itself an integral over a statistical distribution and it is possible to interchange the order on the integrations in equation (9.20) – in other words we can take the expectation inside the time integral. We find expectations such as $E[D(s) \cdot S(s)]$ and $E[R(s) \cdot D(s) \cdot S(s) \cdot h(s)]$.

We would like to be able to take expectations of terms separately and multiply them together (for example, the expectation of the discount factors times the expected survival probability). We can only do this if the various terms are independent. We shall assume that:

(1) interest rates and survival probabilities are independent
(2) interest rates and recovery rates are independent
(3) recovery rates and default rates are independent
(4) if we include the counterparties then we need to assume that the buyer, writer and reference entity survival (and default) are independent.

Note that we cannot assume that the survival product and hazard rate are independent:

$$E[S(s) \cdot h(s)] \neq E[S(s)] \cdot E[h(s)].$$

---

[7] If 'value' is the market value then the statistical distributions are the 'risk-neutral' distributions and we are using the 'risk-neutral measure'.

The first assumption is reasonable – although hazard rates are strongly correlated with the economic cycle, and so are interest rates but only with a significant lag, so the correlation can reasonably be taken to be zero. Likewise the second assumption is reasonable. The third assumption is less reasonable – there appears to be a direct (negative) correlation between recovery rates and hazard rates. Nevertheless it is an assumption we need to make. The fourth assumption is also unreasonable generally – spreads (and hazard rates) tend to be positively correlated and we would anticipate that survival probabilities will be correlated. We therefore drop the counterparties from the equation by assuming that they are risk free. (We shall return to correct valuation including counterparty risk in Part IV.) We shall also test the significance of these approximations in section 9.7.

If we define

$$\overline{D}(t) = E[D(t)]$$
$$\overline{R}(t) = E[R(t)]$$
$$\overline{S}(t) = E[S(t)]$$

then we can rewrite equation (9.1) as

$$V(t) = \int_t^T [1 - \overline{R}(s)] \cdot \overline{D}(s) \cdot E[S(s) \cdot h(s)] \, ds - p \int_t^T \overline{D}(s) \cdot \overline{S}(s) \, ds \qquad (9.21)$$

We cannot take the expectation of the two terms in the above separately because the survival probability is a function of the hazard rate – there is a correlation which we cannot reasonably ignore. But if we define λ by

$$\lambda(s) = -\frac{\partial \overline{S}(s)}{\partial s} \quad \text{or} \quad \overline{S}(s) = \exp\left[-\int_t^s \lambda(x) \, dx\right] \qquad (9.22)$$

and we note that

$$E\left\{h(s) \cdot \exp\left[-\int_t^s h(x) dx\right]\right\} = -E\left\{\frac{\partial}{\partial s} \exp\left[-\int_t^s h(x) \, dx\right]\right\}$$
$$= -\frac{\partial}{\partial s} E\left\{\exp\left[-\int_t^s h(x) dx\right)\right]\right\}$$
$$= -\frac{\partial}{\partial s} \overline{S}(s) = \lambda(s) \cdot \overline{S}(s)$$

then equation (9.21) becomes

$$V(t) = \int_t^T [1 - \overline{R}(s)] \cdot \overline{D}(s) \cdot \overline{S}(s) \cdot \lambda(s) \, ds - p \int_t^T \overline{D}(s) \cdot \overline{S}(s) \, ds \qquad (9.23)$$

We see that the valuation formula has the same form as the deterministic formula[8] (9.11) and the λ function (9.22) looks just like a deterministic hazard rate. We call λ the pseudo-hazard rate. The discount, recovery and survival factors are now interpreted as expectations, and the pseudo-hazard rate is a complicated function of other expectations. λ is neither a hazard rate nor an expectation of a hazard rate – it looks and feels like a hazard rate in (9.23) but it is not. Nevertheless, fitting the above equation to market data is exactly as before, except we are modelling the pseudo-hazard rate rather than the hazard rate. Nothing has actually changed

---

[8] We have set the accrued to zero.

in our modelling formulae for CDS (and for bonds) except that we now explicitly recognise that any of the variables are stochastic. Only the interpretation of the result has changed – the implied pseudo-hazard rate is different from the actual hazard rate and this has to be recognised in situations where volatility of hazard rate is relevant. In addition, we do not know the initial value of the hazard rate.

9.5 CALIBRATION TO MARKET DATA

9.5.1 Calibrating to CDS and to Bonds

If we want a model to value credit derivatives it makes sense to calibrate to CDSs. The 'hazard rate' is then the 'implied' rate of credit events as appropriate to CDS documentation. On the other hand, if we wish to use the model to value bonds it would make more sense to calibrate to bonds and get an 'implied default rate'. We would expect the two rates to be different (see Chapter 11). Sometimes we do not have the luxury of the choice: there may be no CDS data for the name. For example, 'high-yield' entities (often young companies in a rapidly changing and competitive economic environment) will have perhaps one bond in issue only, and typically that bond will be callable (and possibly convertible). The name probably does not trade in the CDS market, but may figure in a CDO structure, so calibration of some form has to be performed.

The choice of calibration data has an impact on how we perform that calibration. For example:

1. Rich CDS data set (say 1, 2, 3, 5, 7, 10-year maturities). We would choose a six-parameter hazard rate function (say piecewise linear with constant short and long stubs) so that we can replicate all the input data exactly.
2. Single CDS data point (say 5 years). We would choose a one-parameter function (perhaps a constant hazard rate or, better, take the shape of the CDS curve from similar spread (and industry) names) to fit the CDS level exactly.
3. CDS and bond data. If several CDS maturities are available we would usually use these alone. However, we may have one CDS data point (say 5 years) and bond data at 2- and 10-year maturities. We may wish to replicate the CDS level and the curve shape information from bonds. We could fit a two-parameter hazard rate curve reproducing the CDS level and giving a best-fit to the slope of the hazard rate curve implied by the bond data.
4. Bond data only (several bonds – say 5[9]). We may increase the bonds spreads to estimate the CDS–bond basis (see Chapter 11), and fit a low-parameter model (say 2 or 3) in order to average out liquidity effects.
5. Single bullet bond. We would fit a one-parameter model to bond price, then adjust the level to estimate the basis.
6. Single callable bond. See Chapter 11.

Note that 'calibration to bonds' does *not* mean taking the bonds spread and assuming that this is the CDS spread, then calibrating to this notional CDS – as is commonly but erroneously done. It means using the bond price, and the bond price function (9.16) under the default and recovery model, to imply a hazard rate.

---

[9] In such circumstances (a rich bond universe) it is likely that CDSs trade. However, we may wish to explicitly model bonds separately from CDSs in such circumstances in order to track the average basis.

9.5.2 Implied Hazard Rates

'Implied' means derived from prices of financial products. Financial economists also call these 'expected' rates – in the sense of a statistical expectation. It is not necessarily a good estimate of future hazard rates ('anticipated' rates) in the same way that forward interest rates are a biased estimator of future interest rates. Prices for financial products contain an estimate of forward rates and the investor gets a reward for taking on the risk of uncertain forward rates. We use 'implied' rates in the pricing of complex derivatives because they reflect the cost of our hedge.

9.5.3 Calibrating to Bonds: Multiple Solutions for the Hazard Rate

We saw in section 9.3 that the bond price under the default and recovery model may be consistent with two hazard rates (if recovery is positive). This will typically correspond to a price marginally below the recovery rate. Additionally, given an assumed recovery rate the floor for a bond price is generally slightly below this recovery rate. Figure 9.2 shows the situation for one bond under a constant hazard rate model. At prices slightly below the assumed recovery of 20 there are two hazard rates, consistent with that price and recovery.

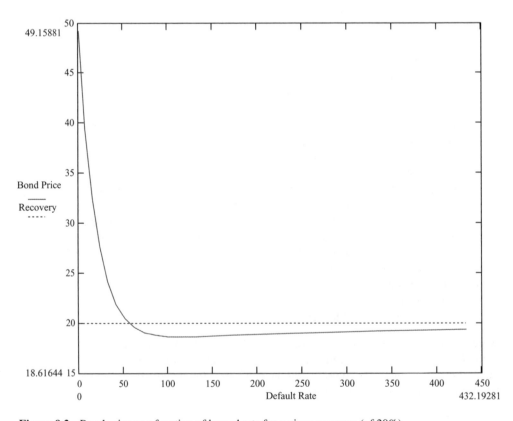

Figure 9.2   Bond price as a function of hazard rate for a given recovery (of 20%)

Table 9.1 Bond sensitivity to hazard and recovery rates at various bond prices (5-year bond with assumed recovery of zero)

		Price sensitivity to changes in default and recovery	
Spread	Dirty price	1% change in RR	1% change in default rate
40	100.40	0.02	5.01 (5-year bond)
400	85.38	0.17	4.20
1 000	66.29	0.36	3.16
2 000	45.41	0.57	2.06
3 000	32.67	0.69	1.39
4 000	24.50	0.78	0.97
5 000	19.15	0.83	0.70
10 000	8.42	0.93	0.20
Infinite	0.00	1.00	0.00

The situation becomes more complicated when we are calibrating to several bonds and we have a multifactor hazard rate curve. Then we potentially have multidimensional surfaces of solutions to the hazard rate curve when prices are around the recovery assumption.

9.5.4 Calibrating to Bonds: Implied Recovery and Hazard Rates

An interesting and useful application of the price model to bonds is to derive information on implied recovery rates. The bond price sensitivity formula (derived from (9.16)) shows that sensitivity to hazard rate drops, and sensitivity to recovery rate rises, as the hazard rate increases. This should be intuitively obvious – at very high hazard rates we have seen that the bond 'trades on a recovery' basis: changing the assumed recovery rate will give an almost equal change in the bond price, but changing the hazard rate by 1 bp will have almost no impact. The opposite is true when the hazard rate is very low. See Table 9.1.

When spreads are 'high' it becomes possible to calibrate to several bonds using a simple hazard rate curve and treating recovery as a parameter to be fitted. Note that we can also partially calibrate to recovery when fitting to several CDSs of different seniorities. Figure 9.3 and 9.4 compare

(1) a linear hazard rate curve together with an assumed recovery of zero, and
(2) a constant hazard rate curve and an unknown recovery rate

fitted to Russian bond data in 2000. In both cases a two-parameter model is being fitted, and the model is a 'best fit' minimising the sum of square price errors. It turns out that the latter case – fitting to recovery and a single hazard rate – gives a markedly better fit than assuming recovery of zero and fitting a higher order hazard rate curve.

9.5.5 Implied Hazard Rate Curve and No-Arbitrage

The implied hazard rate should be positive at all times – the model should not allow for re-incarnation – and mathematically it is required for a time-changed Poisson process. Permitting negative hazard rates can produce problems in implementations (particularly under

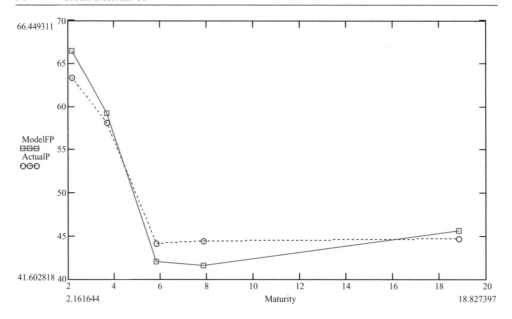

Figure 9.3   Zero recovery, two factor hazard rate curve fitted to distressed debt: Rms error = 2.1%

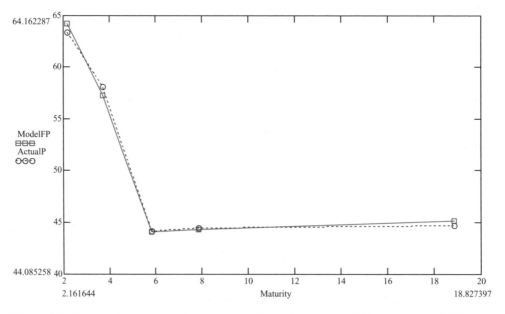

Figure 9.4   Constant hazard rate and recovery rate: implied recovery = 26%, rms error = 0.6%

some simulation approaches). If negative hazard rates arise after calibrating to input data, then this indicates the presence of arbitrage opportunities. A simple example serves to illustrate corresponding inconsistencies at the CDS premium level.

Example

Given a 3-year CDS of 50 bps and a 5-year CDS of 60 bps then there are constraints on where a 4-year can trade. The default and recovery model interpolates a sensible value based on a hazard rate curve, and will probably come up with a number around 55 bps. The actual 4-year CDS may differ from this level but there are quite tight constraints on the no-arbitrage premium levels. If we enter 3-, 4- and 5-year CDS levels into a pricing model, then the calibration will alert us to an arbitrage if the implied hazard rate is negative at any point. Suppose the 4-year CDS traded at 35 bps: if we bought this contract we would pay a total of 140 bps over the 4 years, which is 10 bp less than if we buy the 3-year CDS. In other words, at this price the fourth year is not only free but the counterparty actually pays us to take on our risk!

Exercise
Show that, with the above 3- and 5-year spreads the 4-year CDS must be between about 37.5 bp and 75 bp to avoid an arbitrage.

9.6   CDS DATA/SOURCES

9.6.1   Survey Data

The 'credit pyramid' in Chapter 4 outlines one of the major problems related to the credit and credit derivatives market – lack of good-quality data, both in terms of coverage and reliability, arising from the relative lack of liquidity in the markets. The last 10 years has seen rapid growth in credit derivatives, with a concomitant increase in the amount of data available from market deals and via brokers. In the past, banks have relied on their own internal databases of CDS data collected from front offices and brokers. This is not sufficiently complete for the banks, and does little to help other institutions dealing less frequently in the CDS market.

As part of the process of supplying banks and other institutions with good independent market data to help in the pricing and monitoring of deals and risk, several data services have developed. Some examples are as follows.

1. Several credit derivatives brokers supply CDS (and other) data based on quotes and trades that have been seen.
2. Lombard Risk, through their ValuSpread product, supplies CDS mid-levels and recovery assumptions based on participating banks mid-office reports.
3. Mark-it Partners supplies CDS data derived from partner banks (13 major investment and commercial banks) and nearly 30 other contributing banks and institutions. Data is sourced primarily from banks' front-office (trading) desks directly from the systems which feed the firms' books of record.

Mark-it Partners supplies[10] the following (as of June 2004).

---

[10] Quoted from Mark-it Partners marketing material.

Daily credit pricing that is independently validated, accurate and robust.
Automatic data cleaning algorithms reject poor quality data.
Poor data includes: stale data, flat curves and outliers.
Approximately 30% of daily CDS data and 20% of bond data is rejected.

Over 12 000 CDS credit curves constructed daily (by entity, tier of credit, currency and documentation clause) across 2500 entities and tiers of debt

Historical data includes more than 3 years of daily CDS spreads, 2 years of syndicated loan prices and one year of cash history. All can be plotted against other CDS or cash securities or to back-test credit and capital models.

Over 10 000 daily cash prices on a universe of 25 000 cash securities and over 3400 Par and Distressed syndicated loan prices on North American and European issuers.

Cash securities are time stamped and then asset swapped to enable LIBOR-based spread analysis.

Mark-it Partners aggregates data across 10 nodes (maturities) of the credit curve and also captures recovery rate assumptions for each contributor.

In addition they provide data on industry and rating sector portfolios. Figures 9.5 and 9.6 show the geographical and rating breakdown of the volume of data.

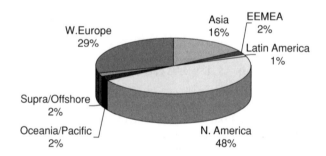

Figure 9.5   CDS data breakdown by region (*source:* Mark-it Partners)

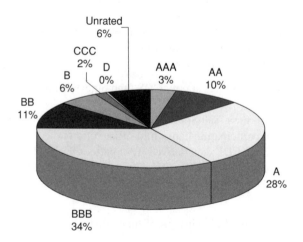

Figure 9.6   CDS data breakdown by rating (*source:* Mark-it Partners)

9.6.2 Data Engineering

Data engineering is the process of taking poor-quality data and extracting 'best guess' estimates of the correct data – correcting for errors in the data – and of missing data. In the context of credit derivatives this can mean the following:

(a) Filling gaps in the time series.
(b) Filling a full term structure of CDS quotes.
(c) Producing CDS curves for names where no, or little, data is available.

Survey data in some cases requires data for each name covered and at each maturity. On the other hand, partial data may be received and data engineering techniques used to produce the data required. These various steps require different approaches.

Initial 'Quality' Test on the Data

The idea is to identify and reject bad or suspect data points. A standard approach for any time series is based on the change from yesterday compared with the market average. In the case of CDS spread – where a 200 bp name one day may be 1000 bp the next – this can lead to many false rejections. CDS premia exhibit jumps which are valid changes. The test described above might be amended and used as a tool to improve the data history by identifying sudden jumps which are quickly reversed. Even here correct data might be rejected.

Missing Time Points

Available data can be used to produce an index CDS premium. Indices may be very broad – all corporate investment grade names – with the advantage that index changes from day to day will be very little influenced by the appearance of new names in, or disappearance of old names from, the index. On the other hand, the index may be narrow – specific to US autos rate A – but then large spurious jumps from day to day will arise as names are added or removed from the index.

Once an appropriate compromise index has been produced, percentage index changes can be used to estimate today's CDS level for a name where no data is available, based on yesterday's level and the percentage index change (for the index appropriate to the name). Clearly such a process is an estimate which gets progressively worse as time goes on. The underlying assumption is that the name follows average market moves.

CDS Curve Generation

Yield curve modelling techniques can be applied to describe the shape of the CDS curve for those entities where CDS premia at several maturities are seen. Fortunately CDS curves tend to follow similar patterns across most names – upward sloping and levelling off at long maturities for low and medium spread names, and downward sloping and levelling off, for high spread names. The following functional form illustrates the approach and can be extended to give a more accurate description of a curve (Chaplin, 1998; Anderson et al., 1996):

$$f(t) = A + B \cdot \exp(-\alpha \cdot t) \tag{9.24}$$

A and B are chosen to fit the curve while α can be chosen to reflect the overall curvature – defined in terms of the half-life (HL) of the levelling out of the curve:

$$\alpha = -\ln(0.5)/\text{HL} \tag{9.25}$$

A half-life, which is proportional to the spread, can give a good fit for most CDS curves from AAA up to B-rated names.

Once curves are calculated for different ratings or spread bands, an average curve can be selected – defining A and B. Given a single CDS level for a name the half-life is defined, and the A parameter can be adjusted so that the curve passes through the known data point. The process can be refined to use an earlier known curve data for the name.

Missing Names and Seniorities

A common problem is to price a collateralised loan obligation (CLO) related to entities and/or debt which does not trade. Internal ratings can be used to map names with no market data to generic CDS curves for that rating. The adjustment to 'loan' seniority from 'senior unsecured' data is generally based on recovery assumptions.

9.7   MODEL ERRORS AND TESTS

We shall review some of the assumptions made in the process of building the model (9.16), and attempt to assess the significance of some of these.

9.7.1   Recovery Assumption

The impact of the assumed recovery rate, and of changing this assumption, on the implied hazard rate is huge. This will similarly have a huge impact on the value of digital CDSs (see Chapter 14), but typically only a tiny one on CDS values (the impact is zero on an at-market deal). Figure 9.7 shows the implied default rate for a range of assumed recovery rates and a given CDS to which to calibrate.

9.7.2   Interest and Hazard Rate Correlation

This can be tested by setting up a model where both interest and hazard rates follow correlated diffusion processes. Let h be the hazard rate, r the interest rate, with drifts μ and standard deviations σ, then define lognormal processes

$$\frac{dh}{h} = \mu_h \cdot dt + \sigma_h \cdot dz_h \tag{9.26}$$

$$\frac{dr}{r} = \mu_r \cdot dt + \sigma_r \cdot dz_r \tag{9.27}$$

where $E(dz_h \cdot dz_r) = \rho$ is the correlation between these variables.

We can use the above model to give the CDS values of several maturities, and compare the results when 0 or 50% correlation is used. Figure 9.8 shows the results based on 1m simulations with a 10% interest rate volatility and 50% hazard rate volatility.

We conclude that – at least for investment grade names – interest rate and hazard rate correlation does not have a significant impact.

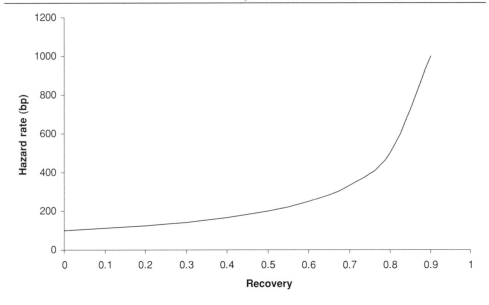

Figure 9.7   Implied hazard rate for a range of assumed recovery rates

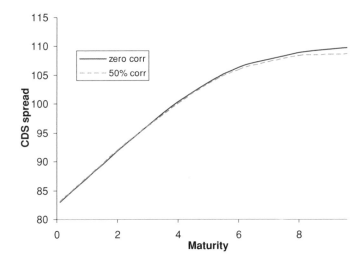

Figure 9.8   Impact of interest rate and hazard rate correlation on CDS pricing

9.7.3   Reference Name and Counterparty Hazard Rate Correlation

The reader should note carefully the final paragraph of this section.

Assume that the buyer is risk-free, but now include the writer risk as well as the reference entity risk, using a lognormal default rate model with correlated Wiener processes (similar to equation (9.26)). We choose two risks with nearly flat default rate curves – the reference name at 82 bp and the counterparty at 123 bp, and use this simulation model to evaluate the premium that should be paid for the reference entity CDS where there is a correlated risky counterparty.

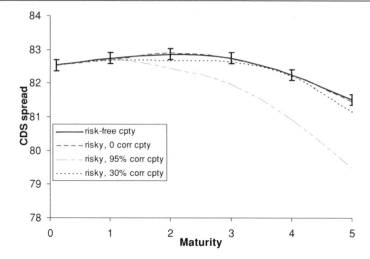

Figure 9.9   The impact of a risky counterparty on CDS pricing when spreads are correlated

Theory says that, with zero correlation, counterparty risk should have zero premium impact on continuously paid premiums – and this is what we see in Figure 9.9: the curves for a risk-free counterparty, and a risky uncorrelated counterparty, are well within the simulation error bars.

Default rate correlation has almost no discernible impact (well within bid/offer spreads) on CDS pricing for investment grade pairs and 5-year CDSs at spread correlations levels up to 95%, and less than 1% impact up to 60% correlation.

On the other hand, there is a discernable impact on very long-life (25-year) and high spread names (around 1000 bp or more) (not shown). Although intuitively we expect correlated spreads to lead to higher risks that both names default in a certain time, the problem is that the default event is a sudden and surprising event. Widening of the spread on the remaining name does not significantly raise the possibility of a default within the remaining period of interest, at least for investment grade names.

The above results should be treated with care. We have shown that, if the reference name and counterparty have correlated spreads, *and those spreads follow diffusion processes*, then there is negligible impact in the pricing of CDS deals. However, the transition matrix, and experience in credit markets, tell us that spreads follow a more violent process than a diffusion. A jump process would be a better model. Part IV returns to this topic, armed with a better model – and comes to quite different conclusions.

9.7.4   Interpolation Assumptions, and the Pseudo-hazard Rate Versus Stochastic Hazard Rate

Interpolation assumptions can clearly have a large impact on valuation results. Suppose a 2-year CDS on a reference name stands at 100 bp, and the 5-year is at 150 bp. If we own a 3.5-year CDS and use a piecewise linear hazard rate model, we find that the implied fair value CDS premium for the 3.5-year maturity is very close to 125 bp. On the other hand, if we use a piecewise constant hazard rate assumption (not very sensible), we will find the 3.5-year

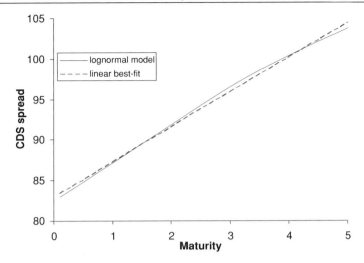

Figure 9.10 Linear pseudo-hazard rate versus stochastic hazard rate with drift

CDS fair value premium is 150 bp. The difference of 25 bp is a gross error but can easily be produced with a poor choice of interpolation function.

Other forms of interpolation function (an exponential formula, for example) will generally lead to minor differences in CDS values. A simple reserve can be based on the use of an alternative interpolation routine and looking at valuation differences.

A more subtle question arises through the use of the pseudo-hazard rate model as opposed to a full stochastic model. Under the former model we have a near linear CDS curve if we assume a linear hazard rate curve. The latter model produces a sloping CDS curve if we have a stochastic hazard rate with a drift. How accurately does a linear pseudo-hazard rate curve fit the values arising from the stochastic model? Figure 9.10 shows the result of 1m CDS pricing simulations with 75% volatility.

Over a 5-year span there is an rms error of under a 1 bp. Over a 10-year span with a best-fit linear curve there is an rms error of under 3 bp (not shown).

9.8   CDS RISK FACTORS; RESERVES AND MODEL RISK

We summarise below the various risk factors we have discovered through the above analysis.

9.8.1   Captured and Hidden Risks

Risks Captured by our Model

1. Default event risk.
2. Default rate and recovery rate risks, now and forward.
3. Interest rate risks.
4. Repo rate term structure risks where bonds are valued or used for calibration or hedging.
5. Bond/CDS basis – if we use separately calibrated hazard rate curves for bonds and CDSs.

Risks not Captured by The model (Hidden Risks)

1. Correlation between interest rates and default rates.
2. Correlated counterparty risk.
3. Interpolation methods for default rate and interest rates.
4. Delivery option.
5. Liquidity.
6. Volatilities of CDS premia, of interest rates, and of recovery.
7. Correlation between foreign exchange rates and hazard rates (relevant to cross-currency hedging).

9.8.2   Limits

Limits can be set on default event exposure to control unhedged event risk. These limits can be on a name, a class (US 'AA' corporates), a currency, or book(s). Digital (recovery rate) risk can be captured by changing recovery assumption, recalibrating, revaluing the books, and having limits on the difference. Term structure risks can be controlled by having limits on spread sensitivity in maturity buckets. Repo risk: what is the impact of repo risk and how does it affect hedges?

9.8.3   Reserves against Implementation Errors

Our model is a complicated interpolation procedure to value trades. Reserves are usually taken against each trade to reflect:

(a) 'errors' in the implementation of the model – for example, recovery assumptions or poor choice of hazard rate function;
(b) reserves for model risk – the hidden risks (see section 9.8.4).

Typical examples of the former set of reserves are:

1. Bid–offer spread if the model is marked to mid.
2. Unknown recovery.
3. Interpolation.

Bid–Offer Reserve

When marking to model one can take fit to bid side data to get a bid, or fit to mids and make an adjustment (reserve) at the end. The bid–offer reserve or adjustment is one that should clearly be taken by both the trader and the institution: all other reserves arguably belong to the institution only.

In principle, bid–offer is name and maturity dependent. Some active names and maturities may have near zero bid–offer spread; others may have a 30% spread. Increasingly traders seem to take a name-by-name approach to marking their books explicitly estimating the bid–offer spread.

Marking on a deal-by-deal basis may overestimate the reserve. Well-hedged positions should be subject to a significantly narrower reserve (see Part I).

Recovery Reserve

Recovery is a key arbitrary number with almost no impact on some types of trades and huge impact on others (digitals). A reserve per name can be calculated by shifting the recovery assumption to 0, or up 30% (with some practical upper limit), recalibrating and taking the worst change in the position value. This captures the large recovery risk in digital positions as well as the small recovery risk in vanilla trades.

Should the recovery reserve be netted across names? In a diversified portfolio it can be argued that overestimates in one area will be compensated by underestimates in another area. The mean will have less uncertainty. On the other hand, the mean recovery rate changes markedly over time. Even in non-recession years the mean moves 10% or so.

On the portfolio as a whole the impact of the reserve should be less than the sum of all the individual reserves. On the other hand, we know that the average recovery across a broad portfolio does vary over time – so a minimum recovery reserve on a portfolio can be set by shifting all recoveries simultaneously by (say) 10%.

Hazard Rate Interpolation Reserve

Pricing a 2-year CDS off a 5-year quote is subject to risk from the unknown shape of the curve – review the exercise at the end of section 9.2. The uncertainty increases as the deal moves further from the calibrating instruments. Clearly the interpolation reserve could be very large if inappropriate choices of hazard rate functions are taken.

Where active investment grade names are concerned, a rich data set and a linear interpolation curve will give rise to insignificant errors except at the short and long end. One way to set an interpolation curve would be to use the form of the curve derived from engineered data and best-fit to the actual data for the name.

The reserve should be greater for inactive or atypical names (names where there is reason to believe that the risks are fundamentally different over time from other names of similar rating or industry). An extreme would be to base the reserve on a flat versus a generic curve shape. This would overestimate the reserves for a portfolio of such risks.

Repo

This only matters where 'special' bonds are used for calibration. It does not apply to corporate debt except in very exceptional circumstances. The amount assumed can be stressed to zero or up to an arbitrary amount, recalibrated and revalued. It is additive across the book.

Basis

The basis may be captured by separate calibration to bonds and CDSs resulting in a mark-to-market change as market levels change. The only reserve needed is to cover the error in its estimation, and this will already be included primarily in the interpolation reserves.

9.8.4   Model Reserves

We can divide these into

(a) reserves for known simplifications in the model, and
(b) into unknown deficiencies in our model.

The known deficiencies are listed in 9.8.1, and reserves can be implemented based on the analysis of these deficiencies in section 9.7. We mention a few further points.

Claim Amount Reserve (for Sovereigns)

Alternative claim amounts can be used in calibration and pricing to reflect the unknown reality of the recovery process for sovereigns.

Liquidity

This is partly captured by the bid–offer spread. Post-default liquidity is reflected in a potentially wide range of recovery rates for that name and seniority. An explicit reserve for this may be considered.

Unknown deficiencies tend to be handled by an arbitrary formula – perhaps a percentage of the expected loss, or a percentage of notional depending on rating and maturity. Once a decision is made to trade a certain product by an institution, then model reserves would appear to be the responsibility of the institution rather than the trader.

10

CDS Deal Examples

We now look at a range of applications of the valuation formulae established above. The majority of these applications arise from trading or hedging strategies, and a thorough understanding of the analysis of these examples reveals the sources of risk in the deals and how best to control this risk.

Elementary Trading Strategies

At this point the reader should review the elementary trading strategies discussed in Chapter 8 in the light of the valuation and sensitivity results derived in Chapter 9. In particular, note that the value of a long protection position increases as the current (market) CDS premium increases – equation (9.12). Thus a bearish view (expecting CDS premia – or bond spreads – to widen) of a particular name can be implemented by buying protection on that name. A bullish view can be reflected by selling protection or by buying bonds.

The following examples are divided into two parts: (a) purely CDS trades and (b) bond and CDS trades. A fuller analysis of CDS/bond (basis) trading is given in Chapter 11, some other CDS applications are covered in Chapter 12, and trading using Credit-Linked Notes (CLNs) is covered in Chapter 13.

Risk Charts

In this chapter we illustrate trades, with a 'risk chart' (Figure 10.1) showing the spread sensitivity and the default event sensitivity. These are intended only to give a quick visual impression of the trade – they are not exact, nor do such charts in any sense replace a full risk report (which would include risks other than just these two). We shall assume 50% senior recovery, and 0% subordinated recovery where required. Positive spread risk means we make money when spreads rise, and positive event risk means we make money on a credit event. For example, a bearish trade on FMC implemented by buying USD 10m protection in 5-year maturity is shown in Figure 10.1.

10.1 A CDS HEDGED AGAINST ANOTHER CDS

10.1.1 Cross-Currency Default Swap Pricing and Hedging

An investor wishing to take GMAC risk but wishing to invest in EUR has limited choice – most debt is in USD or CAD and only around 2% is in EUR. A bank could create EUR GMAC debt synthetically by producing a CLN linked to GMAC in EUR (see below) effectively buying 5-year (say) GMAC protection in EUR. The bank could hedge this by selling protection to the same maturity on GMAC in USD. What price differences should there be, and what is the correct hedge, for long CDS protection in EUR hedged by short CDS protection in USD (or any other pair of currencies)?

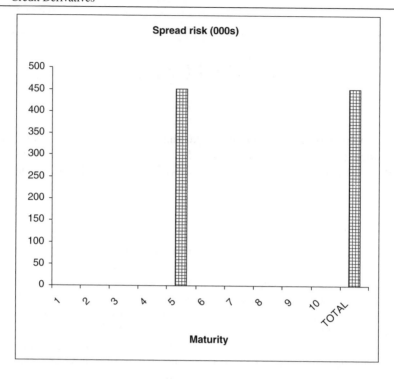

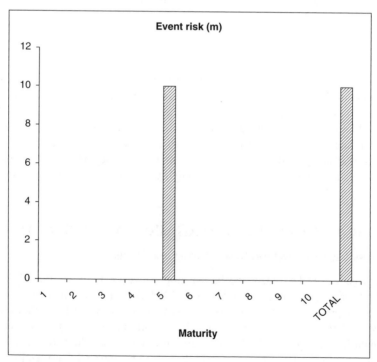

Figure 10.1   Risk chart for the bearish trade example

Case A: Constant Hazard Rate/Constant Forward FX Rate

First assume that the hazard rate is constant. Equation (9.15) says that the CDS premium is the hazard rate for GMAC times the loss given default – there is no mention of currency or interest rates in this equation. The hazard rate gives the rate of default for the entity GMAC, and the recovery is the recovery rate on (senior unsecured) GMAC debt (all currencies of senior unsecured debt rank equally in default so have the same recovery). The implication is that the USD CDS premium and the EUR CDS premium should both be the same. In practice we can see the USD CDS premium in the market – say 200 bp, we assume a recovery rate – say 40%, and calculate a hazard rate 200/0.6 = 333.3 bp (3.333% p.a.). Given this hazard rate we can calculate the CDS is any currency = 333.3 × 0.6 = 200 bp.

So the theory (with a constant hazard rate) implies that the CDS premia are identical in USD and EUR. If we buy 20m EUR protection at 200 bp, we should sell USD protection at 200 bp (although, of course, the bank will try to source protection cheaply and sell it expensively), but in what size?

If default occurs immediately we deliver 20m EUR of defaulted debt into the protection. In practice on the long we would deliver EUR 20m worth of the cheapest USD or CAD debt (since this is almost all that is available) into the protection. We should make sure that we know what debt we will be delivered to us on the short protection hedge before we have to decide what debt we want to deliver[1] – we may be able to find something cheaper but we cannot rely on it. Subject to this documentation requirement, we also want to make sure that the nominal amount delivered to us is the amount we need to deliver into the protection. If we are delivered USD debt, then the amount is just the size of the USD protection we have written.[2] We want this amount to be financially equal to EUR 20m/EUR USD where EUR USD is the number of EUR per USD at the delivery notice date. We do not know what this amount will be but if the forward exchange rate is equal to the spot exchange rate (at all dates) then the expected exchange rate is just this rate. If the rate is 1.25, then we need to sell USD 16m protection as a hedge. On default, we get delivered 16m USD debt which, if the rate turns out to be 1.25, is EUR 20m worth of debt – the exact amount we need to deliver into the long protection. We receive EUR 20m cash which converts into USD 16m and which we pay to the owner of the USD protection we sold.

The actual exchange rate may be higher or lower than this but the expected value is 1.25. Even with volatile exchange rates the currency risk we are taking is small. If, a day after we implement the EUR 20m trade (hedged with USD 16m short protection) the exchange rate changes to 1.20, then our EUR 20m protection is equivalent to USD 16.667m, so we need to sell a further USD 0.667m of protection. But under the assumption of a constant hazard rate curve we sell the re-hedge amount at the same premium of 200 bp. The total income on the new total hedge therefore continues to exactly match the outgoing on the bought protection.

If hazard rates are stochastic we know (by assumption) that the expected spread is constant, so although re-hedging will lead to profits or losses (i.e. surplus or deficit on the premium cashflows) the expected loss is zero. We can also see that there are risks associated with how the exchange rate and the currency rate might change together (FX and hazard rate correlation risk).

---

[1] It is the owner of protection who has the choice.
[2] If we are delivered debt in another currency the nominal amount is determined by the current exchange rate (at the time the delivery notice is given stating what debt has been chosen): so is the size of the USD protection sold times the number of units per USD of the currency of the delivered debt.

Case B: Constant Hazard Rate/Forward FX Rate Curve

If we now assume that the forward FX rate is time dependent (determined by the structure of the interest rate curves in the two economies) then the correct hedge amount to be short of at time t is EUR 20m/EUR USD(t) in order to cover the default event risk. If the EUR is rising then we will be selling more and more USD protection as time goes on. Note that at any moment we are paying out 200 bp on EUR 20m of protection = EUR 0.4m, and we will be earning 200 bp on USD 20m/EUR USD(t) = USD 0.4m/EUR USD(t) = EUR 0.4m, so there is no income loss or gain under a constant hazard rate curve as long as we remain default event hedged.

Case C: Hazard Rate Curve/Constant Forward FX Rate

If the exchange rate is constant then the hedge ratio is fixed (apart from unexpected changes in the FX rate which may be either way). The two premium rates are set on day 1, and again the two premia will be the same. The premium is determined by equation (9.11) with $V = 0$, and because the forward FX rate is constant this implies that the interest rate curves are identical, so that equation (9.12) is the same whether we are looking at USD or EUR – hence the CDS premia are identical.

Unanticipated exchange rate moves will cause re-hedging to be done at different CDS premia from the initial premium (since the CDS is shorter and there is a hazard rate curve), giving a profit or loss. The expected value is again zero. Similarly for unanticipated hazard rate moves.

Case D: Hazard Rate Curve/Forward FX Rate Curve

Now let us assume that both the hazard rate and the FX rates are functions of time. In order to cover the default event risk, the hedge ratio at any time is still EUR 20m/EUR USD(t). But now the new hedges we put on are no longer earning 200 bp because the hazard rate curve is not constant, so the forward CDS premia will change – if the curve is upward sloping then the future USD CDS sales are at a higher CDS premium. These higher amounts will generate an excess income over the EUR cost. This implies that the CDS premium in EUR should be more than 200 bp. This is consistent with equation (9.11). Where the hazard rate is non-constant then a dependence on the interest rate curve enters in (9.11) and the existence of an FX rate curve also implies that the discount curves in EUR and USD are different.

First we shall try to get a 'feel' for the impact of this on EUR CDS pricing and on our future hedges. Suppose that EUR interest rates are 2% and USD rates are 3% – this interest rate difference implies an FX curve with the exchange rate (EUR per USD) falling from spot 1.25 to 1.19 at 5-year maturity (EUR strengthening). The hedge sold rises from USD 16m to 16.8m. The CDS spread is changing, but to first order the income is going to be around 200 bp. At the end of year 5 we need to sell an additional USD 800 000 protection, earning an additional USD 16 000. This income is in addition to the fixed USD 16m × 200 bp = USD 320 000 p.a. on the initial hedge amount, and the total income is worth USD 336 000 × 1.19 = EUR 400 000, the same as our cost. We have to take into account the expected change in the hazard rate in order to see the second-order impact. Suppose that the hazard rate is rising linearly from 0 to 667 bp in five years' time (this has a current average of 333 bp, hence a CDS premium of 200 bp approximately). In the final year the average hazard rate is 600 bp, implying a CDS premium of roughly 360 bp. Thus the fourth year produces a risk of 16.6m and an income of

$$\text{USD}(320\,000 + 6400 \times 3.6) \times 1.19 = \text{EUR } 408\,000$$

The excess income will average around EUR 4000 per annum, or around 2 bp – in other words, we should be paying around 202 bp for EUR protection if 200 bp is correct for USD (this, of course, relies on the relative interest rates used in this example and the steep hazard rate curve assumed).

Let us now look at the deal from the point of equation (9.11). The fair-value premium at time t is given by

$$\int_t^T (1 - R) \cdot D(s) \cdot S(s) \cdot \lambda(s)\,ds \Big/ \left[\int_t^T D(s) \cdot S(s)\,ds \right]$$

The only difference between USD and EUR is the lower discounting (by an assumed 1% p.a.) for the EUR. This gives more weight to the higher hazard rates (at greater maturities) so should give a higher premium for the EUR CDS – as we obtained above. An approximate calculation is given in the spreadsheet 'Part II section 3.xls' worksheet 'FX and CDS curve' and indicates roughly 2 bp per annum less for the 5-year EUR CDS compared with the USD CDS. (Note the significant error in the calculation of the USD CDS premium in the spreadsheet arises from the crude numerical integration. This error is similar in both USD and EUR calculations; the difference in the results is quite close to the accurate answer. Accurate calculations require much more accurate numerical integration: results from accurate calculations are quoted in Table 10.1.)

Table 10.1 shows the impact of different hazard and interest rate curves on CDS pricing in one currency relative to a base currency (with a flat 3% interest rate curve). The table incidentally shows the impact of quarterly premia (in arrears with a proportion) compared with continuous premia.

Table 10.1   Cross-currency pricing (relative to base currency with flat 3% interest rate curve); CDS paying quarterly in arrears with proportion to default date

CDS in base currency	Interest rates in second currency	CDS in second currency
200 bp flat; 40% recovery	3% flat	200 bp
	2% flat	199.7 bp
		(if premia were continuous then the second currency CDS would also be 200 bp exactly)
100 bp at zero maturity, rising to 200 bp at 5-year	3% flat	200 bp
	2% flat	100 bp rising to 200.6 bp
	6% flat	100 bp rising to 198.2 bp
	1.5% rising to 4% at 5-year	100 bp rising to 199.4 bp
1000 bp at zero maturity, falling to 500 bp at 5-year; 20% recovery	7% flat	1000 bp falling to 519.8 bp

Other Causes of Currency-Related Premium Differences

The above example related USD and EUR. For these two currencies – and for all major currency pairs – the relationship predicted above is observed in practice (Figure 10.2). This has not always been the case for bonds – in the mid-1990s in bond spreads for JPY and USD debt of the same reference entity differed substantially. It was not possible to short the expensive bonds (and go long the cheap bonds to set up an arbitrage) and the CDS market did not exist in sufficient size to allow a synthetic trade to be set up. However, where an active two-way CDS market exists such differences should not persist.

Hedging Based on Sensitivity Rather than Default Event

The examples above have discussed hedging in terms of default event hedging. Typically hedging will be done on a 'sensitivity' rather than 'event' basis. Results are similar, although much more calculation intensive, and are not given here.

Note on Cross-Currency 'Book' Risks

An investment grade trading or investment book of CDS deals which is net long protection in one currency and short in another runs a risk whose expected value is zero (subject to the CDSs being correctly priced). If forward FX exposure is unhedged and FX rates follow forward rates, then the book will be consistently selling (or buying) protection in one currency. Unexpected moves in either FX rates or all CDS levels will lead to an unanticipated profit or loss on FX rehedging on the net book position.

From a book perspective net cross-currency positions should be limited to an amount with which the institution is comfortable. Examining a representative CDS book and stressing the exchange rate, CDS level, and interest rates in one economy, may indicate an unanticipated FX risk of (say) 0.2% of notional.[3] Naked exposure limits may be set at around 1% of gross notional – so if cross-currency hedging accounted for 10% of naked exposures, this would use up only around $10 \times 0.2 = 2\%$ of the naked exposure limit. Results depend on currencies, CDS levels, etc. Additionally, an institution would wish to look at the unanticipated risk associated with the above – which will be significantly more restrictive.

10.1.2   Back-to-Back Trades, Default Event Hedges and Curve Trades

Typically a front book trader will find he has acquired or sold protection on a specific name (say Ford Motor Credit) to a certain maturity (say 5 years). What risk should one hedge – default event or spread (hazard rate) risk? There are various alternatives available to hedge emerging front book positions or to put on a deliberate risk position.

Back-to-Back Hedge

Where protection has been obtained cheaply (perhaps via a credit-linked note sold to a client), an exactly matching deal – same maturity date, size, currency and reference name – in the opposite direction removes default event, spread and interest rate risk. Only counterparty risk

---

[3] Looking at Table 10.1, the premium 'error' is (say) around 4 bp for the book or 0.2% of notional if they are 5-year deals.

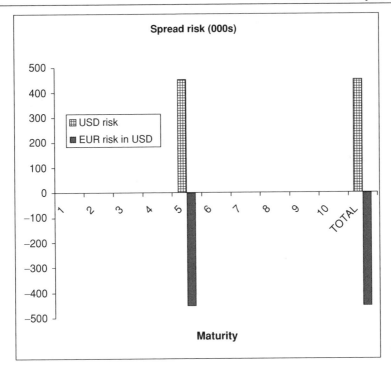

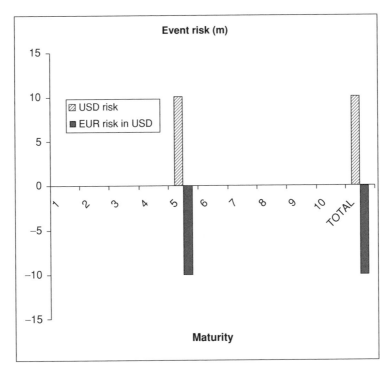

Figure 10.2   Risk chart for cross-currency trade hedged at the same maturity

remains, arising from the chance that the buyer of protection defaults after CDS premia have narrowed.

Default Event Hedge/Spread Directional Trade (Figure 10.3)

A purchase of JPY 1bn of 5-year protection could be hedged by selling the same amount of 3-year protection. If a credit event occurs within the three years, then debt delivered into the protection sold is, in turn, delivered into the protection bought (subject to documentation ensuring that sufficient notice is obtained on the debt to be delivered). If the 5-year protection costs 200 bp, then the 3-year protection may raise 150 bp. This leaves an income loss (**negative carry**) of 50 bp per annum for three years, together with the final two years' cost of the long protection. Of course the expected forward protection on the remaining two years is around 275 bp but there is no guarantee that the 2-year CDS will raise this in future. The risk reports will also show a significant spread risk in this case: as spreads rise, the long 5-year protection will make more money than the 3-year trade loses. This is a bearish trade on spreads while being default event neutral.

Alternatively, if the name is highly risky, 5-year protection may cost 1000 bp p.a. but 3-year protection may raise 1400 bp – leaving a total income deficit of only 800 bp. The residual spread risk will be a small proportion of the risk arising from the 5-year deal alone.

CDS Spread Hedging/Curve Trade (Figure 10.4)

A longer CDS has a greater sensitivity to a shift in the hazard rate (or spread) curve. The spreadsheet 'Chapter 10.xls' worksheet 'spread hedging' calculates the hedge ratios for a 5-year with a 3-year (and vice versa) CDS under a flat hazard rate curve. (The Mathcad sheet 'Chapter 9 and Chapter 19 hedge theory.mcd' gives the mathematical formulae and also performs the calculations.) Long 5-year protection at 200 bp (say) could be hedged by selling approximately 160% of notional in three years at 150 bp raising 240 bp – covering the cost of the 5-year protection and leaving a **positive carry** of 40 bp. If no credit event occurs during these three years, 120 bp will have been earned, and protection can be sold in three years' time for the remaining two years to earn more income. The hedge runs a significant default event risk during the first three years. In addition, the trade is exposed to changes in the shape of the curve. If 5-year spreads rise more than 3-year spreads, a profit is made – the trade is a **curve steepener**.

Note that the hedge ratio (of 160% in this case) changes over time – in one year's time it is more like 400%. The hedge is **dynamic**.

Consider for a moment an equity options trader who has written 3-month at-the-money (forward) call options on GBP 10m of Unilever Plc. The trader could delta hedge this position by buying 5m worth of Unilever shares (the option delta is 0.5). A small move in the price of the shares will see equal and offsetting changes in the value of the shares and the options. Yet a default event of Unilever will see the shares fall to practically zero – a loss of GBP 5m – which the option premium taken in will only be of the order of GBP 0.2m.

For two main reasons, an equity trader generally does not worry about the default event. First, the positions are hedged by other options as fully as possible, so *residual* risk to the share price is actually small. Extreme moves in share price are considered in reporting risk on the options book – although often not explicitly the default event. The second is that high-quality (investment grade) names are regarded as default risk remote.

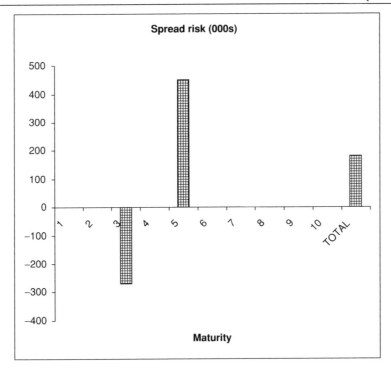

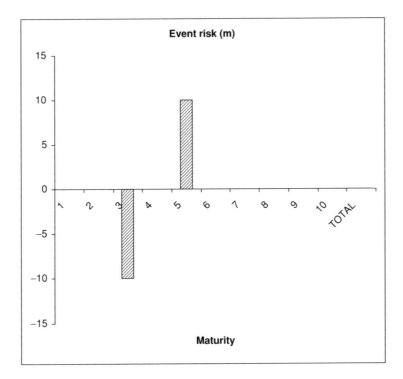

Figure 10.3   Risk chart for event-hedged spread trade

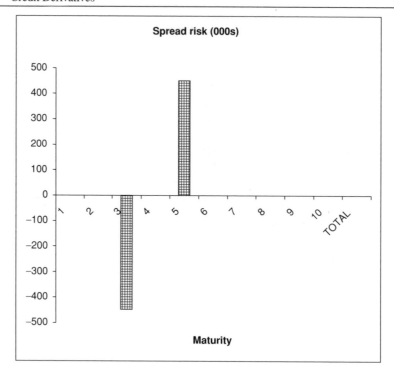

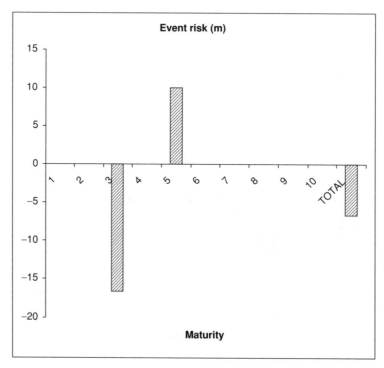

Figure 10.4   Risk chart for curve trade

The same philosophy generally extends to the CDS book – investment grade names are generally seen as default risk remote and a significant default event risk can be carried in each name as long as spread risk is small. On the other hand, 'emerging market' names – where spreads are wide and default risk is substantial – will tend to have much tighter default event risk limits.

10.1.3   Hedging both Credit Event and Spread Risk Simultaneously

Is it possible to hedge both default event and spread risk?

Typically a desk trading investment grade CDS will hedge spread risk which will usually leave a net default event risk (and the desk loses money on credit events typically). The reader should note that it is theoretically possible to hedge both credit event risk and spread risk under certain assumptions (Figure 10.5). In principle, a long 5-year protection position in FMC could be hedged by short positions in both 3-year and 7-year CDSs. We require that the nominals are chosen so that the default event risk and the spread sensitivity are both zero. The two simultaneous equations can be solved to give the hedge nominals.

Suppose we own one nominal of FMC. Then we can sell notional N_1 of the 3-year CDS and N_2 the 7-year CDS (we suppose, for simplicity, the net value of all three CDSs is currently zero – i.e. they are fair market trades). We require:

$$N_1 \times (1 - R) + N_2 \times (1 - R) = (1 - R) \tag{10.1}$$

in which default event losses are equal;

$$N_1 \times S_1 + N_2 \times S_2 = S_0 \tag{10.2}$$

in which trade and hedge sensitivities (S) are equal.

This gives

$$N_1 = (S_2 - S_0)/(S_2 - S_1) \quad \text{and} \quad N_2 = 1 - N_1 \tag{10.3}$$

If the CDS curve moves up or down in parallel, (10.2) ensures that there is no net profit or loss to first order. Also, on a credit event (and subject to the usual documentation conditions), the nominal delivered equals the amount we have to deliver (10.1). There is a solution to the equations as long as the sensitivities of the hedges are not equal (10.3).

Suppose we were to use a 1-year and a 10-year CDS as the hedges? Or suppose we are hedging a 2-year CDS with a 3-year and a 5-year, what problems do you foresee?

Equation (10.2) assumes that the CDS spread curve undergoes parallel moves. In reality this is not the case, so hedging as above is flawed in practice. The example given – 5-year versus 3- and 7-year – is reasonable but the other examples will lead to large curve risk and large hedge notionals. Attempting to hedge slope risk with a third CDS will simply introduce curvature risk – 5-year spreads rise 10 bp, but 3-year spreads rise 12 bp and 7-year rise 10 bp, whereas the slope hedge anticipates a 9 bp change. We could hedge this by adding a fourth CDS, but then there is 'twist' risk ... and so on. The CDS curves are not as well arbitraged as the LIBOR curve, so shape changes do not necessarily follow a predictable pattern. On top of this, spread moves often include jumps – not infinitesimal moves.[4] Hedging both credit event

---

[4] Equation (10.1) ensures that we are hedged to the ultimate jump, but intermediate moves may be different from both extremes of (10.1) and (10.2).

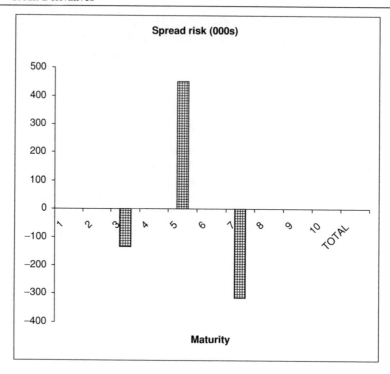

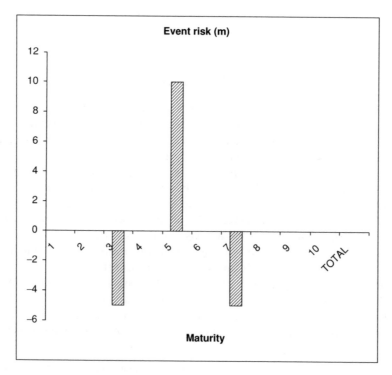

Figure 10.5   Risk chart for default and event hedge

and spread risk is not a practical possibility generally, and we shall revisit this topic when we discuss book hedging.

10.1.4 Seniority Mismatch

Consider a reference entity where both senior and subordinated debt trades – typically such entities are financial entities (banks or insurance companies). A long protection position on junior (= subordinated) debt in EUR 10m against a short position in the same notional amount of senior debt can at worst lead to no loss in the default event. For example, if senior recovery[5] is 50% then junior recovery is less than this. Long junior CDS gets more than par-50% on a credit event and the sold senior CDS only has to pay par-50%. In the worst case debt delivered into the short position can be delivered into the long position if necessary. It is more likely that we can sell the defaulted senior debt in the market at a higher price than it costs to buy junior debt to deliver into the long protection position (Figure 10.6).

The same trade in reverse (long senior protection, short junior) can suffer a maximum loss of 10m. Junior debt may be trading at near zero post-default, yet senior debt may be close to par.

As junior CDSs are more risky than senior CDSs, they carry a higher premium. Figure 10.7 shows some junior and senior CDS premia on financials (data from 2003). Based on around 50 names, subordinated CDSs typically traded at around twice the senior CDS premium. Why should this be?

Suppose the senior CDS trades at P_{sen} and the junior CDS at P_{sub}, and assume a recovery of R_{sub} on the junior CDS. Then (from equation (9.15)) the implied hazard rate for the entity is $P_{sub}/(1-R_{sub})$. This hazard rate relates to the entity not the seniority, so the senior premium and recovery (again from (9.15)) are related by $(1 - R_{sen}) = (1-R_{sub}) \times P_{sen}/P_{sub}$. If $P_{sen}/P_{sub} = 0.5$, then we get the relationship between junior and senior recovery rates shown in Table 10.2.

In particular the ratio of CDS premia is inconsistent with a senior recovery rate of less than 50%. Suppose, for example, (based on fundamental research on the company), you think senior recovery is likely to be only 20%, and junior recovery is 0%. The market is being optimistic on senior risk so the senior CDS premium is too low. We should therefore buy senior protection and sell junior protection. Suppose we buy 10m senior protection at 50 bp, and sell X of junior protection (to the same maturity – typically 5-year) at 100 bp. On a credit event, if our recovery assumptions are right, we make $10m \times (1 - 0.2) = 8m$ on the senior protection, and lose X on the junior. We are default event hedged if $X = 8m$. We have a positive cashflow of $8m \times 100$ bp $- 10m \times 50$ bp $= 30\,000$ p.a. (Such a trade may be capital intensive for certain institutions if the capital required to finance the positions is much greater on junior than on senior debt, which may also be a hidden factor in the pricing of junior debt.)

10.1.5 Trade Level Hedging and Book Basis Hedging

The trades in sections 10.1.3 and 10.1.4 above are initiated by the trader based on a view of recovery rates for that name. The deals do not lead to any default event risk within the internal risk reports if the trader's recovery assumptions are also reflected in the risk reporting recovery assumptions. This is also true of spread (hazard rate) risk (equation 9.18). If the risk reports are generated using different recovery assumptions, from the trader's assumptions, then a spread

---

[5] Remember that recovery here means 'one month post-default bond price'.

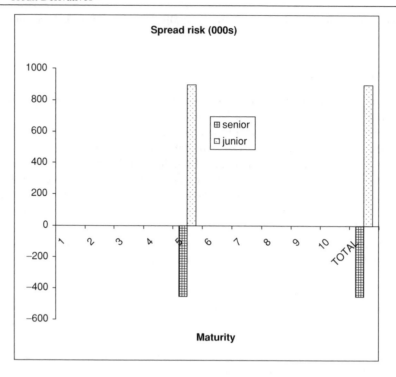

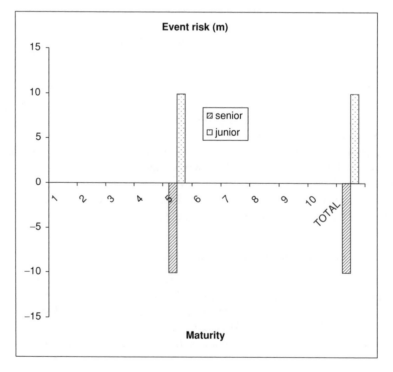

Figure 10.6   Risk chart for cross-seniority trade

Table 10.2 Implied senior recovery rate when sub-CDSs-trade at twice the junior CDS premium

Junior recovery assumption	Implied senior recovery rate
0	0.5
0.2	0.6
0.4	0.7
0.6	0.8
0.8	0.9

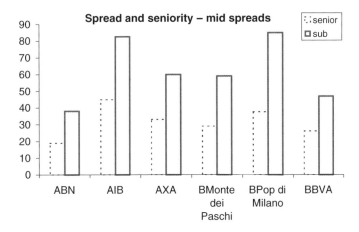

Figure 10.7 Senior and sub-CDS premia (sample financial data, 2003)

risk will appear. This will be aggregated with other spread risks and unless the trader is aware of the source of the net spread risk then that risk will automatically be hedged out, largely negating the intended effect of the trader's recovery rate hedge. It is therefore essential that recovery (and other) assumptions used for reporting be kept in line with the trader's assumptions, or that risk is not aggregated for certain trades. We discuss this topic in more detail in Chapter 18.

10.2 INTRODUCTION TO BOND HEDGING

10.2.1 Default Event Hedging

Loans may be non-assignable (they cannot be sold) so CDSs represent a potentially attractive way to remove the economic risk[6] of the loan without selling the bond. If permission of the borrower is sought to sell the loan this may damage the bank/client relationship, whereas a CDS deal is less conspicuous, and a portfolio CDS (CDO) deal is less judgemental about specific borrowers.

It may also be attractive to hedge bond positions by a CDS – perhaps as part of a term structure strategy, or to reflect a short-term view. Suppose you own USD 10m nominal of a

---

[6] A loan plus CDS of matching maturity into which the loan is deliverable eliminates the default event risk (and also the mark-to-market risk) sufficiently well that the risk is seen to be no longer that of the borrower under the loan but that of the CDS counterparty. The economic risk to the borrower has gone, although the loan remains on the bank's books.

5-year FMC bond priced at par. What CDS would you use, and how much would you buy, to protect against the default event risk over the next year? If the bond is priced at 80, or at 120, how would your answer differ?

If we buy USD 10m of a 2-year (or 10-year) CDS, then on default at any time in the next year we can deliver the bond and get USD 10m. We are fully event hedged in this case. If the bond is priced at 80, suppose recovery on default is 50% and, for the moment, think in terms of a cash-settled CDS. If we own a 10m CDS then, on the default event, we gain $10m - 5m = 5m$ on the CDS but only lose $8m - 5m = 3m$ on the bond. We need to buy only 6m notional of the CDS in order to be hedged. Alternatively, if the bond is priced at 120 we lose 7m on the default event and need to buy 14m of the CDS to be hedged. In fact the correct hedge ratio against the default event is given by

$$CDSnotional = bondnotional \times (P - R)/(1 - R) \qquad (10.4)$$

Unless the bond price is par, the correct hedge ratio requires an estimate of the recovery rate – hence generally *we cannot hedge the default event with certainty*.

Commercial bank loan portfolio managers generally do not mark their loans to market, so they stand on the books at the issue price – typically close to par. Also the manager does not have to hedge the risk of the change in value of the loans. A notional for notional hedge is often appropriate for such portfolios. In addition, if it is required to reduce regulatory capital under current regulations, then the CDS life needs to be at least as long as the bond life.

Most market-traded CDSs are on senior debt (exceptions being financials where subordinate CDSs also actively trade). It may be necessary for a loan portfolio manager to buy CDSs on senior debt (rather than cheaper loan CDSs). On the default event, the loan is potentially deliverable into the CDS (since it is more senior than senior bonds), although the portfolio manager would generally do better by buying defaulted bonds to deliver and keep the loans on the books to get the ultimate recovery.

10.2.2   Spread Hedging

If we assume that the CDS and the bond are priced off the same hazard rate curve, then we can use the sensitivity formulae of Chapter 9 to calculate the hedge ratio. For bonds priced at par the bond sensitivity is almost the same as the CDS sensitivity for a CDS of the same maturity – so a spread hedge (which is one for one) and a default event hedge are the same, and we hedge both risks at the same time. If prices are away from par then the hedge ratio needs to be calculated from the formulae.

In practice, bonds and CDSs do not move together – the difference is referred to as the basis. This is investigated further in Chapter 11.

Figure 10.8 shows a risk chart for a 4-year bond spread-hedged with a 5-year CDS. This leaves an event risk (not shown) and the more important 'basis risk'. A change in the CDS premium may be accompanied by a different change in the spread on a like maturity bond. This difference is a change in the basis.

Basis risk is the same in magnitude as naked spread risk. Although we would expect the basis to be constrained, it can move very sharply in the short term. Limits on basis risk often impose tight constraints on basis trading by banks.

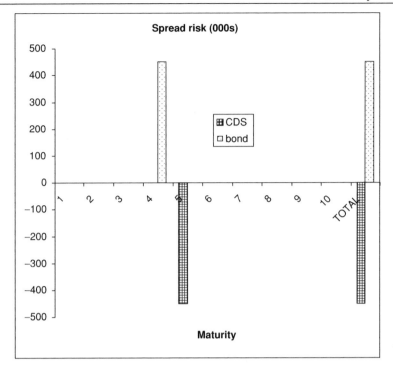

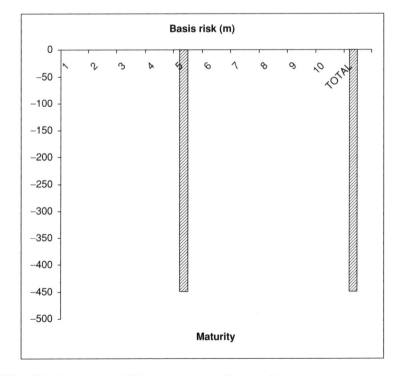

Figure 10.8   Risk chart bond and CDS spread hedge with basis risk

10.2.3 Convertible Bonds and Equity Risk

Convertible bond traders typically buy convertible bonds to strip the equity conversion option out and sell a matching option at a higher price. This leaves the trader with an exposure to the underlying credit over the life of the deal (typically there are several conversion dates when the bond and the risk will cease to exist, and the underlying bond itself may also have embedded calls and puts). Ideally the trader wishes to buy protection on the name which knocks out on conversion of the bond or on call or put. There then remains pure interest rate risk which can be hedged with interest rate swaps and with swaptions (with some residual risks related to conversion dates and the contingent unwind cost on the default event).

CDS contracts with matching knock-out features do not trade – standard CDSs being bullet contracts. Typically the convertible desk will consider buying a bullet CDS to the final maturity date of the bond, but this may be too expensive. The question of pricing a matching structured CDS is left as an exercise. [*Hint:* Build a tree to evaluate the call and put possibilities. The equity price also needs to be modelled in a consistent way in principle – an approximation could be obtained by taking a lognormal equity price model to determine when and whether conversions occur. The dates and probabilities can be incorporated into the call and put tree, and the credit event risk can then be priced off this tree.]

10.3 HEDGE AND CREDIT EVENT EXAMPLES

We review some cases of 'defaults' from the perspective of a CDS protection owner, and also a bond and CDS owner, to see how the CDS and the hedging process worked in practice.

Sudden Default

Fiugre 10.9 shows a (low coupon) bond price in the run up to the sudden default by Enron. Prior to October 2001 the price was stable; there was a lurch down and partial recovery as hints of problems appeared, followed by a sudden drop to a very low price towards the end of November when bankruptcy was announced over a weekend.

Exercise 1

Suppose in January 2001 you owned USD 10m of an Enron bond (say the low-priced bond in the chart) and USD 10m of 5-year CDS protection. How would the protection have worked over the credit event and how much would you have made? Suppose it was 1-year protection? How much notional would be required to hedge the position?

Answer: The bond could be delivered into the (1-year or 5-year) CDS to obtain USD 10m; the bond position was worth around USD 6m at the beginning of October. The loss on the bond position, if it was sold in the market, would be around USD 5m, while a 10m holding would make around USD 9m – giving a USD 4m profit. With the benefit of hindsight a CDS position of about 5.5m notional would have been sufficient to protect the bond.

Protracted Spread Widening

The charts in Figure 10.10 show the gradual decline of Marconi shares to near zero over a period of years, accompanied by the gradual decline of an 8-year bond to a price of around 30.

GPC   N248 **Corp**   **GPC**
ENRON CORP   ENRNQ 0 02/21-04   D E F A U L T E D
                              Trade Line ENRNQ 0 02/07/21 Corp   1/11
        Range 8/22/01 – 5/22/02   Period D Daily
Upper Chart: 1 Trade Line   Moving Averages   Source BGN
             N No additional graph(s)   1) News

Australia 61 2 9777 8600   Brazil 5511 3048 4500   Europe 44 20 7330 7500   Germany 49 69 920410
Hong Kong 852 2977 6000 Japan 81 3 3201 8900 Singapore 65 212 1000 U.S. 1 212 318 2000   Copyright 2002 Bloomberg L.P.
                                                                                          G487-485-0 23-May-02 17:50:44

Figure 10.9   Sudden default: Enron.
Source: Bloomberg L.P. Used with permission.

Even at the end of the chart period a credit event had not occurred (subsequently a restructuring was announced).

Exercise 2

Suppose in early 2001 you bought GBP 10m of the 9-year bond at a price of par, and simultaneously bought 10m 9-year CDS protection. How would the CDS have protected you during the period shown? Suppose it had been 10-year or 5-year protection? How much 5-year protection would you have needed to protect the value of your investment?

Answer: Although no credit event had occurred over the period shown, the CDS would have provided value protection. At a price of 30, bonds were trading 'on a recovery basis' – imminent 'default' was expected. CDS contracts expected to cover the time horizon of the default would likewise have a capital value of par minus recovery – around 70 points. All three maturity CDSs would have provided full capital protection. Initially the value of the 5-year CDS would have increased less quickly than the bond's value fell since it was of lower duration. At some point the effective duration of the 5-year CDS would actually have exceeded that of the longer CDS and the capital value of the 5-year CDS would have moved rapidly to 70 as the bond price decline continued.

Technical Default

Figure 10.11 shows the price of a (high coupon) Railtrack bond over the period when it was announced that the company was being 'put into administration' (a credit event but not a default on debt). The bond price reacted but remained above par.

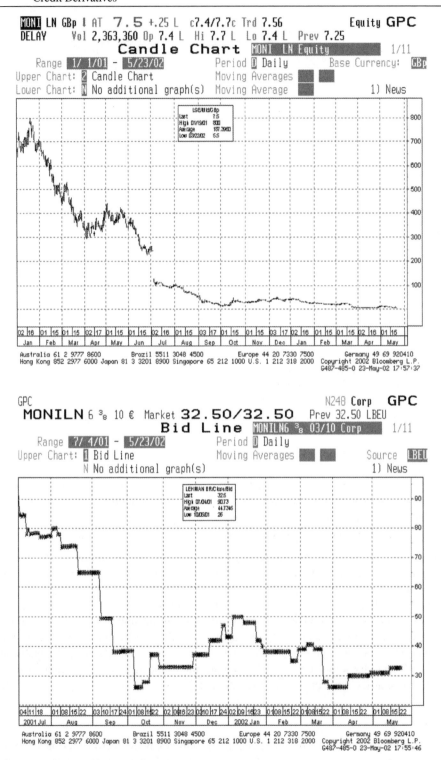

Figure 10.10   Slide into 'default': Marconi.
Source: Bloomberg L.P. Used with permission.

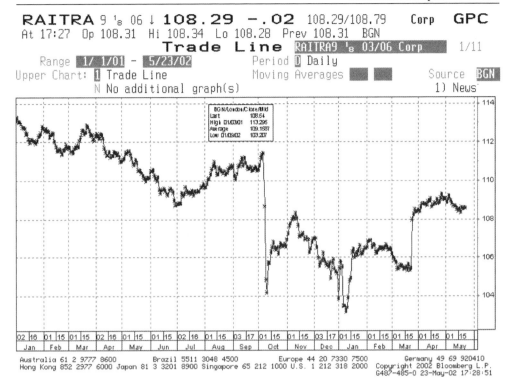

Figure 10.11   Non-default credit event: Railtrack.
Source: Bloomberg L.P. Used with permission.

Exercise 3
Suppose (a) you owned the bond and an equal notional of CDS protection. How would it have protected you? (b) Suppose you owned a convertible priced at 60?

Answer: (a) It wouldn't unless you could find bonds below par to deliver. (b) The only below par bonds were convertible – see section 2.1 in Chapter 2 for discussion of this case.

11

CDS/Bond Basis Trading

If we wish to trade bonds against CDSs or vice versa (basis trading), or calculate VaR for a portfolio, then we need to understand how the (z-)spread on a bond relates to the CDS premium, and how a change in one relates to a change in the other. The default and recovery model has been developed with a single hazard rate driver for one entity. In this chapter we look at the practical aspects of the basis, the factors driving the basis, and how the default and recovery model can be enhanced to model bonds and CDSs more realistically.

We define the 'basis' as the CDS premium expressed in basis points less the bond z-spread (for a specific bond and identical maturity CDS) (see section 11.3 below). Basis is bond and maturity specific.

We saw in Chapter 9 that if a bond which

(a) has a single maturity (a bullet bond – see 11.5)
(b) is an FRN
(c) is not, and never will be, special on repo at any date in the future (see 11.2 and 11.9)
(d) is priced at par (see 11.4)

and is hedged by a CDS which

(e) has the same maturity as the bond
(f) is triggered by exactly the same events which trigger default on the bond (see 11.8)
(g) has only that bond as the deliverable instrument (see 11.6)
(h) pays par plus accrued on that bond if a credit event occurs (see 11.7)

then we can set up an arbitrage trade implying that the basis is zero. We see below that deviations from the above assumptions can introduce a positive, negative, constant or variable basis. In addition, a basis may emerge related to new issuance or other market-related factors – which we incorporate in a 'liquidity' element of the basis.

Under the above conditions a bond with a z-spread above par presents an easily arbitraged trade (buy the bond on repo and buy the CDS) which generates a riskless profit. Factors giving rise to negative basis tend to quickly produce arbitrageurs reducing the basis to a fair level. CDS spreads above bonds do not lead to a simple arbitrage – it is not easy to short issues via the repo market. (This is one reason that the CDS market developed.)

11.1 BOND VERSUS CDS: LIQUIDITY

Liquidity is the 'fudge factor' left when everything possible has been explained. Variable elements of the basis largely fall under this heading. However, one explanation for a change in the basis relates to market movements generally. If spreads start to move rapidly, a CDS is used as the liquid instrument in which to place bets on, or hedge, spread movements. The CDS tends to react more quickly than bond spreads, so the basis initially increases as spreads rise, and decreases (possibly becoming negative) as spreads fall.

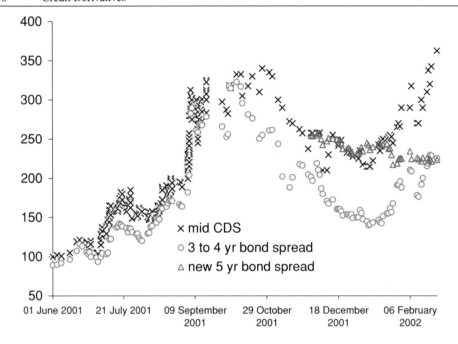

Figure 11.1   Alcatel 4- to 5-year bond spreads and 5-year CDS

This factor is variable in magnitude and sign. There is a relationship to market movements, and to new bond issues which are 'priced to go'. A bond that is priced cheaply in order to secure funds for the company will reduce the basis (and may make it negative) until the issue has been fully absorbed. Figure 11.1 shows CDS and similar maturity bond spreads, and variations in the basis can be seen, particularly around the time of the new 5-year issue and shortly afterwards as spreads widen rapidly.

11.2   BOND REPO COST

We saw in Chapter 9 that (for the situation described above, but where the bond is special on repo) the CDS premium should be the bond spread plus the amount special on repo. If the CDS premium remains fixed but the bond becomes special on repo, then the spread on the bond should decline.

For example: suppose the 5-year CDS is 500 bp, and the deliverable bond is not special on repo, then the z-spread should be 500 bp. Suppose the bond now becomes 200 bp special on repo.[1] The bond can now be lent out, against which cash collateral is received and on which interest at LIBOR minus the amount special has to be paid. The cash can be used to pay off the loan taken out to buy the bond – saving LIBOR. Net income, therefore, increases by 200 bp, so the bond spread should drop to 300 bp.

It is rare for corporate (non-sovereign) debt to go special, but in 2002 5-year France Telecom CDSs were trading at 475 bp whereas the comparable bond was at 290 bp – and special on

---

[1] To the maturity of the trade.

repo – while other similar maturity debt was trading around 480 bp. A corresponding situation arose over Commerzbank data at around the same time. Sovereign (non-domestic) debt, on the other hand, often goes special on repo.

Repo is a bond-specific element of the basis. It can be independently measured (although this requires access to a repo trading desk).

11.3   BOND SPREAD MEASUREMENT: z-SPREAD NOT ASSET SWAP SPREAD

We define the basis relative to the z-spread. Asset swap spread will show a different relationship to a CDS premium. For bond prices substantially away from par the asset swap spread will be further away from the CDS premium than the z-spread (see Part I).

11.4   BOND PRICE IMPACT

If we know that the recovery on a given entity is R, then debt priced at R is effectively risk-free. If the entity defaults we are going to get R back. Of course the pull to maturity means that the price should rise above R later and there is forward credit risk (only a 'perpetual' would not have forward risk under a constant hazard rate). In contrast, highly priced debt (perhaps because it carries a high coupon) carries much greater risk. The spread on low-priced debt should therefore be low, while that on highly priced debt should be relatively high.

Table 11.1 shows how the (z-)spread on bonds (with 2% and 5% coupons) relates to the CDS spread at various levels of the CDS spread. Note that the coupon effect is considerable at high spread, with a 5% coupon bond trading at roughly 800 bp while the CDS should be at 1000 bp.

Above par bonds should have a spread above the CDS and below par bonds should have a spread below the CDS (ignoring other factors).

Note, from equation (9.17), that if recovery is assumed to be zero then the z-spread is equal to the hazard rate (which in turn is equal to the CDS premium). In practice, because we do not know the recovery rate, we cannot be sure of the basis impact of the bond coupon.

Table 11.1   CDS and bond spread: theoretical coupon effect (5-year, 50% recovery)

CDS premium	5% coupon bond		2% coupon bond	
	z-Spread	Basis	z-Spread	Basis
100	100.5	−0.5	94.5	5.5
200	197.3	2.7	185.7	14.3
300	288.3	11.7	272.2	27.8
400	376.0	24.0	353.9	46.1
500	459.3	40.7	431.0	69.0
600	538.1	61.9	503.0	97.0
700	612.6	87.4	571.6	128.4
800	682.9	117.1	635.3	164.7
900	749.0	151.0	694.8	205.2
1000	811.2	188.8	750.3	249.7
2000	1323.8	676.2	1155.6	844.4

Given a recovery assumption we can fit the default and recovery model to the bond price (9.17) to get a bond-implied hazard rate. This then gives a bond price implied CDS premium (from 9.15), and this can be compared with the actual CDS to get a *coupon adjusted basis given a recovery assumption.*

11.5   EMBEDDED OPTIONS IN BONDS

Callables are treated in more detail in Chapter 15. We restrict our discussion here to the impact of embedded options on the basis.

Bullet bonds – bonds with a single maturity date – represent a large proportion of investment grade debt. Callable bonds (which may be redeemed early at the issuer's option) or puttable bonds (which may be sold back to the issuer at a predetermined price prior to the final maturity date) are also common. These embedded options on fixed coupon bonds may be triggered by either interest rate or credit spread moves. Suppose interest rate volatility is 10% (on a lognormal basis), with the yield level at 4%, then the basis point volatility is $0.1 \times 4\% = 40$ bp. Spread volatility varies with the reference name (maturity, seniority, etc.): Table 11.2 shows some typical volatility levels based on individual CDS curves during the 2001–2003 period. (CDS data is used rather than bonds because of the constant maturity of the CDS and the better quality of the data.)

The bond option is driven by the price which, in turn, is driven by the yield. We therefore need the yield volatility and a yield model in order to price the option. The yield volatility will depend on the LIBOR yield volatility, the spread volatility, and the correlation between the two. Table 11.3 shows some results at various spread and correlation levels.

[Calculations are in 'Chapter 11.xls'.]

We can see that the volatility of the bond yield is considerably higher than the volatility of LIBOR rates and, at higher spreads, the spread volatility dominates the LIBOR volatility. For a 5-year bond (duration of, say, 4) the price volatility of a par bond will be about 4% if the

Table 11.2   CDS volatility: and bp (Figures are only indicative)

Spread level bp	% volatility	Bp volatility
100	85	85
500	50	250

Table 11.3   Spread volatility, LIBOR/spread correlation and yield volatility

Spread	Spread vol.	LIBOR/spread corr.	Yield vol.
100	85	−.5	74
100	85	0	94
100	85	.5	111
500	250	−.5	233
500	250	0	253
500	250	.5	272

spread is 100 bp, and about 10% if the spread is 250 bp. The value of a 1-year at-the-money price option is about 40% of the price volatility – that is, 1.6 points on a 100 bp spread name and 4 points on a 250 bp name. These price differences correspond to a spread change (= basis change) of about $1.6/4 = 40$ bp and $4/4 = 100$ bp respectively: the callable trading on a wider spread than a comparable bullet by these amounts. American options running to the maturity date of the bond will be even more valuable.

It is clear that embedded options will have a very substantial impact on the pricing of the bonds and on its basis to a similar maturity CDS. We briefly discuss models to estimate this basis in Chapter 15. It should be borne in mind that, although the implied volatility on the LIBOR (swap) rate is easily obtained, there is currently no source of implied volatility for the spread or CDS premium on a particular name. Given that spread volatility is typically the most important variable in driving the basis, then the uncertainty in that volatility means that basis adjustments for callables will, at best, be crude.

11.6 DELIVERY OPTION IN CDS

If there is no delivery option (i.e. there is a specific deliverable) then the owner of protection may find he has paid the premium for no protection. In the mid-1990s more default swap contracts had been written on specified deliverable instruments (of certain Korean bonds) than there was debt available to deliver. When a default occurred the price of the debt would rise to high levels as owners of protection tried to buy the debt to deliver into the CDS.

The delivery option reduces the risk of such a situation recurring – and reduces the risk of bond squeezes being engineered. The tangible benefits of the option are two-fold:

1. Post-default trading may be at very different levels (within the same seniority) as certain investors are forced to dump bonds ('post-default illiquidity').
2. Since the CDS payoff is par, but bond prices should be recovery of (par + accrued), a greater net gain is made by buying bonds with little accrued.

There is little data to asses the former. The large standard deviation of recovery rates we saw in Part I is largely driven by the recoveries across different names. Data giving the standard deviation of defaulted bond prices for a defaulted entity is generally not easily available, and many defaults are of names with only a single traded bond. Looking at a small number of specific defaulted names suggests that this arbitrage is generally relatively small, usually being within the (wide) bid–offer spread.

The latter factor is easier to get comprehend. Suppose, no matter what the timing of the default, there is always a bond with zero accrued. The (theoretical) price in the market is then R, where R is the recovery rate.[2] Suppose also there is always a bond with 8% accrued. Then the theoretical price is $R \times 1.08$. If we owned such a bond we could sell it in the market, buy the zero accrued bond for R, deliver that bond into the CDS, and end up with $1 + R \times 0.8$. Assuming an average recovery of 50% then the delivery option gives us 4% more than if we did not have the option.

Of course this analysis will vary by name. For an entity with a rich universe of deliverable debt the accrued component of the delivery option may be worth 4–5% of the CDS premium.

---

[2] Actually the situation is a little more complex than this. The 'recovery rate' is the one-month post-default bond price averaged over the debt for that name. Since defaulted bonds are quoted including accrued, R includes an average amount of accrued. The zero coupon bond should therefore have a price of R less the average accrued.

In other cases there may (currently) be only one deliverable bond, so the option will have a low value – some value coming from the possibility that other debt may be issued in the future.

The delivery option in total may be worth around 5% of the CDS premium. This number will be relatively fixed over time but will vary according to name.

11.7   PAYOFF OF PAR

The CDS pays par on the occurrence of a credit event, whereas the risk on a par bond is actually par plus accrued. Given an assumed recovery rate R, then the risk on the bond is greater than that on the CDS by an amount that varies over time but whose average is $(1 + A/2 - R)/(1 - R)$ greater than that on the CDS. The CDS premium should therefore be less than the par bond spread by around 5% of the spread.

11.8   TRIGGER EVENT DIFFERENCES

Trigger events for default swaps are a superset of the default event for bonds. The default event is typically failure to pay, whereas credit events for the CDS also include filing for protection from creditors and restructuring. On either of these events deliverable debt can be delivered into the CDS for par. Bonds will not necessarily be trading at low prices (e.g. Railtrack) but any debt that meets the deliverability requirements and is trading at a low price (perhaps because it carries a low coupon and has a long life) can be delivered in return for par.

CDS premiums should therefore exceed bond spreads. The greater the chance of a restructuring and the more there is low coupon debt issued by that reference entity, then the more the CDS premium should exceed par bond spreads.

It is difficult to estimate the financial impact of this trigger level difference. It will depend on the type of restructuring clause that is included, and also will depend on the reference entity. For example, implicit government support may make a default event unlikely, but bond spreads and CDSs will asses the impact of potential restructuring in different ways – the CDSs being driven by the event risk and the presence of low-price bonds, while bonds would be driven by the event risk and the outstanding maturity on those bonds.

Some investment bank studies have suggested that the premium for the wider trigger event may be as much as 25%. In cases where CDSs have traded with different trigger events the market seems to indicate that the widest trigger event set is worth about 10% more than the default event only as the trigger event.

11.9   EMBEDDED REPO OPTION

Imagine the situation described at the beginning of this chapter and suppose we could buy the bond on the same spread as the CDS, then we actually have a free option on the forward repo rate. If the bond goes special at any time in the future we can lend the bond out to earn an additional income of the amount that is special for as long as the bond remains special on repo.

Generally repo has not been a significant factor on corporate debt in the past – but this is not true for sovereign debt. Where there is a risk of a significantly special repo rate occurring in future, then we would expect the CDS premium to exceed the bond spread by at least the value of this option on the repo rate.

Table 11.4 CDS/bond basis – factors and approximate magnitude

Factor	Description	Approximate magnitude (% CDS premium or bp) and sign (positive means CDS > z-spread)
Choice of spread	z-Spread is preferred to (par–par) asset swap spread	Nil for par bonds; asset swap spread > z-spread above par; asset swap spread < z-spread below par
Liquidity	1. Market direction and volatility related 2. New issue related 3. Other – fudge factor	Variable in magnitude and sign
Repo	Bond specific amount special on repo	+ Amount special in bp
Bond coupon	Coupon affects price affects risk affects spread	Nil at par; 200 bp when CDS = 1000 bp
Embedded options	Bond calls and puts	Variable; explicitly model the option
Delivery option	Accrued effect at delivery; post-default liquidity effect	+ 5%
Trigger differences	Restructuring and other non-bond-default triggers	+10%
Par payoff	CDS pays par whereas bond risk is par plus accrued	−5%
Embedded repo option	Zero cost bond + CDS position allows the bond owner to enter a repo trade if the bond becomes special	+ 1% or less
TOTAL	For bullet par bonds	+ 10% (5–30%) + amount special +/− liquidity

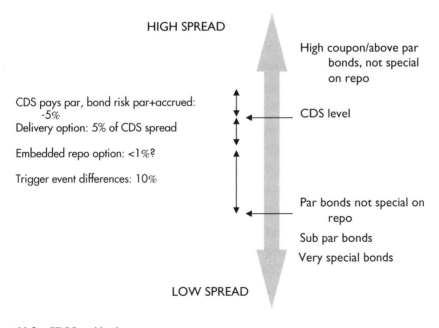

Figure 11.2 CDS/bond basis

11.10   PUTTING IT ALL TOGETHER

Table 11.4 summarises the influences we have discussed in this chapter and gives approximate magnitudes. Note that the magnitudes are entity, bond and maturity specific, and change over time, so the figures are intended to be an indication of the rough magnitude only. Figure 11.2 summarises the relationships.

12

Forward CDS; Back-to-Back CDS, Mark-to-Market and CDS Unwind

12.1 FORWARD CDS

A forward start CDS is like a vanilla CDS except that risk does not begin until the start date – say two years' time – and lasts until (say) seven years' time. In the event of a default in the first two years the contract terminates. No premium is paid or starts accruing until the forward start date.

How would you hedge a EUR 10m position using vanilla CDSs?

The obvious choice is a long 10m 7-year protection position (at 350 bp say) and a short 10m 2-year one (at 250 bp). In the event of default in the first two years then, as long as our documentation is correct, we can deliver the bond we get delivered on the 2-year short position into the 7-year long position, the forward CDS we have written knocks out, and we have no net capital gain or loss.

However, because the 2- and 7-year CDS premia are different, the premium cashflows leave an unhedged risk arising from these premium differences, starting at zero and rising to a maximum of 200 bp after two years. After two years the premium on the forward CDS starts (at a higher rate than the 7-year CDS: say 407 bp) while the premium on the 2-year CDS has ceased – a positive cashflow starts to reduce the accumulated negative cashflow from the first two years' life of the deal. (See Figure 12.1)

How does the exposure appear in the books? (See 'Chapter 12 .xls' sheet 'forward CDS'.)

Day 1: There is no value difference: the value of the forward CDS and the 7-year and 2-year CDSs are all individually zero if the premium is 'at market'. (We look at sensitivities below.)
Day 2: Net premium is paid which appears in the P&L as a negative accrued. The value of the forward CDS now exceeds the value of the hedges by an equal and opposite amount (other things being equal). The default event exposure will show a small negative – corresponding to the loss of the mark-to-market value of the CDS positions.

On day 1, with the proposed hedge, the sensitivities do not sum to zero, so the trade – even on day one – is not delta hedged. One way of obtaining a delta hedge on day 1 is to sell only 93% of the 2-year CDS – even then the sensitivity gradually becomes more and more mismatched. (See 'Chapter 12 .xls'.)

We can see that there are problems with the proposed hedge – it does not hedge the capital risk (except on day 1) and it does not hedge the spread risk of the deal (even on day 1). In fact there is no practical hedge that eliminates either capital risk or spread risk at all times during the life of the deal. *Any hedge has to be dynamic.*

Typically, if the name is investment grade then hedging is likely to be spread delta hedging. The sum of the sensitivities to a parallel shift in the hazard rate or spread curve is zero. This means that, initially, the hedge ratios are different from 100% in the shorter maturities (if the 100% hedges are implemented, a sensitivity mismatch is detected at the end of day 1 and this

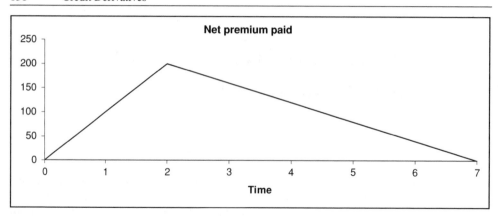

Figure 12.1   Net exposure on a long 7-year CDS, short 2-year CDS, and short '5-year 2-years forward' CDS position

mismatch may then have to be hedged on day 2). Day-by-day the sensitivities change by a small amount. Each day the trades are marked-to-market and net sensitivity is calculated. The sensitivity mismatch arising from this deal may be well within limits set for trading. Over time the sensitivity may exceed the limit and re-hedging is required. In practice the deal will not be viewed on its own but in aggregate with many other deals and a book hedging policy will be followed. (See Chapter 17.)

12.2   MARK-TO-MARKET AND BACK-TO-BACK CDS

Suppose we sold a France Telecom 5-year CDS, receiving 300 bp for protection two years ago, and a current 3-year CDS is at 100 bp on that name. What is the value of the deal?

In order to calculate the above we look at the fair market premium for a 3-year CDS, take our recovery assumption and calibrate the model, and use the implied hazard rate to value the cashflows under the deal as described in Chapter 9. (See 'Chapter 12 .xls' sheet 'valuation calc'.)

If we assume 50% recovery we find a value of +55 000 per 1m notional: 'plus' because we are receiving 300 bp, whereas if we took out a new deal we would only receive 100 bp. The number makes approximate sense – the 200 bp excess premium for three years is worth a little less than 2% × 3 = 6% of notional.

But suppose we had assumed 0% recovery – we find the trade value is +55 800. And if we assumed 90% recovery the value is +49 000 (a range of roughly 10% of the value).

For non-investment grade names the valuation is even more uncertain. A name that has a 1000 bp 3-year spread (otherwise the same trade details) has a value of −172 000 per 1m at 0% recovery, −150 000 at 50% recovery and only −70 000 at 90% recovery.

The value of the trades on our books is uncertain – very uncertain at an individual deal level for high-yield names. Looking at the (investment grade) book as a whole, the value of the book is uncertain to the extent that the recovery rate differs from the actual average recovery rate across the book. If we assume 50% recovery, it is plausible that this is in error by 20%. So the value of the investment grade vanilla CDS book is inaccurate to a few percent because of the unknown recovery rate.

Suppose (on the France Telecom deal above) we did a back-to-back deal with another counterparty to attempt to lock in this profit. We write protection for three years for a premium of 100 bp. Ignoring the counterparty risk we have effectively secured a positive cashflow of 200 bp per annum for three years *contingent on the survival of France Telecom*. The value of this cashflow is uncertain (it is the same value as the mark-to-market of the original deal since the 100 bp deal currently has zero value – on any recovery rate assumption). The back-to-back deal is a way of locking in a profit of favourable spread movements. How much value is locked in can only be determined precisely once the deal has terminated (through default of maturity) – a credit event tomorrow means that no profit is realised, but if France Telecom survives to the maturity of the trade the maximum 600 bp is earned.

12.3   UNWIND CALCULATION; OFF-MARKET TRADE VALUATION AND HEDGING

An alternative to the back-to-back deal is an 'unwind'. In some cases there is a third option. Consider the following deal. Suppose you bought 5-year protection on Ford Motor Credit two years ago at 100 bp. The current 3-year CDS premium is 400 bp and you want to take profit. In this case we could buy a 3-year life bond to generate the excess spread income.

On this deal we could eliminate the risk to the reference name on a trade in one of the following ways:

1. Enter into a *back-to-back trade* with another counterparty. Earn 400 bp on sold protection and an excess of 300 bp over bought protection. If you ensure that the notice of delivery on the written protection is before the notice you have to give on the bought protection, then there is no delivery risk. Again the present value of the premium excess is around 8.5%.
2. Go back to the original counterparty and ask for an '*unwind* price' – a sum that the counterparty pays to you to terminate the contract at the payment date.
3. Buy a 3-year bond. The bond gives a return equivalent to (approximately) 400 bp over the funding rate, and 300 bp return over funding and default protection. A total of 900 bp of 9% of face value – with a present value of about 8.5% say. In practice this is the least likely approach because of mismatching dates and risk.

In case 2, how much should the counterparty pay in order to effectively 'tear-up' the original CDS deal?

Looking at the options 1 and 3 above, it is clear that the 900 bp is earned only if the reference entity (and the counterparties) survives the remaining three years. If default occurs tomorrow there is no profit.

The calculation of the unwind price is exactly the same as the mark-to-market valuation calculation described above. (See the unwind calculation in Chapter 12 .xls'.) Given our recovery assumption (of say 20%) we calibrate to FMC and find the implied hazard rate is 500 bp per annum. The current fair value premium is 400 bp whereas we are paying only 100 bp, so the value is the value of this premium excess over three years. We need to discount each payment at LIBOR, and we need to multiply by the survival probability. We expect to be offered 7.887% to unwind the trade.

The counterparty actually offers us just over 7%. Why? Valuation and the unwind value is a recovery dependent figure, as we have seen. The counterparty is assuming a 70% recovery for FMC, which implies a much higher rate of default – hence a lower probability of receiving all the cashflows. Taking a 99% recovery assumption means that default is highly probable and the unwind price becomes a mere 0.74%. All answers are correct given the assumptions – the problem is that there is no determinant of the correct recovery assumption.

How can the trader argue for a better unwind value? Some parties ask for the counterparty's recovery assumption every time a new trade is put on. In the above case the counterparty may have been using 40% at the time the trade was put on. Of course the counterparty can reasonably argue that times have changed, and so have its recovery assumptions. This can easily be checked against recent deals done with that counterparty.

A second argument relies on the growing availability of survey data on recovery assumptions being used in the pricing of CDSs by the investment banks – for example, products from Mark-it Partners, Lombard Risk's ValuSpread, and others reporting the participants' assumptions for recovery rates. Again this does not force the counterparty to use the market average, but it acts as an argument against using outlandish assumptions.

A further argument can be used in special cases. Note that the value declines as the recovery assumption increases. Suppose that the reference entity is Marconi, which was bought at 250 bp some years ago and in 2001, when the spread had risen to 4000 bp, you decided to unwind. Your calculation assumes 30% recovery and suggests a value of 51.5% of notional. The counterparty offers just less than 1% of notional (arguing that it thinks recovery is going to be very high, and is using a 99% recovery assumption). In this case a much stronger argument can be used. Marconi debt is trading around 'on a recovery basis' of 30 (bond prices are similar, irrespective of maturity) at this time. This is consistent with a recovery level of 30% and imminent default. Recoveries greatly above this level cannot be consistent with the bond prices and the default and recovery model. In addition, in this case the alternative of buying a 3-year bond at 30 is an attractive alternative – on the credit event the bond is delivered and par received, while if there is no default the high return is achieved.

P&L assigned to the trades is open to debate – it depends on the recovery assumption used. On any individual deal the actual profit achieved will exceed the expected P&L if the reference entity does not default (and losses will also be greater in magnitude). On the other hand, if the reference entity defaults early, a lower P&L will be achieved. The actual P&L on the book will agree with that expected if defaults are as expected, and the recovery rates average out to be equal to the assumption used in the daily valuation of the deal.

12.4 'DOUBLE-TRIGGER CDS'

We discuss some further forms of this trade in more detail in Parts III and IV. For the moment we shall consider some of the simpler applications of this deal – where the only credit risk is the counterparty risk.

A great deal of banking business is in the form of interest rate swaps, cross-currency swaps, forward FX deals, asset sales, etc., where there is a risk to the counterparty to the deal. On day 1 the deal may have a mark-to-market of zero (the interest rate fixed and floating legs initially have the same capital value) but it may move away from this over time as interest rates rise, or the deal's initial value may be far from zero (e.g. an asset sale with delayed payment). On both types of deal there is (at least) a potential future exposure to the counterparty ('the buyer'): a default of the counterparty to the swap or asset sale leaves the seller with an exposure to the underlying asset which has to be unwound at market rates.

The seller therefore has a contingent exposure to some financial variables (e.g. interest or exchange rates) triggered by the default of a counterparty. The size of this exposure is neither constant nor a deterministic function of time. A CDS that pays an amount related to the value of some financial product on the default of a name is referred to as a 'double trigger' or 'variable exposure' CDS.

The valuation formula for such a product is similar to equation (9.11) – only the payoff function is different. We assume that the premium is paid as a single up-front payment for simplicity: a better course in practice is to relate the premium to the then current exposure so that as risk increases, so does premium income. Let $F(t)$ be the present value of the contingent reference asset (e.g. the forward swap unwind cost) at time t, and the survival and hazard rate functions refer to the reference entity – the counterparty to the deal. $F(t)$ may be positive or negative; and we have implicitly assumed that there is no correlation between the financial factors driving this valuation function and the hazard rate function for the reference name. Note also that the risk is digital.

$$V = \int_0^T F(x) \cdot S(x) \cdot \lambda(x) \, dx \qquad (12.1)$$

Typically, deals between professional counterparties are collateralised so that the forward exposure is only the mark-to-market change over a short period (7–14 days) while the counterparty failure is discovered. For collateralised deals the main concern is possible correlation between the market moves and the risk of the counterparty defaulting (and the formula above is not suitable for this problem).

Double-trigger CDSs appeal to banks with uncollateralised counterparty exposures. Putting such a deal in place may indicate an unattractive level of disclosure about the bank's business to a potential competitor.

We shall return to this topic and the question of correlated counterparty risk in Part IV.

13

Credit-Linked Notes

13.1 CLN SET-UP; COUNTERPARTY OR COLLATERAL RISK

In a **credit-linked note** (CLN) the buyer of protection (seller of the note) transfers credit risk to an investor via an intermediate bond-issuing entity. This intermediary can be the buyer's own treasury or a third party's treasury using a **limited recourse note programme**, or via a **special purpose vehicle** (SPV).

The former route is conceptually simpler, and is cheaper to use once the note programme is set up. The purpose of the limited recourse note programme – a set of legal documentation and an issuing process – is to make it clear to investors and others that the failure of the note to provide the full cashflows (for example, on a credit event of the reference entity) does not constitute a default by the issuing bank.

It is helpful to think in terms of a simple CLN, where the embedded risk is exposure to (say) Ford Motor Credit. The note may mirror CDS terms and conditions – it may have a 5-year life, paying LIBOR plus (say) 250 bp (or it may be a fixed coupon note), but it will terminate early if FMC suffers a (CDS) credit event. In that case coupons on the note cease, and the investor receives the notional on the note less an amount determined by the issuing bank – CLNs are typically cash settled. The terms embedded in the note may (and often do) differ in detail from those of a CDS. For example, a specific bond may be referenced for the purposes of calculating the cash amount; accrued interest may not be paid up to the date of default; or a non-standard set of credit events may be used.

The process of issuance is for the bank to embed the terms of the note in the CLN issue document required under the issuance programme; the note is sold to investors (at a price that may be different from par); cash is received by the issuing department and deposited internally with the bank's internal treasury department.

The CLN is a funded instrument which offers the end investor (the buyer of risk) synthetic credit exposure to the reference entity (FMC), and gives the bank credit protection on the reference entity but no counterparty exposure.[1] The exposure to the reference entity is synthetic because the issuer is not the reference entity but the originating institution. It should be noted that, from the investor's point of view, the note gives the investor direct exposure not only to the reference credit but also to the issuing bank. Although the risks are simplified from the bank's point of view, they are actually more complicated from the investor's point of view (compared with direct investment in the reference entity's debt). The investor loses some or all of his investment on the first to default (within the life of the note) – either the reference entity or the issuing bank. (We return to this viewpoint later.)

The CLN issued via a limited recourse programme is summarised in Figure 13.1.

An alternative issuing process is via an SPV. The SPV is a third party – usually independent of both the originating bank and the investor(s) – usually a company (corporate entity) often

---

[1] If the price is below par there is still no counterparty exposure but the protection obtained is a variable amount and is less than the notional of the CLN.

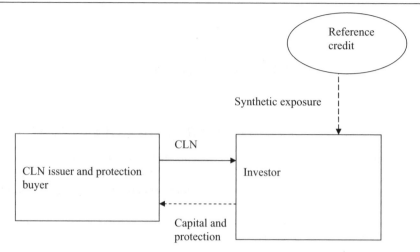

Figure 13.1   CLN via a limited recourse programme

owned by a charity and established in an offshore financial centre. The process is somewhat more complicated. The SPV issues the note described above via its own issuance programme (not necessarily limited recourse programme) to the investor(s). Cash received is invested, typically in high-grade and/or diversified assets (usually debt). In addition, the SPV enters into a contract with the issuing bank providing (say) 5-year CDS protection in return for a premium. This situation is summarised in Figure 13.2.

The bank now has the protection on FMC it requires, but obtained from a corporate (non-bank) entity – the SPV – to which it has counterparty risk. The bank is closely involved with the SPV (perhaps providing administrative or investment services), and as the SPV is well collateralised (often rated AAA), the counterparty risk is regarded as very small. Nevertheless the bank indirectly carries both default risk on the collateral and also some mark-to-market collateral risk (see below).

The investor now has synthetic exposure to the reference entity, to a portfolio of high-grade assets (but no direct exposure to the originating bank), to the SPV and to any third party obligations the SPV may have, including the CDS and any interest rate swap contracts with the originator.

The protection buyer eliminates counterparty risk to the investing institution – for example, it becomes possible to buy protection on Bank X from its parent company. This can be useful in restructuring certain subsidiary bank portfolios. Counterparty risk to the SPV and its underlying collateral is substituted.

There is a **credit event** under an SPV CLN (embedded risk on a single reference name).

On the reference entity credit event, or at maturity, collateral is liquidated. In the former case, collateral is sold to generate cash and, if there is sufficient, par less the recovery on the reference entity debt is paid to the original bank. Collateral risk is also borne by the investor – excess cash may be less than the recovery amount if the collateral was below par. The investor also bears collateral risk at maturity if there is no default event.

What is the risk that the collateral is insufficient to cover the loss on the reference entity (i.e. collateral is insufficient to meet the SPV's obligations under the default swap contract with the originating bank)?

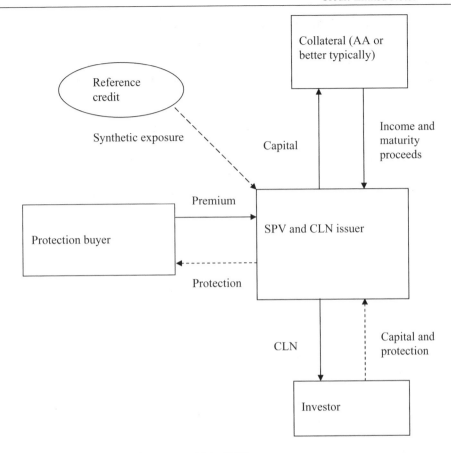

Figure 13.2   CLN via a special purpose vehicle (SPV)

The payoff required on the CDS is $100 - R$. Let us suppose that the SPV collateral has value V at the time of the reference entity credit event. V may be less than par because of adverse market moves on, and defaults in, the collateral pool. If $(100 - R) > V$, then there are insufficient funds to pay the amount promised on the CDS. This is the equivalent of an American put on the collateral at $100 - R$. If the collateral is of short life, diversified and high-grade, and R is not close to zero, then this will have a negligible value. Generally it can be estimated using traditional options theory. We can model the collateral prices as a function of spreads and interest rates and we should introduce a distribution of recovery values, R. The risk is concentrated in the area of R near zero. Let's do a very crude calculation. For SU debt approximately 10% of recoveries will be below 10%. The chance of high-quality collateral falling below 90% is small – partly arising from default event risk. The risk of a loss of 10% may be 2% (including the (say) 5-year default risk on the collateral) – giving a risk to the originating bank on the CDS of about $10\% \times 2\% = 20$ bp if a credit event occurs. The chance of a credit event on a 250 bp reference entity (assuming zero recovery) is roughly 12% over a five-year trade. In other words, the bank would expect to pay below the market rate for the CDS protection it is buying by a figure of the order of $12\% \times 20$ bp $= 2$ bp.

13.2   EMBEDDED SWAPS AND OPTIONS

The CLN, particularly if issued via an SPV, may also include embedded interest rate or currency swaps. For example, if collateral is in both fixed and floating forms, and in various currencies, swaps will be used to hedge out the interest rate and FX risk but introduce *contingent* interest rate and FX risk. Typically contingent swap risk is carried by the investor – any loss on unwinding these swaps between the SPV and the bank on the occurrence of a credit event on the reference entity comes out of the collateral before any residual amount is paid to the investor.

If the reference risk is bond with embedded options (callable or convertible, for example) then these risks will also be embedded in the CLN. Typically such notes would be issued to fund and hedge the convertible desk's activities and a back-to-back hedge by embedding the risks into the CLN is the most attractive route for the bank.

13.3   COSTS

A limited recourse programme is expensive to set up (of the order of EUR 50 000-100 000) but once established the marginal costs are low: EUR 10 000 or less. An SPV is set up for each deal and has roughly a similar cost to those for a limited recourse programme. These costs are reflected in the terms of the CLN to the investor.

13.4   APPLICATIONS

We have already seen that the elimination of counterparty risk can be important, and here a CLN (or fully collateralised deal) is the obvious choice.

Large single name deals are more frequently done via a CLN. A bank may be seeking EUR 1bn protection on XYZ Company. Sourcing via CDS is difficult (dealing size is normally EUR 10m-25m), whereas the investor group for notes is wider and there is a larger sales force available within the bank.

Investors may be seeking an exposure to a particular US reference name but a risk denominated in EUR and to a specific maturity. The reference entity may have no EUR debt or no debt of the appropriate maturity. A CLN allows a bank to manufacture synthetic XYZ debt to meet the investor's requirements. This was the case for Ford Motor Credit, which at one time had little EUR debt. This then leaves the bank with a hedging problem that is easily handled on a book basis.

Where the bank is seeking protection via a CLN, but the bank is regarded as high risk, the investor is likely to prefer the use of an SPV to a note issued on the bank's own balance sheet. For example, if the bank borrows at 50 bp over LIBOR, then this is a significant risk compared to other investment grade entities and may be unacceptable to the investor despite the additional spread the investor receives. In addition, the product becomes a significant 'first-to-default' risk and creates booking and monitoring problems.

The main applications of CLNs are in the structuring of more complex credit derivatives – we look at an example below – either for single reference names or for protection on losses between certain levels on a reference portfolio (a 'funded' tranche of a CDO).

There will be capital benefits or regulatory implications for the bank. Where a CDS protects a reference name the risk weighting (under Basle 88) is reduced to 20% (as long as the counterparty is an OECD bank). If a CLN is used, then cash resides in the bank rather than an SPV, and covers the risk weighting and more. If an SPV is used then there is no reduction of regulatory capital (the SPV is a corporate and gets 100% weighting) and no capital is raised.

13.5   CLN PRICING

13.5.1   Basic Pricing

Consider the following example: 5-year Fiat trades at 150 bp in the CDS market. The issuing bank's treasury borrows at LIBOR − 5 bp for five years' USD or, alternatively, suitable collateral can be found paying LIBOR + 10 bp after swap costs. What spread can the bank offer on a USD 10m or 100m CLN via its limited recourse note programme, or via an SPV?

If the bank issues the CLN at par off its own book then the hedge it puts in place and associated costs are as follows:

(a) Pay the set-up costs out of the capital received. The set-up costs are (say) EUR 10 000 and this translates to about 2 bp per annum on the 10m note, or 0.2 bp on the 100m note.
(b) Write Fiat EUR CDS protection at 150 bp (we are ignoring bid–offer spreads).
(c) Deposit funds with its treasury department at LIBOR −5 bp.
(d) If the CLN is fixed coupon, then arrange an internal interest rate swap paying floating and receiving fixed.

The cashflow is matched between the hedges and the CLN if the CLN pays LIBOR plus 150 bp − 5 bp − 2 bp = 143 bp for the 10m note (144.8 bp for the 100m note). Additionally the bank has a cross-currency position to hedge and charge for – see Chapter 9.

If the bank issues via an SPV, then

(a) the set-up cost of the SPV corresponds to 10 bp (1 bp) for the 10m (100m) note
(b) the CDS protection earns 150 bp as before
(c) the collateral spread is +10 bp
(d) and the cost of the risk that the collateral is insufficient to cover the loss given default on the reference entity is approximately 2 bp,

giving a CLN spread to LIBOR of 148 bp and 157 bp respectively for the 10m and 100m notes.

13.5.2   CLN Pricing Model

From the bank's point of view the cashflows arising from the note are the promised payments subject to the reference entity survival plus payment of the recovery amount contingent on the credit event. The formula is identical to pricing the reference entity's debt (using a hazard rate appropriate to the CDS market if the CDS triggers are used).

From the investor's point of view the promised payments are contingent on the joint survival of the reference name and the issuing bank, and the recovery amount is contingent on the default of the reference entity and the survival of the bank.

From the investor's perspective this may present both booking and valuation problems. Although the CLN looks like a bond it holds two risks and booking the CLN as a bond on the underlying, ignoring the counterparty risk, is technically incorrect. Booking needs at least to record the existence of counterparty risk, and risk reporting should report this risk (at the very least the nominal exposure). Full valuation needs the methods of Part III since the reference name and the issuing bank represent a correlated two name portfolio in general. However we can easily develop pricing results in the case of zero correlation.

There are two sets of cashflows under the note:

1. Promised cashflows – coupons and maturity amount. These are valued by discounting the cashflow (off the LIBOR curve) and multiplying by the probability of the joint survival of the reference entity and the counterparty to this date. If these two entities are uncorrelated then this is just (the probability of reference name survival) times (the probability of counterparty name survival). We know these survival probabilities by calibrating to CDS data for these two names, given a recovery assumption.
2. Contingent cashflows:
   (a) The recovery on reference entity debt in the event of reference entity default before the counterparty.
   (b) The recovery on the CLN in the event of counterparty default before the reference entity.

We can now make several useful deductions:

(A) Let us first assume that recovery on both names is zero. Then item (2) above is zero; the hazard rate is just the spread, and we can see that the CLN value is just the promised cashflows discounted at LIBOR plus the sum of the reference name and counterparty spreads.
(B) If we assume that only the counterparty recovery is zero, then recovery on the reference debt appears and again we are valuing the risky cashflow using the credit bond valuation formula (9.16) except that the LIBOR curve is shifted by the counterparty spread. The result is *approximately* the same as discounting the promised cashflows at LIBOR plus the sum of the reference name and counterparty spreads.
(C) If the counterparty recovery is also non-zero, then a further recovery term appears.
(D) Generally we assume that recovery on counterparty debt is non-zero but also assume that recovery on the CLN will be zero (as it is not traded debt, it may be difficult to find a buyer). In this case we can see that the CLN is *approximately* the same as discounting the promised cashflows at LIBOR plus the sum of the reference name spreads and counterparty *hazard rate*.

The final result should be noted.

The Mathcad sheet 'Part III N2D CDO CLN price and hedge.mcd' includes code for CLN valuation in the general correlated case (using the results of Part III), and uses this code to value a CLN with a correlated counterparty in addition to the uncorrelated case.

13.6 CAPITAL GUARANTEED NOTE

Any (credit-related) risk can be embedded into a CLN. A very simple CLN will embed a single vanilla CDS and it is easy to reflect the CDS settlement terms (physical) in a cash payoff on the CDS related to the recovery of the underlying. As a deal gets more and more complex, reflecting the 'recovery on reference debt' element of an embedded CDS becomes more difficult to describe, and it becomes more common to embed a digital risk. In this section we look at one example of a more complex CLN, where the embedded risk may be a single reference entity risk or a more complex instrument, and risk is embedded in digital form.

CLN Description

The CLN has a 20-year maturity, carries a fixed coupon of 6% and, for the first five years only, bears credit risk to a specific reference entity. If there is a credit event on the reference entity during this period, coupons immediately cease (although a proportion may be paid to the credit event date). Par is returned at maturity whether or not a credit event has occurred.

Pricing and Valuation

We can write the formula for the value of the CLN on day 1 (assuming the CLN is sold at par). If we assume, for simplicity, that coupon g is paid continuously, we have

$$1 = g \int_0^5 v(t) \times S(t) \, dt + g \times S(5) \int_5^{20} v(t) \, dt + v(20) \tag{13.1}$$

where v is the discount factor and S the survival probability for the reference entity. The equation states that the market price is equal to the sum of:

(1) the value of the coupon over the first five years weighted by the probability that the reference name survives to each payment date during that term;
(2) the value of the coupon over the 5–20-year period, contingent only on the fact that the reference name survives to the end of five years; and
(3) the value of par at maturity.

For a given reference entity and LIBOR curve we can solve this equation, knowing the survival probabilities and discount factors, to find the fair-value coupon g on the CLN. Note that if the reference entity is risk-free $[S(t) = 1]$ then the coupon is the 20-year swap rate. The spreadsheet 'Chapter 13 .xls' implements the above formula for general risk and maturity periods. If the reference entity CDS is 200 bp, and the assumed recovery rate is 30%, then we find a coupon enhancement over the 20-year life of 50 bp. Figure 13.3 shows how the amount of protection bought under the note varies over its life, and shows the value of the final capital amount (assuming 4% interest rates).

Note that the enhanced coupon continues for 20 years in the event of no default, and that protection is in digital form.

Hedging

Per 100 nominal there is a digital protection amount falling from an initial value of slightly over 60 to a little over 50 just before the 5-year risk-termination date. At time t in the future ($t < 5$ years) the amount of protection is just the value of the outstanding coupons that will not be paid following the credit event. This is

$$g \int_t^{20} v'(s) \, ds \tag{13.2}$$

where the prime indicates that the discount factors are those appropriate at time t (i.e. the forward discount factors).

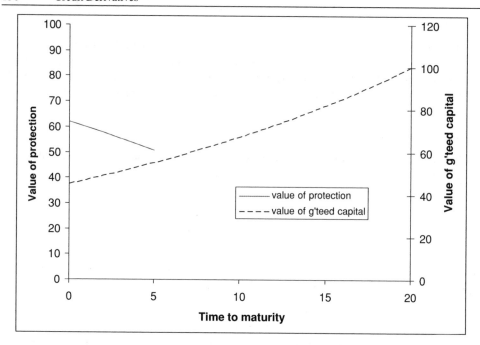

Figure 13.3   Value of protection and guaranteed capital amount

For simplicity we shall assume an average 55 digital protection (an accurate hedge calcu-lation will take into account the exact protection, the exact life and the corresponding spreads available in the CDS market for the various maturities). Given the recovery assumption of (say) 30%, then the 55 digital protection can be hedged by selling vanilla protection on $55/(1 - 0.3) = 78.5$m per 100m CLN. The trader can therefore enter into the following hedging deals once the CLN is sold:

1. Sell 78.5m 5-year vanilla protection on the reference entity at 200 bp, generating an income of 1.57m per annum for five years.
2. Enter into an interest rate swap with the IR swap desk, paying an initial capital amount of par, plus 1.57m quarterly for five years to receive par at maturity and a fixed coupon for 20 years.

On default of the reference name the fixed cashflows (excluding the maturity amount) have to be sold for a capital sum – this introduces a *contingent interest rate risk*: a loss is suffered if interest rates rise. This capital sum has to settle par minus recovery on the 78.5m vanilla CDS sold – whose expected cost is $78.5 \times (1 - 0.7) = 55$m. This introduces a (large) *recovery rate risk*.

During the life of the deal interest rate moves (and possibly changing recovery rate assumptions) will cause a changing net exposure to the reference name which will be re-hedged.

Exercises

1. What is the impact on the coupon of reducing the final maturity (for a fixed 5-year risk period)?
2. What is the coupon impact of using a more risky reference entity?
3. If the CLN carries a floating coupon, what impact is there on the initial hedges and on the risks?

The reference risk in the capital guaranteed CLN could be a first-to-default basket, the 'equity' protection of a synthetic CDO, a portfolio of CLNs, or any other credit risk.

14

Digital or 'Fixed Recovery' CDS

14.1 PRODUCT DESCRIPTION

A digital CDS is similar to a vanilla CDS except that the payment in the event of a credit event is not par in exchange for defaulted debt (or par less recovery), but par. Similarly, a fixed recovery CDS is a CDS where the payment on the occurrence of a credit event is par less the agreed recovery.

The difference between a digital (sometimes called a 'binary') CDS and a fixed recovery CDS is merely documentation. For example, consider a digital CDS in EUR 10m on Fiat, subject to a premium of 600 bp. A fixed recovery CDS on EUR 12.5m with an agreed recovery of 20% pays $12.5 \times 0.8 = 10$m in exactly the same circumstances and conditions as the digital. The correct premium for the fixed recovery CDS is $600 \times 10/12.5 = 480$ bp, giving the same monetary premium for the same monetary protection in both cases.

Digital products are not very important in their own right – very little trading takes place in a simple digital CDS. Generally a digital CDS does not form a natural hedge for many risks – most risks being in the form of bond or loan assets with an unknown recovery or equity risk where a full loss is taken on the credit event but the forward exposure is unknown. The key feature of digital CDS in valuation and risk management terms is the strong recovery rate sensitivity of the value of these products.[1]

Digital risk arises in two main forms:

1. Off-market vanilla CDS positions and non-standard premium streams have a small recovery sensitivity (which increases further the more the premium stream differs from the current fair value quarterly-in-arrears premium). In particular, a mature book of vanilla CDS positions will have a small digital risk.
2. Structured credit products, particularly in CLN form, often have embedded digital risk. Examples are the capital guaranteed note (section 13.6), a CLN with exposure to the 3% to 5% of losses on a reference pool, and counterparty exposure on an interest rate swap. We shall also see in Part III that portfolio products have a significant recovery rate risk.

A recovery stress on the individual reference name, together with recalibration and revaluation, reveals the level of digital risk in the books.

14.2 PRICING, HEDGING, VALUATION AND RISK CALCULATIONS

14.2.1 Simple Pricing

Given that a vanilla 5-year CDS is trading at 200 bp, where would you price a digital?

---

[1] This may seem counter-intuitive. We know the price of a vanilla CDS from the market. The payoff is par minus the unknown recovery, but the chance of a credit event has to be inversely proportional to par minus recovery to justify the CDS premium. The digital CDS pays par but is driven by the same recovery-dependent chance of default. Hence the digital premium is recovery dependent.

Our calibration for that name might assume a 50% recovery, leading to a 4% default rate. On the occurrence of a credit event the vanilla pays $100 - 50 = 50$ while the digital pays 100, so the digital should be subject to a premium of 400 bp. But suppose we had assumed that recovery would be 0%. The digital has the same payoff as the vanilla so the premium should be 200 bp. If the reference asset were a secured loan we might assume that recovery is 90%, and then the digital would pay 10 times as much as the vanilla CDS and should be priced at 2000 bp.

There is no way of either knowing or hedging effectively the digital risk (until such time that digital products trade actively). Faced with the prospect of doing a single isolated deal in a digital CDS, a trader would naturally take a cautious view of the recovery risk and make a wide bid–offer spread. On the other hand, if you regularly dealt in such instruments, and had a large diversified portfolio on the books, then you would be much more comfortable quoting close bid–offer spreads on digitals. This happens when constructing CLNs with an embedded digital risk.

14.2.2   Recovery Assumptions

In the case above we should note a substantial difference between the status of the recovery rate assumptions for vanilla CDS and those for digital CDS products. We saw that a vanilla CDS has little valuation sensitivity to the recovery assumption (section 12.2) – so the actual recovery assumption is not very important. However, the simple example above shows that the fair value premium, and therefore the trade valuation, changes dramatically as we change the recovery assumption.

From the perspective of credit event risk, let us consider a portfolio where a 100 m short in autos is hedged by a 100 m long in utilities. Suppose we assume a 50% recovery across all senior secured names, and suppose, for simplicity, that the CDS premia are all 100 bp, then it follows that all names are subject to a hazard rate of 200 bp. But if, in reality, autos are subject to a 30% recovery rate (hence 133 bp hazard rate), utilities are subject to an 80% recovery rate (hence 500 bp hazard rate), and defaults are as expected (1.33 autos for every 5 utilities), then the results are as follows.

Vanilla CDS book: net loss $= 1.33 \times 0.7$ (autos) $- 5 \times 0.2$ (utilities) $= 0$
Digital CDS book: net loss $= 1.33 - 5 = 3.67$.

If we are trading digital risks we should put much more effort into making realistic recovery assumptions. (This does not mean that we have to trade 'digital' products as such – for example, portfolio credit products contain significant recovery (digital) risk.)

14.2.3   Valuation and Hedging

The valuation formula can be derived as in section 10.1 – we simply have to drop the recovery cashflows from equation (9.11) – the value of a long digital protection is

$$V(t) = \int_t^T D(s) \cdot S(s) \cdot \lambda(s) \, ds - p \int_t^T D(s) \cdot S(s) \, ds \qquad (14.1)$$

We can immediately see that if the hazard rate is a constant then the premium equals the hazard rate for a fair value trade.

Embedded digital protection in structured CLN products ultimately has to be hedged using vanilla CDS. For simplicity, consider a single name digital CDS where the vanilla trades at 100 bp. If we assume zero recovery, then a long 10 m digital risk is hedged by a short 10 m CDS (the payoffs are both 10 m), whereas if we assume 90% recovery then 10 m digital is hedged by a 100 m vanilla position. In reality, on an investment grade portfolio, we will typically hedge spread risk, not default event.

Exercise
Consider hedging digital CDS from the spread sensitivity perspective. Compare sensitivities derived from equations (14.1) and (9.1).

14.3   TRIGGER EVENT DIFFERENCES

In the mid to late 1990s Enron attempted to develop a market for digital CDSs among corporate clients. They called these products 'bankruptcy swaps' and they were triggered by default or 'filing for protection from creditors'. They therefore had significant documentation differences compared to vanilla CDS, which would have further complicated hedging. (The market in bankruptcy swaps did not prove to be popular.)

Current embedded digital CDSs tend to reflect the terms and conditions of vanilla CDSs or, where differences occur, they tend to favour the origination bank.[2]

---

[2] 'Documentation trading' – where essentially back-to-back trades are used to capture favourable documentation differences – was a common feature of the CDS market before standardisation of documentation took place. It is now largely confined to structured products in CLNs.

15
Spread Options, Callable/Puttable Bonds, Callable Asset Swaps, Callable Default Swaps

The biggest problem with spread option products is the lack of an open market and the lack of any source of 'implied' spread volatility. This may be changing in the portfolio area – with the introduction of options on the iTraxx CDO tranches – but single name spread options remain a narrow market, and largely restricted to embedded 'conservatively' priced options.

15.1 PRODUCT DEFINITIONS

15.1.1 Vanilla Spread Options and Variations

A credit spread option is an option on the spread of a 'defaultable' bond (e.g. the yield on Fiat 6.125 May 08) over a reference yield (e.g. the interpolated EURIBOR swap rate). At maturity (European) or at any time up to maturity (American), a credit spread put (call) gives the buyer the right but not the obligation to sell (buy) the defaultable bond at the price implied by the strike spread and the reference yield. For example, the bond may be trading at 150 bp currently, the option may be a European put exercisable in one year's time at a z-spread of 250 bp. The holder of the bond may also hedge the fixed coupons with an interest rate swap – so interest rate moves have equal and opposite impacts on the bond and swap. If spreads on the bond rise to 400 bp in a year's time, then the bond plus interest rate swap value will decline below the initial price. Instead of selling the bond at a 400 bp spread the option buyer can sell at 250 bp through the option, effectively making a profit of 150 bp relative to selling in the market.

Spread Option Cashflows

Suppose DKB sells a one-year European call to BoA on the Fiat bond at an exercise z-spread of 150 bp for a premium of 40 bp p.a. quarterly. We suppose BoA also enters into a forward (starting in one year's time) interest rate swap related to the bond where BoA pays fixed, so that interest rate moves on the intended forward holding of the bond are hedged out (Figure 15.1).

If the spread in the market at expiry is above 150 bp then it is cheaper to buy the bond in the market, but if the spread is, say, 100 bp the price calculated on a z-spread of 150 bp is less than the market price and the option will be exercised (Figure 15.2).

Exercises

1. How much profit (approximately) is made in the above example?
2. Suppose it was a put option and spreads widened to 500 bp?

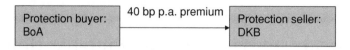

Figure 15.1   Spread option cashflows: pre-expiry

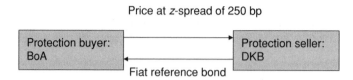

Figure 15.2   Spread option cashflows

Product Variations

- Premiums may be paid up-front or in swap form.
- The reference rate may be on a specific bond – generally a government issue. This introduces several new risks: the repo on the reference bond, and idiosyncratic price movement of the reference bond.
- The option may be cash settlement – if exercised the writer pays the difference between the price of the underlying at the exercise spread, and the market price, to the buyer.
- A put may knock-out on default, in which case an owner of the bond and the option is left with a worthless option and a defaulted bond. Otherwise the option is usually immediately exercisable on default.
- The option may be on a default swap instead of a bond. The call (put) option gives the buyer the right to sell (buy) the CDS at a predetermined spread. (Put/call terminology is used in a way consistent with the risk implication of an option on a bond.)

Exercises

Suppose you write a European call exercisable in two years' time on a (then) 5-year CDS on GMAC at 300 bp. The option is exercisable early in the event of default (defaulted debt is delivered for par).

1. How would you hedge the credit event risk before the exercise date?
2. What would the price difference be between a CDS call option without/with the knock-out?

15.1.2   Related Embedded Products

Callable Asset Swaps

The asset swap desk has the option to terminate the asset swap at par at any time prior to the maturity date. If the spread on the underlying asset has narrowed substantially, the reference bond (which is owned by the desk as a hedge against the asset swap) will have risen in price. Without having the call feature embedded in the asset swap, the desk does not benefit from the price rise of the bonds since the bond is economically owned by the asset swap counterparty through the asset swap. If the desk can terminate the asset swap at par, then the bond can be sold at market price (and the interest rate swap unwound) to yield a profit. (Note that a rise in interest rates will not significantly harm the profit arising from the spread narrowing, since adverse bond price movement arising from the interest rate risk is almost exactly offset by the interest rate swap held by the desk.)

Callable Default Swaps

A callable CDS is a vanilla CDS with the added feature that the buyer of protection has the right to terminate the CDS (at any time or at certain dates) on a narrowing of the fair market CDS premium below the trigger level for the option. This allows the buyer to terminate the CDS and replace it with a cheaper CDS.

A callable CDS and a callable asset swap are financially similar – the difference being the basis risk between the asset swap reference asset and the CDS on the reference name of the same maturity. Similarly, a spread put option on a bond is closely related to a puttable default swap.

A seller of a CDS with the option to terminate the swap if the spread widens beyond a certain level will do so if that level is breached. The termination could be followed up with a new sale at a wider spread or the name may be considered too risky (in which case any long CDS held as a hedge may be sold for a substantial profit). From the CDS buyer's point of view the embedded option removes much of the benefit of the CDS – sudden default being protected – so the premium would have to be substantially below the vanilla CDS premium. An alternative is to allow the CDS premia to ratchet up (driven by spread levels or ratings) rather than allow protection to terminate.

Commercial bank **standby facilities** or a **facility**: an agreement to lend a certain amount of money at an agreed spread over LIBOR at any time up to a specified date in the future. This is equivalent to the potential borrower owning a credit spread put option on its own debt. Usually the facility knocks out in the event of a default.

15.1.3 Bond Price Options

A price option on a credit bond has the same format as a price option on a government bond. In the case of put options the question of the occurrence of a default before the option date has to be addressed. Price options are driven by both interest rate and spread movements.

A yield model is needed to value bond price options. This may be constructed by modelling the LIBOR curve and the reference entities hazard rate (or spread) curve, together with a correlation model, or may be driven by a one factor model for the yield. Typically a Hull–White model is used or a binary tree implementation of a lognormal yield model. The tree approach discussed in section 16.2 (for the hazard rate) can trivially be applied to the yield.

The key problem in pricing all spread-related options is the unobserved implied volatility. For bond price options there is the additional problem of the yield/spread correlation required to calculate yield volatility.

Correlation Note

Note that the bond's yield and the LIBOR rate will have very different correlations according to the level of spread. At a low spread, the yield on the bond and the LIBOR rate are almost identical, so the correlation is close to 100%, but at very high spreads the yield is at a similar level to the spread, so the yield and the LIBOR rate correlation will tend to the spread/LIBOR correlation. Yield/LIBOR correlation therefore varies hugely with the level of spread. On the other hand, the correlation between the LIBOR rate and the reference entities spread would not appear to have any particular relationship to spread level and is regularly assumed to be zero. If it is necessary to have a two factor model, LIBOR and spread with a constant correlation corresponds to a LIBOR and yield model with a complicated correlation structure – the former approach is preferable.

15.1.4   Applications

At one time – when CDS documentation was unclear and market participants were unsure whether they could incontrovertibly establish whether a credit event had occurred – deep out-of-the-money spread puts were used as an alternative to default swaps. As a reference entity went into default and the bond prices fell, the spread on the bond could always be calculated. If prices fell very low, then the option could be exercised.

What is the payoff difference of these two contracts in this case?

Take a 5-year FRN priced at par and paying a 100 bp spread. Let us assume that you own a spread option with a strike at 600 bp exercisable at any time up to one year from now. Also assume a 50% recovery and that default occurs tomorrow. The CDS would pay $100 - R = 50$. The FRN priced 500 bp away from current par value has an approximate price of 80, so the gain on the spread option is $80 - R = 30$. Note that the deep out-of-the-money spread option protects the price of the bond at the exercise spread. A hedge ratio against default swaps is recovery dependent.

Commercial banks are active writers of spread options (standby facilities and irrevocable lending commitments) and in principle buying a spread put option would allow them to hedge their risk. In practice this almost never happens.

1. Commercial banks generally run such positions in a 'buy and hold' portfolio. Marking to market is not required and risk management is through portfolio diversification and 'knowing your client'.
2. Spread options remain conservatively priced – in other words, hedging standby facilities with spread options is expensive compared with the commercial banks' own assessment of risk (although this is usually not based on an options pricing model).

The largest application of such options is embedded into bonds, into asset swaps and into CDSs. Ideally, spread options would allow the investor to hedge risks and take views on the market in a more flexible or tailored way. This will not happen until a more open market in spread volatility develops.

15.2   MODEL ALTERNATIVES AND A STOCHASTIC DEFAULT RATE MODEL FOR SPREAD OPTION PRICING

15.2.1   Model Approaches

The model described in Part I, based on transition matrices (calibrated to the reference entity in question), is capable of calculating the forward prices of credit risky assets whether in default or non-defaulted. Forward spreads are one of a handful of values only, and the underlying hazard rate model is a pure jump process. It is driven by the Normal Copula, and has similarities to the portfolio pricing techniques described in Part III.

An alternative approach is to model the underlying hazard rate process as a stochastic process – following some sort of diffusion process. This will allow for an infinite range of forward
spreads. Remember that the CDS pricing and calibration formulae discussed in Chapter 9
remain valid, even if the hazard rate is stochastic, as long as the hazard rate moves are uncorrelated with interest rate and other moves. However, the CDS calibrated hazard rate is not the
true stochastic hazard rate but the pseudo-hazard rate valid for the CDS pricing only. (If we
also wish to introduce an interest rate/hazard rate correlation, then we must also rework our
CDS and other pricing formulae.)

A discernible difference between these two alternative models arises, for example, if we
consider a short-dated option. Suppose the underlying spread is 80 bp for a BBB rated name.
Under a diffusion model with a 100% volatility in one month's time there is approximately
a one in a thousand chance that the spread will exceed 150 bp (about 3 standard deviations
away), whereas under the TM approach there is around a 1.5% chance of a spread of 200 bp
or more. (See the TM probabilities in 'Chapter 2 and Chapter 15.xls'.)

On the other hand, bank and insurance company names tend to have very low ratings
volatility – a TM-based approach may overestimate the chance of a significant change in the
spread.

The TM model has been described previously in the context of simulated spreads for bonds
in a portfolio – and exactly the same process can be applied here. We now describe a simple
stochastic hazard rate tree implementation of the second model alternative.

15.2.2 Hazard Rate Tree

A simple version of a tree model (see, for example, Jarrow and Turnbull, 1996) is described
and implemented in the Mathcad sheet 'Chapter 15 stochastic hazard rate.mcd'.

We use a recombining binary tree for hazard rates (see Figure 15.3). For simplicity the
hazard rate, λ, is assumed to be a constant (although the formulae can easily be amended for
any expected hazard rate curve). The hazard rate can increase in any time interval to λu with
probability C (conditional on no default), or to λd with probability $1 - C$. The logarithmic

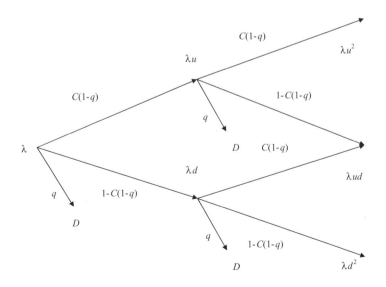

Figure 15.3   Hazard rate tree

variance is assumed to be σ^2 per annum, which gives rise to a formula for u. We then calculate C in terms of u [$C = 1/(u + 1)$] and find u in terms of σ. The tree is a trivial recombining tree for the hazard rate conditional on no default. If q is the default probability in the time interval Δt then the unconditional probability of an up-move is $u \times (1 - q)$, and similarly for a down-move.

We now have a three-legged tree. At each step the hazard rate may move up, down, or the reference entity may default. To price a bond (for example) we evolve the hazard rate tree to the maturity of the bond (where the price is 100 on the non-default nodes of the tree). We then work backwards ensuring that, at each step, the value of the bond is the expected value of the three alternative one-step-forward bond prices discounted back, together with any coupon to be paid.

The same hazard rate tree and similar pricing formulae can be used to get the CDS premium. Note that, for both bonds and CDSs, we have a process of trial and error in order to calibrate the hazard rate in order to produce the correct bond or CDS price. It is not accurate to use the pseudo-hazard rate obtained from CDS calibration.

The tree now has bond, or CDS, values at each of its nodes. We can now use these values to calculate the value of European or American call options on these underlyings.

15.2.3   Callable High-Yield Bonds

The implementation referred to in 15.2.2 actually calculates the option value for a price option on a callable high-yield bond. This follows the process described in Chapter 11 – the spread volatility (a guess based on historical volatility) is combined with the LIBOR volatility (from swaptions) and a correlation (assumed to be zero) to get a yield volatility for the bond. In this case the bond is a high-yield bond, and the volatility is dominated by the spread volatility. We assume that interest rates are constant and model the stochastic hazard rate only in order to estimate the embedded option value.

15.3   SENSITIVITIES AND HEDGING

Spread (or yield) options have hazard rate, recovery and interest rate sensitivities as do CDSs and, additionally, sensitivity to the hazard rate volatility. Since the mark-to-market levels are largely unknown, offsetting or hedging one deal with another is highly uncertain. Typically a risk control view of such a position would be to impose large reserves – reflecting uncertainty in value – and tight limits on outstanding positions. Buying options is usually handled by writing off the value of the premia (and marking to intrinsic). The trading desk is then limited in the trades it can do involving selling options – hampering liquidity – but is able to buy cheap (low premium) options – hence the growth in embedded bought options.

The development in the standardised CDO market (see Part III) and options on CDO tranches may provide some help in assessing mark-to-market levels of volatility, though the conversion from implied volatility on portfolios and tranches of portfolios to individual name volatilities is not trivial.

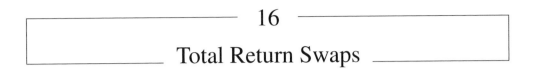

16

Total Return Swaps

16.1 PRODUCT DEFINITION AND EXAMPLES

A **total return swap** (TRS) is an off-balance transaction in which the **payer** pays the **receiver** the total return on a reference asset (be it positive or negative) from the effective date to the 'fixing' date in return for a floating leg, usually LIBOR plus a spread. Cashflows – such as coupon payments – are usually paid to the receiver on the dates the reference asset makes those payments. A TRS may be arranged with several intermediate fixing dates before maturity. In this case usually the terms of the TRS may be the same as if each sub-period was a TRS in its own right done at fair market terms, effectively terminating and restarting a new TRS at each fixing date. We shall only consider a TRS with a single total return payment date.

The payer is often called the buyer of protection, as the TRS will compensate the payer for negative performance of the reference assets. If the asset declines in price, the payer pays a negative amount – i.e. receives a payment from – the receiver. In particular, if the asset defaults, a large payment is made by the receiver to the payer, and the contract terminates with a proportionate floating payment from the receiver.

Similarly, a receiver of the total return is often called a seller of protection, as the swap will expose him or her to negative performance of the reference assets.

On default of the underlying, settlement can be cash or physical.

Counterparty risk is initially zero but increases as the reference asset moves away from its forward price curve. Counterparty risk may be positive or negative. Periodic cashflow dates (short maturity) reduce counterparty risk.

Before expiry the reference asset cashflows are passed to the receiver (Figure 16.1). At expiry, default or on a fixing date the capital gain since the last fixing is paid, in return for the floating payment. The contract terminates at the expiry or default date (Figure 16.2). There may be an option to terminate at the fixing date – which is worthless if the TRS is remarked to current levels and terms at each fixing date.

What restrictions should there be on the reference asset? There should be a readily available market price, and the ability to deal in the size of the contract at that price. For example, the following would normally be acceptable:

1. US Treasury bond – typically up to several billion USD.
2. Alcatel 5.875 05 – typically up to EUR 10m.
3. Alcatel equity – up to the typical dealing size.
4. A forward delivery of oil – up to the typical dealing size.

16.2 APPLICATIONS

Total return swaps were traditionally used between banks where one bank had exceeded its balance sheet limits and another had balance sheet available. A TRS allowed the former bank to remove the asset from its balance sheet while maintaining economic ownership of the asset.

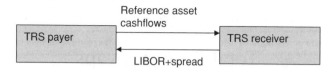

Figure 16.1   Pre-expiry: the reference asset cashflows are passed to the TRS receiver

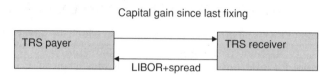

Figure 16.2   On expiry, default or a fixing date

Usually the deals were of large size (USD 1–2bn not being unusual), often on very liquid assets (US Treasuries), often originated by one bank selling the asset to the other bank (buying it back at the end of the deal), and usually the TRS deal was for less than three months' life. From the perspective of the bank with available balance sheet, the TRS is viewed as a 'balance sheet rental' trade.

Recently the TRS has been used more by hedge funds. The TRS allows the fund to have economic exposure to the underlying asset without having to finance it. Alternatives include dealing in an economically similar but unfunded asset – such as writing a CDS. This presents problems for some hedge funds because, as unregulated and possibly also high-risk corporate entities, they are unattractive counterparties for a bank buying protection – without substantial collateral being in place. Another alternative is buying the asset and financing it by doing a repo trade – we have seen that this is essentially the purpose of a TRS.

A further application is to allow an investor to obtain economic ownership of an asset that he or she would otherwise not be allowed to buy. For example, assets within a certain country may only be legally owned by residents' of that country. A domestic bank could buy the assets and grant economic ownership (and funding) via a TRS.

16.3   HEDGING AND VALUATION

16.3.1   Pricing and Hedging

The payer may set up a hedge as follows:

1. Buy the reference asset at the market price P.
2. Enter into a repo trade with the asset as collateral for repo rate r for the term of the TRS. (If this term repo is not possible in practice, a rolling short-term repo can be entered into, or the bank may finance the asset off its own balance sheet at its funding rate for the period.).

We can see that a TRS is the purchase of the asset and a funding trade performed one step removed. The TRS payer, rather than the end investor, is taking risk on the funding rate – if indeed the investor were able to do the trade personally.

The payer then pays cashflows as follows:

1. Cashflows on the reference asset are paid to the 'receiver' as they are received.
2. At the fixing date, the reference asset is marked to bid, P_{fwd} (or sold if it is the expiry of the deal or the asset has defaulted), and the price gain $P_{fwd} - P$ paid to the receiver.
3. The repo rate is paid on the repo transaction based on the initial reference price.
4. LIBOR plus a spread, X, is received on the initial capital in the trade (P). (An alternative is to base the premium on the notional of the deal – this is just a rescaling exercise.)

The net cashflow on a single period TRS is LIBOR $+ X - r$. Thus a fair market price is achieved if X is minus the amount special on repo.

Even in the single period TRS there are risks. A term repo rate may not be available – and the bank will have to estimate the repo cost on a rolling basis. On the other hand, if the bank is financing the trade off its own balance sheet then it will know this cost. Secondly, if a default event occurs on the reference asset, any term funding transaction will have to be unwound at prevailing rates.

A multi-period TRS will continue but now the bank is not financing the initial price, P, but the fixing date price, P_{fwd}. The initial hedge could take into account the expected price change and the expected funding cost.

In practice the spread paid by the TRS payer will be above the fair value spread. A charge is made for access to the balance sheet, access to restricted markets, or access to funding which will be as large as the market will bear and will be chosen to generate a target return on capital for the payer.

16.3.2 Valuation

If we value the deal which expires at time t, where an asset cashflow c is expected at time t_0, then the value of the assets (bond, repo and TRS cashflows) is made up of the following:

1. The bond, current value P_t and a loan of P.
2. The cashflow c is exactly matched by an outgoing cashflow, so has no valuation impact.
3. A recovery arising from a credit event is exactly matched by an outgoing cashflow, so has no valuation impact.
4. A credit event forces unwinding the repo trade at then current market rates. We would normally assume that the repo follows the forward repo curve, so the expected unwind cost is zero.
5. A payment of the total return amount at the maturity date if the name survives.
6. The repo payment of the loan plus interest at the repo rate if the name survives.
7. A receipt of LIBOR plus the spread on the initial capital if the name survives.

$$V = P_t - P + (P_{fwd} - P) \cdot S(t) \cdot d(t) + P \cdot [(1+r)^t - 1] \cdot S(t) \cdot d(t)$$
$$- P \cdot [(1+L+X)^t - 1] \cdot S(t) \cdot d(t) \tag{16.1}$$

where $d(.)$ are discount factors off the LIBOR curve, $S(.)$ is the survival probability of the reference entity, L is the LIBOR rate and X is the spread.

Note that if we are performing the valuation at the outset then $P_t = P$ and the value is zero if $r = L + X$ as before.

17
Single Name Book Management

The aim of 'book' or 'portfolio' management is to understand and then to control the risks. Risk is related to potential changes in value, and this can be assessed in two different ways:

1. A **level/duration/convexity** approach. We may describe the full functionality of the value function by the values of all the derivatives of that function to all inputs. The first-order derivatives are variously called 'PV01', 'sensitivity', 'duration'. Second-order derivatives include 'convexity'. Book risk can be measured by the values of these derivatives – typically we only look at derivatives of second or third order. If a derivative is close to zero, then the book is hedged. On this approach a one-year and a 20-year trade will both contribute risks to these measures (sensitivity, convexity, ...) and will add to (or net against) each other. Note that risks beyond second order can be significant (in a 1-, 5-, 30-year CDS deal spread hedged and convexity hedged – the 'twist' risk would be very large).
2. A **bucketing** approach. We look at sensitivities only (first-order changes only) but only aggregate risks on 'similar' trades (e.g. both 5-year BBB rates US names). Typically a one-year and a 20-year deal would not lead to an aggregated risk position.

We have already illustrated the bucketing approach in Chapter 10 with the simplified 'risk charts'. The subject of this chapter is how to risk control and manage these CDS positions in practice.

17.1 RISK AGGREGATION

Credit derivatives books or portfolios within an investment bank or other institution are generally separated into main product categories. Here we look at the 'single name book'; we look at the 'correlation (portfolio products) book' in Part III, and the 'counterparty risk book' in Part IV.

The single name CDS book contains all vanilla CDS contracts arising from market-making (client-driven) activities, proprietary trading or investment, and in-house hedging activities – for example, hedges done between books (e.g. the CDO traders will hedge residual name risk with the CDS traders). A separate single name (spread) volatility book will also be created to hedge volatility risk – residual single name spread risks will be passed down to the single name CDS book either explicitly via intra-desk deals, or implicitly at the risk level.

Managing the single name book requires the calculation of risks according to the pricing model of Chapter 9 (or the institutions preferred model). Typically these involve interest rate risk (generally very small and we shall not discuss it further), spread or hazard rate delta risk, of default event risk, or recovery rate risk. Risk is calculated on an individual name basis. The trade is assigned to a bucket and a bucket may be defined as follows:

1. Reference entity
2. Maturity: for example, 0–6 months, 6 months–1 year, 1–2 years, 2–4 years, ...
3. Geographical region: North America, Europe, emerging market, ...

4. Currency
5. Industry: for example, using rating agency industry groups
6. Rating or spread range
7. Seniority
8. Others.

Buckets define a cell in a matrix into which trade sensitivities are posted. The natural next step is aggregation of risks. The risk charts in Chapter 10 illustrated the risks at the individual deal level, and an aggregation by maturity and across all maturities for certain types of deals. In practice, aggregation for a given name will be across all CDS (or bond) deals on that name.

An aggregation hierarchy might be as follows:

1. Name, currency, seniority and maturity
2. Name, currency and maturity
3. Name and maturity
4. Name
5. Industry and rating (by currency by seniority by maturity, and aggregates of these)
6. Region and rating (etc.)
7. Rating and maturity
8. Rating
9. All (e.g. a single spread sensitivity aggregated across all trades).

Risk limits are imposed on the various captured risks and certain buckets. In addition, reserves are held (i.e. capital is set aside) against risks not captured by the model but inherent in the deal. Generally the reserves are small on the single name book – the largest being the bid–offer spread if this is not factored explicitly into the valuation process; another example is liquidity risk.

We briefly review some of the trades discussed earlier and highlight some further features of these deals and implications of the risk control approach.

Example 1: Naked Risk

Risk is allocated to a bucket. Within that name this is the only risk so the view (for the currency and seniority) of the deal is as in Figure 10.1. As we progress up the hierarchy – say to the industry, rating, currency, seniority and maturity bucket – we may find that the risk from this long protection deal is offset by other (effectively short protection) deals.

In other words, within the bucketing and risk limit approach adopted, naked exposure in different but similar names offset each other. Our rules allow us to hedge FMC with GMAC, for example.

Example 2: Cross-Currency Risk

Figure 10.2 showed the position for a trade in a particular name where long risk in one currency was offset by short risk in another. Within the bucketing approach we may be looking at an offset of short 5-year Fiat CDS in USD offset by Fiat EUR protection in 3- and 4-year maturities, or long non-Fiat protection (e.g. other autos in USD).

Note also that the risk is dynamic, driven by interest rate moves. Cross-currency hedging can be controlled to a greater extent by having tighter limits on bucketed risk within a specific currency. Thus, if the autos A and BBB limits are EUR 40 000 per bp in 5-year Euros, and a similar amount in USD, then cross-currency hedging is limited to 100m (100m × 0.0001 × duration of 4).

Example 3: Curve Risk

Figure 10.4 shows the net risks for a curve trade on a specific name. Suppose the trades had been done (with the appropriate delta hedge ratios) in 1-year versus 10-year. What difference does this make?

The risk with curve trades is that spreads may not move in parallel but the curve tilts adversely. This risk is clearly greater in a 1/10 maturity trade compared to a 3/5 maturity trade. Clearly the bucketing picture for that name will be different with the risks being in very different parts of the maturity range. We can control the magnitude of these trades by putting tight limits on the exposure within each bucket, not at the specific name level but at the industry, rating, currency, and seniority level. Similar curve trades in various names will aggregate to large bucketed positions: the risk can be reduced by having curve steepeners on some names offsetting flatteners on others – or by having smaller positions.

Note that the hedges for a curve trade and the 'forward CDS' deal (section 12.1) are dynamic. Fixed hedges will give rise to an emerging spread risk (at the total level, and changing spread risks in each maturity bucket for that name). Mismatches will appear at the individual name level and also in buckets as risks are aggregated.

A portfolio management approach allows:

(a) emerging risks on some deals to be automatically offset by emerging risks of the opposite sign on other deals, and
(b) reduction of risks by hedging aggregated emerging risk more frequently than is practical at the single name level.

Example 4: Cross-Seniority Risk; Digital Risk

Figure 10.6 shows the position for a cross-seniority trade. Within the 'all seniorities' bucket, net spread risk does not know whether it came from senior, subordinated, loan or other exposure.

One way to pick up and control cross-currency hedging is through the default event risk measure. Based on assumed recoveries, the deals offset; but if we stress recoveries to 0% and 100% separately for different seniorities, we find a worst-case loss of zero on this deal. On the other hand, if the portions were reversed, the risk charts would be essentially the same, but the stress results would show a worst-case loss on the notional of the short subordinated protection – arising from senior recovery 100%, giving no gain on the long position; and junior recovery to 0%, giving a full loss on the short position.

Likewise, the aggregated spread risk bucket does not know whether the risk came from vanilla CDSs or digital risks. We can establish this by changing our recovery assumptions on all names, recalibrating, revaluing all the deals, and recalculating the bucket risks. Large movements in the bucket risk will reveal the presence of digital exposures from whatever source – including off-market CDSs, embedded digital products and cross-seniority trades.

17.2   CREDIT VaR FOR CDS

We saw in Chapter 6, how to use an (adjusted) transition matrix to simulate both default events and forward spreads. The transition matrix can be adjusted to replicate CDS premia rather than bond spreads in the obvious way. (The TM gives the default probability by year, hence we can calculate the value of a payoff contingent on the default event and a payoff contingent on survival (the premium stream).)

The approach described there can be applied equally well to a CDS portfolio where we generate the capital proceeds arising from credit events before the time horizon, and the forward value of all CDS positions (aggregated by rating).

18

CDS and Simulation

Single name CDS products are easily handled by closed form models (such as those described in section 9.5). In 18.2 we briefly look at simulation applied to single name CDS products. This is not of great importance in its own right, but serves as a simple introduction to some of the simulation techniques of Parts III and IV, and enables us to understand some of the key concepts in a relatively simple context.

In addition, in section 18.3 we describe an interesting way to use the simulations to obtain not just product price but also – from a single simulation set – the hazard rate (spread) sensitivity of the CDS.

First we state a few more results from the Poisson process which are of relevance now and later.

18.1 THE POISSON MODEL AND DEFAULT TIMES

If the hazard rate is constant, the expected time to default is

$$T = \int_0^\infty t \cdot \lambda \cdot \exp(-\lambda \cdot t)\mathrm{d}t = \frac{1}{\lambda} \tag{18.1}$$

We can also show that the standard deviation of the default time is $1/\lambda$.

If we imagine simulating default times (see section 18.2) then the average of these simulated times will tend to T, and the standard deviation will also tend to T.

Note also that, given our assumption that the hazard rate is constant, if the name has survived in H years (a given time horizon), the hazard rate is still λ – in other words, the forward expected default time at H is still T. Therefore, if we take all the simulated default times, exclude those that are less than H, then the average of the remainder will still be T.

Results are more complicated if the hazard rate is a function of time. For many thought experiments the use of a constant hazard rate is sufficient.

18.2 VALUATION BY MONTE CARLO SIMULATION

For a given name and hazard rate we shall simulate the default time for that name. We also ignore counterparty risk, assume premia are payable continuously, and that the interest rate is constant. The process is as follows:

1. Pick a random number from any convenient distribution.[1]
2. Find the cumulative probability associated with that number.

---

[1] In the case of a single name we have much more freedom in the choice of random number generation than we have for more than one name, where we need to be more careful over the choice of random number generator and how these numbers are used.

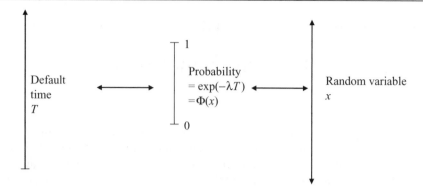

Figure 18.1   Normal random variable to default time.

3. Associate that probability with the probability of survival up to a certain time – the default time.
4. Given the default time t we know whether a capital payment (of $1 - $ recovery) is made (if $t <$ maturity $[M]$ of the CDS), and when the premium stream stops.

The simplest example is where we use a uniform distribution. See 'Chapter 18.xls' worksheet 'CDS simulation' for an implementation of these examples. Pick a random $x \in [0, 1]$. Since the distribution is uniform, the probability of getting a number of x or less is just x itself. So x is the probability of survival up to time t. If we assume the hazard rate to be constant[2] (i.e. there is no CDS term structure), then we have

$$x = \exp(-\lambda t) \qquad \text{hence} \quad t = \frac{-\ln(x)}{\lambda} \tag{18.2}$$

Alternatively, if we had chosen x from a Normal distribution then we would have to calculate the probability of seeing an x or less – using the cumulative Normal distribution – and our formula would become

$$t = \frac{-\ln[\Phi(x)]}{\lambda} \tag{18.3}$$

Generally, under the Normal distribution but for a general hazard rate curve, we have

$$\Phi(x) = \exp\left[-\int_0^t \lambda(s)ds\right]$$

Techniques for solving the above equation for t, depend on the functional form chosen for the hazard rate. The process is illustrated in Figure 18.1.

Now we value the cashflows for that simulation. Remember, we now know when the default takes place – each simulation is a realisation of the universe; we know precisely what happens and when; when the premium stream is terminated and when the capital payoff is made (if at all). Under one simulation everything is deterministic since all the uncertainty is reflected in

---

[2] In the case of a time-dependent hazard rate the formula becomes implicit for the time t (where x equals the probability in equation (9.6)) and we have to find efficient numerical procedures to obtain the default time from the simulated random number.

Table 18.1 Simulated CDS premia using different distributions

Generating distribution	Mean	StDev
Uniform	99.92	0.2
Normal	99.70	0.3
Exponential	99.97	0.1

the universe of all simulations, so valuation only requires discounting. If t is less than the CDS maturity then the benefits value is

$$B = (1 - R)\exp(-rt) \tag{18.4}$$

otherwise it is zero.

Similarly the value of premia paid until the earlier of the default time and the CDS maturity is

$$P = \frac{1 - \exp[-r\min(t, M)]}{r}. \tag{18.5}$$

Now we repeat the process, adding to the value of benefits and premium stream for the value arising from this new simulation. We repeat many times – typically around one million simulations for a single name – and calculate the average (=expected) benefits value (and standard deviation), the average (=expected) premium value (and standard deviation), then finally the fair value premium (and standard deviation) or the net value of the trade (for an existing deal with known premium).

The process is very simple, requiring only a few lines of code to implement, and is illustrated in the 'Chapter 18.xls' spreadsheet.

Table 18.1 gives the results of implementing the above process 1m times for a single name with hazard rate 0.02 and recovery of 50%. The correct CDS premium (for continuous premia) is 100 bp.

Note that there is nothing special about using the Normal distribution in the case of simulation for a single name (or many uncorrelated names).

Exercise
Prove that under the simulation process described, the mean and standard deviation of the default time are the inverse of the hazard rate.

Take any (piecewise analytic) statistical distribution $f(x)$ with cumulative distribution $F(x)$. If we select x randomly then the default time is given by $t = \{-\ln[F(x)]\}/\lambda$. The expected value of t is

$$E(t) = -\frac{1}{\lambda}\int_0^1 \ln[F(x)]f(x)\mathrm{d}x = -\frac{1}{\lambda}\int_\infty^0 y\exp(-y)\mathrm{d}y = \frac{1}{\lambda}$$

where we have made a change in variable $y = \exp[-F(x)]$. The integral on the right-hand side has been evaluated by integration by parts to give the required answer. Similarly evaluating the expectation of the squares of the default time allows us to calculate the variance, and we get the required answer.

Notes On Credit Simulation

(A) We simulate default time. This is very different from most simulation procedures in finance where a variable (for example, interest rates) is simulated along a time path. A single simulation produces a series of interest rates at different times – which are then used in product valuation. Simulation of default time – a single simulation – produces all relevant values for the product. This is much faster than path-based simulation but is only applicable to certain products. For example, it is not directly suitable for spread option products (we look at some modifications in Part III).

(B) A single simulation is a realisation of a particular universe. Producing many simulations is like looking at many possible universes or outcomes – only one of which actually occurs. Pricing based on the average of many simulations (also pricing off closed-form models) disguises the fact that the outcome may be very different from the expected result. This is an important point when we trade F2D protection hedged by single name CDSs. The realised P&L from the rehedging activity may be very different from expected.

18.3   SENSITIVITY

We could calculate the sensitivity of the CDS value to a change in the hazard rate (or spread) as follows:

1. Shift the hazard rate (by, say, 10 bp) .
2. Recalculate all the default times (using the same set of random numbers used in the first set of simulations).
3. Recalculate the expected benefits value and the expected value of the premium stream, hence the expected value of the trade.
4. Subtract the value on this set of simulations from the value obtained on the first set, and divide by 10 to get the sensitivity per basis point (to an up-shift in hazard rate).

This is the process generally used when calculating sensitivities of complex CDO products. The uncertainty in the sensitivity is higher than the uncertainty in the valuation itself and we generally need to use more simulations when calculating sensitivities than just doing a valuation. Note that, if we had used a different set of random numbers in the shifted simulations, then the uncertainty would be even greater and we would have to use many more simulations to get a reliable estimate – it is good practice to reuse the same random numbers to generate the default times under the shifted hazard rate. Peculiarities of that random number sequence tend to cancel.

   There is another way to calculate sensitivity which does not require recalculation of default times under a second simulation. We can extract for information from each simulated default time to produce the sensitivity as follows and as shown in Figure 18.2.

   Note that if the hazard rate is shifted and default times are recalculated, then every single default time in the valuation simulation run is shifted to an earlier default time by a factor depending on the hazard rate and the shift (equation (18.2) or (18.3)).

$$t_{\text{shifted}} = -\frac{\ln[F(x)]}{\lambda + \Delta \cdot \lambda} = t\frac{1}{1+\Delta} \approx t - t \cdot \Delta \tag{18.6}$$

For every default time that is shorter than the trade maturity, the payoff value increases because it is paid slightly earlier, and the premium stream is less because it is slightly shorter. For each

Simulated defaults times for a 5-year CDS

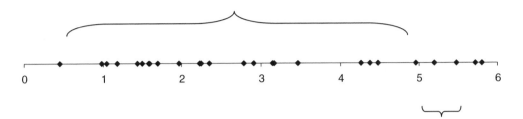

Simulated defaults: increasing hazard rate shortens
default time and increases CDS value

Near defaults: increasing
hazard rates shifts these
into the default region

Figure 18.2   Simulated default times and the impact of shifting the hazard rate

such default the increase in benefits value is just

$$\Delta B = B \cdot r t \Delta \tag{18.7}$$

and the change in the premium value is the loss in premium discounted by the time to default

$$\Delta P = -t \cdot \Delta \cdot \exp(-rt) \tag{18.8}$$

The two terms above give us the change in value arising from the shortening in the default time of those defaults that occurred before maturity. In addition, there are defaults that occur just after maturity that will shorten to just before maturity. All those default times between M and $M + M \cdot \Delta$ will now give rise to a benefits payment and an increase in the benefits value of

$$B_{\text{new}} = (1 - R)\exp(-rM) \tag{18.9}$$

and a reduction in premium whose value is

$$P_{\text{new}} = -\frac{M}{2}\Delta \cdot \exp(-rM). \tag{18.10}$$

We can evaluate these terms at the same time as we perform the simulation for value, and the sensitivity is then

$$S = \sum_{\text{defaults}} [B \cdot r \cdot t \cdot \Delta - t \cdot \Delta \cdot \exp(-rt)]$$

$$+ \underbrace{\sum_{\text{nearDefaults}} \left[(1 - R)\exp(-rM) - \frac{M}{2}\Delta \cdot \exp(-rM)\right]}_{\sim \cdot \Delta \cdot \lambda} \tag{18.11}$$

Part III
Portfolio Products

19

Nth-to-Default Baskets

Nth-to-default (N2D) products are the small portfolio product both in terms of number of reference names and the size of the deal. Trading volumes are high compared with bespoke CDO deals but in nominal exposures typically of less than EUR 25m. Trading is almost entirely in first-to-default. These products provide a means of trading 'correlation' on small numbers of reference entities.

N2D products are modelled using the same mathematical framework as that for CDOs – only product cashflows differ – and are a useful tool for testing and understanding many features that are applicable to both sets of products.

19.1 PRODUCT DEFINITION AND FEATURES

19.1.1 First-to-Default Product Definition and Example

A first-to-default (F2D) swap is similar to a plain vanilla credit default swap. However, a first-to-default swap gives credit protection on a list of reference names instead of just one reference name, and will result in a pay-out after the first default only. The contract then terminates.

The typical contract pays par on the first credit event in return for ('physical settlement') debt issued by the reference name that suffered the credit event. Premia are paid quarterly in arrears with a proportion up to the default date.

Documentation

Documentation follows CDS documentation. A reference obligation is given for each reference name; documentation is changed slightly to clarify the contingent payment made on the first credit event, and termination of premium and future obligations on that event. The question of mergers is discussed below.

Premium Quotation Basis

It is usual to quote the premium as a percentage of the sum of the CDS premia of the component names. CDS spreads may vary a little over a few hours or days – while a potential trade is being discussed – but the F2D premium will remain close to a certain percentage (which varies according to the underlying reference names) of the sum of premia. When documentation is signed the actual premium in basis points per annum – not the percentage of the sum – appears.

Example

JPMorgan (say) sells EUR 10m 5-year F2D protection on a five reference entities – Allied Domecq Plc, Ford Motor Credit, Delphi Corp., Lehman Brothers Holdings Inc., and ThyssenKrupp AG – in return for a fixed premium of 362 bp p.a. In the discussions prior to

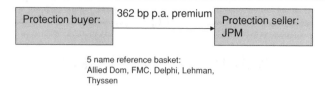

5 name reference basket:
Allied Dom, FMC, Delphi, Lehman,
Thyssen

Figure 19.1   First-to-default basket: pre credit event

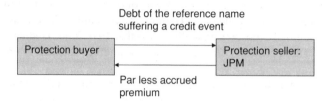

Figure 19.2   First-to-default basket: credit event

signing the deal the sum of CDS premia on the individual names was around 600 bp, and the premium would have been indicated as (say) 60%. The buyer pays the 362 bp premium to JPMorgan quarterly in arrears until the earlier of the deal maturity or a credit event on one of the names (see Figure 19.1).

Suppose a credit event occurs on Delphi before the maturity of the trade (Figure 19.2). JPMorgan pays EUR-10m in return for defaulted debt of Delphi. The protection buyer pays a proportional premium up to the date of default. The contract then terminates. No further protection on the remaining four names exists under the contract.

Note: N2D baskets should not be confused with 'average baskets' (see Part II). Both of these products are sometimes confusingly referred to as 'baskets'. An EUR 10m average basket on the above names would initially cost 600 bp and, if the Delphi CDS premium was 140 bp, then on a Delphi credit event, EUR 10m Delphi debt would be delivered and the average basket would continue in EUR 10m on (each of) the remaining names, subject to a reduced premium of 460 bp.

19.1.2   Documentation and Takeovers

A new feature of portfolio trades is the merger or takeover risk. A CDS trade usually provides protection on the reference name or its successors (i.e. protection continues on the resulting entity after a merger or takeover – as defined by the ISDA 'successor' language or similar). A particular problem of portfolio products is that a merger of two of the names in the reference pool results in a smaller basket (one name fewer). Current documentation treats mergers in one of two ways:

1. The documentation does not make any particular provision for the event of merger of two or more names in the basket. Note that a credit event of the successor entity may be pointed to as a credit event of both of the predecessor entities, so such an event would trigger a second-to-default contract at the same time as a first-to-default contract.
2. There may be replacement provision. This may operate along the following lines: one side suggests a list of potential replacement names and the other side selects from that list. The list may be restricted in rating, industry or spread – for example, any name on the list must

have the same industry group as either of the merged entities, and the same rating as either of those entities had at the time the trade was done, or the suggested replacement names must have similar spreads to the merged entity.

The ISDA N2D confirmation gives the counterparties the choice of 'no replacement' or of 'with replacement'. Under the ISDA replacement provision, the replacement entity must be in the same industry group, and have a (bid) spread no greater than 110% of the spread on the name it is replacing (as determined by a dealer poll conducted by the protection buyer). The buyer must deliver a list of three or more eligible names to the seller within 10 business days of the successor event, and the seller then has five days to select the replacement entity.

What trading opportunities does a replacement clause open up? On a merger event, the side that draws up the list has a contingent option (triggered by merger) to suggest names with a relatively wide spread. The restrictions in the clause are designed to limit the value of this contingent option. In addition, the nature of the basket can be changed – the buyer of protection would like to increase the diversity[1] of the basket (which increases the value of the deal to the buyer) while the seller would like to reduce the diversity (which reduces the value of the deal).

What risk is present if there is no replacement clause? The reduction of the number of names itself causes a drop in the value of the deal. Take the example in 19.1.1, and assume that two names merged. The sum of CDS premia for the reduced number of names is now (say) 480 bp, and the fair value premium for the basket drops to (say) 300 bp, so the buyer is now paying 62 bp above fair value. There is a further pricing impact: a four name basket is seen as different from a five name basket (there is less diversity) and is therefore priced rather differently. We shall see that the implied correlation on smaller baskets tends to be higher than on larger baskets, reducing their value to a buyer. The pricing correlation would rise, so the fair value premium would drop further as a percentage of the sum of spreads. Hence the value of the deal to the buyer will drop (on the above example this might give rise to a further drop in the fair-value premium to 285 bp). A merger will therefore cause a significant downward jump in the value of the basket, related directly to a reduction in the number of names and also to a change in the pricing correlation. The combined effect is that, on merger events with 'no replacement', the F2D writer makes a mark-to-market profit and the buyer makes a loss.

One of the leading market-makers in this product argues that a 'no replacement' clause is preferable, primarily on the grounds that (where replacement applies) if a long basket is hedged with a short basket on the same names, then after a merger and replacement the two baskets could refer to different portfolios. (In addition there is a 'consistency' argument: standard CDO contracts do not have a replacement clause.)

19.1.3   Second (and Higher)-to-Default

An *n*th-to-default product is similar to an F2D except that nothing is paid on the *i*th credit event if $i < n$. If the basket reaches the *n*th credit event then defaulted debt is delivered in return for the notional amount (less accrued premium) and the contract then terminates.

Example

Suppose, on the above reference pool, JPMC wrote EUR 10m second-to-default protection for 140 bp. The deal is unaffected by the first credit event (Delphi) – except that it now effectively

---

[1] For 'diversity' we can also read 'correlation'.

becomes a F2D on the remaining names. The premium continues at 140 bp on EUR 10m until maturity, or until a second credit event occurs if earlier. Suppose FMC suffers a credit event after Delphi and before the maturity of the deal. Then the debt of FMC is delivered to JPMC in return for par (less accrued premium) and the contract terminates.

19.2   APPLICATIONS

In practice only F2D products trade frequently. Typical notional exposure is the same as (single name) CDS deals – around 10–20m, and 5-year deals are the most common. F2D baskets are regarded as the vanilla correlation trading product. They give a 'geared' exposure – in the above example the writer is taking on risk to reference names with an average spread of 120 bp, yet gets paid 362 bp.

19.2.1   Correlation Trading

The main application of F2D baskets is as a means of trading 'correlation' risk. Pricing of a F2D basket is dependent on not only the individual risks, but also the way in which credit events on one name relate to credit events on another. We refer to the relationship as 'credit event correlation', 'credit correlation' or just 'correlation'. In section 9.8 we discussed the correlation of hazard rates and we would intuitively expect that this should be the source of the 'correlation' behind F2D products. It turns out (Chapter 21) that this is indeed the case, though for practical reasons we choose to implement a model not by correlating hazard rates but by correlating default times.

We shall see how F2D can be used to trade correlation once we have developed a pricing model in Chapter 21.

19.2.2   Mergers

F2D baskets can also be used to trade merger views – see section 19.1.2 above. Writing baskets including potential merger candidates, and with 'no replacement' clause, gives a mark-to-market profit on a merger event on the short protection trade. Deals can be hedged by buying protection 'with replacement'. If the premium differential is less than the jump in premium expected on a merger (which can be calculated) times the probability of the merger (a guess) times a discount factor dependent on the timing of the merger, then an overall profit is made.

19.2.3   Standard Baskets

F2D products can include any names that the buyer and seller agree to trade. Certain baskets or types of baskets have become popular and some market-makers regularly quote prices on certain baskets. Following the introduction of the CDX indices the market agreed (July 2004) to quote certain five-name baskets made up from the most liquid names within certain indices. The F2D baskets quoted are as follows:

1. Basic industries
2. Diversified – including high-volatility names
3. Diversified – excluding high-volatility names
4. Financials

5. Consumer products and retail
6. TMT (Telecoms, Media, Technology)
7. Energy.

Table 19.1 gives the current constituents and shows indicated CDS and basket premium levels at the time.

Such baskets allow the investor to trade sector views combined with correlation views. For example, if one's view is that the TMT spreads are high and will narrow relative to basic industries, then a short F2D on TMT hedged with a long F2D on basic industries benefits if TMT spreads narrow, and benefits further if the implied correlation increases (this further reduces the fair-value premium on the basket).

Exercise
A 5-year CLN in USD 10m, issued at par, has as its underlying risk the 'first-to-default' out of a list of seven names. On a credit event on any one of the names the note terminates and the investor receives nothing. How would you hedge the CLN and, if the F2D costs 630 bp, what spread would you expect to pay on the CLN? If the CLN is capital guaranteed with a 15-year life, 5-year risk, what would the premium be?

In the remainder of this chapter we shall look at some special cases of correlation that allow us to calculate some significant results and will teach us a considerable amount about pricing generally.

19.3   PRICING: ZERO AND 100% CORRELATION

Special cases – where exact solutions are known – are of interest in their own right and also useful as limiting cases to test more sophisticated models. These special cases allow us to perform tests on our correlation model (Chapter 21) and the Monte Carlo implementation. In addition, the zero and 100% correlation cases provide further insight into how correlation products work and also how our model treats them – with some surprising conclusions. (In addition the 'semi-closed form' pricing approach for correlated portfolios can give very accurate answers in special cases – see Chapter 22 and 'Chapter 22 Normal Copula closed form N2D pricing.mcd'.)

For readers who wish to skip the mathematics below we summarise the key results:

1. Zero correlation
   (a) For a fair value F2D where the two names are uncorrelated, and where the hazard rates are constant, we see that the first-to-default premium is the sum of the premia for the individual CDS contracts. See *Exercise 1*.
   (b) The F2D hedge ratios are less than 100% in each name. See *Exercise 3*.
   (c) The S2D premium is positive – so an F2D and an S2D product on two reference names costs more than the sum of the CDS premia – and the hedge ratios are positive. See *Exercise 4*.
   (d) The sum of the hedge ration for the F2D and the S2D is greater than 100% of the notional for each name in the basket. See *Exercise 6*.

2. 100% correlation
   (a) The F2D contract is identical to a CDS on the higher hazard rate name, and the S2D is identical to a CDS on the lower hazard rate name.

Table 19.1 Standard F2D baskets and sample quotes

			STATIC DATA				
F2D basket name	Basic industries	CP and retail	Energy	Financials	TMT	Diversified / inc HiVol	Diversified / exc HiVol
Name 1	Ford Motor	Altria Gp (Philip Morris)	Duke Energy	General Electric Cap Corp	AT&T	Ford Motor	Dow Chemical
Name 2	Bombardier Capital	Albertson's	Halliburton	CIT Group	Time Warner	Altria Gp (Philip Morris)	Sears Roebuck
Name 3	Delphi	Sears Roebuck	FirstEnergy	Countrywide	Electric Data Systems	Halliburton	Duke Energy
Name 4	Dow Chemical	Safeway	Dominion Resources	American Intl	Motorola	Loews	General Electric Cap Corp
Name 5	Intl Paper	Tyson Foods	ConocoPhillips	Capital One	Verizon Comms	AT&T	Verizon Comms
			MARKET DATA				
Bid – offer	680–710	360–385	185–200	137–147	540–570	650–680	250–265
Bid – offer % total	80–83	69–74	64–69	66–71	72–76	80–83	84–89
Implied correl.	33–27	48–40	62–54	63–56	48–40	29–23	32–23
Mid spreads							
Name 1	175	172	48	27	335	175	48
Name 2	438	63	76	51	80	172	132
Name 3	133	132	77	51	234	76	48
Name 4	48	67	61	20	59	57	27
Name 5	59	85	28	60	44	335	44

(b) Since recovery is unknown on specific names, the premium for the F2D may be anywhere between the lower spread name and the higher spread name. The sum of the N2D premia remains equal to the sum of the CDS premia.

(c) The hedge ratios for the N2D contracts sum to 100% in each name.

19.3.1 Zero Correlation Case – Exact Pricing from the CDS Model

Consider the first-to-default product. For simplicity we assume that the hazard rates are constant (i.e. there is no CDS term structure), and the interest rate is also constant. We also ignore counterparty risk at the moment. The formulae illustrate the case for a basket of two names, but the generalisation to many names is straightforward.

Since the names are uncorrelated, we have the following results from basic probability theory:

1. The joint survival probability of name A and name B is the product of the survival probability of A and the survival probability of B.
2. The probability (density) that A is the first-to-default at time t is the probability that A survives until t, times the probability that B survives until t, times the hazard rate of A.

The following formulae are implemented in 'Chapter 9 and Chapter 19 hedge theory.mcd'.

F2D Valuation

Assume premia are paid continuously (which is a good approximation to the typical premium schedule for 'quarterly in arrears with a proportion to the default date'). Real world implementation would take the details of premium payment and day-count conventions into account, but the differences are small and do not invalidate the key findings below.

A unit of premium $p.\Delta t$ is paid at time t if both A and B survive until t (with probability $S_A(t) \times S_B(t) = \exp(-\lambda_A t) \times \exp(-\lambda_B t)$). Its value is obtained by discounting at interest rate r [$D(t) = \exp(-rt)$]. The value of the premium stream up to the maturity T is therefore

$$P = p \int_0^T \exp[-(\lambda_A + \lambda_B + r)t] \, dt = \frac{1 - \exp[-(\lambda_A + \lambda_B + r)T]}{\lambda_A + \lambda_B + r} \tag{19.1}$$

The contingent benefits arise if both names survive until time t, then either A or B defaults at time t. This gives rise to a payment of $(1 - \text{recovery})$, and this payment is discounted at the interest rate r. Hence the value of the contingent benefits is

$$B = \int_0^T \{(1 - R_A)\lambda_A \exp[-(\lambda_A + \lambda_B + r)t] + (1 - R_B)\lambda_B \exp[-(\lambda_A + \lambda_B + r)t]\} \, dt$$

$$B = [(1 - R_A)\lambda_A + (1 - R_B)\lambda_B] \frac{1 - \exp[-(\lambda_A + \lambda_B + r)T]}{\lambda_A + \lambda_B + r} \tag{19.2}$$

Recall that, under the assumptions we are making, the single name CDS premium is equal to hazard rate times loss given recovery (equation (9.15)). Hence the net value of a long position in an uncorrelated F2D (equation (19.2) minus (19.1)) is

$$V = (CDS_A + CDS_B - p)\frac{1 - \exp[-(\lambda_A + \lambda_B + r)T]}{\lambda_A + \lambda_B + r} \qquad (19.3)$$

For a fair value F2D where the names are uncorrelated, and where the hazard rate is a constant, we see that the first-to-default premium is the sum of the premia for the individual CDS contracts:

$$p = \mathbf{CDS_A} + \mathbf{CDS_B}.$$

Exercise 1
How can this make sense? We are paying as much for an F2D, which terminates at the maturity date, or the default of either name, as we would for two individual CDSs which give the same protection up to the earlier default date yet gives continued protection on the remaining name after the first defaults.

The answer is in our assumption that the (pseudo-)hazard rates are constant. When the first name defaults then, given our assumption, we can purchase protection on the remaining name at the same premium rate as if we had bought it at inception. Hence F2D protection plus the potential future purchase of single name protection at a known price gives the same protection at the same cost as two single name CDS contracts.

This result clearly is not valid if there is a term structure to credit spreads for a single name – though the error is typically quite small.

Exercise 2
Given the above pricing result how would you hedge an uncorrelated F2D basket?

The hedge ratios are **not** 100%. For a notional holding (long of protection, say) in an F2D basket we can hedge by selling notional amounts of CDS_A and of CDS_B (all trades are assumed to be done at a fair market price). For the moment we shall concentrate on hedging out hazard rate sensitivity (equivalently spread risk). In order to be hedged the portfolio must show no sensitivity to changes in the hazard rate (spread) on either name. We can calculate the sensitivity of the F2D from the value formula above, and compare with the CDS sensitivities – this gives two equations for the notional amounts in the two CDS contracts. **The F2D hedge ratios turn out to be less than 100%** (even though – at zero correlation – the correct premium for the F2D is the sum of the CDS premia).

Exercise 3
Why are F2D hedge ratios not 100% even at zero correlation?

The answer ultimately rests on the fact that the incidence of cashflows is different under an F2D compared with the portfolio of CDS contracts. If we were dealing with contracts where the premium is paid as a single up-front amount (given by the value of contingent benefits) we get the intuitive result that the F2D up-front premium is the sum of the CDS up-front premia but we would still find the F2D hedge ratios are not 100%.

If we view the F2D as two CDS contracts less a forward contingent purchase (at a known annual premium rate) of a CDS on the surviving name, then we can see immediately where the difference in sensitivity comes from. It is the contingent forward CDS deal which differentiates the F2D from the two CDS prior to the default of one name. We would therefore expect the F2D hedge ratios to decline as we look to higher spread names (because the contingent forward deal is more and more likely to be triggered). The reader can check this in the 'Chapter 9 and Chapter 19 hedge theory.mcd' sheet, or by implementing the formulae in Excel.

S2D Valuation

Three cases give rise to a premium stream:

1. Both names survive to time $t \leq T$.
2. Name A defaults at time $t_1 < t$ and B survives to $t < T$.
3. Name B defaults at time $t_1 < t$ and A survives to $t < T$.

This gives us the value of the premium stream p_2 for the second-to-default:

$$P_2 = p_2 \left\{ \int_0^T \exp[-(\lambda_A + \lambda_B + r)t]\, dt + \int_0^T [1 - \exp(-\lambda_A t)] \exp[-(\lambda_B + r)t]\, dt \right.$$

$$\left. + \int_0^T [1 - \exp(-\lambda_B t)] \exp[-(\lambda_A + r)t]\, dt \right\}$$

(19.4)

We can expand and simplify this to get

$$P_2 = p_2 \cdot \left\{ \frac{1 - \exp[-(\lambda_B + r)T]}{\lambda_B + r} + \frac{1 - \exp[-(\lambda_A + r)T]}{\lambda_A + r} - \frac{1 - \exp[-(\lambda_A + \lambda_B + r)T]}{\lambda_A + \lambda_B + r} \right\}$$

(19.5)

A capital payoff is made in one of two cases:

1. Name A defaults at time $t_1 < t$ and B defaults at $t < T$
2. Name B defaults at time $t_1 < t$ and A defaults at $t < T$.

This gives the value for the contingent benefits of

$$B_2 = \int_0^T [1 - \exp(-\lambda_A t)] \exp[-(\lambda_B + r)t] \lambda_B \cdot (1 - R_B)\, dt$$

$$+ \int_0^T [1 - \exp(-\lambda_B t)] \exp[-(\lambda_A + r)t] \lambda_A \cdot (1 - R_A)\, dt$$

(19.6)

Expanding, integrating and simplifying gives

$$B_2 = \text{CDS}_B \frac{1 - \exp[-(\lambda_B + r)T]}{\lambda_B + r} + \text{CDS}_A \frac{1 - \exp[-(\lambda_A + r)T]}{\lambda_A + r}$$

$$-(\text{CDS}_A + \text{CDS}_B) \frac{1 - \exp[-(\lambda_A + \lambda_B + r)T]}{\lambda_A + \lambda_B + r}$$

(19.7)

So the capital value of a long protection S2D deal in these circumstances is

$$V_2 = (CDS_B - p_2) \cdot \frac{1 - \exp[-(\lambda_B + r)T]}{\lambda_B + r} + (CDS_A - p_2)\frac{1 - \exp[-(\lambda_A + r)T]}{\lambda_A + r}$$

$$-(CDS_A + CDS_B - p_2)\frac{1 - \exp[-(\lambda_A + \lambda_B + r)T]}{\lambda_A + \lambda_B + r} \tag{19.8}$$

The fair value new CDS premium is given by finding the p_2 which makes the trade value zero. Examples are given in the Mathcad example sheet.

Exercise 4
The above formula gives a non-zero S2D premium. Clearly the S2D has some value and so has a positive (non-zero) premium no matter how remote the probability that both names default. Consider two portfolios (of the same maturity):

1. A CDS on name A and a CDS on name B; both names are subject to 100 bp premia
2. A F2D on names A and B at 200 bp, and a S2D on names A and B at 8.8 bp.

In the zero correlation case, if I buy first-to-default and second-to-default protection I am paying more than the sum of the two CDS premia. Both portfolios – FSD plus S2D or CDS$_A$ plus CDS$_B$ – give the same capital protection: why should the F2D plus S2D portfolio cost more?

It is true that the two portfolios have the same capital (contingent payoff) flows in all cases – whether there are no defaults, whether A defaults and B survives, whether B defaults and A survives, or whether both default before the maturity date. But the premium flows are different. We have seen that the F2D premium is a high number ($=$ the sum of the CDS at zero correlation); the S2D premium is typically a low number – much less than the lower of the CDS premia in the case of zero correlation. Imagine for a moment that the F2D plus S2D premium is the same as the sum of the CDS premia. If no defaults occur, the same premium is paid on both portfolios. But in any other event, after the first name defaults, less premium is paid on the S2D contract than on the remaining CDS (whichever name survives). Hence the premium in the case where both names survive has to exceed the sum of the CDS premia. (This argument is true at any correlation except 100%.)

Exercise 5
Prove that if the interest rate is 4% and recovery is assumed to be 50% then the S2D premium above is 8.8 bp.

Exercise 6
Do the F2D plus S2D hedge ratios add to 100%?

No. At this stage the result probably does not surprise you. For 1000 bp and 2000 bp names and a 5-year F2D and S2D together we find that the hedge ratios are approximately 105% in the first name and 120% in the second. At 100 bp and 200 bp we find 103% and 107%.

19.3.2   100% Correlation: Exact Pricing

We shall use the default time simulation process of Chapter 18. We simulate 100% correlated defaults, and then value various portfolio products. What does this mean?

We saw in Chapter 18 that we could obtain a default time from a random number (equation (18.3) reproduced below). If default times are 100% correlated then this means that we use the same random number to generate the default times for names A, B, ... – a single random number x generates the default times for all the names i in the portfolio:

$$t_i = \frac{-\ln[\Phi(x)]}{\lambda_i}$$

Note that if name A has a 1% hazard rate, and name B has a 2% hazard rate, then name A defaults after twice the time it takes B to default. For example, if the randomly generated probability is 0.015, then A defaults after $-\ln(0.15)/0.01 = 420$ years, while B defaults after $-\ln(0.15)/0.02 = 210$ years.[2]

Suppose A has a higher hazard rate (lower survival probability and shorter simulated default time) than B. Then the probability that A and B survive to time t is just the probability that A survives to time t. If we are looking at F2D and S2D contracts; then the F2D is triggered if and only if CDS_A is triggered, and the S2D is triggered if and only if CDS_B is triggered. Thus the F2D *is* CDS_A and therefore has the same premium and is exactly hedged by a 100% holding in name A, and the S2D *is* CDS_B.

We can also follow through the probability formulae to calculate the premia and hedge ratios explicitly – this is done in the 'Chapter 9 and Chapter 19 hedge theory.mcd' sheets. In this case the sum of the basket premia is equal to (and not greater than) the sum of the CDS premia.

Recovery Uncertainty

There is one oversimplification we have made which is particularly relevant at 100% correlation. Consider the following.

Exercise 7
At 100% correlation, calculate the F2D and S2D for a two name basket where name A has 100 bp CDS, and name B has 200 bp CDS. When is the F2D premium 100 bp, and the S2D premium 200 bp? Is an F2D premium of 184 bp possible (maintaining the 100% correlation assumption)?

The F2D premium may in fact be anywhere between 100 bp and 200 bp and the S2D is then 300 bp minus the F2D premium. If we assume that both names have 40% recovery, then the hazard rates (from equation (9.15)) are $0.01/0.6 = 0.01667$ and $0.02/0.6 = 0.03333$. Name B has the higher hazard rate and therefore defaults first, so F2D premium $= 200$ bp and S2D premium $= 100$ bp. But suppose B is junior debt while A is a secured bank loan: we might assume zero recovery for B, but 80% recovery for A. This gives a hazard rate of $0.02/1 = 0.02$ for B, and $0.01/0.2 = 0.05$ for A. A has the higher default rate and defaults first, so F2D premium $= 100$ bp and S2D premium $= 200$ bp.

---

[2] This may make no intuitive sense and/or the model may seem to be nonsensical. Nevertheless this is a result of the mathematical model. The question whether this is or is not a realistic model is discussed later.

Table 19.2   F2D and S2D pricing under recovery uncertainty (100% correlation)
The CDS on name A is assumed to be 100 bp, and on name B is 200 bp

Assumed recovery A	Implied hazard rate A	Assumed recovery B	Implied hazard rate B	F2D premium	S2D premium	Probability
0.0	100 bp	0.0	200 bp	200 bp	100 bp	$0.25 \times 0.25 = 0.0625$
0.4	167 bp	0.0	200 bp	200 bp	100 bp	$0.55 \times 0.25 = 0.1375$
0.9	1000 bp	0.0	200 bp	100 bp	200 bp	$0.2 \times 0.25 = 0.05$
0.0	100 bp	0.4	333 bp	200 bp	100 bp	$0.25 \times 0.55 = 0.1375$
0.4	167 bp	0.4	333 bp	200 bp	100 bp	$0.55 \times 0.55 = 0.3025$
0.9	1000 bp	0.4	333 bp	100 bp	200 bp	$0.2 \times 0.55 = 0.11$
0.0	100 bp	0.9	2000 bp	200 bp	100 bp	$0.25 \times 0.2 = 0.05$
0.4	167 bp	0.9	2000 bp	200 bp	100 bp	$0.55 \times 0.2 = 0.11$
0.9	1000 bp	0.9	2000 bp	200 bp	100 bp	$0.2 \times 0.2 = 0.04$

However, what we have so far is a modelling oversimplification. We are assuming a recovery rate and deriving an implied hazard rate from CDS data. In the case of CDS pricing (Section 9.5) we saw that this was possible and reasonable as long as recovery and hazard rates are independent – and then the recovery rate is just the (statistically) expected recovery rate. But now we are valuing more complicated products and the presence of recovery uncertainty should be considered.

We implement the recovery uncertainty model of Part II section 9.2. Imagine the following. Both A and B have an expected recovery of 40%, but we have an uncertainty (standard deviation) of 30%. We can model this by assuming 0, 40% or 90% as possible recovery rates with probabilities p_0, p_{mean} and $1 - p_0 - p_{mean}$. We have two equations for the mean and standard deviation to solve in two unknowns:

$$0.4 = p_{mean} \cdot 0.4 + (1 - p_0 - p_{mean}) \cdot 0.9$$

and

$$0.3^2 = 0.4^2 \cdot p_0 + 0.5^2 \cdot (1 - p_0 - p_{mean})$$

We find $p_0 = 0.25$ and $p_{mean} = 0.55$ (and $p_{90} = 0.20$). If we assume that recoveries on A and B are independent, then we can perform nine different pricings and get the results shown in Table 19.2.

The expected premium for the F2D and S2D respectively are therefore

$$200 \times (0.0625 + 0.1375 + 0.1375 + 0.3025 + 0.05 + 0.11 + 0.04) + 100$$
$$\times (0.05 + 0.11) = 184$$

$$100 \times (0.0625 + 0.1375 + 0.1375 + 0.3025 + 0.05 + 0.11 + 0.04) + 200$$
$$\times (0.05 + 0.11) = 116$$

Note that the sum is unchanged, but hedge ratios for the F2D are 84% name B and 16% name A.

We can see that different assumed recovery rates for different names, or uncertainty over the recovery rate, means that the premium for an F2D under 100% correlation may be less than the highest individual CDS premium.

Extending this method to higher dimensionality products rapidly becomes unmanageable. For a three name basket we need 27 valuations, four names require 81 valuations, and 12 names require over half a million valuations. A practical solution is to perform a small number of simulations for some randomly chosen combinations of recoveries (the random choices being driven by the probability of that combination of recoveries).

Exercise 8
Show that recovery uncertainty has no impact when correlation is zero.

20
Collateralised Debt Obligations

Collateralised debt obligation (CDO) deals, which were started in the late 1980s, usually related to US high-yield reference names. Originally they were collateralised bond obligations (CBOs), then structures related to loans were introduced (collateralised loan obligations – CLOs), then structures related to bonds and loans (CDOs), and finally synthetic or partly synthetic structures on a much wider class of underlying reference risks.

A CDO is best thought of as a product that provides protection on some or all of the 'tranches' of losses on a reference pool of risks (i.e. on instruments which define the magnitude of losses on the occurrence of a credit event). The terms 'tranched default basket' (TDB) or 'tranche of protection' are often used and are a better description of the tranches of protection that form the underlying product. Occasionally a 'single tranche of a CDO' is misleadingly referred to as a 'single tranche CDO'. CDO may be used to refer to the entire structure of all tranches and the reference pool (and hedges), or may just refer to a single tranche.

It should be noted that the reference pool does not need to exist as an actual portfolio 'hedging' the CDO. Typically that reference pool merely defines the risk – the CDO is the protection on losses relating to that reference pool. Note also that there are usually no substitution rights on mergers of names in the reference pool.

In this chapter we shall define the CDO structures and look at various forms of CDO covering a range of applications. In addition we shall look at some standard portfolios and tranching structures.

20.1 STATIC SYNTHETIC CDO

20.1.1 Product Definition

A **reference pool** is a list of credit risky entities and related assets. The list defines the legal entities on which the risk is taken, and defines the asset, the size of the exposure, and how the loss is to be determined, should a credit event occur.

The reference pool is **static** if, once it has been defined and a deal done on that reference pool, no additions or substitutions of reference entities or assets occur. Only credit events affect the pool, reducing the number of entities and assets covered.

A reference pool is **synthetic** if some or all of the instruments defining losses are non-cash assets. Examples include CDSs or legal agreements transferring risk between one body (typically a commercial bank) and another body (typically an SPV). We shall look at a variety of examples later.

For the purposes of this section think of a **static synthetic reference pool** as a fixed list of CDS deals. Such a pool is typically long of risk only. Note that the reference pool is merely a list of reference entities and/or assets. It need not exist as a portfolio of assets owned by an investor.

A **tranche of protection** (also called a 'tranche', a 'CDO tranche', or – rather misleadingly – an 'nth loss piece') on the reference pool with **attachment points** $[a, b]$ reimburses losses between $a\%$ and $b\%$ on the total notional of the pool. The **notional size** of the tranche is the percentage size multiplied by the notional size of the reference pool.

Example 1

The [3%, 6%] tranche on a EUR1 bn reference pool of 125 reference entities covers losses from EUR 30 m up to EUR 60 m related to that reference pool.

The collection of all tranches (collectively covering 0–100% of losses) is referred to as a **CDO**. Many varieties of CDO will be described in this chapter, and many variations in the product.

The tranches of protection also go under a variety of different names which carry less information than knowing the attachment points.

1. The **first loss piece** (FLP) of a CDO absorbs the losses up to a predefined percentage of the sum of the notional on a portfolio of reference names. It is the [0, b] tranche of a CDO, also called the **equity piece**. The latter term has come into use because in some structures the originator of the deal 'retains' (i.e. writes protection on) the equity piece and also keeps all residual income after paying contractual costs. In this case the originator of the deal is more like an equity shareholder, rather than a bond holder, in that the return is very uncertain.
2. A **mezzanine** or **second/third/...loss piece** starts to absorb losses once the first loss piece is exhausted. Mezzanine tranches may also be called 'junior' (more risky') or 'senior' (less risky).
3. The **senior** piece is the least risky [a, 100] tranche. If the senior tranche is rated AAA, and if the reference pool could suffer several defaults before the senior tranche loses its AAA status, then it is referred to as **super senior**. The tranche adjacent to the super senior tranche is then sometimes called the **senior** tranche.
4. Actual names used in the CDO documentation vary – synthetic static CDOs are increasingly giving just the attachment points. Cash deals and older transactions may give the tranches names – A, B, C, ... being typical albeit unimaginative names.

Usually there are 3–7 tranches of protection covering the entire nominal of the portfolio, though single tranche [0, 100] CDOs are now common (and often thought of, incorrectly, as average baskets). If a deal is a single tranche then the attachment points of the other tranches are irrelevant.

Figure 20.1 and Table 20.1 illustrate the above for a standardised tranching structure based on the iTraxx[1] portfolio. Every reference entity exposure is the same notional size – say 8m to give a total notional on 125 names of EUR1 bn. Note that the reference pool is an index portfolio managed by International Index Company. The CDO tranches are products traded by various banks based on the index portfolio.

The protection writer of the tranche receives a premium – this is covered in more detail in the following section.

Impact of Credit Events on the Junior Tranches

Suppose a deal is done on 9 July 2004 for a maturity of 20 September 2009, and credit events on reference names occur during the life of the deal. Each reference name accounts for 0.8%

---

[1] iTraxx indices are managed by International Index Company, and are described in more detail in section 20.2 below.

Reference pool	Tranching
	[0, 3%] 'equity tranche'
Portfolio of 125 reference 5-year CDS deals of equal size	[3%, 6%]
	[6%, 9%]
	[9%, 12%]
	[12%, 22%]
	[78%, 100%]

Figure 20.1   Standard tranching structure based on the iTraxx reference pool

of notional and suppose that recovery is 30% on the first, fourth, seventh, etc., default, 50% on the second, fifth, eighth, and 70% on the others, so credit events causes a loss of

$$0.8\% \times (0.7, 0.5, 0.3) = (0.56\%, 0.4\%, 0.24\%)$$

The impact of the defaults on the junior tranches is given in Table 20.2.

Impact of Credit Events on the Senior Tranches

Example 2

Suppose the first-loss-piece of a CDO is 2%, and suppose a default amounting to 1% of notional (one name out of 100 in the reference pool) occurs and the loss to the FLP is 0.5%. The notional of this tranche reduces from 2% to 0.5%. The notional of the reference pool is 99% of the original amount. Suppose there is a single mezzanine tranche of 3%, and a senior tranche of 95%. After this first exposure the total protection is 1.5% + 3% + 95% = 99.5%. The mezzanine piece still protects 3% of the original notional; the senior piece also seems to protect 95% of the original portfolio. If the entire portfolio defaulted, with 50% recoveries, then the equity and mezzanine tranches would suffer a further 4.5% loss, and the senior piece would suffer the balance, (99% × 0.5) − 4.5% = 45%. The outstanding notional on the senior piece (50%) would remain – even though there was no surviving portfolio to protect – and the senior piece would continue to receive premium (a reward for no risk at this stage).

Although some CDO senior tranches are documented as above, more frequently the following procedure is applied. For every credit event affecting the reference pool, recovery amounts are deducted from the notional exposure of the senior tranche. In the above example, after the first default, the senior tranche reduces to 94.5% of notional and, if all names default, the

Table 20.1 Partial listing of the reference pool for the DJ iTraxx portfolio (June 2004)

Autos	Consumer cyclicals and non-cyclicals	Energy	Financials
AB Volvo	AB Electrolux	BP Plc	ABBEY National Plc
Bayerische Motoren Werke AG	Accor	E.on AG	Aegon NV
Compagnie Financiere Michelin	Boots Group Plc	Electricidade de Portugal, SA	Allianz AG
Continental AG	Compass Group Plc	Electricite de France	Assicurazioni Generali – SPA
DaimlerChrysler AG	Deutsche Lufthansa AG	Endesa, SA	Aviva Plc
GKN Holdings Plc	Dixons Group Plc	Enel SPA	AXA
Peugeot SA	GUS Plc	Energie Baden-Wuerttemberg AG	Banca Intesa SPA
Renault	Hilton Group Plc	Fortum OYJ	Banca Monte dei Paschi di Siena SPA
Valeo	Kingfisher Plc	Iberdrola, SA	Banco Bilbao Vizcaya Argentaria, SA
Volkswagen AG	Koninklijke Philips Electronics NV	National Grid Transco Plc	Banco Comercial Portugues, SA
	LVMH Moet Hennessy Louis Vuitton	Repsol YPF SA	Banco Santander Central Hispano, SA
	Marks and Spencer Plc	RWE AG	Bayerische Hypo-und Vereinsbank AG
	Pinault-Printemps-Redoute	Scottish Power UK Plc	Capitalia SPA
	Sodexho Alliance	Suez	Commerzbank AG
	Thomson	Technip	Credit Suisse Group
	British American Tobacco Plc	Total SA	Deutsche Bank AG
	Allied Domecq Plc	Union Fenosa, SA	Dresdner Bank AG
	Cadbury Schweppes Plc	United Utilities Plc	Hannover Rueckversicherung AG
	Carrefour	Vattenfall AB	HSBC Bank Plc
	Casino Guichard-Perrachon	Veolia Environnement	ING Bank NV
	Diageo Plc		Lloyds TSB Bank Plc
	Gallaher Group Plc		Muenchener Rueck AG
	Groupe Danone		Swiss Reinsurance Company
	Henkel KgaA		The Royal Bank of Scotland Plc
	Imperial Tobacco Group Plc		Unicredito italiano SPA

Table 20.2   Impact of defaults on the two junior tranches in Example 1

Credit event number	Loss	Outstanding protection on the [0, 3%] tranche	Outstanding protection on the [3%, 6%] tranche	Outstanding protection on the [6%, 9%] tranche
0		3%	3%	3%
1	0.56%	2.44	3.00	3.00
2	0.40%	2.04	3.00	3.00
3	0.24%	1.80	3.00	3.00
4	0.56%	1.24	3.00	3.00
5	0.40%	0.84	3.00	3.00
6	0.24%	0.60	3.00	3.00
7	0.56%	0.04	3.00	3.00
8	0.40%	0.00	2.64	3.00
9	0.24%	0.00	2.40	3.00
10	0.56%	0.00	1.84	3.00
11	0.40%	0.00	1.44	3.00
12	0.24%	0.00	1.20	3.00
13	0.56%	0.00	0.64	3.00
14	0.40%	0.00	0.24	3.00
15	0.24%	0.00	0.00	3.00
16	0.56%	0.00	0.00	2.44
17	0.40%	0.00	0.00	2.04

senior tranche suffers losses of 45% (total portfolio loss less 2% + 3%), and has a remaining notional of zero (95% − 45% losses −50% recoveries).

Note that, since premium is usually related to notional outstanding, the former treatment of losses and recoveries is advantageous to the senior tranche writer (and therefore the premium should be lower).

20.1.2   Premium Waterfall

Associated with the tranche's notional size is a premium. As the remaining notional reduces, the premium on the tranche also reduces. We use the term 'premium waterfall' to describe how this happens. The term 'waterfall' is used later to describe a more complicated related feature for 'cashflow CDOs'.

Premium is generally expressed as a percentage of (or number of basis points applied to) the notional of the tranche. In example 2 above the [2%, 5%] mezzanine piece is an initial USD 30m notional (absorbing losses from 20m to 50m) if the reference pool is USD 1bn of risks. If it was subject to an initial premium of 250 bp, then the premium would initially be USD 750 000. After five defaults with 50% losses (= 25m losses since each notional reference name exposure is 10m) the mezzanine tranche would reduce to 25m and the premium would typically remain at 250 bp on the outstanding notional, so reduce to USD 625 000.

Premia are typically quarterly in arrears with a proportionate premium related to the losses occurring during the quarter and the credit event dates (similar to vanilla CDSs). Similar variations in premium occur, with different frequencies being common. Occasionally premia are fixed amounts independent of defaults (guaranteed to maturity, the equivalent of an up-front premium with no rebate).

Exercise 1

Suppose a 5-year reference portfolio has 100 reference names, each of which has the same 200 bp CDS premium, and we assume 50% recovery for all names. Approximately how many defaults would you expect to occur and what size tranche would be just wiped out by this number of defaults? How much variation in the number of defaults would you expect and what other tranches would be affected by this variation? Suppose we assumed that recovery was 0%, how much would this affect the results?

Hint: On a single name the hazard rate is given by equation (9.15) and the survival probability over five years is given by equation (9.6) (with constant hazard rate) – roughly these are a 4% default rate and an 82% survival/18% default probability over five years. If all defaults are independent then the expected number of defaults is given by the binomial distribution and is $100 \times 18\% = 18$ defaults or 9% losses. The standard deviation of the binomial is $\sqrt{(100 \times 0.18 \times 0.82)} = 3.8$, so we would anticipate between roughly 10 and 26 defaults or between 5% and 13% losses (taking two standard deviations).

Exercise 2

Suppose the premium on the 1% equity tranche of a risky underlying 5-year portfolio is 200% (200 00 bp). How much premium is paid to that tranche over its life? What risks are there to both the buyer and the seller of protection, and how might the risks be lessened?

Hint: In one year twice the notional size of the tranche is paid in premium if there are no defaults. Consequently, the equity piece is expected to have a short life.

The equity tranche is subject to a variety of further premium variations. Often the premium is a combination of a fixed up-front amount (say 40% of notional) and an ongoing 'small' premium of, say, 500 bp. The premium on the FLP of the iTraxx/CDX-based CDOs are of this form.

A further variation of equity premium is as follows. For each reference name there is an agreed premium: name A 200 bp, name B 20 bp, name C 35 bp, name D 60 bp, ... The initial premium on the equity piece may be 10% of a 3% notional = EUR 3m on a EUR 1bn reference portfolio. On default of name A (the first-to-default) the reference portfolio suffers a notional loss of income of 200 bp × EUR 10m = EUR 200 000. The premium on the equity piece reduces by this amount to EUR 2.8m. Default of name B causes the premium to reduce further to EUR 2.78m, etc.

The above 'equity premium waterfall' typically reduces more slowly than the previously described percentage of outstanding notional. Theoretically the equity tranche may be wiped out, although the premium being paid is still a substantial proportion of the original amount. Usually the premium terminates when the tranche is exhausted.

20.1.3 Documentation; CDO Set-Up

No standard format for CDO contracts exists. Unlike a CDS contract, which is usually a few pages long, CDO documentation may be several hundred pages long (for each tranche). Documentation for synthetic static CDOs tends to be shortest – a little longer than a CDS contract – and usually appends a list of terms unique to the CDO structure.

Tranches of protection on a CDO may be bought or sold off a client's own balance sheet. An alternative is to set up the CDO structure through a Special Purpose Vehicle (SPV: see Part II, section 13.1, and below). The latter usually applies to collateralised structures, often cash structures, and sometimes all tranches (or all but the equity piece) of protection are bought. We shall look at a variety of examples later.

20.1.4   CDO Tranches; Funded and Unfunded Tranches; 'Buying' and 'Selling'

The reader should see a CDO tranche as a deal in its own right (which indeed it is) not requiring the existence of any further structure. There may be no other tranches of protection bought or sold – perhaps just a single mezzanine tranche on a reference portfolio. In addition the reference pool of assets may not (and typically does not) exist as an actual portfolio held on someone's books. A typically 'CDO deal' amounts to only some of the tranches of protection being bought or sold. It is very rare for a reference portfolio of assets to be bought, and all tranches of protection to be bought from third parties.

A tranche of protection may be split into many transactions ('deals') all ranking *pari passu* with each other. A deal may be set up in two forms:

1. A premium is paid in exchange for capital protection paid as and when a credit event occurs – known as 'CDS style'.
2. The protection is embedded into a credit-linked note which carries a fixed or floating coupon (which includes the tranche premium) in return for the notional exposure of the deal (though sometimes CLNs are priced below par).

Recall that the sale of a CLN by bank X corresponds to the purchase of protection by bank X. Buying protection via CDS style deals may be accompanied by the sale of CLNs related to the same tranches, to achieve the same object.

'CDS style' deals related to a CDO are also referred to **unfunded deals**, while CLN deals are **funded deals**.

Exercise

For a given reference pool of assets, what is the economic difference between the following?

1. A [3%, 6%] tranche related to a USD 1bn sized pool of which 15m is in CDS form and 15m is in CLN form, the two deals ranking *pari passu*.
2. A [3%, 6%] tranche related to a USD 500m sized pool which is in CDS form, and a [3%, 6%] tranche related to a USD 500m sized pool which is in CLN form (the two deals are unrelated other than having the same reference pool).

Answer: None.

'Buying' and 'selling'

Often investors think in terms of CLN (funded) structures and, treating a CLN as a bond, talk in terms of 'buying a tranche' when what is meant is the purchase of a CLN with embedded CDO risk. For investors, 'buying' means buying risk – corresponding to buying *a* bond – and therefore writing protection. For non-funded deals particularly the meaning of 'buy' or 'sell' has to be clarified by adding 'risk' or 'protection'.

20.1.5   Relationship to *n*th-to-default

We saw in Chapter 19 that *n*th-to-default products are generally first-to-default for a notional amount of EUR/USD 10–20m on 2–10 reference names. In contrast CDO deals may be for any tranche of protection (high risk to low risk), and typically refer to a reference pool of EUR/USD 500m–5bn and between 50 and 500 reference risks.

Despite these large differences in deal characteristics, there is a close theoretical relationship between the two products. Consider a portfolio of N reference names – it does not matter what N is; we shall take $N = 10$ for illustration. Suppose each risk is of 10m giving a total notional of 100m. Suppose all recoveries are 0%. The first default gives rise to a loss and would trigger an F2D contract (of, say, 10m size). It would also wipe out the capital protection granted by a 10% equity piece (and the premium on the equity piece would terminate). The second-to-default would trigger an S2D contract (again of 10m) and would wipe out a 10% junior mezzanine tranche.

Thus if recoveries are zero an 'nth-to-default contract (in $100/N$ notional) is identical to an $[(n-1) \times 100/N, n \times 100/N]$ tranche of a CDO, for $n = 1, \ldots, N$, where N is the number of reference entities in the pool.

If recoveries are not zero the 10m notional F2D pays par in exchange for defaulted debt – so effectively pays 5m if recovery is 50%, and the deal then terminates. If we make the equity piece 5m so that it terminates on the F2D, then there is a difference in the premium rates because the F2D is based on 10m while the equity piece is based on 5m. There is therefore still a close correspondence but not an exact match between the contracts if recoveries are not zero. This correspondence is useful for code testing.

20.1.6   Arbitrage CDOs

Synthetic static CDO structures have been used by investment banks since the late 1990s. Typically these were based on a reference portfolio of 100 investment grade names which are liquid in the CDS market and usually either entirely EU or entirely North American names. The investment bank would typically buy protection on mezzanine tranches 'cheaply',[2] buy protection on the large senior tranche (in order to limit its own capital usage) at a 'fair price' or slightly above, and **retain** the equity risk – effectively obtaining protection on all tranches.[3] 'Retaining' the risk effectively means that the originating bank is writing protection on that tranche to the desk originating the deal. Typically it does not enter into a contract with itself to do so, but simply owns the risk by not buying protection. Often it will allocate internal capital to the full extent of the equity tranche – effectively paying a 100% notional up-front premium. Usually this is done by valuing the risk at notional in the bank's accounts. Some banks will value the risk using a model such as that described in Chapter 21.

The originating desk now owns all tranches of protection and enters into a hedge where it sells protection on all the underlying names. The set-up is illustrated in Figure 20.2.

The desk receives premia on the individual name CDS deals, and pays premia on the tranches. Any excess of the income on the CDS over the cost of protection is retained by the desk (i.e. the originating bank). If the equity tranche is not wiped out by losses then any excess capital

---

[2] We shall define 'fair price' and what we mean by 'cheap' in section 20.3.
[3] Some banks have favourable regulatory treatment, which means that they do not have to source protection externally. Those that do need to, and who find a potential writer of protection in the form of an insurance company, may face further complications. Capital reduction was only obtained if the protection was via an OECD bank, so it was often necessary to 'wash' the deal through an OECD bank with favourable regulatory treatment, which in turn dealt with the insurance company (often through an SPV).

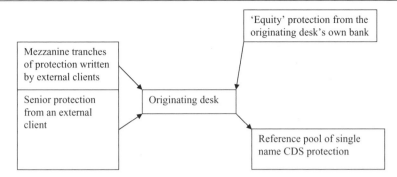

Figure 20.2 Static synthetic arbitrage CDO set-up

is released back to the bank at maturity. Such deals could generally be done to yield a profit and became known as 'arbitrage CDOs'.

Example

Suppose the average spread on 100 names is 100 bp with 10m exposure each. The initial income is 1bn × 1% = 10m per annum. Tranching may be 3% (retained), 7% at 200 bp (average over several tranches), and 90% at 10 bp. The cost of the external tranches is

$$70m \times 2\% + 900m \times 0.1\% = 1.4m + 0.9m = 2.3m$$

leaving an excess of 7.7m and an exposure of 30m – an effective premium of just over 25%. The best case result would be no default, in which case the bank loses no capital and earns 7.7m × 5 years. The worst case is immediate defaults of all names – in which case the 30m capital is lost.

Exercise
Calculate the expected profit using the CDO valuation software ('CDO pricer.xls').

Hint: The expected profit is the net value of the assets held. The individual reference CDSs (traded at fair market premium) have zero net value. The tranches will have been dealt in at prices different from the fair market premium.

The question of hedging the structure above is discussed in section 21.5.2. The obvious (default event) hedge of 10m notional in each reference name (in the above example) may lead to a large (30% or so) mismatch in terms of spread risk depending on the amount and form of the premia paid for the tranches – and in particular for the equity piece.

20.2   INDEX PORTFOLIOS AND STANDARD CDO STRUCTURES

Although the iTraxx and CDX portfolios are used to create nothing more than static synthetic CDOs, we describe these products, their background and related products in a little more detail. The key difference between these index products and 'bespoke'[4] static synthetic CDOs is that

---

[4] A deal based on a list of reference entities, and a tranching structure, chosen to suit the client.

the former actively trade in the secondary market, whereas the latter are typically primary trades only.

These indices and products based on them are the key liquid CDO trading products, are currently the data source for 'implied correlation' data, and are the primary hedging vehicle for correlation and other risks arising from bespoke CDO transactions.

20.2.1   Background and Terminology

Background

Credit portfolio indices and standard portfolio CD products largely developed over the last five years. The iTraxx and CDX products outlined below were introduced in 2004. The indices are managed by International Index Company (IIC), and replace the TRAC-X (Morgan Stanley & JPMorgan) and iBoxx indices that were set up and managed by groups of banks and other institutions. These latter indices were introduced in 2003, replacing earlier products such as Morgan Stanley's 'TRACERS', and rapidly became popular. The latest versions of these indices will change over time, but most of the general features described below are shared with their legacy products and will probably be inherited by successors.

The 'indices' are sets of reference entities chosen by IIC based on CDS trading volume data supplied by around 20 banking institutions – see the Appendix for details. Trading on these indices, and on tranched CDO products based in these indices, takes place between counterparties (banks and other institutions) and does not involve IIC.

Index Structures

The motivation for developing CD products based on an index is to meet the needs of traders and investors who require a portfolio hedge or a portfolio exposure. The index product allows trading in relatively small size[5] yet gives exposure to a diverse portfolio of risks. As such it is a quick and low-cost means to get diversified exposure to spread risk. It also provides a clear index of the performance of credit markets. An index provides a liquid, efficient, convenient and transparent means of trading general credit risk.

Standard tranche products are of major benefit to the professional institutions structuring credit solutions for clients. Where the bespoke client structure introduces correlation, the presence of an actively traded CDO gives a means to hedge the correlation risk embedded in the client structure using a liquid and relatively tightly priced standard instrument. They also provide transparent pricing information on implied correlation and its relationship to tranches for a relatively diverse portfolio.

The construction of the indices, and the products based on them, is discussed in more detail in section 20.2.2 onwards. First, we present some terminology.

Average Basket, Portfolio CDS and Single Tranche CDO, CDO Tranches

Index-based CDS contracts are actually set up as single tranche CDOs rather than pure average baskets. An average basket (see Chapter 8) will have a premium rate associated with each

---

[5] If an investor deals in a 9m [3%, 6%] tranche then the reference pool is 300m, and the notional of each underlying reference entity is $300/125 = 2.4$m. Since the tranche itself is a liquid-traded product the counterparty hedges with that product rather than with many small deals in the underlying reference names.

reference name; after default of that reference entity the total premium paid on the basket reduces by the premium rate associated with the defaulted name multiplied by the notional of that name. In practice, index-based CDSs are [0, 100] tranches ('single tranche CDOs'), and have a premium rate defined by the portfolio at the outset.[6] A default of a single entity does not affect the premium rate – the total premium falls by the rate applied to the notional for the entity defaulting. Thus the usual set-up for an index CDS is more correctly described as a CDO on the reference portfolio, where the CDO has a single tranche only. (Note that the term 'single tranche CDO' is often used to mean a '[a, b] tranche' rather than a [0, 100] tranche.)

20.2.2   Composition of the Indices

The single name CDS market has strived to build up liquidity in as broad a range of underlying names as possible. The portfolio credit market has simultaneously developed CDOs based on portfolio structures. The indices managed by the International Index Company (IIC) are known as the iTraxx (European and Asian names) and CDX (North American names and managed CDS Indexco) are based on the most liquid names in the single name CDS market selected from a range of industry sectors. The reader is reminded that the detail of the make-up of these indices is likely to change: the current (August 2004) make-up of these portfolios is described in more detail in the Appendix. Key features are:

1. The indices are based on active names in the CDS market – market-makers are committed to providing daily data to enable the calculation of the index (being the average CDS premium).
2. A variety of indices are maintained: from a diversified investment grade portfolio of 125 names, to sector portfolios of 10–30 names, a 25-name subordinated financial portfolio, high premium and sub-investment grade portfolios. All names are equally weighted in each CDS-based index.
3. Reference portfolios are redefined every six months, are of standard 5- and 10-year maturities (to IMM dates), and are known as different 'series'. Deals related to 'series 1', for example, may be rolled into 'series 2' (on market terms at that time) when the next series is introduced, or the 'series 1' deal may be held to maturity (with the original list of reference names of course remaining unchanged).
4. The average CDS premium X is calculated at inception and is defined to be the premium for the single tranche CDO based on that portfolio. Deals done on the portfolio will change hands with the payment of a capital sum (representing the off-market value of the CDO and a 'basis' – see below).

20.2.3   Single tranche [0%, 100%] CDO Products

Funded and Unfunded Forms

Currently all the portfolios trade on a single tranche basis. The trade gives protection on the entire portfolio covering all losses between 0 and 100% subject to a predefined premium rate levied on the remaining notional only. All names in a reference portfolio have equal weightings. The 'portfolio' defines the reference pool, and the initial premium on the single tranche CDO

---

[6] The premium is the average spread. Even at outset this is not the correct 'fair value' premium, but trading takes place with an exchange of capital up-front.

is also defined when the portfolio composition is first announced. Deals may be in unfunded (CDS) form, or funded.

Example

Quoted from International Index Company:

> Counterparty buys €10m DJ iTraxx Europe Exposure in Unfunded/CDS Form
>
> *No Credit Event*
>
> - At issue of a given series, assume credit spread ('premium') of 45 bp
> - Market maker pays to counterparty 45 bp per annum quarterly on notional amount of €10m
> - With no Credit Events, the counterparty will continue to receive premium on original notional amount until maturity
>
> *Credit Event – Physical Settlement*
>
> - At issue of a given series, assume credit spread ('premium') of 45 bp
> - Market maker pays to counterparty 45 bp per annum quarterly on notional amount of €10m
> - A Credit Event occurs on Reference Entity, for example, in year 3
> - Reference Entity weighting is 0.8%
> - Counterparty pays to market maker $(0.8\% \times 10\,000\,000) = €80\,000$, and market maker delivers to counterparty €80 000 nominal face value of Deliverable Obligations of the Reference Entity
> - Notional amount on which premium is paid reduces by 0.8% to $99.2\% \times 10\,000\,000 = €9\,920\,000$
> - Post Credit Event, counterparty receives premium of 45 bp on €9.92m until maturity subject to any further credit events.

Note that the predecessor 'Euro TRAC-X' 100 name index suffered a credit event when Parmalat defaulted at the end of 2003, triggering a capital payment and a reduction in the outstanding notional on the junior tranche. The index then continued with 99 names and 99% of the initial notional.

The funded form would carry a Euribor+45 bp spread and mirrors the above: on a cash-settled credit event the investor receives the recovery amount and the notional of the note is effectively reduced by the defaulting notional (0.8%).

Initial Premium

We can see intuitively that the 'correct' premium for a single tranche CDO should be slightly below that for an average basket. Generally the higher spread names are expected to default first, which will reduce the premium on the average basket faster than a [0, 100] tranche. The effect is not large because the constituents have broadly similar spreads. For a 100 name equally weighted 5-year index with average spread of 60 bp and spreads in the 20–100 bp range, the average basket premium is initially 60 bp and the [0, 100] tranche premium is 59 bp. A new tranche deal may carry a 60 bp premium but will change hands with an additional capital payment up front.

Secondary Trading

Since the premium on the (single) tranche is fixed, secondary trading takes place with the payment of an up-front premium.

Calculation of the capital value of index protection should be performed within a CDO valuation tool, to correctly take into account the premium waterfall. Suppose the deal is traded on a premium date five years before maturity, where the (fixed) premium on the index is 60 bp but, because average spreads have risen, the fair premium for the tranche has risen to 70 bp. The approximate calculation is to discount the 10 bp excess quarterly premia at interest rates (say 4%) plus the hazard rate as if the CDO were a single reference entity (i.e. assume a 40% recovery so the hazard rate is $0.7/(1 - 0.4) = 1.17\%$, and we then discount at 5.17%) to give 0.44%. The capital value according to the Copula CDO pricing model may be 0.40%. Errors increase the more the diversity of spreads increases.

In addition to this difference between the average spread and the correct premium for the single tranche CDO, there will also be a 'basis' between where the product actually trades and the theoretically correct premium. Quoting from JPMorgan 'Credit Derivatives Strategy (Reproduced by permission of JPMorgan Securities Ltd): Introducing DJ iTraxx Europe Series 1', June 2004:

> As a note of caution, we have to emphasise that the DJ iTraxx index will not be trading exactly in line with the average of the single name CDS. Broadly there are two reasons for this. Firstly, there is a Basis to Theoretical between traded DJ iTraxx and the spread derived from the underlying CDS within it. Secondly there is the difference between the theoretical DJ iTraxx spread and the average spread level of the single name CDS.... the basis [to theoretical] has traded in a range between −8bp and +11 bp from July 2003 until today.

20.2.4 Standard Tranched CDO Structures: iTraxx and CDX

The large (125 name) European and North American name portfolios are additionally traded with a non-trivial tranching structure – these individual tranches trade actively, and also certain super tranches (e.g. the [3, 100]) constructed from them. The tranche attachment points are as follows (see Table 20.3).

1. iTraxx portfolio: these tranches are [0, 3], [3, 6], [6, 9], [9, 12], [12, 22]
2. CDX portfolio: these tranches are [0, 3], [3, 7], [7, 10], [10, 15], [15, 30]

From the point of view of a deal done on a specific reference portfolio (series) the CDO is a static synthetic deal. In two years' time when the deal has three years outstanding life there

Table 20.3 Example indicative quotes on the iTraxx Europe (July 2004)

5-year/tranche	Bid	Ask	Implied correlation
[0, 3] (+500 bp p.a.)	29.5%	31.5%	21%
[3, 6]	179 bp	199 bp	3%
[6, 9]	78 bp	84 bp	14%
[9, 12]	45 bp	50 bp	21%
[12, 22]	21 bp	25 bp	30%

10-year/tranche	Bid	Ask	Implied correlation
[0, 3] (+500 bp p.a.)	47.5%	51.5%	20%
[3, 6]	443 bp	483 bp	46%
[6, 9]	199 bp	229 bp	86%
[9, 12]	128 bp	143 bp	12%
[12, 22]	69 bp	79 bp	29%

may not be current average spreads quoted by market makers (and currently there is no plan to quote such spreads). Then current spreads will refer only to then current (5- and 10-year) series. Many traders and investors will roll their deals into the new series as it is announced.

Applications of Standard CDOs

The portfolio products (single tranche CDOs) can be used to go long or short protection (bearish or bullish of the underlying synthetic bonds). This can be used as a hedge, as an outright directional play, or as part of a sector trade using the smaller sector-based portfolios as described earlier (Part II, section 8.4).

The tranched CDO products define fair value market levels in those CDO tranches. **Most importantly, an active market in CDO tranches allows banks to create CDO structures tailored to clients' needs and put an effective hedge in place**. We discuss this in more detail in section 21.6.

20.2.5   Index Options and Modelling spread

The market for options on tranches of the iTraxx and CDX portfolios is less well developed and less active than that on the tranches themselves.

Product Description

- A limited range of maturity dates trade (the next and the following roll dates for the underlying portfolios).
- At-the-money forward strike only.
- European option.
- Up-front premium.
- Physical settlement (the buyer of the option is delivered a position in the underlying tranche; if the strike premium is different from the tranche premium then a capital sum is payable).
- If credit events on the underlying have already occurred then the protection can be immediately triggered leading to a capital payment or receipt.
- 'Call' is similar to a bond call – it is the right to buy risk/sell protection; similarly a 'put' is the right to buy protection; straddles also trade.

Example

Suppose the premium on the iTraxx [0, 100] is 51 bp mid. Assume the portfolio is a single name CDS with a gently upward sloping CDS curve. We can calculate the forward CDS premium in six months' time – suppose this is 55 bp. Prices for the options might be:

- Straddle: 50–70 cents
- Put: 30–40 cents
- Call: 20–30 cents

We can get a rough sanity check on these numbers as follows. At 55 bp the equivalent up-front premium (=expected loss) is about $55 \text{ bp} \times 4.5 = 2.5\%$ where we assume the 'duration' of the portfolio is 4.5. The volatility of the portfolio premium (and spreads) might be 50% per annum – for a six-month option the volatility of the forward value of the up-front premium is

$50\%/\sqrt{2} = 35\%$. An at-the-money option under the Black–Scholes model has a premium of 40% of the cash premium times the volatility for the period: $0.4 \times 2.5 \times 0.35 = 35$ cents (for either the call or the put). This is at the high end of the market quote, which implies that the volatility used was a little less than 50%.

> **Exercise**
> What is the implied volatility on the above straddle?

Typically these options are priced using the Black–Scholes model. We discuss the errors with this approach below.

Volatility

Volatility of the tranche premium is the key new variable driving the price of the option. This in turn is driven by the volatility of the CDS premia on the reference names, conditional on no default, and on the distribution of defaults up to the exercise date.

If default times on the portfolio were uncorrelated, then we could correctly price an option on a tranche as follows:

1. Simulate defaults using the uncorrelated Normal Copula.
2. At the exercise date, independently simulate forward spreads on non-defaulted names using an assumed spread distribution and volatility.
3. Valuation at the forward date can take into account defaults which occurred before the exercise date (the payoff under the portfolio protection can still be claimed), and the value of the portfolio protection on the remaining names.

Choice of the stochastic hazard rate process is completely open to us because all the reference entities are independent in the above situation. If, instead, we assumed all the names were 100% correlated, then if one of the names (the highest spread name if all the recovery rates are equal) defaults before the exercise date, then all the other default times are known precisely. In particular, the forward hazard rate process on the remaining names is known. In the general case, where there is some default time correlation, we need a forward hazard rate process that is consistent with the defaults that have actually occurred and with the remaining future defaults implied under the Normal Copula. The more defaults that have occurred on a particular simulation the more likely will there be several further defaults during the life of the deal – so the higher the implied spread levels on those names at the exercise date. See section 21.1 for more discussion of this topic.

We need a hazard rate simulation process which is consistent with the default time simulation model. There are two current approaches:

1. Use an Archimedean Copula. It is then possible to build in a hazard rate process consistent with the Copula (but having the unrealistic implications of Archimedean Copulae) (Schönbucher and Schubert, 2001).
2. Use the (calibrated) transition matrix approach (described in Part I), replacing the portfolio by a portfolio of seven spread levels (effectively defining our own ratings).

An alternative is an extension of the BET approach described in section 20.4. For each industry (or other 'tag') replace the actual number of holdings by a smaller number of uncorrelated holdings that have the same hazard rate, recovery rate and notional size. Then use the multinomial distribution to simulate defaults and survival to the exercise date. For the surviving names we simulate forward pseudo-hazard rates (by industry) using any convenient distribution (say lognormal). We can then calculate the forward value of the underlying tranche or portfolio.

20.3   CDO TERMINOLOGY AND VARIATIONS

In section 20.1 we discussed applications of the CDO structure where the underlying reference pool is static and synthetic – both arbitrage CDOs and index products. In this section we describe a variety of other variations in, and applications of, the CDO format. Most of the products described in this section exist with many different variations of detail. We aim to highlight the general form of the product, special issues faced for this form, and some ways of handling those issues. Section 20.3.1 defines a few terms frequently used in subsequent sections. Section 20.3.2 and following look at a variety of alternative CDO structures.

20.3.1   OC and IC Tests; WARF; Diversity Score

Coverage Tests

The following tests are the most commonly applied portfolio tests. In principle, any other test could be incorporated into a 'cashflow CDO' to trigger income diversion to a 'reserve' or 'collateral' account. An example of another test is the average spread on the portfolio, or the spread on any bond, compared to a predefined level.

Interest Coverage (IC) Test

The original form of the test came from the bond and loan market where it acted as a constraint on the issuance of debt by a company. The basic idea is to compare the collateral income to the outgo committed to that tranche and anything senior to it; the excess of income over servicing costs is called the **excess spread**.

Over-collateralisation (OC) Test

One definition is to take the ratio of the par amount of non-defaulted debt in the reference pool, plus expected recoveries on defaulted debt, to the tranche nominal for *pari passu* and senior tranches. The ratio has to exceed specified levels (greater than unity) which typically increase as we look at more senior tranches.

Variations in definition exist – for example, expected losses may be deducted from the numerator.

WARF Test

The calculation of WARF (weighted average rating factor) is described below. It is a measure of the average rating on the portfolio: for example, a rating factor of 360 corresponds to Baa2 on 5-year bonds. The WARF falling below a predefined level on a portfolio test date may trigger the diversion of excess cashflow to the reserve account.

Reserve or Collateral Account

The above tests, or other tests, may trigger diversion of excess cashflow into the 'reserve account' (also called an 'over-collateralisation' account). Funds in the reserve account may be released if defaults start to occur – the reserve account effectively acting as a new junior tranche to the extent that it holds any assets. Alternatively, funds in the reserve account may be used to repay tranches early (**amortising principal**).

WARF Calculation

Ratings are replaced by numerical rating according to the maturity of the individual asset. The numerical rating is weighted by the notional holding of the asset, and the sum over all assets is then divided by the total notional:

$$\text{WARF} = \frac{\sum_{i=1}^{n} N_i \cdot nr_i}{\sum_{i=1}^{n} N_i}$$

where *nr* is the numerical rating taken from the table of Moody's 'idealised' default probabilities – see Table 20.4.

Diversity Score and Calculation

This uses a Moody's defined table to derive the 'diversity score', D, for a portfolio. Apart from being used as a quantitative measure of a portfolio, the diversity score is a key step in Moody's 'binomial expansion technique' (described in section 20.4) used to analyse the default risks in a portfolio. The calculation steps are as follows:

1. Calculate the average notional exposure, A
2. Calculate a weighting for each name, $w = \text{minimum}(1, \text{total\_notional}/A)$.
3. For each industry group (of the Moody's defined groups) calculate the weight W for that industry by summing the above w's for each name in that industry.
4. Using the lookup table (Table 20.5) go from the industry weight W to the industry diversity score d.
5. Sum the d's over all industries to get the portfolio diversity score, D.

20.3.2   Cash and Cashflow CDOs

A **cash** CDO is one where the reference portfolio is physical assets – bonds or loans – and the reference portfolio actually exists as a 'risk' or 'hedging' pool. The key problem associated with cash CDOs is the ragged nature of bond maturities compared with the single maturity of the CDO. How is the excess (or deficit) of protection term to be handled in terms of premium paid and risk taken? Solutions include

(a) building up a cash reserve as bonds mature, and reducing the exposure for longer bond positions to maintain duration risk, and/or
(b) partial early maturity of the tranches with a reduction on notional and premium (*amortising principal*).

Table 20.4 Moody's idealised default probability

Moody's rating					Year					
	1	2	3	4	5	6	7	8	9	10
Aaa	0.0001%	0.0002%	0.0007%	0.0018%	0.0029%	0.0040%	0.0052%	0.0066%	0.0082%	0.0100%
Aa1	0.0006%	0.0030%	0.0100%	0.0210%	0.0310%	0.0420%	0.0540%	0.0670%	0.0820%	0.1000%
Aa2	0.0014%	0.0080%	0.0260%	0.0470%	0.0680%	0.0890%	0.1110%	0.1350%	0.1640%	0.2000%
Aa3	0.0030%	0.0190%	0.0590%	0.1010%	0.1420%	0.1830%	0.2270%	0.2720%	0.3270%	0.4000%
A1	0.0058%	0.0370%	0.1170%	0.1890%	0.2610%	0.3300%	0.4060%	0.4800%	0.5730%	0.7000%
A2	0.0109%	0.0700%	0.2220%	0.3450%	0.4670%	0.5830%	0.7100%	0.8290%	0.9820%	1.2000%
A3	0.0389%	0.1500%	0.3600%	0.5400%	0.7300%	0.9100%	1.1100%	1.3000%	1.5200%	1.8000%
Baa1	0.0900%	0.2800%	0.5600%	0.8300%	1.1000%	1.3700%	1.6700%	1.9700%	2.2700%	2.6000%
Baa2	0.1700%	0.4700%	0.8300%	1.2000%	1.5800%	1.9700%	2.4100%	2.8500%	3.2400%	3.6000%
Baa3	0.4200%	1.0500%	1.7100%	2.3800%	3.0500%	3.7000%	4.3300%	4.9700%	5.5700%	6.1000%
Ba1	0.8700%	2.0200%	3.1300%	4.2000%	5.2800%	6.2500%	7.0600%	7.8900%	8.6900%	9.4000%
Ba2	1.5600%	3.4700%	5.1800%	6.8000%	8.4100%	9.7700%	10.7000%	11.6600%	12.6500%	13.5000%
Ba3	2.8100%	5.5100%	7.8700%	9.7900%	11.8600%	13.4900%	14.6200%	15.7100%	16.7100%	17.6600%
B1	4.6800%	8.3800%	11.5800%	13.8500%	16.1200%	17.8900%	19.1300%	20.2300%	21.2400%	22.2000%
B2	7.1600%	11.6700%	15.5500%	18.1300%	20.7100%	22.6500%	24.0100%	25.1500%	26.2200%	27.2000%
B3	11.6200%	16.6100%	21.0300%	24.0400%	27.0500%	29.2000%	31.0000%	32.5800%	33.7800%	34.9000%
Caa1	17.3816%	23.2341%	28.6386%	32.4788%	36.3137%	38.9667%	41.3854%	43.6570%	45.6718%	47.7000%
Caa2	26.0000%	32.5000%	39.0000%	43.8800%	48.7500%	52.0000%	55.2500%	58.5000%	61.7500%	65.0000%
Caa3	50.9902%	57.0088%	62.4500%	66.2420%	69.8212%	72.1110%	74.3303%	76.4853%	78.5812%	80.7000%

Table 20.5 Industry diversity score

Number of firms in the same industry	Diversity score	Number of firms in the same industry	Diversity score
0	0.00	4.95	2.67
0.05	0.10	5.05	2.70
0.15	0.20	5.95	3.00
0.95	1.00	6.05	3.03
1.05	1.05	6.95	3.25
1.95	1.50	7.05	3.28
2.05	1.55	7.95	3.50
2.95	2.00	8.05	3.53
3.05	2.03	8.95	3.75
3.95	2.33	9.05	3.78
4.05	2.37	9.95	4.00
		10.05	4.01

Another solution is covered in section 20.3.4 below. An additional related problem is that cashflow (coupons and maturity amounts) received on the collateral pool, and liability payments (tranche payments plus taxes, fees, and swap fees), are spread over a period of a year with payments concentrated on certain days. A solution here usually requires a cashflow account that has an initial sum (part of the overall collateral or a loan) and into which positive and negative cashflow is directed.

A further problem for cash CDOs where the 'collateral' (reference) pool does not already exist as a real portfolio, is how to build up that pool once protection and capital (funding) is obtained. Typically such portfolios have a **ramp-up** period during which the assets are acquired. This may range from three months to a year, depending on the type of collateral and its illiquidity.

Note that cash CDO structures will typically have embedded interest rate and FX swaps. Contingent risk on these will usually form part of the effective loss for the associated name on a credit event.

Cash CDOs primarily have application in the hedging of existing pools, or in allowing such pools of physical assets to be created (see 20.3.4 below). Commercial banks or other hedgers could create a cash CDO on their own balance sheet related to their portfolio of commercial loans. Typically, however, commercial banks use synthetic structures partly because of the greater flexibility they give.

20.3.3 Cashflow Waterfall

The terminology **cashflow CDO** was coined for certain cash structures where income generated by the 'asset' (reference) pool was used in a certain way to service the CDO structure. The **cashflow waterfall** describes in detail how this income is used. This usually includes the use of 'quality' tests (such as income coverage or over-collateralisation tests described above) and diversion of income into a **reserve** (or over-collateralisation) **account**. A cashflow waterfall can actually be applied to any type of CDO – the reference pool can include synthetic assets and need not exist as a real portfolio. The previously described premium rules for CDO tranches could be described by a trivial waterfall structure, but some synthetic CDOs have recently included a complex waterfall structure. The objective of a non-trivial waterfall structure and reserve accounts is to improve the quality (reduce the risk) of certain tranches of the CDO.

The Waterfall

Positive cashflow is credited to a cashflow account. The waterfall describes the priorities of application of funds from that account in any one period. Typically from highest priority to the lowest the waterfall implements the following priorities (highest first).

1. Payment under third-party financial transactions – such as interest rate and FX swap payments (these typically match the cashflows on the bond assets so have to take priority).
2. External fess and expenses – taxes, rating agencies, legal, reporting and paying agents fees, ...
3. Investment adviser's fee and structuring agent's fee.
4. Payments to tranches more senior than the equity tranche.
5. Payments to reimburse tranche protection writers for losses they have already suffered.
6. On the failure of specified portfolio tests the diversion of all remaining cash to a reserve account until the test is satisfied (see section 20.3.1).
7. Excess cash is paid to the equity tranche holder.

The equity tranche holder is typically the originator of the deal together with the collateral pool manager. The income they get from the deal is a combination of the high priority fee payments (item 3) and the low priority equity tranche payment (item 7).

Table 20.6 gives an example of how the initial annual waterfall on a cashflow CDO might look. Income is shown net of funding costs and after the payment of interest and FX swaps (priority 1 in the waterfall). The portfolio is assumed to generate an average of 100 bp on 1bn notional initially. As credit events occur, income drops. Portfolio tests (item 6) may start to fail and cashflow is diverted to the reserve account rather than paying equity. Further defaults may eliminate the equity tranche and defaults may take money from the reserve account or start to hit the senior mezzanine tranche. In principle the CDO may reach a state where the

Table 20.6 Cashflow CDO – initial waterfall

Item	Income	Net cashflow
Asset cashflow after funding costs and after swap payments	$1bn \times 100\ bp = 10m$	10m
External fees	$-0.05m$	9.95m
Investment adviser's fee	$-1m$	7.95m
Structuring fee	$-1m$	
Super senior tranche	$-850m \times 10\ bp = 0.85m$	7.10m
Senior tranche	$-70m \times 25\ bp = 0.175m$	6.925m
Mezz. B	$-30m \times 200\ bp = 0.6m$	6.325m
Mezz. A	$-20m \times 500\ bp = 1m$	5.325m
Reimbursement of tranche losses	0	5.325m
Diversion to reserve account	0	5.325m
Payment to equity tranche holders	5.325m	0

equity tranche has been used up, no other tranches have been hit by losses (or have been hit but subsequently reimbursed), and the portfolio tests are passed. In that case the equity tranche holders continue to receive excess cashflow.

20.3.4 Managed CDOs

In contrast to a static CDO, a **managed CDO** has a reference pool which is **dynamic** – it changes over time – and is managed by a credit portfolio manager. Reference pools are usually cash assets though they may include synthetic risks (CDS, TRS) and may also include long protection positions. Note that the ability to manage the CDO can be used as a partial solution to the ragged nature of the cash maturities – as a bond matures an alternative risk can be substituted.

Substitution Rules

Such structures require controls or rules under which reference risks might be changed. If the originating institution is the buyer of protection, and manages the pool, then it may be advantageous to put highly risky names into the reference pool. For example the institution may have illiquid risky assets elsewhere on its books and wishes to obtain default protection. These substitution risks are handled in a variety of ways:

1. The originating institution and the portfolio manager usually take the first loss risk.
2. Substitution may be limited to replacing maturing bonds, or may allow the sale of one bond before maturity and the purchase of another.
3. Risk limits: the pool as a whole may have to maintain an average weighting better than a certain level, a spread below a certain level, or a WARF better than a certain level on a substitution.
4. Asset types may be constrained to bonds or loans or may have a maximum exposure to other types of risk (such as mortgage-backed securities or tranches of other CDOs).
5. Concentration limits may apply: there may be maximum percentage exposures (by notional, or notional weighted by spread or WARF) on industry groups (e.g. a maximum of 10% by notional in any group); the portfolio may have to maintain a 'diversity score' of (for example) 40 (a measure of the lack of concentration in the portfolio – see section 20.5 below).
6. Over-collateralisation, interest coverage or other tests may have to be passed for a proposed substitution to be allowed.
7. The manager may be required to remove assets if their rating falls below a certain level (e.g. Baa3).

Only if all the substitution rules are satisfied can the substitution be made.

Managed CDOs offer investors access to credit portfolio management. As such one of the key deciding factors is the skill of the manager. An alternative application is to seek protection on a dynamic portfolio that already exists. For example, the credit trading desk of a bank holds long (and occasionally short) positions in a large portfolio of reference entities. Typically risk is held for a short period – less than three months and often much less than that. If a credit event occurs while the desk is long, it suffers a large loss. Using CDS to protect risk would be difficult because of the turnover required and the bid–offer spread to be paid. A dynamic CDO offers an attractive solution where the trading desk could limit its losses (by retaining a small equity piece).

Note that a CDO managed under tight (or lax) constraints is by no means guaranteed to outperform a static CDO. The debate about the value of active management is as valid in the context of credit portfolios as in equity and other portfolios. It is generally agreed that credit managers are more effective at avoiding defaults in a portfolio than is a static portfolio – but by the time a credit is removed its price may have fallen to the recovery level, or even below, or the name ultimately may not default. The impact on portfolio performance of a requirement such as item 7 above, or of active management as a whole, is not necessarily positive.

20.3.5   High-Grade and High-Yield CDOs

Generally reference pools for CDOs are divided into investment grade (BBB or better, usually with an average rating around Baa2) or high yield. Although the principles behind the CDO are the same for any underlying bond or CDS assets, the quality of those assets will affect the tranching structure markedly.

Exercise 1 in section 20.1.2 above can be reworked using an average spread of 50 bp, when we find expected losses of about 2%, or using an average spread of 400 bp when we expect losses of almost 20% over the 5-year life of a portfolio. For the former portfolio the equity tranche may be less than 3% in size, and the super senior piece may be more than 90%, while the latter portfolio may have an equity piece around 15% and the super senior piece may be less than 60% of the notional.

20.3.6   Reference Assets

CDOs have been constructed with a variety of reference assets – not just bonds, loans and CDS but including the following:

1. Debt in any form – synthetic bonds.
2. Contingent debt – including commercial bank facilities and guarantees.
3. Other CDOs or structured credit risks.
4. Mortgage portfolios, credit card portfolios.
5. Lease contracts or trade receivables.
6. Equity.

Terminology and valuation techniques will vary according to these variations. For example a CDO of CDO tranches[7] requires (in principle) a 'look through' valuation to the assets underlying each CDO since a single reference name may appear in several reference pools. This can present logistical problems if the CDOs are dynamic. In addition, a reference CDO does not suffer a credit event – if funded it repays less than par at maturity – so 'credit event' calculations have to be reworked in terms of the outstanding notional of the CDO tranche.

20.4   TRANCHE RATINGS AND BET

The rating agencies provide a ratings service for some or all of the tranches of a CDO and other credit structures. The asset may be required to be rated by investors as part of a due diligence process and may be a prerequisite before they are able to buy a tranche. The rating agencies make it clear that the process of rating any sort of deal is not a purely mechanical one of entering data into a formula and getting the rating. This can be a problem for structurers – not

---

[7] Sometimes called a CDO squared or a CDO^2.

being sure what the final rating will be until the rating agency provides it just before the product launch. Structuring a deal efficiently generally requires knowledge of the ratings that will be applied to tranches since this will influence the premium that has to be paid to investors (writers of protection). The structurer tries to minimise overall cost by adjusting tranche sizes and the reference portfolio (thereby changing the tranche ratings and affecting the premium that will have to be paid on the tranche).

However, the agencies have become more transparent and more formulaic (at least for static synthetic structures) – for example, S&P will supply its 'CDOevaluator' software to market participants. Generally, the rating agencies' methods are historically driven: ratings are used, together with historical default and recovery rates, as the basis for the determination of the expected losses on a tranche. Historically these ratings have driven the pricing of CDO tranches, and the cost of obtaining protection in tranched form has often been less than can be earned in spread on the underlying portfolio (leading to 'arbitrage CDOs'). 'Value' was generally found in the mezzanine area.

We describe below Moody's Binomial Expansion Technique (Moody's, 1996). This has been expanded and enhanced compared to the simplified version described (Moody's, 2003).

Moody's Binomial Expansion Technique (BET)

The aim of the approach is to replace the actual correlated portfolio by an uncorrelated one which otherwise has the same general risk characteristics. Calculating expected defaults (and tranche losses) for an uncorrelated portfolio is a trivial application of the binomial distribution (item 4(a) below).

1. Calculate the diversity score, D, for the portfolio (section 20.3.1).
2. Calculate the WARF (section 20.3.1).
3. From the 'idealised default rates' table, the WARF gives the average default probability, q, over the life of the deal for each notional entity in the diversified pool of D names. For calculations that default, probability may be increased by a stress factor depending on the tranche to be rated and depending on the desired rating for that tranche.
4. Calculate the expected loss on the portfolio assuming that the D notional reference entities have the same notional exposure (the average exposure, $A = \text{total\_notional}/D$).
   (a) The probability of n defaults is (the 'binomial distribution')

$$p(n) = \frac{D!}{n!(D-n)!} \cdot q^n \cdot (1-q)^{D-n}$$

   (b) Assume an expected loss, L, from Moody's idealised expected loss table (reproduced as Table 20.7) according to the WARF (and implied average rating). The loss associated with n defaults is nAL.
   (c) The expected loss for the portfolio is $\sum_{n=0}^{D} n \cdot A \cdot L \cdot p(n)$.
   (d) The loss associated with n defaults can also be allocated to each tranche according to the waterfall, and the expected loss for each tranche can then be calculated.
   (e) The expected loss for the tranche can then be equated to the product of tranche size, L and a default rate Q. We can then use the tranche default rate Q and the idealised default probability table, to get an implied rating.

Various steps of the implementation have been refined. The number of defaults can be distributed in different ways over time – for example, with a 50% 'front loading' – to see the impact on tranche valuation.

Table 20.7 Moody's idealised expected loss

Moody's rating	Year									
	1	2	3	4	5	6	7	8	9	10
Aaa	0.0000%	0.0001%	0.0004%	0.0010%	0.0016%	0.0022%	0.0029%	0.0036%	0.0045%	0.0055%
Aa1	0.0003%	0.0017%	0.0055%	0.0116%	0.0171%	0.0231%	0.0297%	0.0369%	0.0451%	0.0550%
Aa2	0.0007%	0.0044%	0.0143%	0.0259%	0.0374%	0.0490%	0.611%	0.0743%	0.0902%	0.1100%
Aa3	0.0017%	0.0105%	0.0325%	0.0556%	0.0781%	0.1007%	0.1249%	0.1496%	0.1799%	0.2200%
A1	0.0032%	0.0204%	0.0644%	0.1040%	0.1436%	0.1815%	0.2233%	0.2640%	0.3152%	0.3850%
A2	0.0060%	0.0385%	0.1221%	0.1898%	0.2569%	0.3207%	0.3905%	0.4560%	0.5401%	0.6600%
A3	0.0214%	0.0825%	0.1980%	0.2970%	0.4015%	0.5005%	0.6105%	0.7150%	0.8360%	0.9900%
Baa1	0.0495%	0.1540%	0.3080%	0.4565%	0.6050%	0.7535%	0.9185%	1.0835%	1.2485%	1.4300%
Baa2	0.0935%	0.2585%	0.4565%	0.6600%	0.8690%	1.0835%	1.3255%	1.5675%	1.7820%	1.9800%
Baa3	0.2310%	0.5775%	0.9405%	1.3090%	1.6775%	2.0350%	2.3815%	2.7335%	3.0635%	3.3550%
Ba1	0.4785%	1.1110%	1.7215%	2.3100%	2.9040%	3.4375%	3.8830%	4.3375%	4.7795%	5.1700%
Ba2	0.8580%	1.9085%	2.8490%	3.7400%	4.6255%	5.3735%	5.8850%	6.4130%	6.9575%	7.4250%
Ba3	1.5455%	3.0305%	4.3285%	5.3845%	6.5230%	7.4195%	8.0410%	8.6405%	9.1905%	9.7130%
B1	2.5740%	4.6090%	6.3690%	7.6175%	8.8660%	9.8395%	10.5215%	11.1265%	11.6820%	12.2100%
B2	3.9380%	6.4185%	8.5525%	9.9715%	11.3905%	12.4575%	13.2055%	13.8325%	14.4210%	14.9600%
B3	6.3910%	9.1355%	11.5665%	13.2220%	14.8775%	16.0600%	17.0500%	17.9190%	18.5790%	19.1950%
Caa1	9.5599%	12.7788%	15.7512%	17.8634%	19.9726%	21.4317%	22.7620%	24.0113%	25.1195%	26.2350%
Caa2	14.3000%	17.8750%	21.4500%	24.1340%	26.8125%	28.6000%	30.3875%	32.1750%	33.9625%	35.7500%
Caa3	28.0446%	31.3538%	34.3475%	36.4331%	38.4017%	39.6611%	40.8817%	42.0669%	43.2196%	44.3850%

The BET approach is an alternative to the Copula model. Instead of making an arbitrary assumption about how defaults are correlated (the Copula method applied to default times, the specific Copula to use, and the choice of correlation numbers or other parameters), Moody's makes an arbitrary assumption about how many uncorrelated names[8] are 'equivalent' to the actual number of names held in each industry (and Moody's assumes that different industries are uncorrelated). The BET method is extremely quick to evaluate – being closed form.

There are steps in the implementation that could be altered – for example using the implied default rates per tranche rather than rating implied default rates or parametrising the mapping of the number of correlated names to the number of uncorrelated names – although the BET approach has not been used for mark-to-model validation.

20.5   SPVs AND CDOs

An SPV may be used to house all or part of a CDO transaction. There are no differences in principle between this application of an SPV and that described for the creation of a simple CLN, in Part II, section 13.1. The SPV may contain the entire transaction – for example:

1. A synthetic CDO may be set up via an SPV. The SPV writes default swaps (the reference pool), and buys tranches of protection from the market. Tranches may be funded – and the SPV owns collateral to back these tranches – or unfunded, in which case there is counterparty risk.
2. A managed CDO may be set up in an SPV. Tranches of protection are sold by the SPV in funded form and capital raised is used to buy the reference pool.

Typically this is not the case – we look at two examples below where the SPV buys and writes protection only on some tranches of the CDO.

Example 1

This example is based on the BISTRO series of 'balance sheet' CDO transactions developed by JPMorgan. The SPV buys funded protection from the market on certain mezzanine tranches of a synthetic CDO – say the [2%, 8%] tranche. In turn it sells protection to the investment bank. In its turn the investment bank sells protection on a 2–100% tranche of the reference pool to a commercial bank. The commercial bank retains the first 2% of risk, and buys protection on the balance of the portfolio from an OECD bank in order to get regulatory capital relief. The investment bank may write the senior protection off its own books, or may buy it from a third party directly. Note that the risk on the reference pool of assets – commercial bank loans and facilities – is passed synthetically via the tranches of protection to ultimate investors through the investment bank plus (for the mezzanine tranches) through the SPV. In this case the role of the SPV is to hold collateral behind the funded notes remote from the investment bank. The transaction is summarised in Figure 20.3.

Example 2

Protection on the super senior tranche of a CDO is to be bought from a certain insurance company in standard credit derivatives form, yet the insurance company is unable to write credit derivatives although it can sell an insurance guarantee. An SPV is set up which buys a

---

[8] Tests show that the correlation implied by Moody's diversity score table varies according to the number of names in the industry, but, for small numbers of names, is equivalent to a default time correlation around 70%.

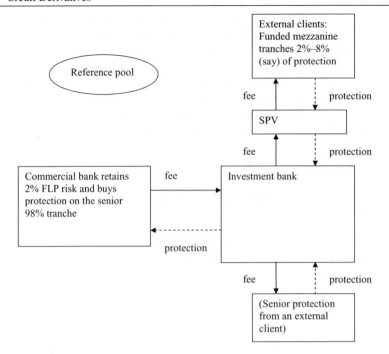

Figure 20.3   SPV holding the funded mezzanine tranches of a CDO

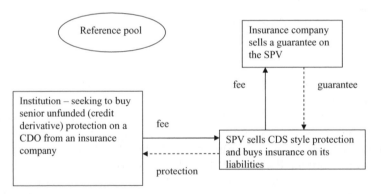

Figure 20.4   SPV holding an unfunded super senior tranche of a CDO

guarantee (on its liabilities) from the insurance company, and the SPV sells unfunded protection on the super senior tranche of the CDO (see Figure 20.4).

20.6   APPLICATIONS

We have covered the following applications above:

1. Access to portfolio credit risk (static index portfolios).
2. Access to liquid CDO tranches giving credit exposure at a chosen level of risk, and also access to CDO tranches for hedging (tranched index products).

3. Arbitrage CDOs.
4. Access to credit management (managed CDOs).

We also mentioned the used of CDOs by commercial banks. We shall expand discussion of this topic and a few other applications in this section.

20.6.1 Balance Sheet CDOs

A balance sheet CDO is used to obtain capital relief (reducing economic risk or regulatory capital) on a pre-existing portfolio of credit risks. Typically the institution seeking protection is a commercial bank and the reference pool of assets contains non-assignable loans and a variety of contingent credit risks (including facilities and revolvers). Typically these are passed synthetically to an SPV which obtains protection in tranched form (or variations along the lines of section 20.5, example 1). Passing the risks synthetically is quick, easy and flexible – allowing a wide range of complex risks and contingent risks to be passed across. (The problem in this case is less about the mechanics of the deal and more about correct valuation for products which do not trade in a secondary market.)

We shall now look at an example of regulatory capital reduction in the context of the Basle 88 capital rules. Changes under the forthcoming Basle II regulations will relate capital more closely to the risk of the assets. Similar structures will continue to be of interest though the sums will change.

Suppose a bank has a EUR 5bn loan and other credit risk portfolio on which it wishes to

(a) release lines
(b) release internal economic capital and economic risk
(c) reduce regulatory capital
(d) increase return on capital.

Suppose the credit risks are subject to a regulatory capital charge of 8% of notional (EUR 400m), and have an average spread of 60 bp generating EUR 30m in income. The current return on capital is 30m/400m = 7.5%. We assume that the bank arranges the following structure:

1. It retains risk to the first 1.5% of losses against which it allocates full capital (EUR 75m).
2. It obtains protection on three tranches covering the remaining 98.5% of risk, arranged via an SPV, with an OECD bank between the commercial bank and the SPV. Tranches and capital required are as follows
   (a) Junior mezzanine of 1% subject to a premium of 500 bp (cost EUR 2.5m; capital required 50m × 8% × 20% [OECD bank] = 0.8m).
   (b) Senior mezzanine of 3.5% subject to 100 bp premium (cost EUR 1.75m; capital required 2.8m).
   (c) Senior tranche of 94% subject to an 8 bp premium (cost EUR 3.76m; capital required 75.2m).

The net income is now 30m −2.5m − 1.75m − 3.76m = 21.99m but the capital required has fallen to 100m + 0.8m + 2.8m + 75.2m = 153.8m and the return on capital has increased to 14.3%. The situation is summarised in Table 20.8.

Internal capital or economic risk will be allocated according to the asset risks. The retained first loss piece is high risk and will be allocated the face amount of capital. The other risks are

Table 20.8 Balance sheet CDO: capital and risk reduction

Asset or liability	Size (EURm)	Spread in bp	Income (cost)	Capital	RoC
Loan portfolio	5000	60	30m	400m	7.5%
1.5% FLP	75	n/a	0	75m	
1% mezz.	50	500	−2.5m	0.8m	
3.5% mezz.	175	100	−1.75m	2.8m	
94% senior	4700	8	−3.76m	75.2m	
Total			**21.99m**	**153.8m**	**14.3%**

counterparty risks to the bank, and capital allocated will typically depend on the counterparty rating.

20.6.2 Diversification and Risk Reduction Trades; a 'Credit Bank'

An insurance single name credit risk portfolio, developed on the basis of familiarity with the local market, may be geographically concentrated – for example, primarily Japanese. The company could write protection on a senior tranche of a portfolio of EU or North American credits (most simply using index products) to obtain geographical diversification at relatively low risk. The reverse trade might appeal to non-Japanese-based insurance companies.

Likewise commercial bank loan portfolios tend to be concentrated both geographically and by industry. An EU bank could reduce its concentration risk at negligible cost by buying CDS protection on individual large exposures and selling protection on an average basket of EU names where no exposure is currently held. Additionally, the bank could obtain protection in tranched form on its remaining risks (releasing lines, etc.) while writing protection on a portfolio again in tranched form. In practice commercial banks currently rarely sell protection because it is not capital efficient and greater income can be obtained from existing clients (a large part of commercial bank income is in the form of fees rather than spread income).

Corporate treasury departments run substantial risks to trading counterparties – products or raw materials may be supplied to clients in large volumes for delayed settlement. Typically the number of counterparties is relatively small and concentrated, and risks are typically rolling short-term risks (though they may extend beyond 12 months in some cases). This leaves them doubly exposed – the loss of a client and the loss of a loan – in the event of the counterparty failure. One theoretical solution is the development of a 'credit bank' – a CDO related to the reference pool of risks obtained synthetically from several corporate entities and other sources. The contributing corporates retain the first loss piece and an SPV obtains tranched protection on the remaining risks.

21

Valuation and Hedging

In this Chapter we concentrate on the theoretical aspects of pricing models and, in particular, the 'Normal Copula', together with hedging issues and model errors. In Chapter 22 we discuss the source and derivation of the correlation numbers, and related issues. Where it is necessary in this Chapter to have a concrete idea of what the correlation is and where it comes from, the reader should think in terms of an 'implied correlation' (similar to the 'implied volatility' used in the Black–Scholes option pricing model).

21.1   DEFAULT TIME CORRELATION

We shall explain the concept of default time correlation by considering simulated default times.

21.1.1   Generating Correlated Default Times

First consider two names that have a default time correlation, ρ. Part I, section 6.3, showed how to obtain the Cholesky decomposition from the correlation matrix and how to generate correlated random Normal numbers using this decomposition. Part II, Chapter 18, showed how to convert a Normal random number into a default time given the hazard rate process (equation (18.3) if the hazard rate is a constant). The spreadsheets 'Chapter 21.xls' and 'Chapter 18.xls' produce correlated default times given CDS premium data and recovery assumptions (under the assumption that the hazard curve is constant), for any correlation.[1] Table 21.1 shows the first few simulated default times for uncorrelated ($\rho = 0$), 70% correlated, and 100% correlated default times.

21.1.2   Intuitive Understanding of Default Time Correlation

In Table 21.1, 'name 2' has a higher hazard rate than 'name 1' so has an expected default time which is before that of name 1. In 8 of the 14 simulations in the first pair of columns (zero correlation), name 1 actually defaults before name 2 – but as only 14 simulations are shown in the table no clear conclusion can be reached.

> **Exercise 1**
> Extend the simulations to 10 000 and show that the expected default time of name 1 is indeed 50 years, and name 2 is 25 years. In particular the average default time of name 1 is greater than that of name 2.

---

[1] Note that setting $\rho = 1$ does not give a correlation matrix (more on this later). We can let the correlation get close to unity but not actually be equal to unity. When we talk about 100% correlation we mean the correlations is very close to unity. (The simulation process can be extended to work with unit correlation but not using the 'correlation matrix'.)

Table 21.1 Simulated correlated default times for 100 bp and 200 bp CDS names with recovery of 50%

No.	Correlation = 0		Correlation = 0.7		Correlation = 1.0	
	Name 1	Name 2	Name 1	Name 2	Name 1	Name 2
1	24.5	29.8	30.4	9.3	37.0	18.5
2	1.6	9.7	14.5	11.0	127.2	63.6
3	14.1	37.8	3.1	4.1	3.6	1.8
4	9.9	1.9	10.1	4.1	36.0	18.0
5	47.8	25.6	20.3	15.3	1.7	0.8
6	3.1	20.4	112.5	63.8	75.3	37.6
7	30.4	3.3	67.3	26.1	7.8	3.9
8	5.9	6.1	21.3	7.9	156.2	78.1
9	6.1	43.1	193.9	16.2	45.6	22.8
10	75.8	26.7	43.3	26.7	31.8	15.9
11	63.3	20.9	29.2	14.8	44.8	22.4
12	12.7	35.6	10.5	5.8	17.7	8.8
13	1.7	23.0	24.6	26.3	70.5	35.2
14	76.3	15.4	5.8	4.4	59.3	29.7

If we set the correlation to 70% then 12 out of the 14 simulations show name 1 defaulting after name 2, and if we set the correlation to 100% then – on every simulation run – the default time of name 1 is twice that of name 2.

Exercise 2

Extend the simulations to 10 000 and show the following:

(a) At both 70% and 100% correlation the expected default time of name 1 is indeed 50 years, and name 2 is 25 years. In particular the average default time of name 1 is greater than that of name 2.
(b) At the three correlation levels what proportion of name 1 defaults is after name 2?
(c) Using formula (18.3) explain the 100% correlation results.

We conclude that *changing the correlation has no impact on the expected default time of a particular name*, but does have something to do with how defaults of one name relate to defaults of another.

We can think of a single simulation as a roll of the dice which tells us the complete future of the universe (for these two names). We know what these two default times will be once we have cast our random numbers. If we think of many simulations we are actually thinking about many separate universes in which the two names default. By looking at the default time of name 1 and the default time of name 2 as random variables, we can calculate the correlation of the observed default times in the usual way.

Of course reality is totally different from the above. There is just the one universe in which name 1 and name 2 default and, if we wait until they have defaulted, even then we cannot calculate their default time correlation. Thus although the concept of default time correlation is mathematically valid, it is not observable in a direct way.

How can we calculate the default time correlation of two names? We postpone this discussion until Chapter 22.

The extension of the above process to any number of names is mathematically trivial in principle.

Why do we use a model based around such an obscure and unobservable quantity? We have already touched on alternative possible models – for example, correlated hazard rate processes, possibly with jumps. The answer to the above question is that the model based around correlated default times is very quick to execute – even if we simulate default times – whereas a simulated hazard rate process requires simulating over time intervals which is slow, and also presents substantial problems (at least in terms of run-time) for the calibration of each single name CDS. Using such a hazard rate simulation and calibration process, it may take 24 hours to price a single CDO tranche, whereas by the default time model it can take one hundredth of a second (if a 'semi-closed form' approach is taken – see later). Against this enormous practical advantage of the Normal Copula default-time model we are stuck with a model in which we have no direct means of observing the key input.

21.1.3 Spread Implications of 100% Default Time Correlation

We have seen above (exercise 2(c)) that, at 100% correlation, the default times are in the precise relationship to the inverse of the hazard rates.

What happens to spreads and CDS levels during this process? If we look at the deal in, say, five years' time, what does the model tell us about the CDS premia on the surviving names?

Take the 100% correlated column in Table 21.1. If name 2 has defaulted but name 1 has not (simulation number 7) we know precisely when name 1 will default – in this case a further 2.8 years. The hazard rate function in this case has changed completely – the hazard rate is zero up to 2.8 years' time when it becomes infinite. We shall return to this question later.

Exercise

Using the simulated default times in columns G and H we can ask questions like: 'if name 2 survives 5 years, what is the expected default time of name 1?'. Working with hazard rates of 100 and 200 bp respectively, show that (columns Q to Y) if name 1 and name 2 have a positive default time correlation then:

1. the expected default time of name 1, conditional on name 2 surviving beyond (say) five years, is greater than 100 years;
2. the expected default time of name 1, conditional on name 2 defaulting before five years, is less than 100 years;
3. the expected default time of name 2, conditional on name 1 surviving beyond (say) five years, is greater than 50 years;
4. the expected default time of name 2, conditional on name 1 defaulting before five years, is less than 50 years.

(Increase the number of simulations to ensure that you get significant results.)

What does this say about the forward (conditional) hazard rates (and spreads) of name 1 and name 2? The Copula model implies a correlated jump process for spreads, and pseudo-hazard rates and, implicitly, hazard rates.

21.2   THE NORMAL COPULA

The process described above, taking a correlation matrix, generating independent Normal random numbers and converting them into correlated random numbers, then producing correlated default times, is an application of the 'Normal (or Gaussian) Copula'. The Normal Copula model is the industry standard valuation procedure among investment banks and others for the valuation of portfolio credit derivatives – nth-to-default baskets, CDOs and default swaps with correlated counterparty risk. We describe Copula methods more generally later – here it merely carries the implication that the Normal distribution is being used to produce correlated default times when the only information we can observe is the (unconditional) spread curve for individual names. The Normal Copula is a very simple and a rather special case of Copulae.

We need to know no more about the Normal Copula than we have seen already:

(a) Generate correlated Normal numbers.
(b) Equate the nth name survival probability to the cumulative probability of the nth random number.

We shall return to the topic of other Copulae in Chapter 24, and put the Normal Copula in the context of other approaches. It was first used (although not referred to by the name 'Normal Copula') – as described in Part I – by RiskMetrics Group (Gupton *et al.*, 1997) in their credit risk analysis. David Li (2000) first identified and used the Normal Copula to generate default times and price correlation products, other Copulae have been used by various researchers, including Schönbucher and Schubert (2001). A review of the Copula approach in the context of other models is given in Finger (2000).

Default Time versus Rating Simulation

Note that the default time approach using the Normal Copula described above, and the approach for simulating forward ratings using the Normal Copula, described in Chapter 6, are related but not identical. If we choose a time horizon for a portfolio (say one year) and simulate forward ratings for a portfolio, then some names will default but most will survive and migrate to another (or stay the same) rating. Consider again two names where the default time correlation is 100%. On those default time simulations where one name has defaulted we know when the other name will default. But in the rating simulation[2] a wide spread name might move into default, but a 100% correlated AAA name would probably remain AAA.

> **Exercise**
> Review Part I, section 6.2, and think through the process of rating simulation in the context of a CCC and a AAA name.

What is the AAA name's expected default time at our time horizon? It is certainly not determined by the rating simulation approach, in contrast to the default time simulation approach. We conclude that, although they use the same methodology, the rating simulation and the default time simulation approaches are different and will produce different answers.

---

[2] The transition matrix can be calibrated to the two names to give the correct spreads.

21.3   PORTFOLIO PRODUCT PRICING UNDER MONTE CARLO SIMULATION

The process of calculation product values for nth-to-default and CDO tranches is mathematically trivial, given a set of simulated correlated default times. In certain circumstances there are alternative (semi-closed form) solution methods (discussed in more detail in section 22.3). The simulation technique is easy to understand and to apply. It will handle a general correlation matrix whereas semi-closed form implementations will not, and will handle many 'tag' correlation matrices (see Chapter 22) more quickly than the semi-closed form approach. The valuation formulae under simulation can also be trivially extended to handle many cashflow CDOs with OC, IC and other tests, and handle the operation of reserve account or tranche amortisation rules.

The key point to understand about valuation using simulated default times is that default time uncertainty, and correlation between names, is handled by the simulation process. Within a given simulation the survival probability of a name up to its default time is unity, and zero after the default time. Each set of simulated default times for the names in the portfolio is a realisation of the universe – there is now no uncertainty left. The default times generate a certain set of cashflows, and all we have to do is value those cashflows using the LIBOR-based discount factors.

We shall illustrate valuation of both products by example.

21.3.1   N2D Baskets

We illustrate the process for a two name basket and a first-to-default contract – larger baskets and higher N2D contracts are handled by a trivial extension of the procedure. Suppose the product maturity is N years, and suppose we assume recoveries of R_1 and R_2 for name 1 and name 2 respectively. During the simulations we keep track of the value of capital payments (the 'contingent benefits stream', B, also called 'the capital value' or 'expected loss'), and the value of premium payments (paid at a rate of 1 bp per annum – the 'premium stream', P). It is also useful to keep sum-of-square terms to allow us to estimate the standard deviation of the expected value we calculate. In section 21.5 we shall show how to extend the process to give spread sensitivities.

Simulation: Let the simulated default times be T_1 and T_2 years, then there are three possible cases[3]:

1. $T_1 \leq N$ and $T_2 > T_1$: generating a capital flow of $1 - R_1$ at time T_1, and premiums ceasing at time T_1.
2. $T_2 \leq N$ and $T_1 > T_2$: generating a capital flow of $1 - R_2$ at time T_2, and premiums ceasing at time T_2.
3. $T_1 > N$ and $T_2 > N$: generating no capital flow and premiums ceasing at time N.

The valuation formulae will depend on the yield curve, day-count and other conventions. We shall take the simplest case of a constant zero coupon rate, r, and ignore day-count conventions. Then the cashflows increment the values of the contingent benefits, B, by

1. $(1 - R_1) \times \exp(-r \times T_1)$
2. $(1 - R_2) \times \exp(-r \times T_2)$
3. 0

---

[3] Default times are simulated to around 16 decimal places – nanosecond accuracy. We ignore the possibility $T_1 = T_2$.

and increment the value of the premium stream, P, by

1. $[1 - \exp(-r \times T_1)]/r$
2. $[1 - \exp(-r \times T_2)]/r$
3. $[1 - \exp(-r \times N)]/r$

respectively.

We repeat the process many times, using a new pair of simulated default times for each repetition. Finally we can calculate the expected value of the benefits as B/n, and of the premium stream (per bp of premium) as P/n, where n is the number of simulations. The simulated product value is

$$V = \frac{B}{n} - x\frac{P}{n}$$

where x is the actual premium paid on the deal. Alternatively, for a pricing, we can set $V = 0$ and calculate the fair value premium.

21.3.2   CDO Tranches

To value a CDO tranche we need only the simulated default times (and discount curve). The only difference between N2D and CDO products is the cashflows generated by credit events. Consider a tranche with attachment points $[a, b]$, life T, and a reference pool of N names. Given a set of default times for the names in the reference pool these are first sorted into increasing order. We suppose a reference entity j has notional exposure N_j in the pool and defaults at time t_j with recovery R_j, and define two functions of time:

1. The initial notional of the tranche minus losses to date, $E(t)$, and the notional of the $[0, a]$ base tranche $E_0(t)$. We know $E(0) = b - a$ in percentage terms. For each default the loss $N_j \times (1 - R_j)$ reduces E_0 by the amount of the loss or to zero. If there is any excess of the loss over the reduction in the junior tranche, then E reduces by this excess. When the $[0, a]$ base tranche is exhausted, all defaults lead to an excess equal to the loss and reduce E by this loss.
2. The notional for premium calculation, $N(t)$. If the tranche is not the senior tranche then $N(t) = E(t)$. For the senior tranche only, the notional for premium calculation typically follows
   (a) $N(t_j+) = N(t_j-) - N_j$ if the loss hits the senior tranche (the tranche notional drops by loss plus recovery) and
   (b) $N(t_j+) = N(t_j-) - N_j \times R_j$ if the loss hits junior tranches only (the tranche notional drops by recovery), and the obvious extension if the loss happens to hit both junior and senior tranches).

The values of the contingent benefits, and of the premium stream, under the tranche are then given by

$$B = \sum_{i=1}^{N} \text{if} \ \ [t_i < T, N_i \cdot (1 - R_i) \cdot \exp(-r \cdot t_i), 0] \tag{21.1}$$

$$P = \int_0^T N(t) \cdot \exp(-r \cdot t)\, dt \tag{21.2}$$

and the deal value is $V = B - pP$, where p is the actual premium being paid (and $V = 0$ for a fair value deal).

Exercise
What tests could you apply to check consistency of the simulation program across products? What extremes would you test?

Some possibilities are:

(a) N2D and CDO with one name should relate to the underlying CDS.
(b) N2D with two names and correlation of 0 and 100% has known values.
(c) N2D and CDO with particular tranches and zero recovery assumption should generate the same fair value premia.
(d) At very high spreads and zero recovery all tranches will default. If interest rates are zero then the benefits values will tend to the notionals.
(e) Select a set of simulated default times and check that the program cashflows are correct.
(f) Check the pricing of CDO tranches against market traded index products (iTraxx or CDX tranches).

21.3.3   The Number of Simulations

In practice it is best to do a few 'housekeeping' activities:

(a) It is often useful to generate random numbers using the same seed, so that different valuations for the same product with minor changes, can be compared.
(b) If we calculate the sum of square values for the contingent benefits and premium streams, then we can estimate not just the mean but also the standard deviation of the results, and hence get a standard deviation of the resulting deal value or fair value premium.

If we increase the number of simulations n by a factor of 100, then the standard error of the result falls to about one-tenth of its previous value. The number of simulations we need to perform will depend on the accuracy required. Typically for a two name basket, 1m simulations are usually sufficiently accurate for valuation; and for a 100 name basket, 20 000 simulations are sufficient (roughly 2m simulated defaults in both cases). For CDO tranches – and for N2D above F2D – an addition influence comes from the seniority of the tranche. We find that the absolute error of the calculation decreases as tranche seniority increases, but the percentage error increases.

21.3.4   Variance Reduction Techniques

The process described is known as 'crude' Monte Carlo. There are well-documented techniques for reducing the number of simulations required (hence speeding up calculations) (Jäckel, 2003). Such methods may be useful in a production environment. Crude Monte Carlo has the advantage of simplicity and easy estimation of errors. We mention three variance reduction techniques that can be useful.

1. Control Variate: Simulations are used to generate the value V_1 of the actual product and a similar product V_2, where an accurate answer VA_2 is known. The error $VA_2 - V_2$ can then

be used to adjust V_1 to obtain a more accurate estimate. This can be used if the correlation matrix is driven by a single number (so we can use semi-closed form solutions) and

(a) we are comparing a CDO that has a complex waterfall with a CDO that has a trivial waterfall, or

(b) when we want to value a CDO using a complex correlation matrix.

2. Low discrepancy sequences (Jäckel, 2003): Sobol sequences are widely used but are known to have problems in high (around 15 or more) numbers of dimensions.

3. Importance Sampling: For example, in the F2D simulation process for investment grade names, relatively few simulations generate a capital payoff. Importance Sampling is a technique for changing the default distribution to generate more defaults – hence use fewer simulations to get an accurate answer – but make adjustments to get back to an answer appropriate to the actual distribution. Joshi and Kainth (2003) describe the application for N2D products.

The fourth method of speeding up calculation is a hardware solution. Using distributed processing and perhaps 100–1000 idle (during overnight processing) PCs, the calculation time can be reduced by a similar factor.

21.3.5 Complex CDO Structures

CDO of CDOs

Among the reference risks in CDO_A may be tranches of CDO_B.

This can be handled by simulating the universe of all names in the books and calculating the impact of a set of simulations on CDO_B – calculating its maturity amount – and calculating the impact on the valuation of CDO_A of that same set of simulated defaults. (Note that a CDO tranche does not default and, if funded, simply returns a below par amount at maturity.)

One problem with the above approach is that if the correlation required to price CDO_B is c_B, but the correlation appropriate to price a similar CDO to CDO_A (but one which does not have a reference to CDO_B) is c_A, then it is not possible to get a consistent set of simulated default times across all names. A further logistical problem is that the reference pool for B may not be known if it is a dynamic pool at the time a valuation is required.

OC Tests (etc.) and Reserve Accounts

Simulation for cashflow CDOs includes the income generated on the simulated reference pool which accumulates as it is received in the cashflow account. At appropriate dates payments are made from the cashflow account following the waterfall structure to the tranches and other liabilities.

Incorporation of OC, IC, and other tests in the simulation is straightforward in principle. At each test date – based on the reference pool as it is simulated to exist at that date – the test is applied. If the test fails, a cashflow is transferred to the reserve account and payments to the junior tranches are reduced by the transfer to the reserve. At appropriate dates the reserve account is applied to restore tranche exposures, make early redemption payments, etc.

Rating Dependent Premium

The premium for a tranche may be rating dependent. Since rating a tranche is a judgemental rather than a formulaic exercise, this feature can only be handled approximately. A proxy formula for the rating of a tranche can be programmed to operate periodically, based on the simulated pool, and tranche premia adjusted. Such a proxy formula will typically need the forward rating of the reference names. One approach is to tie rating to spread and simulate spread. (We shall return to this topic later.) An alternative is to assume that rating changes and default time simulation are not closely connected, and simulate rating changes separately using the methods of Part I (and a TM closer to historical figures than the implied TM[4]). Approaches along these lines are also slow to execute.

A simpler albeit crude but quicker alternative is to value the tranche assuming the rating is unchanged throughout its life and also assuming rating change is triggered at various forward dates. Separate simulations of rating changes can then be used to find weightings to apply to the above simulated values.

21.3.6 Summary of the Normal Copula Default Time Simulation and Valuation Process

The process is an extension of that described for a single name CDS – we just have more names and an additional step of correlating the Normal random numbers. The process is as follows:

1. Given a correlation matrix R we find the Cholesky[5] decomposition L such that

$$R = L \cdot L^T$$

2. Pick n independent random numbers x_i from a Normal distribution.
3. Multiply the Cholesky matrix by the vector of n independent random numbers – this gives n correlated random numbers z_i from the Normal distribution.

$$z_k = \sum_{j=1}^{n} L_{k,j} \cdot x_j$$

4. Find the cumulative probability associated with each number, $\Phi(z_i)$.
5. Associate that probability with the probability of survival up to a certain time – and get the default time – for each name. $t = \{-\ln[\Phi(z_i)]\}/\lambda$ in the case where the hazard rate is a constant.
6. Given the default times $\{t_i\}$ we can calculate the cashflows under the N2D and static CDO tranche products (with a complex waterfall) and value these cashflows.

21.4 VALUATION EXAMPLES

The aim of this section is to present some graphical and numerical results to show the impact of different correlation on the pricing of portfolio CD products, and to show the impact of various other factors on CDO pricing. Results in this section are based on 10 000 simulations for a 100 name portfolio.

---

[4] One can argue that rating changes are not hedged with 'ratings change products' so we should use the natural measure – historical TM – when simulating rating changes rather than the risk neutral measure.
[5] There are alternative methods such as 'singular value decomposition'. Experience performing over 1000 different CDO valuations has shown the Cholesky decomposition to be stable and accurate.

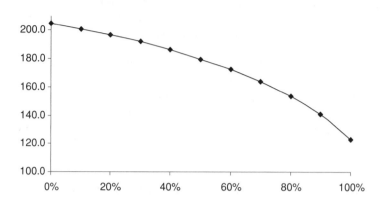

Figure 21.1   Fair value F2D premium on a 5-year two name basket

21.4.1 F2D Baskets

We have already seen the 0% correlation and the 100% correlation results for the fair value premium on a F2D. Figure 21.1 shows the pattern of fair value spread for a two name basket as correlation varies from 0 to 1. We assume that the CDS premia for the names are 82 bp and 123 bp, and we assume that both names have the same recovery. Some further pricing results specific to standard traded CDO structures appear in Chapter 22.

Exercises

1. What happens at negative correlation on the two name basket? If correlation is minus 100%, what does that mean for the simulated random numbers? If the simulated random number means that one name defaults early, show that the other name defaults late. Hence show that the curve in Figure 21.1 continues rise as correlation gets increasingly negative.

2. At minus 100% correlation, the above shows that you would pay more than $82 + 123$ bp for the F2D protection. Intuitively why is this the case? [*Hint*: (a) What is the hedge for the bought protection? (b) If one name defaults within the life of the deal, when does the other default? (c) What can the sold protection be bought back for?]

3. In reality the recovery rates are unknown. What does the Figure 21.1 look like in general terms if we take into account recovery uncertainty?

21.4.2 CDO Pricing: Change of Correlation

First take a 5-year portfolio of 100 names with average CDS premium 100 bp and a standard deviation of premia across names in the portfolio of 29 bp. We assume a recovery of 40% for all names. Table 21.2 and Figure 21.2 show the fair value premia as correlation changes. Note the following:

1. The higher risk tranches have higher fair value premia.
2. At low correlation the equity tranche premium is over 50% of notional per annum, and the premium for the senior tranche is only a fraction of a basis point.

Table 21.2   Fair value tranche premia and correlation

Tranche	Size	Premium and Correlation				
		0	10	20	30	40
Equity	3	5302.4	3775.9	2908.2	2315.0	1872.3
m1	3	1236.6	1079.5	971.1	879.5	790.5
m2	3	132.7	370.5	439.3	460.6	463.0
m3	3	3.0	123.2	214.7	268.5	294.8
m4	10	0.0	17.0	58.1	101.1	137.4
Senior	78	0.0	0.0	0.7	2.9	6.7

Tranche	Size	Premium and Correlation				
		50	60	70	80	90
Equity	3	1517.5	1226.9	971.5	739.1	530.3
m1	3	704.4	624.0	543.3	462.8	375.7
m2	3	446.9	424.4	395.7	360.7	308.4
m3	3	308.2	312.0	308.2	295.9	268.7
m4	10	166.2	188.0	203.5	211.9	212.1
Senior	78	12.0	18.8	26.7	36.3	48.7

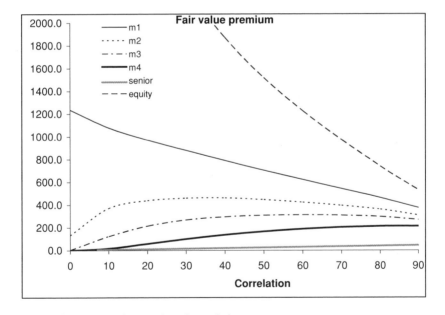

Figure 21.2   Fair value tranche premia and correlation

3. At high correlation the senior premium is close to the lowest CDS premium on the portfolio, and the equity tranche premium is close to the highest CDS premium.[6]
4. As correlation increases, the fair value premium of the equity tranche drops monotonically.

---

[6] This is similar to the N2D result. The precise behaviour for CDO tranches will vary according to the reference portfolio and size of the CDO tranches.

5. As correlation increases, the fair value premium of the senior tranche increases monotonically.
6. One tranche ('m2') has a premium that increases initially, then decreases as correlation increases. In particular, if the actual tranche premium is 400 bp there are two correlation figures ('implied correlation') consistent with this premium – one about 15% and another about 68%.

Note: Where the equity (or other) fair value premia are 'large' the market generally deals using a combination of a 500 bp premium (per annum) plus a non-refundable up-front premium. This has significantly helpful hedging implications (section 21.5).

Exercise
As correlation increases, value shifts from the equity tranche towards the senior tranche – why is this?

Hints:
1. At zero and 100% correlations, what is the appearance of the simulated default times?
2. At zero correlation, how many defaults would you expect to see? How much variation would you expect to see?
3. At 100% correlation, how many defaults would you expect to see? (Why is this the same as in (2)?) How much variation would you expect to see? (Why is this much greater than in (2)?)

21.4.3 CDO Pricing: Change of Tranching

With the same underlying portfolio the table shows the effect of reducing the tranche width and making the tranches more junior. Fair value spread on each tranche increases as the tranche becomes more junior.

A key feature in CDO product design, when producing a bespoke CDO, is the optimisation of tranche sizes and placement in order to obtain the best combination of tranche ratings, cost in the market to obtain protection on each tranche (not the same as fair-value premium), and tranche sizes – to minimise the total cost of servicing all tranches of protection.[7] See Table 21.3.

21.4.4 CDO Pricing: Change of Underlying

A change in the average spread of the underlying portfolio can be compensated for to some extent by changing the tranche attachment points. Table 21.4 shows a changed tranching for a high-spread portfolio compared with the portfolio above. In both cases we express the premium as a multiple of the average CDS. In practice the equity piece would be much larger with the aim of getting investment grade ratings on the senior tranches.

Introduction of a Few High-Spread Names

Table 21.5 shows the impact of introducing five names with 1000 bp CDS premium. With unchanged tranching the fair value premium on all tranches increases.

---

[7] The cost of servicing the tranche is the premium actually paid time the value of a 1 bp premium stream – as calculated in equation (21.2). In cases where a junior tranche is retained, the capital allocated (notional of the tranche) can be taken as the equivalent up-front premium for the tranche.

Table 21.3   Tranche size and premium

20% correlation

Tranche	Size	Premium	Size	Premium
Equity	2	3737.6	3	2908.2
m1	2	1516.8	3	971.1
m2	2	838.7	3	439.3
m3	2	489.5	3	214.7
m4	4	245.9	10	58.1
Senior	88	7.4	78	0.7

Table 21.4   100 bp and 500 bp portfolios: tranche premium divided by average CDS

20% correlation

Tranche	Size	Premium/100 bp	Size	Premium/500
Equity	3	29.08	3	27.02
m1	3	9.71	7	8.86
m2	3	4.39	6.5	4.20
m3	3	2.15	10	1.89
m4	10	0.58	8.5	0.64
Senior	78	0.01	65	0.03

Table 21.5   The impact of five wide spread names

	100 bp av portfolio		Five 1000 bp names		
20% correlation	Tranche	Premium	Premium	New tranching	Premium
Equity	3	2908.2	4350.1	5	2895.8
m1	3	971.1	1437.7	3	842.1
m2	3	439.3	652.8	3	402.0
m3	3	214.7	315.9	3	200.4
m4	10	58.1	84.9	10	52.9
Senior	78	0.7	1.0	76	0.6

Exercise
Assuming zero default time correlation, what is the expected number of defaults from these high-spread names?

If we increase the equity tranche size by 2% and reduce the senior tranche by the same amount, then we find that the spreads on the new tranching for the new portfolio is now very similar to the old one.

Change in Recovery Assumption

If we take the 100 bp average spread portfolio and, instead of assuming a single average 40% recovery for every name, we assume the recoveries are 0%, 40% and 80% (evenly distributed

Table 21.6 Flat 40% recovery assumption versus 0/40%/80% recovery assumption

20% correlation	Size	$R = 0.4$	$R = 0/0.4/0.8$
Equity	3	2908.2	3007.2
m1	3	971.1	948.9
m2	3	439.3	407.6
m3	3	214.7	191.5
m4	10	58.1	48.1
Senior	78	0.7	0.5

Table 21.7 Fair value premia at several maturities assuming no defaults

20% correlation	Size	No defaults		
		5-year premium	3-year premium	1-year premium
Equity	3	2908.2	3019.5	3210.4
m1	3	971.1	802.2	424.9
m2	3	439.3	298.4	97.3
m3	3	214.7	124.0	27.3
m4	10	58.1	26.9	2.5
Senior	78	0.7	0.1	0.0

across the names and across spread levels), then we find a significant (at the 95% confidence level on each tranche) shift in value from senior tranches to the equity tranche. See Table 21.6.

21.4.5 CDO Pricing: Change of Maturity

With the 100 bp average portfolio, 40% recovery, and the same tranching, the fair value premia on senior tranches drop as the CDO shortens *assuming* that no defaults and no change in spread occurs. Table 21.7 shows the fair value premia at shorter maturities for the same underlying portfolio.

21.5 SENSITIVITY CALCULATION AND HEDGING

In this section we consider the calculation of a variety of risk (sensitivity) numbers and simplistic hedging methods. We return to this topic again when we look at some specific deals and we consider correlation book management. The principles and methods described here are appropriate to both CDO tranches and N2D baskets.

21.5.1 Dynamic Hedging: Spread Risk

Principles

Pick a name in the reference pool. If the CDS premium on the name changes from one day to the next, then the portfolio product (CDO tranche or N2D basket) will also change in value.

If we own unit amount of the portfolio product and α of the CDS on the reference name, then the portfolio value is

$$P(x, t) = V(x, t) + \sum_{i=1...n} \alpha_i C_i(x_i, t) \tag{21.3}$$

and the change in the value of the portfolio is zero if

$$\alpha_i = -\frac{\partial V / \partial x_i}{\partial C_i / \partial x_i} \tag{21.4}$$

where V is the value of the CDO tranche, C is the value of the CDS, and x is the CDS premium. A discrete approximation replaces the derivatives by finite differences, with Δ denoting the change in value. We may take the differential form – the hedge ratio is the rate of change in the value of the tranche with respect to the CDS – or we may take a finite change such as 10 bp up on the CDS (or we may take the average of up and down moves).

The change in the value of the tranche for a given change in the premium on an underlying name is referred to as the **name (spread) sensitivity**, the **name [or micro] delta [or PV01]**. If we shift all names in the portfolio simultaneously, the change in the tranche value is sometimes referred to as the **macro delta**. The change in name sensitivity as spreads change is the **name (spread) convexity** or **micro convexity**, while the change in macro delta as spreads change is sometimes called the **macro (spread) convexity**.

Implementation

The CDS or bond sensitivity may be derived from a formula (Part II, Chapters 9 and 10). Generally the tranche or N2D sensitivity is calculated numerically (even under 'semi-closed form' solutions).

Bumping Method

For each reference name we first calculate the sensitivity of the hedge (CDS or bond) instrument by shifting the premium or spread, recalibrating (to give two sets of hazard rates for each name – the 'base' hazard rate and the 'shifted' hazard rate), and revaluing the CDS or bond.

Valuation of the tranche depends on the method used for pricing: simulation or closed form.

1. *Simulation.* For each set of correlated random numbers generating N default times (where N is the number of names in the reference pool) we also generate another N default times (using the same random numbers) using the shifted hazard rate. Each set of default time gives rise to $N + 1$ values for the tranche – the base value where the base hazard rate curves are used for all names, and N values where each name's base curve in turn is replaced by its shifted curve. The sensitivity of the tranche to a shift in a reference name's spread is then found by differencing the two relevant tranche valuations. Note:
   (a) It is important to use the same random numbers to simulate the base and the shifted default time.
   (b) Since we are taking differences in Monte Carlo simulated values, we need to use a greater number of simulations to get an accurate answer. If 10 000 simulations are required for a pricing – which might take one second – 1m simulations may be needed for sensitivity calculation which takes nearly three hours for a 100 name portfolio.

2. *Semi-closed form.* Semi-closed form methods use numerical integration but can only be applied when the correlation matrix has a certain form (in particular a single non-trivial correlation number will do) and the CDO does not have a complicated waterfall. Then the tranche is priced using the base and shifted hazard rate curves and a difference in values is calculated. Calculation time for the sensitivities is reduced to a few seconds. This has been one of the main practical reasons (but not the only reason – more complex correlation matrices do not necessarily give better prices) for quoting implied correlations based on a trivial correlation structure.

Approximate Method

The same procedure described in detail for the single name CDS case (Part II, section 18.2, equations (18.6) onwards, and Figure 18.2) can be applied to get the sensitivities for each nth-to-default basket to the rth reference entity. The procedure is only a little more complicated. All existing N2D events triggered by the rth name contribute to an increase in value of the N2D if the hazard rate on name r is increased. We obtain an estimate of an increase in the value of the N2D arising from new events by looking at cases where the $(N - 1)$2D is triggered and the N2D is not triggered, and finding those simulations where the rth name lies within Δ of the life of the trade.

The procedure is implemented in the Mathcad sheet 'Part III N2D CDO CLN price and hedge.med' (for the case of assumed equal recoveries) for nth-to-default baskets.

Hedge Ratios for CDO Tranches

We compare the hedge ratios for two CDOs which differ only in that, for the former CDO, the equity tranche receives a 1200 bp premium while the latter receives 500 bp. The reference portfolios for each are 125 investment grade names, and the tranching is the same. Hedge ratios are calculated using a flat 20% correlation across all tranches. Tables 21.8 and 21.9 show the minimum, average and maximum hedge ratios applicable to each name (expressed as a percentage of the notional of that name in the reference pool). Note that, for the equity tranche, all three figures are higher for the former portfolio than for the latter. The tables also show the hedge ratio for each name to each tranche (for a subset of the reference pool). The former portfolio has an average hedge ratio around 117%, while the latter is around 106%. In particular, the hedge ratios do not sum to 100%. Equivalently, a spread hedged CDO is not event hedged.

Note also that the higher spread names have a higher hedge ratio to the equity tranche, and a lower hedge ratio to the senior tranches, while the lower spread names show the opposite phenomenon.

Why do the hedge ratios not sum to 100? If the premium for protection on all CDO tranches was paid up-front, and the premia on CDS deals were also paid up-front, then the sum of the two (all CDO tranches, and all CDS) would be equal. We would also find the hedge ratios sum to 100%. The capital flows from the CDO and the hedging CDS deals are identical no matter how the premia are paid if the CDO tranches are in aggregate hedged by a 100% notional position in each reference CDS. However, a standard CDO tranche has a premium paid quarterly in arrears. Think about the equity tranche – with a premium of 1200 bp. As defaults occur this premium stream rapidly drops, whereas the sum of the CDS premia falls much more slowly. There is a difference in the premium profile between a CDO and a portfolio of CDS, and this causes hedging differences. Reducing the ongoing equity premium brings the sum of hedge

Table 21.8 CDO tranche hedges – high premium equity tranche

TRANCHE →	Total	Hedge ratio (% name notional)						Name CDS
		[22, 100]	[12, 22]	[9, 12]	[6, 9]	[3, 6]	[0, 3]	
min		0.1	2.6	4.2	10.6	27.2	53.2	
average		0.3	4.7	6.3	14.0	30.3	62.1	
max		0.5	7.0	8.3	16.7	31.4	72.2	
Reference entity								
Lafarge SA	117.9	0.2	4.2	5.9	13.5	30.1	64.0	50
Linde AG	117.8	0.3	4.9	6.6	14.4	30.7	61.0	35
Lloyds TSB Bank Plc	117.2	0.5	7.0	8.3	16.7	31.4	53.2	12
Marks & Spencer Group Plc	116.8	0.1	2.6	4.2	10.6	27.2	72.1	121
Metro AG	117.9	0.2	4.0	5.7	13.2	29.9	64.8	55
Muenchener Rueckversicherungs AG	117.7	0.3	5.3	6.9	14.9	31.0	59.2	28
National Grid Transco Plc	117.9	0.3	4.6	6.3	14.0	30.5	62.2	41
Pearson Plc	117.9	0.3	4.5	6.2	13.9	30.4	62.6	43
Peugeot SA	117.8	0.3	4.7	6.4	14.1	30.5	61.8	39
Pinault-Printemps-Redoute	117.2	0.1	2.6	4.2	10.6	27.5	72.2	119
Portugal Telecom International Finance BV	117.8	0.3	5.0	6.7	14.6	30.8	60.5	33
RWE AG	117.7	0.3	5.4	7.0	15.0	31.0	59.0	28

Table 21.9 CDO tranche hedges – 500 bp premium equity tranche

TRANCHE →	Total	Hedge ratio (% name notional)						Name CDS
		[22, 100]	[12, 22]	[9, 12]	[6, 9]	[3, 6]	[0, 3]	
min		0.1	2.6	4.2	10.6	27.2	43.2	
average		0.3	4.7	6.3	14.0	30.3	51.0	
max		0.5	7.0	8.3	16.7	31.4	59.9	
Reference entity								
Lafarge SA	106.6	0.2	4.2	5.9	13.5	30.1	52.7	50
Linde AG	106.8	0.3	4.9	6.6	14.4	30.7	50.0	35
Lloyds TSB Bank Plc	107.2	0.5	7.0	8.3	16.7	31.4	43.2	12
Marks & Spencer Group Plc	104.4	0.1	2.6	4.2	10.6	27.2	59.8	121
Metro AG	106.5	0.2	4.0	5.7	13.2	29.9	53.4	55
Muenchener Rueckversicherungs AG	107.0	0.3	5.3	6.9	14.9	31.0	48.5	28
National Grid Transco Plc	106.8	0.3	4.6	6.3	14.0	30.5	51.2	41
Pearson Plc	106.7	0.3	4.5	6.2	13.9	30.4	51.5	43
Peugeot SA	106.8	0.3	4.7	6.4	14.1	30.5	50.8	39
Pinault-Printemps-Redoute	104.9	0.1	2.6	4.2	10.6	27.5	59.9	119
Portugal Telecom International Finance BV	106.9	0.3	5.0	6.7	14.6	30.8	49.6	33
RWE AG	107.1	0.3	5.4	7.0	15.0	31.0	48.3	28

ratios down (it may even be less than 100% if the equity premium is zero). Traders who prefer a statically hedged synthetic CDO will either

(a) retain the equity piece – ongoing premium of zero, or
(b) buy equity protection paying a substantial up-front premium and paying a much lower ongoing premium.

These hedge differences can be very substantial – on long-dated high-yield reference portfolios the delta hedging portfolio initially may be 50% larger than the notional size of the CDO. Reducing the ongoing equity premium brings the sum of hedge ratios down (it may even be less than 100% if the equity premium is zero).

Hedging in Practice

We shall illustrate some conclusions that can be drawn from the concept of hedging spread sensitivities and the above formulae applied to an F2D product. Similar results apply to CDO tranches.

Time Decay

Suppose we are long 10m F2D protection on two names, so CDS hedges will be sold. The hedge ratios might be 70% in one name and 60% in another – i.e. we sell 7m CDS protection on the former name and 6m on the latter. The income from the hedge will generally not be equal to the premium on the F2D. As the trade matures we find that the hedge ratios increase (assuming constant spreads) and generate an increasing income from larger sold CDS positions (albeit at declining CDS levels arising from the slope of the typical CDS curve). Figure 21.3 show the net premium income from the dynamic hedge (the initial position is the rhs of the chart at five years to maturity).

In the early years more is being paid for the F2D protection than is the expected cost of that protection – and the situation reverses in later years. This is an example of **time sensitivity**, **time decay** or **theta** for a portfolio product. The time decay can be defined as the change in value of a portfolio CD as the time to maturity reduces (by a specified interval).

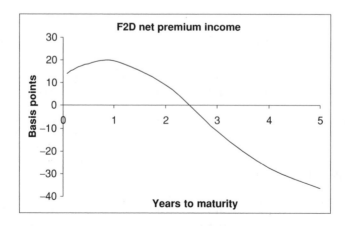

Figure 21.3   First-to-default protection and hedges: net premium income

Table 21.10 F2D hedges and changes

		Spread changes	Hedge ratios (%)
Day 1	Name 1		70
	Name 2		70
Day 2	Name 1	+10	68
	Name 2	+10	68
	Name 1	−10	72
	Name 2	−10	72
	Name 1	+10	76
	Name 2	−10	66
	Name 1	−10	66
	Name 2	+10	76

Spread Correlation and Volatility Risk

For simplicity take a two name basket, at 70% correlation the premium is around 80% of the sum of CDS spreads. We examine the hedges in two pairs of situations: if spreads move up or down simultaneously, or if one moves up and one down.

1. Simultaneous 10 bp moves cause a change in the hedge ratio in the opposite direction. If spreads rise we find we have smaller CDS hedge positions so have to buy back hedges at higher spreads. This leads to a loss on rehedging whether CDS premia rise or fall, as long as they move together. The greater the move, the greater the loss.
2. Opposite moves cause an increase in the hedge on the name whose premium has risen, and a reduction on the one that has fallen. We have to buy back some of the CDS whose premium has fallen – leading to an immediate profit – and sell some more of the CDS whose premium has risen[8] – leading to a profit again.

The supposed spread changes and impact on the hedge ratios are summarised in Table 21.10.

Dynamic spread hedging of a N2D or CDO tranche is subject to a risk to spread correlation and spread volatility – the higher the correlation and volatility the greater the loss (on long F2D positions), the lower the correlation the higher the profit.

Why do spread correlation and volatility not figure in the pricing model? Figure 21.4 shows the results of simulated dynamic (costless) hedging where the hedges are calculated under the default time Normal Copula model, and where hazard rates follow a lognormal random walk process. The pricing correlation for the two name F2D is 60%, and the spread correlation under the simulations is between 0 and 100%. The expected rehedging profit is expressed as a corresponding error in the premium (a positive, meaning that the premium charged on the F2D was too high and led to a profit). A 75% spread volatility was used.

We find that the expected rehedging cost is zero if the spread correlation and the pricing correlation are the same; if spread correlation turns out to be lower than pricing correlation, we make an expected profit on long F2D and equity CDO tranches through dynamic hedging; and

---

[8] One might sell more notional at the same premium – below market levels – and also take an up-front premium to compensate. Thus a positive cashflow is generated. If premia remain at expected levels this cashflow will turn into profit.

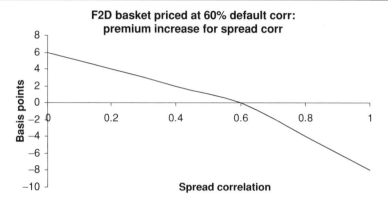

Figure 21.4   Long F2D dynamically spread hedged in different spread environments

if spread correlation turns out to be higher we make a loss. This is often used as an argument that the default time correlation should be the spread correlation – if it is not, then a significant pricing element is missing from our model.

Note that individual simulation paths can lead to substantially different P&L results from the expected value. *In other words a trader who spread hedges a book that is predominantly long of protection on F2D or equity CDO tranches, using CDS contracts as the hedge, is running a substantial risk to spread correlation* (even if the products are correctly priced). This risk is effectively captured by the book's (default time) correlation risk – see below.

Also note that rehedging is done daily: changes in short-term spread correlation can have a big impact on P&L.

Default and Spread Jump Risk

Consider, for example, a long protection F2D position on two names hedged by short positions (say 70%) in each CDS. According to the default time correlation model, on the early default of name 1, the spread on name 2 jumps substantially. Seventy nominal bonds delivered into the short CDS protection are passed (together with a further 30 bought in the market) into the long F2D protection – resulting in a capital gain of 30 × (1 − recovery). However the short CDS on name 2 has to be unwound. Within the model world this should have jumped in spread, and the unwind therefore leads to a capital loss. The expected value of this capital loss will be similar to the expected capital gain on the defaulted name – but there is not an exact match.

More importantly, does this pattern of behaviour occur in practice? To the extent that the model says the jump in spread occurs at the instant that the correlated name defaults, this is unrealistic. But consider a basket on telecoms bought in 2000. As telecom names suffered a rapid increase in spreads, a long F2D basket would have suffered substantial rehedging losses from the delta rehedging in the highly correlated environment. The default of one of the names in the basket may then lead to no further widening in spreads, but would give rise to a capital profit on the defaulted name (as long as the hedge ratio was less than 100%). This profit would offset to a greater or lesser extent the loss realised in the run up to default. It can therefore be argued that the default time correlation model correctly captures the broad features of the correlated default process, although the timing is wrong.

21.5.2   Static Hedging: Default Event Risk

In the context of single name default swaps a 'default event hedge' is simple to understand. For example, a 5-year long USD 10m protection position on GMAC can be default event hedged by selling USD 10m of a 3-year CDS on the same name. On a credit event, debt delivered into the short position can be delivered into the long position, and the USD 10m received on the long position can be used to pay off the short.

Unfortunately 'default event hedging' does not have such a clear meaning in the context of credit portfolio products. We illustrate the problem with some examples and consider two alternative means of defining and calculating 'default event risk'.

'Back-to-Back' CDO

Typically a bank which sets up a CDO structure and obtains protection on all the tranches sells protection on all the underlying CDS contracts to the full notional amount in the reference portfolio. A credit event on a reference name will lead to a loss of (say) 6m on a 10m notional exposure, and protection on this loss is obtained from the tranches. This is often called a 'back-to-back' hedge, and is also a **default event hedge** in the sense that *capital flows are perfectly hedged*. It is also a static hedge – the CDS hedge size is the fixed notional in the reference pool, and is the constant amount on which the CDO provides credit event protection.

Event Risk on a Single Name

Another way of thinking of default event risk is as follows. Consider a specific name in the reference pool – name 1. Suppose name 1 defaults. What is the change in the value of all the tranches? We can then choose a notional exposure for the hedge, so that the change in value of the hedge equals the change in value of the tranches. (We could apply this idea equally to a single tranche rather than an entire portfolio, or we could apply it to an nth-to-default position.)

This definition has some surprising consequences. Think of a CDO and all the tranches of protection and the reference pool of CDS, and suppose that all trades are done at fair value premia. If we make a reference name default then the CDS on that name in the reference pool has a jump in value – approximately the loss-given default if the premium is low. The equity piece has a jump in value arising from the loss-given default (LGD) and now the premium on what remains on the tranche is below the fair market premium. So the hedge ratio for the equity tranche alone is greater than 100%. The remaining tranches have all now degraded – their lower attachment point has effectively dropped in relation to the remaining reference pool. So the hedge ratio for all these tranches is also positive.

Table 21.11 illustrates the above concept for a CDO. The reference pool is 100 names with CDS premia ranging from 55 bp to 250 bp and recoveries from 15% to 40%, and 20% correlation is assumed. Tranches are assumed to be paid the fair value premium. The table shows the 'default event' hedge ratios for each tranche for a 55 bp name and a 250 bp name, calculated by assuming immediate default of that name (and no change in the remaining CDS premia) and recalculating tranche values. Not that the hedge ratios, and the total, are quite strongly dependent on the correlation used and the tranche premia.

In addition, there is the problem with the approach in that we cannot force a specific name to default immediately, leaving other spreads unchanged, and be consistent with our pricing model.

Table 21.11   CDO 'default event' hedge ratios (impact of immediate default)

Tranche	Hedge ratio (% reference notional)	
	250 bp name	50 bp name
0–3	136	138
3–6	36	39
6–9	18	20
9–12	10	11
12–22	11	14
22–100	2	3

The above definition of default event risk may be useful for the calculation of a risk number but is not suitable for hedging purposes. The following approach is preferred.

Expected Event Risk

The 'back-to back' CDO had the property that any capital cashflow triggered by a default event in the reference pool is matched by a cashflow in the tranches. Thinking of the default time simulations, for each name we can see whether (and by how much) the default hit the equity tranche, the junior mezzanine tranche,..., etc. We can calculate the expected value of the impact of default of name 1 on each of the tranches. We know that the sum of these expected values is equal to that for the CDS (since cashflows are identical). The value for each event is the discounted value of the LGD less the discounted value of the premium stream up to the default date (for narrow spread names we could ignore the latter term without much loss of accuracy since it is small compared with the LGD).

The following definition of default event risk is consistent with the model and has more natural properties. It can be thought of as the expected impact of the default event on each tranche compared with the impact on the underlying CDS.

The 'default event risk' for the kth tranche (or, similarly, kth-to-default contract) to the ith name in the basket is given by

$$\text{DEHR}(k, i) = \frac{\sum\limits_{\text{simulations}} \text{TDB}(k, i)}{\sum\limits_{\text{simulations}} \text{CDSB}(i)}$$

where

- CDSB(i) denotes the value of the capital payoff less the premium stream arising from the CDS for those cases where name i defaults before maturity, and
- TDB(k, i) denotes the value of the capital payoff less the premium stream arising from the kth tranche for those cases where name i defaults before maturity.

For example, for a CDS, each simulation gives rise to the following valuation term:

$$\text{CDSB}(i) = (1 - R_i) \cdot \exp[-r \cdot T(i)] - p_i \frac{1 - \exp[-r \cdot T(i)]}{r} \quad \text{if } T(i) < \text{contract life}$$

$$= 0 \text{ otherwise}$$

Table 21.12   CDO 'default event' hedge ratios (impact of expected default)

Tranche	Hedge ratio (% reference notional)	
	250 bp name	50 bp name
0–3	29	38
3–6	22	25
6–9	16	15
9–12	12	9
12–22	16	11
22–100	5	2

Table 21.13   Correlation sensitivity of CDO tranches (EUR per 1bn)

Tranche	+1% correl sensitivity
[22, 100]	5 069
[12, 22]	51 737
[9, 12]	46 987
[6, 9]	64 962
[3, 6]	31 851
[0, 3]	−216 106

where R_i is the assumed recovery on name i and $T(i)$ is its time of default. The formula for TDB(k, i) is similar (we need to take into account the amount by which the tranche is hit). Such an approach is very fast to implement under a simulation environment.

Table 21.12 shows the expected event hedge ratios for the same portfolio as in Table 21.11.

The default event hedge ratios sum to 100% – as does the 'back-to-back' hedge – and there is a marked difference between high- and low-spread names and the event sensitivity of each tranche. The default sensitivity of a tranche (to the default of a single name) is sometimes referred to as the **omega**.

21.5.3   Correlation Risk

Figure 21.2 and table 21.2 show that the fair-value premium depends on the pricing correlation – correspondingly valuation of a portfolio deal will depend on the correlation. There is a sensitivity of value to the pricing correlation. This sensitivity varies according to the tranche – and is typically strongest (per unit of nominal) for equity tranches. Some (mezzanine) tranches may be quite insensitive to even substantial correlation changes. Table 21.13 shows the correlation sensitivities of the portfolio used for Table 21.8 (and assuming a 1bn reference portfolio). Correlation risk is calculated assuming a 1% increase, and is expressed in EUR.

At this level of correlation (a flat 20%) there is a significant level of correlation risk on all the tranches shown. The equity tranche has an opposite sensitivity to all the others – increasing correlation takes value from the equity tranche and adds it to the others.

Correlation risk describes the sensitivity of the tranche value to a change in the pricing correlation. There is also an unmeasured exposure to spread correlation and spread sensitivity.

A tranche spread hedged along the lines of section 21.5.1 (using single name CDS) may leave a substantial correlation risk, and the only way to hedge correlation products is with other correlation products.

A deal in a CDO tranche (perhaps a bespoke portfolio and structure for a client) is best hedged by hedging the correlation risk first – for example, using appropriate tranches of standard liquid CDO products (such as CDX and iTraxx tranched portfolios). Once the correlation risk is eliminated, the spread risk can be addressed. A good correlation hedge will usually largely eliminate (bucketed) spread risk. Individual cross-bucket spread risks may remain to be hedged. For example, the bespoke portfolio may have no autos but an excess of finance exposures; when hedged with an iTraxx tranche there will be a net long protection in autos and short in finance. This could be hedged using the iTraxx auto and finance index products (not tranches). Residual large exposures in certain names could then be hedged with CDS.

Following this approach, exposure to correlation changes (and to spread correlation and volatility) is largely eliminated. Correlation sensitivity is sometimes referred to as **rho**.

21.5.4   Recovery Risk

Table 21.6 showed *sensitivity to a change in the standard deviation* of assumed recovery rates. In addition, if we change the expected recovery rate there is a greater sensitivity of tranche values – tranches of a CDO have digital risk. Table 21.14 shows the sensitivity to a 5% increase in assumed recovery rates across all names.

Recovery rate risk has to be hedged by other digital exposure. Hedging CDO tranches initially using other similar CDO tranches will tend to introduce equal and opposite recovery risk, leaving a typically small residual. Of course, spread hedging alone will not achieve this.

21.5.5   Convexity Risks

Credit spreads are not well behaved – jumps in spreads occur on individual names (Xerox, Marconi, and many other examples exist of large overnight spread moves without an accompanying credit event), or on sectors or geographical regions (Telecoms, Autos, Asia). This introduces a large exposure to *spread convexity* risk. Table 21.15 shows convexity risk for a junior mezzanine tranche calculated by shifting all CDS premia up simultaneously by 100. Alternative measure would shift spreads individually and by sectors.

Again Figure 21.2 shows **correlation convexity** risk. Fortunately implied correlation does not appear to show marked short-term changes. On the other hand, investors using historically calculated correlation matrices, especially where unstable calculation methods are employed, will experience large profits or losses arising from correlation convexity risk.

Table 21.14   Tranche sensitivity to recovery rates

Tranche	5% recovery rate sensitivity
[22, 100]	−5 124
[12, 22]	−49 291
[9, 12]	−44 774
[6, 9]	−63 858
[3, 6]	−45 980
[0, 3]	186 455

Table 21.15 Spread convexity: change in hedge ratio for a 100 bp jump in spreads

TRANCHE →	Total	Hedge ratio (% name notional)					
		[22, 100]	[12, 22]	[9, 12]	[6, 9]	[3, 6]	[0, 3]
min		3.7	17.4	9.8	8.0	−9.8	−33.4
average		4.9	18.9	8.7	5.3	−9.3	−36.7
max		8.4	23.6	8.0	2.7	−8.9	−43.2
Reference entity							
Lafarge SA	−8.7	4.4	18.2	8.9	5.9	−8.5	−37.6
Linde AG	−8.2	4.9	18.9	8.6	4.9	−9.7	−35.9
Lloyds TSB Bank Plc	−7.8	5.4	18.3	7.1	2.6	−11.2	−30.0
Marks & Spencer Group Plc	−8.0	3.7	17.5	9.9	8.6	−4.7	−43.1
Metro AG	−7.4	5.4	20.7	9.6	6.1	−9.4	−39.9
Muenchener Rueckversicherungs AG	−8.0	5.2	19.1	8.4	4.4	−10.3	−34.7
National Grid Transco Plc	−7.9	5.2	19.8	9.0	5.3	−9.8	−37.4
Pearson Plc	−8.2	4.9	19.2	8.9	5.4	−9.3	−37.3
Peugeot SA	−8.5	4.7	18.5	8.6	5.2	−9.3	−36.2
Pinault-Printemps-Redoute	−7.3	4.4	19.4	10.5	8.7	−5.6	−44.6
Portugal Telecom International Finance BV	−8.7	4.6	18.0	8.3	4.8	−9.4	−34.9
RWE AG	−8.4	4.9	18.4	8.1	4.3	−10.0	−34.1

Consider the 5–8% tranche of an investment grade CDO referencing 50 EU and 50 Asian entities. This is hedged by appropriate nominals of the 5–8% tranche of two separate CDOs: one referencing the same 50 EU names, and the other referencing the same 50 Asian names. Suppose five EU and no Asian names default over the next year. The tranche of the EU CDO will probably have made capital payments, whereas neither the 100 name nor the Asian CDO tranches have been hit (although the 100 name tranch is now closer to being hit). In this case there is **name convexity** where the trade is subject to a risk to an imbalance in the way defaults occur.

Once more hedging, initially using other similar correlation products, greatly reduces the convexity risks.

21.6 MODEL ERRORS AND TESTS; ALTERNATIVE MODELS

We conclude this chapter with a review of the model, the captured and hidden risks, and some alternative possible modelling approaches.

21.6.1 Captured and Hidden Risks

The model has captured and can explicitly calculate the following risks:

1. Interest rate risk
2. Spread risk on individual reference names
3. Recovery rate risk

4. Event risk
5. Default time correlation risk
6. Convexity risks.

The model as also identified but does not capture

7. Spread correlation risk
8. Spread volatility risk.

Additionally there is model risk related to

9. Choice of correlation
10. Choice of Copula
11. The general form of the model.

Items 1 to 5 have been explicitly addressed above, while 6 to 8 have been implicitly addressed. We shall look at correlation in detail in Chapter 22, and we look at alternative Copulae in Chapter 24. In the remainder of this chapter we briefly look at spread models – revisiting a point touched on in Part II – and we discuss the setting of reserves.

21.6.2   Spread Models

Suppose we wish to price a first-to-default product on a basket of two names. We might initially assume that a stochastic hazard rate process, as described in Part II, section 9.7, would be appropriate. We can use this model to price the individual CDS and a F2D on the two names. If the two names are investment grade and the F2D is a 5-year deal, we surprisingly find that the fair value premium for the F2D is the sum of the two CDS premia – no matter what the spread correlation (assuming a spread volatility of around 100%). Only if we look at long-dated F2D on two initially wide spread names do we find any significant impact from the spread volatility and correlation. Figure 21.6 shows the results for such a model on a 25-year basket of 500 bp and 800 bp names. We conclude that a diffusion model for spreads is incapable of explaining the basket prices we observe in the marketplace.

Indeed spreads do not appear to follow a diffusion process – Figure 21.5 shows three telecom spreads and a relatively common 'explosive' price move (Andreasen, 2001).

Suppose instead spreads are driven by several external factors – world recession or an industry funding crisis (Telecoms, Asia) as well as individual name factors. Suppose these external factors can be modelled by a jump process. The factor can jump up a large amount at a low rate, or down by smaller amounts but at a higher frequency, so the expected hazard rate change is zero. The factor is applied to all default rates for names for whom that factor is relevant. The implied jump process in default rates gives rise to 'default-time' correlation. Figure 21.6 compares the jump process model with Copula prices and prices from the spread diffusion model.

The Copula model prices lie between two sets of 'jump model' prices (one using an arbitrarily chosen large jump, the other with half that jump), and these three price curves are significantly steeper than that derived from the default rate (diffusion) model. Clearly a jump process model is capable of producing similar results to the Copula model. One could argue that the jumps are independently observable, so some real world estimates are available. However calibration of the model is complex – we have to work back from CDS data using the stochastic (jump) process model in order to find the initial hazard rate. The end result is something that is

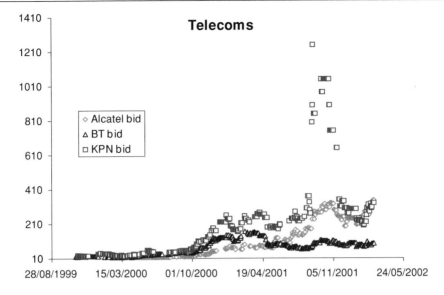

Figure 21.5   Telecom CDS bid spreads

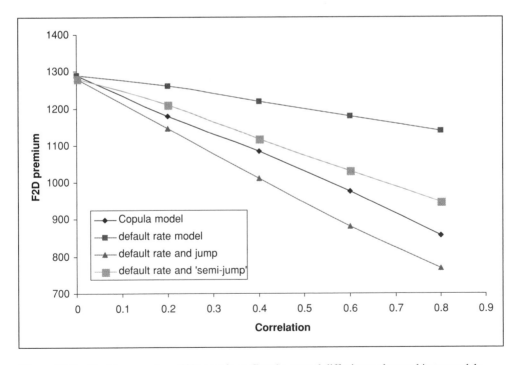

Figure 21.6   Model comparison F2D premium: Copula, spread diffusion and spread jump models

indistinguishable from the Copula model – both curves have strong downward slopes, the absolute levels may differ but that would just mean that the market implied correlations on the two models are different. There does not appear to be any significant advantage in this route, against which there are substantial calculation disadvantages.

21.6.3 Reserves

For a general CDO tranche, marking to model requires the following:

1. Estimation of the marking correlation: this in turn will depend on
    (a) the underlying reference portfolio
    (b) the tranche attachment points
    (c) the maturity of the deal.
2. Single name data and assumptions.

For portfolio products these reserves therefore include the following:

1. A bid–offer reserve if model values are based off mid.
2. A recovery (mean and standard deviation) reserve.
3. The underlying portfolio may differ from the portfolio used to estimate implied correlation – a name correlation reserve.
4. The portfolio tranching may differ from the portfolio tranching on the benchmark portfolio – a tranching correlation reserve.
5. The portfolio maturity may differ from benchmark maturity – a maturity correlation reserve.
6. A model reserve.

Even on liquid products – such as standard CDO tranches – this may mean marking to mid and having a **bid–offer reserve** to effectively mark to the worse of bid or offer. Some institutions take the view that marking to mid on a balanced portfolio does not need such a reserve since a portfolio trade would be done at closer to mid.

The **reference pool reserve** is chosen to reflect the impact on the tranche correlation of having a different reference pool from the CDO structure used to derive implied correlation. For large (60+ names) diversified (diversity score > 30) pools of investment grade names there seems to be little variation in correlation for comparable tranches. Examination of the implied correlations on the CDX and iTraxx portfolios (and predecessor portfolios) shows differences of only a few percent (after adjusting for tranche attachment point differences) for portfolios that have totally different reference entities.

The **interpolation reserve** allows for errors that might be introduced in interpolating a correlation for an 8–11% tranche based on implied correlations on 6–9% and 9–12% tranches. Alternative interpolation routines typically give under 2% correlation errors for intermediate tranches. Equity tranche correlations are more sensitive for homogeneous portfolios, but the equity price may be driven by particular widespread names rather than the correlation on other portfolios. The senior tranche has relatively little correlation sensitivity over the likely range of correlation, though is typically of much larger size, so the EUR sensitivity can be large. However, there is a more active market in senior tranches generally so this tranche may be capable of being priced directly.

The deal on the books may differ from the maturity of the CDO being used to derive the implied correlation. This will give rise to a **maturity reserve**. Comparisons of the 5- and 10-year iTraxx or CDX quotes show relatively little difference. However the situation may be quite different for shorter-dated portfolios where there are currently no market-traded instruments. The development of active shorter-dated indices and tranches would be useful for marking mature portfolios to market.

Finally a **model reserve** may be applied. It can be argued that the Normal Copula is a standard pricing tool and such a reserve is not necessary. But consider a CDO tranche which is spread hedged CDS only. One known model deficiency is the lack of spread correlation and volatility in the model, and the trading strategy is open to this risk.

Other reserves – such as a **convexity reserve** – may be raised. The choice of reserves to include, and their level, depends very much on the trading and hedging strategy of the institution. A book of CDO tranches hedged with similar tranches faces far fewer risks, and needs less reserving than a directional (in correlation) book.

22

The Correlation Matrix

The Normal Copula – and other Copula models discussed in Chapter 23 – is based on parameters we cannot observe directly. Where does the correlation matrix come from and what are the implications of whatever approach is taken?

In the following sections, bear in mind that the result of the process is a *default time* correlation matrix. Some calculations are based on observable data – say, equity returns or spreads, and those correlations of course are equity return or spread correlations – but as soon as that matrix is used in the pricing model described in Chapter 21 they are being used as default time correlations. The model presented in Chapter 21 produces correlated default times, and the inputs are the drivers for that process whether they were taken from equity data, spread data, or are arbitrary assumptions.

Sources of Default Time Correlation

Understanding the source of the default time correlation is likely to provide some help in deriving the correlations themselves.

Look again at Figure 2.1 – default rates over time. As default rates rise in a recession (and expected default times fall – equation (18.1)) then we see more defaults occurring together. RiskMetrics Group (Gupton *et al.*, 1997) use such data to derive the correlation of defaults within a year (a **binomial correlation**[1]), and find correlations in the 0 to 6% range. Such binomial correlations correspond to default time correlations on the 0 to 30% range.

The health of the economy is certainly a major factor[2] driving default time correlation. We have also seen (Figure 21.5) that industries (or geographical regions) may experience dramatic widening or narrowing of their spreads while other parts of the world economy are largely unaffected. We may think of using *equity data* as a rough indicator of moves in the economy and, possibly, moves in default times. Alternatively we may argue that we can identify key *factors* or *tags* (industry, region, . . .) and use a variety of sources to guess at the default time correlation matrix.

Equation (18.1) also tells us that default time correlation and default rate correlation are intertwined. We have already looked at a correlated default rate model (with and without jumps – section 21.6.2) and seen that developing such a model has few practical attractions. Nevertheless, CDS premia or bond spreads (closely related to default rates and default times) may provide a valuable source of data for default time correlation. Secondly, the hedging results in section 21.5 separately underline the importance of *spread correlation* in N2D/CDO product pricing.

---

[1] Binomial correlation is difficult to work with (Li, 2000). Also, if we look at a longer period than a year the correlations starts to increase, and will become unity for a very long interval.

[2] 'Factor' can be interpreted here in the general sense or in the sense of an external data series driving the default rates (and times) – see section 22.6.2.

In the following sections we investigate the above and related issues. Our conclusion is that, for the purposes of valuing and risk-managing CDO positions 'implied correlation' is in principle the only valid correlation to use. Where a source of implied correlation is not available, spread correlation is the more attractive alternative – although there is quite strong evidence that correlations based on data histories do not give market prices for CDO tranches (section 22.5).

22.1   CONSTRAINTS: WHAT MAKES A CORRELATION MATRIX?

Imagine you have three coins, A, B and C. If you toss A and it comes up heads, then B comes up tails – A and B are perfectly negatively correlated. Suppose B and C are also perfectly negatively correlated – what does this imply for A and C? If A comes up heads, then B comes up tails, so C comes up heads – A and C are perfectly (positively) correlated. Any other 'correlation' (a number between -1 and $+1$) does not produce results consistent with the other correlation numbers.

We saw a slightly more realistic and less obvious example in Chapter 6. A more relevant example is the following. Consider a 10 name F2D portfolio. It is not possible that every name is *minus* 20% correlated with every other name. For a 100 name portfolio it is only possible for every name to have a tiny negative correlation (around 1%) with every other name.

What properties does a correlation matrix have? Every number on the diagonal must be unity (everything is 100% correlated with itself); every number off the diagonal must be between 1 and -1; the matrix must be symmetric – the correlation of A with B is the same as the correlation of B with A. But that is not enough. A further condition is that the matrix must be **invertible**.

Suppose we have a three name F2D. Two banks (one US and one EU) are highly correlated – say 0.9 – and the EU bank and a US software company have very low correlation – say 0. What are the restrictions on the third correlation, x, in the matrix below?

$$\begin{pmatrix} 1 & 0.9 & 0 \\ 0.9 & 1 & x \\ 0 & x & 1 \end{pmatrix}$$

It turns out that x must be between plus or minus 43%. Suppose now we have a 100 name correlation matrix, and we did not know 10 of those correlations. How do you find the limits on those remaining correlations?

We conclude the following:

1. Any method used to produce the default time correlation matrix must satisfy the invertibility constraint.
2. Any process using the correlation matrix – such as a 'correlation stress' or correlation sensitivity calculations – which involves changing values in the matrix, must be sure to satisfy the invertibility constraint for the altered matrix.
3. It may be hard to produce a correlation matrix.

There are two simple ways to ensure that the third requirement is met and we give names to these two matrices.

One Factor Matrix

Note that a matrix that has unity on the diagonal, and the same number ρ, where $0 < \rho < 1$ everywhere else in the matrix, is invertible. Any stress of ρ to ρ_2, where $0 < \rho_2 < 1$ will also produce a correlation matrix.

Data Matrix

Also note that any correlation matrix derived from a consistent set of data (say daily returns for every Monday to Friday between 1 January 1997 and 31 December 2004 – with no gaps or omissions) is indeed a correlation matrix whether or not the underlying correlation data is of good quality. However, it may not be possible to stress this matrix by raising every correlation (other than unity) by the same number, delta (for any value of delta) in order to calculate correlation sensitivity.

22.2 IMPLIED CORRELATION

Imagine that an equity options trader wishes to value a portfolio of options covering a range of strikes and maturities. Typically the trader uses the Black–Scholes model, and uses prices of exchange-traded options to derive implied volatilities, then interpolates these volatilities to the strikes and maturities needed, and then prices the portfolio using the Black–Scholes model. Incidentally, the trader may not use that model to help to determine his or her own trading strategy – a stochastic volatility model with jumps may be preferred but, since that is slow to evaluate, the policy is to mark to market using Black–Scholes for valuation purposes. Any other fundamentally different approach – such as using historical volatility estimates – is wrong since the trader needs to know the price at which a deal could be unwound in the market.

The Normal Copula model takes the role corresponding to the Black–Scholes model when it comes to pricing N2D and CDO tranches. Actively traded liquid instruments (iTraxx tranches, for example) are used to calculate an implied correlation for the tranche (perhaps via the corresponding 'base' tranche – see below). Implied correlations are then interpolated and adjusted to come up with pricing correlations for closely related products.

Where 'mark-to-market' and risk calculations are concerned implied correlation is, in principle, the only answer to the question 'Where does the correlation come from?'. However there are practical problems in some cases where alternative approaches may be sought, and we shall address these below.

22.2.1 Index CDO Deals and Implied Correlation

Prices in tranches of the iTraxx and CDX portfolios are quoted consistently and on demand by market-makers. For example, the 7–10% tranche may have a quoted premium of 150/170 bp. In order to calculate an implied correlation we also need

(a) to know the relevant yield curve levels,
(b) to know the CDS premia on all the known underlying names, and
(c) to decide whether to use bid, mid or offer spreads.

Table 22.1   Bid–offer tranche premium and bid–offer correlation

Tranche	Market bid spread	Market offer spread	Bid correlation	Offer correlation
0–3	20%/500	24%/500	26.5	19.6
3–6	150	196	8.7	14.7
6–9	58	74	18.3	22.5
9–12	28	44	23.5	30.0
12–22	14	20	33.3	38.3

Typically the client is required to estimate the current CDS levels behind the market-maker's quote. This will lead to some (small) uncertainty in the calculation of the implied correlation (also called 'compound correlation'). The impact of the premium bid to offer on the implied correlation is indicated in Table 22.1, based on some wide bid–offer data for early TRAC-X trades. Typically calculations are based on a mid-tranche premium and mid-correlation. We describe the process assuming that the client has sufficient and good quality information on the yield curve and CDS spreads.

Given the above data and the market quote, the Normal Copula pricing model is used with a one-factor matrix, and the correlation adjusted until the calculated fair value premium agrees with market levels. The result is the 'implied correlation' (or 'compound correlation') – say 15.8%.

We saw in Chapter 21 that a tranche may have two implied correlation numbers – often quite different values, say 15% and 78% – which give rise to the same premium. Choice of the implied correlation will affect sensitivities of the tranche and has real implications for trading. In practice it will probably be possible to make a consistent choice over time for that tranche – generally the lower value will be consistent with neighbouring tranche correlations and recent unambiguous implied correlations.[3]

A consequence of the 'implied correlation' approach is that names A and B in the reference portfolio have a correlation of, say, 30% when we are looking at a senior tranche, but only 5% when we are looking at a junior mezzanine tranche. Each tranche must be priced using its own correlation, so we cannot generate a consistent set of default times across a universe of names which may appear in many of our trades. In particular, it is not clear how to price a CDO of CDOs, or a CDO with complex waterfall, consistently using implied correlations.

We should note that a tranche may trade on a premium such that no choice of implied correlation will give that amount as the fair value premium. If we take an extreme example where the tranche premium is very small – changing the correlation matrix may produce a minimum fair value premium for the tranche which is significantly above zero. Similarly there is a maximum premium for the tranche as the correlation varies from 0 to 100%. Results are not materially altered by using a different form of correlation matrix (e.g. equity-based correlations). Such situations were common when there was not a transparent market in CDO tranches.

In situations such as the above we conclude that, either the tranches are above or below fair price (there is an arbitrage present), or the model is faulty. Note that tranche premia on actively

---

[3] On the basis of consistency with neighbouring tranche values it is difficult to imagine ambiguity occurring. This would require a high value of equity implied and low value of senior implied (so that mezzanine implied cover a wide range) but then that would mean that the capital value of the CDO is less than the capital value of all the reference name CDSs) Conversely, a low equity implied and a high senior implied would mean the value of the CDO exceeds the value of all the CDSs.

traded CDO tranches, and on F2D baskets, are now generally consistent with the existence of a positive correlation.

22.2.2   Base Correlation

Figures in this section can be reproduced using 'Chapter 22 demo CDO.xls', and the charts are in 'Chapter 22 charts.xls'.

We saw in Chapter 21 that 'base tranches' (tranches whose lower attachment point is zero) have a unique implied correlation. It would seem that if the market quoted base tranche premia, or their corresponding base correlations, then this would solve our problems of non-unique tranche correlations. This is not the case.

Suppose the market quoted fair value premia for base tranches – then base tranche $[0, a_i]$ would be associated with premium p_i, unique implied correlation ρ_i and unique capital value V_i. We can immediately calculate the value of all the (non-base) tranches – for example, the junior mezzanine tranche has value $V_2 - V_1$. Does this imply a unique premium and implied correlation for the non-base tranches?

No. Take the 100 name portfolio with average CDS premium 100 bp. Suppose the 0–6% base tranche has a premium of 1729 bp and an implied correlation of 20%, leading to a capital value of 3.193% of notional. Suppose the 0–9% tranche has a fair premium of 1190 bp and an implied correlation of 21.3% leading to a capital value of 3.705%. Then the [6, 9] tranche has a capital value of $3.705 - 3.193 = 0.512\%$. We find that a correlation of 12.8% (and premium of 400 bp) and 64% (premium 414 bp) both give rise to this capital value.

We conclude that knowing base tranche premia and/or implied correlations (as defined above) does not get round the problem of non-unique non-base tranche correlations.

JPMorgan (12 March 2004) introduced the concept of base correlation, and defined an implementation using their 'standardised large pool model' (JPMorgan, 6 May 2004). The market has developed alternative implementations of the base correlation concept – given market CDS data for the reference pool one approach (used by Bear Stearns, 17 May 2004, and others) is as follows.

1. The equity tranche, subject to the market premium p_E, gives rise to the first base correlation ρ_E (the correlation at which the net value of the tranche is zero). (Equity is the $[0, a_E]$ base tranche and $a_E = 6\%$ for the example CDO above which we continue to work with.) In the process we have calculated the value of contingent benefits ('expected loss'), V_E, for this base tranche: assuming the 1729 bp premium, we find 20% base correlation.
2. Take the premium p_M on the next tranche, and calculate the net value of the first base tranche subject to this premium using ρ_E. This value, V, is positive. (Why? How does p_M compare with p_E?) We find that the value of a 400 bp premium applied to the whole 6% base tranche is 2.454 at 20% correlation.
3. Since the net value of the mezzanine tranche using its implied correlation[4] is zero, the mark-to-market value of the 0–9% base tranche (at a mix of correlations) is $V = 2.454$, from which we can imply a base correlation of 21.5% for the 9% base tranche.

The question now is: Does the process of going from tranche premia to base correlation (by this process) and back again, lead unambiguously back to the starting point? If it does, then this (and similar definitions) form a satisfactory means of interpolating tranche premia.

---

[4] If there is more than one, take the lower (say).

Given the base implied of 21.5% on the [0, 9] base tranche, and 20% on the [0, 6] base tranche, then the net value of a deal on the [0, 6] base tranche at premium x (using 20% correlation), and the net value of a deal on the [6, 9] tranche also at premium x (=0 using the unknown tranche implied correlation), is equal to the value of the [0, 9] base tranche on this same premium (using the 21.5% correlation). We therefore have to solve

$$B_{0,6} - x \cdot P_{0,6} = B_{0,9} - x \cdot P_{0,9}$$

where the left-hand side uses the [0, 6] base correlation, and the right-hand side uses the [0, 9] base correlation. This linear equation has a unique solution.

Base correlations get round the problem of non-uniqueness of 'compound' correlation (and therefore non-unique hedges for the tranche). Hedge ratios for tranches (other than the equity piece) will be different from those derived using compound correlation – since in one case base correlations are kept constant when CDS premia are bumped, and in the other case compound correlation is kept constant. The process does not result in hedge ratios which, over all the tranches, sum to 100% (unlike the 'default event' hedge ratios of section 21.5.2). We can see this since the base and compound correlation approaches are identical for a two tranche CDO, and hedge ratios here generally do not add to 100%.

The method can be extended to the senior tranches iteratively. Note that the most senior tranche cannot be handled by this process. Since the expected losses of all tranches together equals the expected losses of all reference CDS, the final tranche premium is very tightly constrained. This is a feature of an arbitrage pricing model generally and is *not* a consequence of the base correlation approach. In addition we can see that, at each step the range of possible base correlations is constrained by the expected value of that base tranche – the charts and tables in the 'results' sheet of 'Chapter 22.xls' illustrate these points.

One further minor problem with base correlations is that greater accuracy is needed in valuation calculations – this affects both simulation approaches and semi-closed form solutions based around numerical integration. For example, if 10 000 simulations are sufficiently accurate for a single tranche pricing, then 100 000 simulations may be needed if the tranche is to be valued using the base correlation approach. Symptoms of insufficient accuracy (usually appearing on the more senior tranches) are

- Base correlations appearing to decrease as tranche size increases, and/or
- Inability to find a solution for the base correlation of a tranche.

The key point to note in this process is that the only non-zero tranche values used are those that are uniquely defined (base tranches). Non-base tranches have a uniquely defined net value (at either implied correlation if more than one) of zero, and only this is used in the above process. Subsequently, at no point are tranche valuations derived using 'compound correlation': valuations and individual hedge ratios are obtained using base correlations and base values taking differences where necessary to get tranche values.

22.2.3   Interpolating Correlation

Suppose we wish to price or value a [5, 7] tranche of a CDO whose reference portfolio forms the basis of a regularly traded CDO (say the EU iTraxx). Through the procedure described in 22.2.2 we can calculate the base correlations for the [0, 3], [0, 6] and [0, 9] tranches. We can linearly interpolate these to get base correlations for the [0, 5] and [0, 7] tranches. Hence we can calculate the interpolated 'fair' value premium, hence implied correlation, for the [5, 7] tranche (using a formula similar to that in 22.2.2).

The above is not the only interpolation method. No interpolation method is correct and an alternative is needed to, for example, calculate an appropriate interpolation reserve. It seems more sensible to interpolate correlation numbers than spreads because of the lower variation in the former. Using the tranche implied correlations (with a rule to handle the cases where there are multiple solutions) we can interpolate (probably non-linearly) to get an implied correlation, hence premium, for the [5, 7] tranche. We might set a reserve based on differences we observe between the net values of the tranche using the different interpolated premia and correlations.

22.2.4   Portfolio Differences

Reference Names

Large diversified investment grade portfolios tend to be valued using very similar correlations for corresponding tranches. The CDX and iTraxx portfolios allow this difference to be monitored. This difference may be (say) less than 3% for two portfolios which have no reference names in common. Portfolios which are a mix of EU and North American names could use a correlation interpolated between the iTraxx and CDX (base) correlations. We could define a linear relative to measure the distance between the actual portfolio and the iTraxx as (number of names in the actual portfolio (N) but not in iTraxx/N), and use this to interpolate between the iTraxx and CDX correlations.

For portfolios containing names from other regions we can similarly define a dissimilarity index, and use this to establish a reserve for the trade (based on the worst CDX/iTraxx correlation difference times the dissimilarity index).

Maturity

Implied correlations derived from 5-year CDO trades may not be appropriate for a 3-month CDO. Data for 5-year and 10-year CDOs are helpful when looking at intermediate life CDOs, and we could propose alternative simple (because tranching is identical) interpolation methods – for example, linear. For short-life CDOs it would be useful to get indications from the market for tranche valuations. One might also be tempted to look at current spread correlation over the recent period compared with the longer term average. There are some offsetting effects which lessen the importance of the correlation number at shorter maturities.

Exercise
Show that the correlation sensitivity of a tranche reduces as the outstanding maturity falls to zero (with no defaults on the underlying portfolio).

22.3   TAG CORRELATION AND SEMI-CLOSED FORM PRICING

This approach has been followed by S&P for their Copula model, and also by investment banks in the past for the purpose of CDO and F2D pricing. It can produce the most stable correlation numbers and is very quick to set up; it is also closely related to factor model approaches (Xiao, 2003). The approach is illustrated by the following.

We might identify industry (autos, finance, . . .) and region (Americas, Europe, . . .) as relevant factors. If two reference entities belong to the same region and to the same industry then the correlation is 0.3 (say); if they belong to the same region but different industries, the correlation is 0.1; if they belong to the same industry but different regions then the correlation is 0.2; otherwise the correlation is zero.

A further potential problem is that, depending on the number of reference entities and the choice of numbers in the matrix, it may not be a correlation matrix (i.e. it may not be invertible). In addition, it is unclear what the relevance of this matrix is to the calculation of CDO values.

Tag-correlation matrices are primarily of interest because they give rise to the possibility of 'semi-closed form' pricing. The extreme case is where there is just one tag (the 'one factor matrix') – and the matrix has the same form as the implied correlation matrix used in section 22.2. In such cases it is possible to replace the simulation approach by a formula for the N2D/CDO contingent benefits and premium legs (Laurent and Gregory, 2003; Anderson *et al.*, 2003; Mina and Stern, 2003). The formula (an integral formula) unfortunately needs to be implemented numerically. In the case of a single tag accurate numerical integration can be 100–1000 times faster than the simulation methods, and the key advantage is that this allows the rapid and accurate[5] calculation of spread and recovery hedge ratios for each underlying reference entity. The approach is partially described and implemented in the sheet 'Chapter 22 Normal Copula closed form N2D pricing.mcd'.

If we increase the number of tags, the dimensionality of the integral increases, and the time taken to calculate the numerical integral increases exponentially. If a one-dimensional integral requires 20 points for an accurate answer, then a five-dimensional integral may require around $20^5 = 3$ million points. Monte Carlo simulation is one means of performing numerical integrals and is often the fastest method for multidimensional cases (Fishman, 1995), often taken over between four and seven dimensions.

22.4   SPREAD CORRELATION

Spread correlation has some attraction as a source of correlation data since spread correlation and volatility have an impact on trade value, and there are suggestions that the impact is zero (in expectation) if the spread correlation and the pricing correlation are the same numbers.

Calculation techniques are described in section 22.6. We confine our remarks here to data.

The appropriate correlation for a 5-year CDO deal, for example, will be a weighted average of the correlation over the future life of the deal. The weighting is unclear – the capital value of errors will be greater at longer outstanding life. Additionally, as the deal shortens the correlation changes from correlation of 5-year instruments to correlation of short-dated instruments. So it is not clear what historical correlation we should be using. The CDO may be cash referring to specific deliverable bonds, or may be synthetic referring to CDS deals. In the former case we may be tempted to use bond spread data. Bond spreads suffer from a variety of problems:

1. Any data for the actual reference instruments is not directly relevant to the future – shorter-dated – instruments.
2. Idiosyncratic nature of a particular historical bond (because of repo influences, liquidity) which will differ from the reference asset.
3. Decreasing maturity of the bond used as the source of historical data.

---

[5] There is still a problem for small holdings since the process requires the portfolio to be discretised. The smaller the minimum discretised amount, the more accurate, but the slower, the calculation.

4. History is usually limited for any one issue.
5. Data is generally 'noisy'.

Generally CDS data has some advantages for historical analysis:

1. It is relatively clean (assuming it is available).
2. It has a constant maturity.
3. It refers to a greater liquidity instrument.

Once a data source is chosen there will be gaps in terms of the name coverage (there may be no data for some names) and also variable time periods covered (some names may have become liquid at a certain date and there may be no, or infrequent, data before that date).

22.5   ASSET AND EQUITY CORRELATION

Equity data is attractive because it is generally of good quality and often there are long data series. Historical data can be used to derive correlations (based on pairwise analysis or factor analysis – see section 22.6) and will produce a correlation matrix (i.e. it is invertible) if a consistent time period is used for all entities. Among investors, equity-based correlations are probably still the most popular means of deriving a default time correlation matrix for CDO analysis. Against the advantages of convenience, there are the following problems:

1. There is no theoretical equality between equity correlation and default time correlation. (On the other hand, there is a theoretical equality between 'asset correlation' and default time correlation – see below.)
2. If historical data series are over different time periods then pairwise derived correlations may not produce an (invertible) correlation matrix. Factor methods can help to avoid this problem.
3. Sovereigns and private companies, for example, do not have a readily available equity price.

The credit default models described in Chapter 9, and Chapter 21, are referred to as **reduced form models**. They are largely driven by market data (although recovery rates generally are modelled by looking at historical data). An alternative class of models – **structural models** – attempts to relate the value of the firm to the pricing of credit products. Such approaches are used by Moody'sKMV and CreditGrades[TM] (Finger, 2002) to derive a default probability using an asset model (and equity and balance sheet data). The basis of the model is the 'Merton firm model', and the relevant conclusion of the analysis is that, if the Merton firm model accurately describes the behaviour of the risk (subject to some assumptions about what constitutes default), then the asset correlation and the default time correlation are identical. The assets of a firm are impossible to measure on a real-time basis – typically use is made of the fact that assets equal liabilities, and liabilities – consisting of equity and various forms of debt – are easier to measure. Usually this requires a combination of observed market data (the equity price) and balance sheet data to attempt to measure debt levels, so it is still far from real time.

Attempts were made to use both equity and equity option data to imply asset values and obtain asset correlation, but these were eventually abandoned in favour of equity correlation or asset correlation derived from estimated asset data. The 'structural' approach has, at least initially, failed to produce an effective correlation model for credit derivatives and has left many market participants with the impression that equity correlation is an appropriate measure for default time correlation when, in fact, there is no such concrete link.

Table 22.2   Traded US CDO pricing (June 2004): implied versus equity factor-based correlations

Tranche (spread)	Mid premium	Implied correlation	Premium using factor-based equity correlation	Premium using mean equity correlation (30%)
0–3% (150 bp)	45.75% + 500 bp	20%	45.75% + 280 bp	45.75% + 290 bp
3–7% (40 bp)	430 bp	1%	520 bp	530 bp
7–10% (20 bp)	160 bp	16%	230 bp	230 bp
10–15% (10 bp)	69 bp	21%	110 bp	105 bp
15–30% (5 bp)	17.5 bp	28%	21.5 bp	19 bp

It is also worth noting that equity and asset-based correlations do not produce market prices (using the Normal Copula) for liquidly traded CDO products.

In this case the (factor based) equity based correlations (Table 22.2) lead to a very low premium for the equity piece, high premia for the mezzanine tranches and too low a premium for the super senior tranche (not shown). The use of the average equity correlation (30.3%), rather than the pairwise correlations, gives results which are not materially different from the use of a pairwise correlation matrix.

We conclude that equity derived correlations have no theoretical justification and do not replicate market pricing in cases where the latter are known. Asset correlation is difficult to measure and also fails to replicate market prices.

22.6   CALCULATION TECHNIQUES

There is only one valid approach to correlation for mark-to-market and hedging purposes and that is to use the implied correlation obtained from market prices using a 'good' model. The model currently used for this process is the Normal Copula model and implied correlation is obtained as a single number appropriate to the pricing of a particular tranche on its own.

We discuss a few topics here related to historical correlation and its estimation. Most of the following approaches are relevant to investors trying to 'beat the market', and also to the calculation of VaR for a portfolio along traditional lines.

These alternative approaches involve using market data histories (such as CDS premia, bond spreads, or equity returns) and calculating the correlation from that data. Two approaches to historical volatility calculations are desired. As long as a consistent period of time is used for all the time series, and as long as every reference entity has a data value for every date in the time series, then either approach produces a valid correlation matrix.

22.6.1   Pairwise Estimation From Historical Data

Given two time series, the correlation of these series is calculated. For economic time series we generally find that the number calculated by this process is very unstable over time if the time series is 'short' (say, 3–6 months or less) (Taylor, 1986). We would therefore typically take a 'long' time period (say 5–10 years). One advantage of this approach is that we can calculate some sort of error bar estimate around the correlation number as follows. If we divide the 5-year series into (say) 20 quarterly periods, we can calculate the short-term correlation for each quarter, and then calculate the (annualised) standard deviation of the correlation. We can then use this to get a confidence interval around our 5-year correlation estimate. We might alternatively use these standard deviation numbers to determine a stress to apply to the correlation matrix in order to get a stressed pricing or VaR calculation.

Imagine that we wish to perform a VaR type analysis for a portfolio of 5000 reference entities. There are approximately 12.5m time series to analyse for correlation. Many of these time series will be missing for at least part of the period. The chances of producing an (invertible) correlation matrix for all these names directly from pairwise historical analysis are minimal. Even if we manage to produce a correlation matrix with 25m entries, we undoubtedly will need to invert this matrix at some point in our application – and this will prove impractical.

22.6.2 Factor Analysis and Correlation

An alternative approach is to use a 'factor analysis'[6] of the data. This is claimed to give more stable correlation estimates (it is clear that indeed it should do so since it estimates far fewer parameters). It is also the approach followed by RiskMetrics Group and Moody'sKMV for their estimation of correlation.

One approach is as follows. Suppose we initially try to use a single factor to analyse the data. We set up a regression of each data series (5000 series of, say 1000 time points) on the (unknown) factor:

$$X_{i,t} = \alpha_i \cdot F_t + \varepsilon_{i,t} \tag{22.1}$$

where X are the $i = 1, \ldots, 5000$ data series, F is the factor series for $t = 1, \ldots, 1000$, α is the factor for series i, and ε are the error terms for each date and each series. The fitting process is to minimise the errors (in some way that we need not specify for the purposes of our discussion here).

The factor is defined by a single series of 1000 (unknown) values. Each data series has a single regression parameter against the unknown factor. This gives only 6000 parameters to estimate compared with the more than 12m for the approach of section 22.6.1. If our data represents equity returns then the factor will probably turn out to be close to the market average return, in which case the 'factor' is the 'market' – but we did not know this in advance.

We can now add another factor to our regression formula above (keeping fixed the first factor and the regression parameters), and perform an estimation of this second factor in a similar way. Suppose our data series represent auto companies and telecoms companies. Our first factor may turn out to be the average return, and the second factor may turn out to be the out-performance of autos over telecoms. However, the more factors we include the harder it is to identify what these factors represent.

Once we have identified sufficient factors, and we have decided that N provides a good model to the data but $N + 1$ does not add a sufficiently great improvement that it is worth doing,[7] then we have N parameters for each (equity) data series and $5000 \times N$ parameters for all the series. In addition there are N time series for the N factors, plus a residual error time

---

[6] 'Factor analysis', 'principal component analysis (PCA)' and 'independent component analysis' cover a range of related methods, only some of which are relevant here. Our initial objective is to derive the correlation matrix – so methods starting with the correlation matrix, such as PCA, are not useful (Hyvarinen *et al.*, 2001; Jae-On and Mueller, 1978).

[7] There are many ways of doing this and different statisticians have different approaches. A 'scree' test (Jae-On and Mueller, 1978) is one approach – where a chart of the residual error is plotted against the number of factors and if an abrupt change in the slope occurs then this point may be used to select the number of factors.

series for each equity. We typically assume that the residual is insignificant or uncorrelated with the factors.

$$X_{i,t} = \sum_{j=1}^{N} \alpha_{i,j} \cdot F_j + \varepsilon_{i,t} \qquad (22.2)$$

We can calculate the standard deviation and the correlation of the factors[8] (an $N \times N$ matrix). The pairwise correlation of two reference entities (if needed) can then be calculated from the factor correlations.

Once the factors have been derived (with, or without, an interpretation) then entities with short data series, unreliable or missing data, can be incorporated into the universe. If sufficient data is available, the regression factors may be estimated on this basis, otherwise some assumption will be made (such as taking factors for a similar entity).

If we wish to simulate the portfolio on 5000 credits, we simulate the N factors (and uncorrelated residuals) and calculate the simulated equity returns from the factor values and the regression parameters (a residual may also be simulated). It has also been shown that a correlation matrix estimated from factor analysis is more stable over time than one estimated from pairwise histories.

It should be noted that the factor-based approach to calculating the correlations has nothing to do with the appropriateness of the correlation matrix to the task in hand, or to the invertibility of the resulting matrix. 'Factor correlations' are not 'better' if equity or spread correlation is the wrong data to be using. Both methods (22.6.1 and 22.6.2) estimate equity return correlations (or spread correlations depending on the underlying data) and invertibility of the matrix is guaranteed if a consistent time period is used. Neither matrix has anything to do in principle with CDO pricing.

The approach described is rarely used in practice because of the non-linear estimation of the best-fit parameter values. The following are alternative approaches to the calculation of the factor are as follows:

1. Take $F(n, t)$ for $n = 0, 1, 2, \ldots$ to be orthonormal functions of time – for example, the Legendre polynomials or Fourier series. This approach is more suited to cases where some regular time dependency is suspected.
   (http://encyclopedia.thefreedictionary.com/Legendre+polymonial).
2. Assume that the factors are known (market return, sector return, geographical return, interest and FX rates, ...). This produces non-orthogonal factors but is the most common approach for equity return analysis.
3. If the dimensionality is small (a few hundred at most) we might calculate the pairwise equity correlations and then get the eigenvectors and values. These give us the orthonormal factors. The most important factors can be selected and more stable pairwise correlation estimates can be based on these factors.

The factors are now known and we continue as above to derive the regression and residuals for each series. Methods (1) and (2) have the advantage that the factors are meaningful and independently observable, although the process may be inefficient and in some ways less informative. Method (3) produces the same results as the method described but is only suitable for low dimensionality problems.

---

[8] The approach followed will lead to near orthogonal factors.

It can be argued that the tag correlation approach described in section 22.3 is equally valid (when compared to equity correlations) and has many practical advantages.

22.6.3 Impact on Hedging of Using Historical or Implied Correlations

Correlation estimates based on (say) a six month history will vary sharply as a trade matures and shortening time periods are used to estimate the current correlation. These correlation changes will have different effects on the trade and hedges in place, causing rehedging of a position and potential profits or losses. Such rehedging is not tied to the market pricing of the CDO (which is driven by implied correlation) so any mismatch in the hedge ratios is spurious and will generate spurious losses (there being a bid–offer cost of rehedging).

Spurious rehedging can be minimised by minimising the variability of the historical estimates as described above.

23

Other Copulae

We look at other Copulae for three main reasons:

1. Producing correlated default times based on Student's t distribution is commonly talked about in the literature and often used in practice.
2. Having an alternative Copula is a worthwhile model test and risk-control measure.
3. Some other Copulae – in particular Clayton and the 'Archimedean' class of Copulae – give a different perspective on the Normal Copula and its application, and are also discussed frequently in the literature.

Student's distribution is a simple extension of the Normal case, and some useful results are contained in this chapter for relatively little effort. Sections 23.2 to 23.4 are more specialised, but the general reader is recommended to read the 'implications' at the end of section 23.3 at least.

23.1 STUDENT'S t DISTRIBUTION

Student's t distribution is similar to the Normal when the 'degrees of freedom' is large. It is a simple extension of the Normal model in terms of implementation, and is widely discussed in the literature as an alternative to – and an improvement on – the Normal Copula.

Random Numbers from Student's t Distribution with d Degrees of Freedom

1. Generate N correlated random numbers, x, from the Normal distribution as already described, and d independent Normal random numbers X_j.
2. Calculate an independent $s = \sum_{j=1}^{d} X_j^2$ (which is from the Chi-squared distribution with d degrees of freedom).
3. Calculate the cumulative probabilities $t_d(y_i)$ under the Student distribution[1] of $y_i = \sqrt{(d/s)} \cdot x_i$, where $i = 1, \ldots, N$.

The cumulative probabilities in (3) give us the correlated default times

$$T_i = \frac{-\ln[t_d(y_i)]}{\lambda}$$

The code to implement the above is given in the addendum to this chapter.

Applications and Results

If the $N \times N$ correlation matrix in the Student's Copula is a one factor correlation matrix, then we still have two parameters to fix – the correlation and the degrees of freedom. Student does

---

[1] Press et al. (2000).

Table 23.1   Traded US CDO pricing (June 2004) using equity factor-based correlations under Student's Copula

Tranche (spread)	Mid premium	Premium using factor-based equity correlation and df=3	Premium using mean equity correlation and df=7
0–3% (150 bp)	45.75% + 500 bp	45.75% + −20 bp	45.75% + 105 bp
3–7% (40 bp)	430 bp	460 bp	490 bp
7–10% (20 bp)	160 bp	250 bp	245 bp
10–15% (10 bp)	69 bp	150 bp	140 bp
15–30% (5 bp)	17.5 bp	60 bp	40 bp

not help if we want to follow the 'implied correlation' per tranche description (we need to fix the degrees of freedom).

Does the use of Student's t help in the pricing of the TRAC-X portfolio (cf. Table 22.2) if we use equity-driven correlations?

We have one further parameter to play with (the degrees of freedom) so in some sense we should be able to get a better fit than with the Normal distribution. Table 23.1 shows results with 3 and 7 degrees of freedom (and Table 22.2 under the Normal Copula is the same as Student for a large number of degrees of freedom (around 20 and above)). We see that as the degrees of freedom drop the equity tranche and the senior tranche are increasingly mis-priced – the equity premium dropping even more below market price and the senior premium increasing more and more above market price. Only the junior mezzanine tranche gets closer to the market price.

We conclude that Student's t Copula offers no practical benefits over the Normal Copula.

23.2   COPULAE IN GENERAL

Generally a Copula function is a means of generating a distribution for correlated variables (default probabilities) when all we know is the partial distribution (the single name survival probabilities). The general definition has not been necessary for an understanding and use of the Normal and Student's Copulae – indeed their application is quite different from the general approach. More detail on Copulae can be found in Nelsen (1998). Copula functions are a standard tool in actuarial science and other areas, but not common in derivatives until Li (2000) introduced the approach in the mid-1990s.

If $F(x_1, x_2, \dots)$ is a known joint distribution with partials $F_1(x_1), F_2(c_2),..$ Then the Copula function (which is a cumulative probability distribution in its own right) is given by Sklar's theorem:

$$C(u_1, u_2, \dots) = F(F_1 \text{ inv}(u_1), F_2 \text{ inv}(u_2), \dots)$$ (23.1)

In the general case we do not know F but, instead, we can choose any increasing function C on the positive unit interval subject to certain constraints – including

$$C(u, \dots, 0, \dots) = 0, \qquad C(u, 1, 1, \dots) = u.$$ (23.2)

Once we have found a Copula function we need a general method to generate correlated random numbers using the Copula. One procedure is as follows:

1. Generate independent uniform random numbers u, v

2. Convert these to correlated variables u, t through the conditional distribution of v given u, i.e.

$$v = c_u^{-1}(t) \quad \text{where} \quad c_u(v) = \frac{\partial}{\partial u} C(u, v) \tag{23.3}$$

For multivariate Copulae this requires the partial derivatives up to the order of the distribution.

We follow through the general process described above in the case of the Clayton Copula in section 23.3.

In the case of the Normal Copula we know F – it is the multifactor correlated cumulative Normal distribution. F_1 is the one-dimensional cumulative Normal distribution so, if u_1 is a randomly chosen number between 0 and 1, then $F_1\text{inv}(u_1)$ is between $-\infty$ and $+\infty$. If we were to write out C as a function of the uniform variables we would have a very complex (and unhelpful) integral equation. Instead of following this route we skipped the step of generating the u's and generated the $F_1\text{inv}(u_1)$ directly from the uncorrelated random Normal number generator. We also do not follow the process described above to get the correlated Normal random variables, but instead use a trick based on the Cholesky decomposition of the correlation matrix. In summary, the general Copula description is unhelpful in the case of the Normal and Student's Copulae.

23.3   ARCHIMEDEAN COPULAE: CLAYTON AND GUMBEL

Archimedean Copulae can be generated from a function of a single function $\phi(x)$ which has certain properties (basically a continuously decreasing convex function mapping [0, 1] to (infinity, 0]). Given such a **generating function**, we find that

$$C(u_1, u_2, \ldots) = \varphi^{-1}[\varphi(u_1) + \varphi(u_2) + \cdots] \tag{23.4}$$

is a Copula function. Note that a single generating function can be used to generate a Copula function for any required number of correlated variables.

Archimedean Copulae have the property that hazard rates change by a common factor when one name defaults (Schönbucher and Schubert, 2001). Unfortunately this is an unrealistic property for credit risks – a single 'shock' to the financial system does not cause a credit blow out in all names in the same proportion. Nevertheless, the Clayton Copula in particular can be a worthwhile alternative for small portfolios, and is used later as a further model test.

Clayton Copula

The function

$$\varphi(t) = \frac{1}{\theta}(t^{-\theta} - 1), \quad \theta \geq 0 \tag{23.5}$$

is a generating function, and definition (23.4) leads to the Clayton Copula

$$C(u_1, u_2, \ldots) = \max[(u_1^{-\theta} + u_2^{-\theta} + \ldots - n + 1)^{-\frac{1}{\theta}}, 0] \tag{23.6}$$

In order to obtain the nth correlated random number u_{n-1} given the $n-1$ correlated numbers u_0 to u_{n-2}, and an independent uniform random number t, we need to calculate the inverse of the $(n+1)$th derivative. We find

$$u_{n-1} = \left[t^{-\frac{\theta}{(n-1)\theta+1}} \cdot \left(\sum_{i=0}^{n-2} u_i^{-\theta} - n + 2 \right) + n - 1 - \sum_{i=0}^{n-2} u_i^{-\theta} \right]^{-\frac{1}{\theta}} \tag{23.7}$$

Exercises

1. Check the values of the function φ at 0 and 1, and check the monotonic nature of the function.
2. Show that the inverse is $\varphi^{-1}(s) = (s \cdot \theta + 1)^{-\frac{1}{\theta}}$.
3. Hence derive the Copula function. Also show that C is a probability distribution. [*Hint:* Take the one-dimensional case and show that the integral of C over [0, 1] is unity.]
4. Calculate the derivative of C with respect to the first variable and find the inverse of this function – show that it is consistent with (23.7). Repeat for the second, ...

The spreadsheet 'Part III, Chapter 23.xls' implements the above for two names and calculates correlated default times.

Gumbel–Hougaard Copula

The generating function is

$$\varphi(t) = (-\ln t)^\theta, \quad \theta \in [1, \infty) \tag{23.8}$$

leading to the Gumbel–Hougaard Copula

$$C(u_1, u_2, \ldots) = \exp\{-[(-\ln u_1)^\theta + (-\ln u_1)^\theta + \cdots]^{\frac{1}{\theta}}\} \tag{23.9}$$

A closed form for the inverse of the nth derivative does not exist and numerical methods have to be used.

Implications

The Clayton (and Gumbel) Copulae are both driven by a single parameter – whether there are two names in the reference portfolio or 200. Also, in the case of Clayton, the only constraint on the parameter is that it is positive. That parameter clearly is not a correlation. If the parameter to a Copula cannot be interpreted directly as a correlation (or any other quantity directly driven by the reference names), how do we derive its value? The obvious route would appear to be to imply the parameter from the prices of some traded structures.

Once we have accepted the idea that Copula parameters may have to be implied from market prices, we should ask: 'What Copula would be most useful?'

Suppose we are pricing a CDO on 100 reference names with seven tranches: there is one constraint (the sum of the values of the expected losses on all the tranches must be equal to the sum of the corresponding values for the reference name CDS). If we have a Copula with six parameters (and generally, the number-of-tranches-minus-one parameters) then we could fit the market values of all the tranches exactly with one function. Clayton Copula has only one parameter (too few), and the Normal has 4950, unless we impose some other restrictions (far too many). Such Copula functions, which are tractable, are not known, and the Normal Copula remains the simplest flexible approach.

23.4 CLAYTON AT $\theta{=}0$ AND $\theta{=}\infty$

We know that (Part III, section 8.3), for zero and 100% correlated variables, the F2D premium is independent of the Copula. In fact no Copula is needed at all (in the former case independent random numbers give us independent default times, and in the latter case a single random number generates all the correlated default times). It is worth while to confirm that the Clayton Copula reproduces these results in the limit as θ tends to zero and to ∞.

Consider the use of the Clayton Copula to derive the second correlated random variable, v, given two uncorrelated uniform random variables u and t. Formula (23.7) is (setting $I{=}2$)

$$v = (t^{-\frac{\theta}{\theta+1}} \cdot u^{-\theta} + 1 - u^{-\theta})^{-\frac{1}{\theta}} = [1 + (t^{-\frac{\theta}{\theta+1}} - 1) \cdot u^{-\theta}]^{-\frac{1}{\theta}} \qquad (23.10)$$

Using $x^y = \exp[y \ln(x)]$ and the fact that $0{<}u$ and $t < 1$, the right-hand side can be shown to tend to $t - t \cdot \theta \cdot \ln(t) \cdot [\ln(u) + 1]$ as θ tends to zero (see, for example, Hardy, 1999). We can see that v tends to t – so v and u are independent in the limit as θ tends to zero.

As θ tends to infinity, note that the term $1 + (t^{-\frac{\theta}{\theta+1}} - 1) \cdot u^{-\theta}$ is dominated by $u^{-\theta}$, so v tends to $(u^{-\theta})^{-\frac{1}{\theta}} = u$ and the second random variable v is identical to the first, as required.

23.5 MODEL RISK

The key model assumption is that default time correlation drives the pricing of N2D baskets and CDO tranches. We have identified one major drawback in the model – the lack of spread correlation and spread volatility. Another problem is the arbitrary choice of correlation (unless we use 'implied'), and the arbitrary choice of Copula. One test[2] we can perform is to compare pricing under two Copulae. Alternatively we could match market prices using the implied parameters and then compare hedge ratios under two Copulae. In this section we see how prices derived using the Normal Copula compare with those derived from the Clayton Copula.

The Normal correlation parameter varies from 0 to 1 whereas the Clayton parameter varies from 0 to ∞. In order to plot the results on the same chart, we map the Clayton Copula parameter θ to the range [0, 1] by $1{-}\exp(-\alpha \cdot \theta)$, where we choose α so that the F2D prices agree at ($\theta = 0$ and) $\rho = 0.3 = 1{-}\exp(-\alpha \cdot \theta)$. Figure 23.1 shows that the pattern of prices is very similar except at high 'correlation'. Note that, for a portfolio of two names, Clayton is capable of producing the same range of values as the Normal Copula, with the appropriate choice of parameter.

Of course if we have more than two names in the portfolio then the Normal model – with a non-degenerate correlation matrix – will be capable of producing a wider range of values.

We shall see in Part IV that the Clayton Copula produces some larger differences in values for counterparty CDS compared with Normal.

---

[2] Another route would be to use the multinomial BET model outlined in section 9.5.

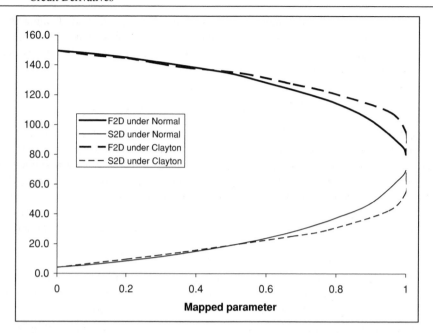

Figure 23.1   F2D and S2D prices under Normal and Clayton Copulae

ADDENDUM

Code for the Cumulative Student's Distribution
(Copyright © 1987–1992 Numerical Recipes Software)

We need the cumulative function $t_d(y) = 1 - I_{d/(d+y^2)}(d/2, \frac{1}{2})$, where $I_x(a, b)$ is the incomplete beta function given by

$$I_x(a, b) = \frac{1}{B(a, b)} \int_0^x t^{a-1}(1-t)^{b-1} dt$$

$$B(a, b) = [\Gamma(a)\Gamma(b)]/\Gamma(a+b)$$

is the beta function, and $\Gamma(z) = \int_0^\infty t^{z-1} \exp(-t) dt$ is the Gamma function.

```
double CMaths::CumStudent(const double y, const double df)
{
  if (y>0) return 1.0-0.5*Betai(df/2.0,0.5,df/(df+y*y));
  else return 0.5*Betai(df/2.0,0.5,df/(df+y*y));
}
double CMaths::Betai(const double a, const double b,
const double x)
```

The incomplete beta function $I_x(a, b)$

```
{
  double bt;
  if (x<0.0 || x>1.0) return(0);
  if (x==0.0 || x==1.0) bt=0.0;
  else bt = exp(gammln(a+b)-gammln(a)-gammln(b)+a*log(x)+
  b*log(1.0-x));
  if (x < (a+1.0)/(a+b+2.0)) return bt*betacf(a,b,x)/a;
  else return 1.0-bt*betacf(b,a,1.0-x)/b;
}
double betacf(const double a, const double b, const double x)
```

continued fraction evaluation – used to calculate the incomplete beta function rapidly

```
{
  double FPMIN = 1.0e-30;
  double aa, c=1.0, del, h, qab=a+b, qam=a-1.0, qap=a+1.0,
  d=1.0-qab*x/qap;
  if (fabs(d) < FPMIN) d = FPMIN;
  d = 1.0/d;
  h=d;

  for (int m = 1; m<100; m++)
  {
        int m2 = 2*m;
        aa = m*(b-m)*x/((qam+m2)*(a+m2));
        d = 1.0+aa*d;
```

```
      if (fabs(d) < FPMIN) d = FPMIN;
      c = 1.0+aa/c;
      if (fabs(c) < FPMIN) c = FPMIN;
      d = 1.0/d;
      h *= d*c;
      aa = -(a+m)*(qab+m)*x/((a+m2)*(qap+m2));
      d = 1.0+aa*d;
      if (fabs(d) < FPMIN) d = FPMIN;
      c = 1.0+aa/c;
      if (fabs(c) < FPMIN) c = FPMIN;
      d = 1.0/d;
      del = d*c;
      h *= del;
      if (fabs(del-1.0) < 3.0e-7) break;

   }
   return h;
}
```

24

Correlation Portfolio Management

The 'correlation book' contains risks arising from portfolio products including N2D baskets, CDO tranches, and portfolio volatility products.

24.1 STATIC AND DYNAMIC HEDGES

Statically (Default Event) Hedged Book

CDO deals may be default event hedged on a static basis as described in section 21.5.2. We saw that a statically hedged deal is not risk free – there is residual delta risk that will give rise to mark-to-market P&L changes. This residual may be minimised through product design, otherwise it can reach high values (equivalent to a naked spread position in 50% of the reference pool notional on a long-life high-yield portfolio).

   If the 'static hedge' is incorporated with other deals in the correlation product book, the residual risk will be automatically and actively delta hedged. For this reason statically hedged deals need to be segregated from the rest of the correlation book to avoid the unwanted P&L arising from rehedging. The owner of the position remains exposed to the spread risk.

Dynamic Delta Hedged Book

We examine the delta hedging of several types of trades, and the consequences of this approach.

Example 1: Long F2D Protection, Long Equity Protection

A position long of protection in a F2D basket is delta hedged by selling single name protection on the individual names in the basket – say around 50–60% notional for each name in the basket depending on the correlation and depending on spread. This brings a strong (short) correlation risk. In addition – as we saw in section 21.5 – it brings a large exposure to spread correlation and spread volatility through future rehedging activity. Similar results apply to an equity tranche – hedge ratios are typically smaller but still substantial. A strategy of forcing the correlation book to have zero single name exposure requires day-to-day rehedging with the single name book resulting in substantial bid–offer payments unless inter-book trades take place at mid-market prices. In the former case the single name book profits from correlation book activity; in the second case the single name book manages emerging single name risks at a potential loss – so some form of P&L sharing or fee payment becomes necessary.

Default and Spread Jump Risk

Consider again the Telecom basket example of 21.5.1. Long F2D protection positions will suffer substantial rehedging loss as spreads widen out in a highly correlated way. Default of a name in the basket may come as a welcome relief – giving risk to a profit on the mismatch in F2D notional and hedge notional – but cannot be relied on.

Example 2: Short Senior TDB Protection

The same principles apply – the position is short correlation and short single name protection.

Senior and equity tranches are also exposed to **extreme event risk** – many defaults on a reference portfolio have a very substantial impact on the value of these tranches. Also, both tranches with their delta hedges are exposed to spread jump risk and delta **convexity risk** – on a sudden large move in spreads the 'delta' hedge ratio is incorrect.

Example 3: Mezzanine TDBs

Mezzanine tranches may be long or short correlation depending on the placement and size of the tranche, the underlyings and the level of correlation. There are some intermediate (mezzanine) TDBs which are relatively insensitive to correlation. This is one way of controlling the correlation risk in the books – deal in those mezzanine tranches which are relatively insensitive to correlation. Clearly this is not appropriate to all mezzanine tranches. This approach does not eliminate the spread correlation risk arising from the delta hedges, however.

Example 4: Put Option on a CDO Tranche

The delta exposure to the reference pool names is subject to further risk: the poorly defined implied volatility for spreads while the product is relatively illiquid. Both correlation risks, and the volatility risk, are present and not resolved by the delta hedging approach.

24.2 CORRELATION BOOK MANAGEMENT

The above examples emphasise that for positions that are only delta hedged, the following risks are unhedged:

- default time correlation
- spread correlation
- spread volatility
- delta convexity
- extreme event risk

in addition to other less serious risks (see section 21.6). A much better strategy to protect the portfolio remains one of hedging correlation in an integrated correlation book. This will leave only residual single name delta risks, and also largely eliminates the spread correlation and volatility risk (except for option products), the delta convexity risk, and can reduce extreme event risk. If the correlation book is allowed large limits on single names but tight limits on delta risk within certain buckets (for example A autos), then the book can run name risk but spread hedge within buckets and avoid delta rehedging problems. How do we hedge correlation and minimise delta and other risks? Consider the following examples.

Example 1: Correlation Hedged Equity Tranche and F2D Positions

A long position in an equity tranche is short correlation – its capital value falls as implied correlation rises. Conversely, a short position in a F2D basket is long correlation. We can hedge the correlation risk on the long equity tranche by selling F2D baskets – *if the correlations move together* – on some underlying names (or on some different names). This will leave long delta risks arising from the equity tranche, and short delta risks on the F2D positions. If these risks fall in the same (single name risk) buckets, then they will net, leaving only a residual delta risk.

Example 2: Correlation Hedged Long Equity and Long Senior Tranches

A long position in a senior tranche is long correlation – its capital value increases as correlation increases. We could hedge the long equity tranche with long senior tranches and – *if the correlations move together* – the correlation risk will be greatly reduced. However, both positions would give risk to positive delta exposures to the underlying names and exacerbate the delta-hedging problem.

There are two further risks in the types of hedges suggested above: basis difference between basket and CDO correlations, and the basis between different tranche correlations. Figure 24.1 illustrates how the implied correlation varied between baskets (of intuitively uncorrelated names) and CDO equity tranches as at December 2003 and July 2004.

We can see that the implied correlation depended quite strongly on the size of the underlying portfolio – F2D baskets on 2–10 names typically having implied correlation in the 40–60% range, whereas 100 name CDOs typically have FLP implied in the 20–30% range. In addition the relationship changed markedly over the time period with quite large declines in F2D correlations.

Figure 24.2 shows the correlation 'smile' as of June 2004. A hedge across materially different tranches can be compared to a curve trade – if correlations shift in parallel there is a hedge, but in reality there is the risk that correlations change senior and junior tranches differently.

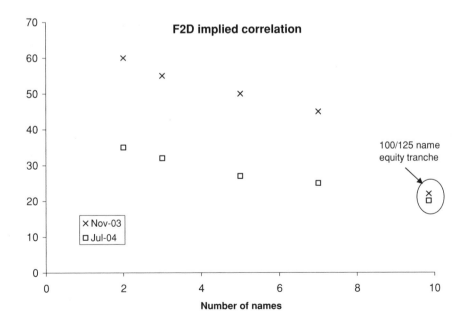

Figure 24.1   Implied correlation on F2D and equity CDO tranches

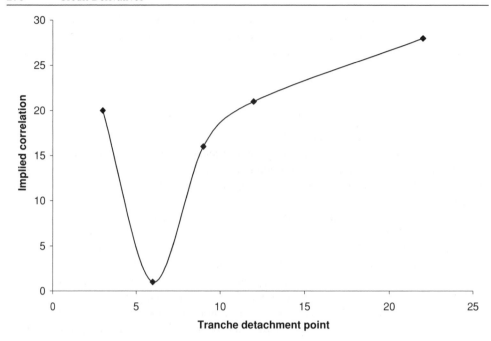

Figure 24.2   The correlation 'smile'

Hedging of correlation risk by tranche buckets is much less risky than hedging with very different types of tranches or products. In practice this means hedging junior CDO tranches with (opposite positions) in other junior tranches, senior tranches with senior tranches, and F2D products with other F2D products. Within each correlation bucket, the net correlation risk is calculated. The net delta risk – not by name but by delta bucket (rating and industry, etc.) – is calculated across all correlation buckets and needs to be hedged.

The growth of index-based CDOs and individually traded TDB tranches (iTraxx and CDX currently) is of major benefit to the correlation risk hedger. Structuring desks can arrange tailored deals for particular clients and hedge correlation risk using appropriate tranches of these index CDOs. The underlying portfolios may differ but large (50+ names) diversified (diversity score 30+) investment grade portfolios tend to be priced very similarly (sections 21.4, 21.6 and 22.2). Tranche differences can also be handled (section 22.2).

There are additional problems with equity tranches related to the granularity of the particular reference portfolio. The equity piece is driven by high spread names (section 21.3) and may come to resemble a F2D basket on these names. In these circumstances an F2D may be a much better hedge than an index CDO based on similar spread names. A special case is where a single name has a very high spread. This will be a key driver of the equity piece: the tranche with a delta hedge on that name then becomes a much better candidate for correlation hedging with index products.

In addition, liquidity in the F2D baskets is now at a level where the active hedging of correlation on small baskets is a realistic possibility.

24.3   CREDIT VaR AND COUNTERPARTY VaR

Portfolio VaR

We conclude this chapter with some comments on portfolio VaR related to credit correlation and portfolio credit derivatives. An objective may be to estimate the worst change in portfolio value with a certain level of confidence ('Total VaR'). Deal values should be estimated by simulation changes in the pricing parameter and repricing. The TM approach to simulate correlated spreads and defaults can be used to obtain the resulting portfolio levels at the VaR calculation date. In order to value CDOs we also need to simulate changes in the implied correlations (probably based on some historical analysis of variability, and changes in the shape of, the implied correlation curve[1]). Each CDO (tranche) can then be revalued using the pricing parameters at the VaR calculation date. Alternative approaches to the calculation exist.

1. We use a single correlation matrix (typically factor-based equity correlations or a one-factor matrix). This fails to correctly mark the deal to market initially and also therefore incorrectly estimates changes in value.
2. We may use a historical TM. This fails to mark individual risks (bonds, CDSs) correctly to market so fails to estimate change in value correctly. Furthermore, the implied volatility of spreads in the historical TM fails to capture the way volatility is priced in the marketplace so will incorrectly assess the risk associated with that volatility.

Suppose we have performed a factor analysis of spreads and identified (say) 20 factors. We could simulate the development of these factors to the VaR calculation date, which then gives us the simulated spreads for each name in a way that is consistent with the factor-based correlation analysis.

An alternative approach would be to replace the actual portfolio by (appropriately weighted) representative entities where there is a one-to-one mapping between reference entity and representative entity, and simulate these. All deals on actual reference entities are replaced by deals on the representative entity.

Either approach gives a manageable correlation matrix and portfolio calculation.

---

[1] Typically a single implied correlation curve would be simulated for (say) 5-year life investment grade CDOs. The correlation for the tranche would be obtained from the curve according to the tranche size and placement. Different maturity correlation curve would typically be deterministically driven by the 5-year curve.

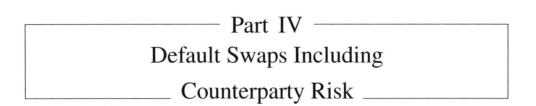

Part IV
Default Swaps Including
Counterparty Risk

25

'Single Name' CDS

We saw in Part III, section 19.3 that, in the case of an F2D where the reference entities have uncorrelated spreads (hazard rates), the valuation formulae are relatively simple. We apply the similar arguments to a CDS with uncorrelated counterparty risk in section 25.1, and with 100% correlation in section 25.2.

We also saw in Part II, section 9.8 that, even where name and counterparty hazard rates are correlated, then the impact of high correlation and high spread volatility is minimal (except at high spreads and very long-life CDS) if the hazard rate process is a diffusion without jumps. However the default time model in Part III, used to price baskets and CDOs, carries the implication that hazard rates follow a jump process. We also saw in Part III that portfolio products exhibit significant default time correlation. So we cannot reasonably ignore the name and counterparty risk without more detailed investigation. Fortunately we can use the correlated default time model to value CDSs, including counterparty risk. We shall illustrate some results in section 25.3.

We revisit the question of alternative Copulae in section 25.4. We look at the effects of collateralisation versus non-collateralised trades in 25.5, and at CDS on a counterparty to a CDS trade (CCDS) in 25.6.

25.1 NON-CORRELATED COUNTERPARTY

Under a default time correlation model, if two names are uncorrelated, then the expected default time of one name conditional on the other name having defaulted is the same as the unconditional expectation. In other words, there is no expected jump in the hazard rate on one name when an uncorrelated name defaults (Part III, section 21.1). Consider the case where we buy protection on a reference name from an uncorrelated counterparty. In the event that the counterparty defaults there is no expected change in the spread on the reference name. The expected replacement cost of the CDS (now that the counterparty has defaulted) is the same as it was the previous night – hence deals on reference names with uncorrelated counterparties have no jump risk on counterparty default. If the deal is collateralised then this also eliminates the risk contingent on changes in the reference entity spread.

If we assume that the (pseudo-)hazard rates on the name and counterparty are constant, and that the counterparty defaults, then we can replace the CDS on the reference name with another (uncorrelated but otherwise similar) counterparty, at the same spread as before. As long as there is always an uncorrelated counterparty available, then we know (on our assumption) that we can always get protection at the same price as before. The uncorrelated counterparty is therefore effectively the same as a risk-free counterparty so the premium we pay to an uncorrelated counterparty must be the same as the premium paid to a risk-free counterparty.

This result is not exactly true (but it is generally a good approximation) in the case where the hazard rates have a term structure. If the (pseudo-)hazard rate of the reference name is upward sloping, then default of the counterparty will be at a time when the replacement cost is above

Table 25.1   CDS premia for a reference entity with risk-free and uncorrelated counterparties (40% recovery)

Reference entity hazard rate	Counterparty hazard rate (flat)	CDS premium – risky counterparty	CDS premium – risk-free counterparty
Flat 2%	0.5%	120.0	120.0
2% now rising to 4% in 5 years	0.5%	178.3	178.5
2% now rising to 4% in 5 years	2%	177.5	178.5
Flat 10%	4%	600	600
20% now falling to 10% in 5 years	4%	947.6	937.8

the previous deal cost. This additional cost can be calculated and weighted by the probability of counterparty default at each date to get an estimate of the impact of dealing with an uncorrelated counterparty in this case. An implementation of formula (9.20) effectively achieves this. The formula for the fair value premium from an uncorrelated counterparty (name 2) on a reference entity (name 1) is (where we ignore the writer's default risk, and D represents the discount factor)

$$
\frac{\int\limits_0^T (1 - R_1) \cdot \lambda_1(t) \cdot \exp\left[-\int\limits_0^t \lambda_1(s)\,ds \right] \cdot \exp\left[-\int\limits_0^t \lambda_2(s)\,ds \right] \cdot D(t)\,dt}{\int\limits_0^T \exp\left[-\int\limits_0^t \lambda_1(s)\,ds \right] \cdot \exp\left[-\int\limits_0^t \lambda_2(s)\,ds \right] \cdot D(t)\,dt}
\tag{25.1}
$$

If the name hazard rate is constant, we see that the integral in the numerator is just a constant times that in the denominator, so the integrals cancel and we get exactly the same premium as in the risk-free counterparty case (as anticipated), but for general hazard rate curves this is no longer true. Table 25.1 shows the correct CDS premium when dealing with a correlated counterparty and when the reference entity has a non-constant hazard rate curve. (Calculations are implemented in the Mathcad sheet 'Chapter 25. mcd'.)

25.2   100% CORRELATION

Recall that, if the default time correlation in a correlated default time model, is 100% then, on every simulation, the default times are in the inverse order of the hazard rates for the names in the product. The highest hazard rate name defaults first, the lowest hazard rate name defaults last.

Consider a CDS on a reference entity written by a 100% correlated counterparty (and assume that the buyer is risk free). We immediately see the following:

1. If the counterparty has a higher hazard rate than the reference entity, then the counterparty will always default before the reference entity and the CDS is worthless.
2. If the counterparty has a lower hazard rate than the reference entity, then the reference entity will always default before the counterparty and the CDS payment will always be made. A CDS written by a 100% correlated but low-risk counterparty is as valuable as a CDS written by a risk-free counterparty! (See Section 25.4 and Figures 25.1 and 25.2.)

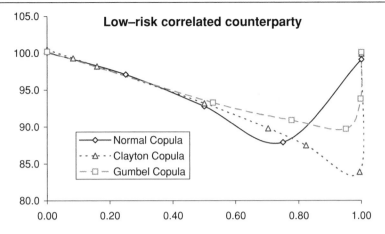

Figure 25.1   CDS protection on a high-risk name from a low-risk counterparty

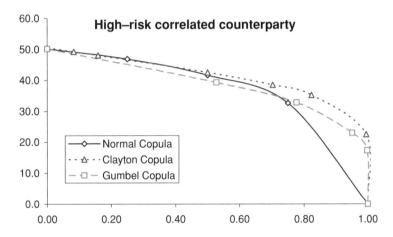

Figure 25.2   CDS protection on a low-risk name from a high-risk counterparty

We saw in section 22.5 that the F2D premium is not the highest CDS spread but the spread on the name with the highest hazard rate. Uncertainty over recovery means that we are not sure which name this is. Likewise, we cannot be sure whether the counterparty is higher risk or lower risk than the reference entity, so we cannot be sure whether the CDS is worthless or worth as much as from a risk-free counterparty!

As in section 22.5, we can model recovery rates on the two names allowing for the uncertainty in the recovery level. Let us assume that expected recovery is 40% and the standard deviation (uncertainty) of recovery is 20%. We can model this (see the Excel spreadsheet 'Chapter 9.xls') by assuming that recovery can take the value 0 with probability 0.11 or 0.4 with probability 0.8, and 0.9 with probability 0.09, we get a 40% mean and 20% standard deviation. We can take all recovery pairs, calibrate each CDS (reference entity CDS = 100 bp, counterparty CDS = 50 bp say, from a risk-free counterparty) to get the hazard rate, and then decide whether the CDS should be priced at zero or the risk-free level.

Exercise

Show that the expected level of the CDS is 91.9 bp.

Hint: How many possible recovery pairs are there? Enumerate these and calculate the probability associated with each pair. Calibrate the risk-free CDS and decide whether the risky CDS is worth 100 bp or 0 bp – then weight the results.

25.3   CORRELATED COUNTERPARTY: PRICING AND HEDGING

The pricing model for a CDS with correlated counterparty risk is very similar to the F2D model. We generate default times for all the parties to the deal in exactly the same way. Given the default times, then a capital payment is made if the reference entity defaults before the maturity of the trade and before the writer and buyer of the CDS. Premia are paid until the first default or the maturity of the trade (if earlier). We generally assume that trade counterparties have zero recovery.

An implementation of the simulation model for counterparty risk is contained in the file 'Part III N2D CDO CLN price and hedge.mcd'.

Table 25.2 shows some results for a low-risk reference entity (100 bp CDS spread) and counterparty (50 bp CDS; we also assume that the writer is risk free). Results are given at a range of correlation levels, and we assume 40% recovery for the reference entity and 0% recovery for the counterparty. We also show the hedge ratios to each name: a long CDS position with the risky counterparty is hedged by selling very nearly 100% of the CDS on the reference name and also by buying a small amount of protection on the counterparty. Results are based on 1m simulations showing a premium standard deviation of 0.3 bp.

Table 25.3 shows the results of a high-risk reference entity (500 bp) and counterparty (200 bp). We assume 20% recovery for the reference entity, and 0% recovery for the counterparty. Results are based on 1m simulations showing a premium standard deviation of 0.9 bp.

Table 25.2   CDS premia with correlated risky counterparty (low-risk entities)

Correlation	CDS	Hedge ratio ref (%)	Hedge ratio cpty (%)
0	100.1	99	0
0.2	98.7	98	2
0.4	96.9	97	5
0.6	94.6	98	10
0.8	92.9	100	17
1	100.1	100	0

Table 25.3   CDS premia with correlated risky counterparty (high-risk entities)

Correlation	CDS	Hedge ratio ref (%)	Hedge ratio cpty (%)
0	499.6	95	1
0.2	487.0	95	4
0.4	474.2	95	10
0.6	463.2	97	17
0.8	461.0	102	22
1	499.4	100	0

Note that the CDS premium cost plus cost of protection on the counterparty is approximately offset by the CDS income on the protection sold. The hedge is dynamic – hedge ratio on the reference entity tending ultimately to 100% and that on the counterparty tending to 0.

25.4   CHOICE OF COPULA

The Clayton Copula is a less unnatural choice where there are only two reference names, such as is the case for counterparty risk where the writer's default risk is ignored. We can value a CDS on a risky reference entity, from a lower risk counterparty, and vice versa, and let the 'correlation' vary from 0 to 1, under the Normal, the Clayton Copula and the Gumbel Copula. We find rather larger differences than in the case of F2D and S2D products. Figure 25.1 and 25.2 show the impact of changing correlation and Copula under the two cases where

(1) the reference entity hazard rate is greater than the counterparty hazard rate
(2) the reference entity hazard rate is less than the counterparty hazard rate.

Note that all three Copulae agree at the 0 and 100% correlation limits. The Normal Copula approaches the 100% correlation limit more rapidly than the other two – from about the 75% area there is a significant divergence in trend and values emerging.

Since recovery is unknown the actual values will be a blend of the above two results as described earlier.

25.5   COLLATERALISED DEALS AND CDS BOOK MANAGEMENT

Typically risky counterparties will be subject to a collateralisation and netting agreement. This will remove mark-to-market exposures as spread levels change, but does nothing to eliminate the theoretical jump risk.

Pricing

Table 25.4 compares the premium for an uncollateralised deal on a 600 bp reference entity from a 160 bp counterparty, with those for a collateralised trade. The results are displayed in

Table 25.4   CDS premia from a risky counterparty: collateralised and uncollateralised deals

Correlation	Uncollateralised deal	Collateralised deal
0	600	600
0.1	594	599.5
0.2	584	598.5
0.3	574	596.5
0.4	563	593
0.5	553	587
0.6	543	579
0.7	537	569
0.8	539	556
0.85	544	546
0.9	556	540
0.95	578	546
0.99	600	600

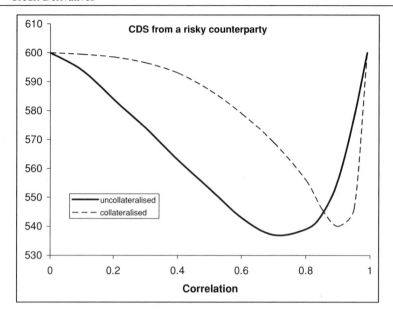

Figure 25.3   CDS premia from a risky counterparty: collateralised and uncollateralised deals

the table and Figure 25.3. Calculations have been done assuming that a collateralised position is equivalent to a rolling two-week uncollateralised deal.

It makes sense that the premium for a collateralised deal should be closer to the premium from a risk-free counterparty – but why was this not the case at high correlations? Embedded in the Normal Copula model is a correlated spread model: spreads can widen-out together, and can widen a long way or can narrow together. The latter must occur more frequently since the narrowing is limited and the expected forward spread is fixed. If spreads widen then collateral is received, and if the counterparty defaults there is a loss on the position because the reference entity spread jumps – but in this case the jump in market value of the CDS is from a wide spread and is limited by the recovery rate. On the other hand, if spreads have narrowed, capital is paid to the counterparty, and if the counterparty then defaults there is a large loss on the CDS position as the reference entity spread jumps from a narrow value.

It should be borne in mind that market prices for CDS contracts relate to deals between professional counterparties – low-risk names and with a collateral agreement in place. Different industry F2D swaps tend to have implied correlations below the 40% level – so the market CDS for, say, an auto reference entity written by a bank will be indistinguishable from the risk-free CDS premium. Where there is strong correlation – banks writing CDS on banks, for example – this will not be the case even for low-risk counterparties.

Book Management

There are two aspects to the risk assessment of trades on the books taking counterparty risk into account. The first is pricing and valuation of the deals. In applying the methodology described above, counterparty jump risk is explicitly taken into account. Valuation is forward looking and reflects the expected value of the deal to the books, but does nothing to report counterparty risk.

The second aspect is monitoring (and potentially hedging) the counterparty exposure. The valuations above report the counterparty exposure synthetically via the hedge ratio. If the deal is off-market, then this value will be large – suppose we are long protection and the reference entity spread has widened out since purchase. For collateralised counterparties the deal hedge ratio will overstate the counterparty exposure since collateral will have been received. In these cases counterparty exposure needs to be calculated using a notional trade where the current market premium is being paid (equivalently reducing the hedge ratio by the collateral received). The counterparty exposure can then be obtained by adding the individual deal (counterparty) hedge ratios referencing that name. This exposure can either be charged for internally (a counterparty reserve) or protection can be obtained.

Counterparty CDS

26.1 PRICING

In Part II we looked at variable exposure CDS – related to interest rate swap or foreign exchange exposures. We now wish to consider default protection on the counterparty to a trade, from another counterparty. This might include protection on the exposure under an interest rate swap with a counterparty C1, or protection on the mark-to-market exposure arising on a CDS on a reference name N written by a counterparty C1, where we wish to obtain protection from counterparty C2. In the former case there is (assumed to be) correlation between the two counterparties only. In the latter case there are three correlated entities (see Figure 26.1).

The former case has been covered theoretically in section 25.3. The only material difference is the variable exposure under the default swap and the counterparties to this trade are likely to be highly correlated – typically banks or wider financial institutions such as insurance companies and hedge funds. The latter case is a three name portfolio. If the trade arises because C1 is 'risky' but C2 is a high-quality counterparty, then we may ignore the C2 risk and the deal becomes a variable exposure CDS with C1 counterparty risk.

In the general case if we think of correlated default times generated under the Normal model then:

(a) We may wish to use a two-factor correlation matrix to explicitly take account of the high correlation between C1 and C2 and the much lower correlation with the reference name N.

(b) If we generate default times T_1, T_2 and T_N, then a payoff under the contract arises if

   (i) $T_1 < T_2$ (the C1 counterpart defaults before the C2 counterparty),
   (ii) $T_1 < T_N$ (the C1 counterpart defaults before the reference name), and
   (iii) T_1 is less than the maturity of the underlying trade.

The payoff in this circumstance is the mark-to-market value of the CDS on the reference name. Valuation is then similar to other portfolio product valuation.

For item b(i) to be the case as often as possible we wish to choose a counterparty C2 whose hazard rate is considerably lower than that of counterparty C1. This is the case if its borrowing spread (or CDS premium) is much lower (intuitive), and if its marketable assets are less (non-intuitive). The latter means that the recovery rate is likely to be lower; hence the hazard rate will be lower.

26.2 COUNTERPARTY CDS (CCDS) BOOK MANAGEMENT

The bank's own counterparty exposures may be the first counterparty risks to be put in a separate book. Generally these are simple variable exposures with little or no correlation between the underlying variable and the counterparty.

Where the underlying contracts are not collateralised there is substantially greater exposure to the counterparty per trade, being the same as the exposure on a collateralised deal plus the

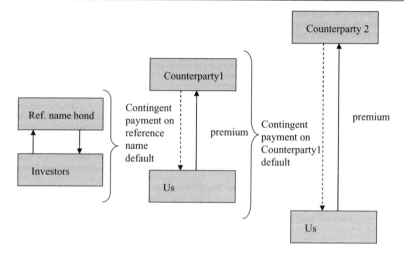

Figure 26.1   Counterparty credit default swap

in-the money value of the trade. As we saw in section 26.1, even collateralised deals still carry counterparty risk for two reasons.

1. If the counterparty fails it takes time to realise that collateral is no longer being posted on the deal, to verify why, and to take steps to close down the deal, declare the counterparty in breach (and set up a replacement deal if necessary). This time period will depend on the institution, but a period of around 10 working days seems to be a typical view of how long this process takes. During this period the market is moving. If (not very conservatively) we assume that the variable driving the value of the underlying contract moves on a random walk, then we anticipate $\sqrt{(10/250)} = 20\%$ of the annual volatility: not insignificant.
2. If the counterparty and the underlying variable are correlated, then default of the counterparty may cause a jump in the related variable and a sudden large movement in the exposure. For example, if the underlying contract is itself a CDS then, according to the correlated default time model, a default of the counterparty causes a jump in the hazard rate on the correlated reference entity.

Collateralised deals (and uncollateralised deals) are subject to possibly significant jump risk. Thus the CCDS book shares risks of the correlation book (correlated name jump risk) together with the vanilla CDS book (significant name exposure).

The second step is to seek protection on the net exposure to these counterparties. This may be crude, based on the maximum (estimated) exposure over the life of the trades, or may be a true variable exposure driven by the actual variable and unknown exposures on the underlying deals.

Risk management procedures appropriate to the correlation book and the CDS book should both be applied. In addition to measuring the single name exposures, the jump risk (on CDS underlyings) can be measured on each trade by looking at default simulations in which the counterparty defaults in the near term, and finding the value of the remaining exposure at the default date of the counterparty. Different underlyings (for example, interest rates, exchange rates, or equity values) need a model of the jump risk between the reference entity default and the underlying. In the case of interest rates and exchange rates this will typically be zero, and equity underlyings can be analysed with the same correlated default model as CD products.

These CCDS contain strong correlation between the counterparty who writes protection (C2) and the counterparty to the underlying deal (C1) – in addition to further possible correlation with the underlying asset or reference name. This strong correlation means that counterparty (C1) exposure will be significant during the life of the trade whether the deal is collateralised or not. The objective within the book is to minimise counterparty exposure but, because of the strong correlation, it is never going to be possible to eliminate this. The conclusion is that the CCDS does not form a complete alternative to good counterparty risk management through diversification.

The Future for Credit Derivatives

In many ways the current developments in credit derivatives echo those of five to 10 years ago, and developments are likely to continue in the following areas for the foreseeable future.

27.1 AREAS OF DEVELOPMENT

Documentation

Standardisation of the CDS contract documentation continues, with debate over 'restructuring' probably not finally settled. The introduction of an ISDA standard format for nth-to-default products in part recognises the higher volume in these deals and will reinforce the product base. A missing area is CDO documentation. The iTraxx (and other standard CDO) products effectively set a standard for tranches of synthetic static CDOs. Documenting managed or cashflow CDOs is likely to remain in the realm of the structurer.

Processing

The top 15 banks currently (Q3 2004) average about 3000 CDS trades per month with a few banks averaging double that figure. The strain on infrastructure is significant and, if not fixed, will hold back the exponential growth in the market for credit derivatives. One of the major contributions to fixing this is a reduction in the need to generate confirmations. The Depository Trust & Clearing Corporation (DTCC) has introduced an electronic clearing service for CDS confirmations to provide automated, real-time matching and confirmation for all standard single reference entity credit default swaps (including North American, European, Asian corporate credits, and sovereign credits), as well as credit default swap indices. An alternative service is provided by SwapsWire.

Basle II

The introduction of a revised international capital framework based on a better identification of risk is now not expected until late 2007, but will carry substantial implications for banks. Realisation that regulatory capital will have to be actively managed will most likely result in a significant new supply of credit risk via credit derivatives. The growth in the market, and expansion of the investor base, should provide an efficient means of distributing and diversifying this risk.

Data

Lack of data has hampered liquidity both for traders and investors who need to be able to monitor their portfolios and mark to market. The development of data resources and, in particular, engineered data to provide continuous independent time series of CDS curves is vital to both groups of users. Data has primarily been for the most liquid investment grade, and emerging market entities, but has started to expand into the high-yield names. Structuring of large portfolios inevitably requires the estimation of CDS premia for many illiquid names. Independent estimates of the spread curve data (for both senior debt and loan-based CDSs) – at least on a portfolio basis by industry sector, geography, and some measure of risk (as a proxy for rating when it does not exist) – would be helpful.

The reference entity database (Mark-it RED) has been a helpful development for deal documentation and will continue to expand its coverage.

Products

Although the basic product range has been largely unchanged for 10 years, there have been many developments of detail, some of which are not yet concluded.

1. The introduction of IMM style maturity dates for CDS has increased liquidity and is now largely copied in the portfolio product area (apart from client-driven deals).
2. The pace of development of standard credit portfolios and indices, together with increased trading on these portfolios and both F2D and CDOs based on them, has increased dramatically over the last two years – and shows no sign of abating.
3. Options on indices (and CDO tranches) are relatively new products and, as yet, have not seen a great deal of investor response.
4. New convexity and correlation products may appear – driven by portfolio differences (name convexity) or tranche differences (correlation convexity).
5. Single name product ideas continue to come forward – equity CDSs and constant maturity CDSs, for example.

Further development of credit index products – perhaps related to mortgage, loan or equity portfolios, as well as the expansion of the CDS indices geographically – is to be expected.

27.1.1   Market Growth and Investors

The credit derivatives market has recently survived perhaps the most dramatic period in terms of numbers of defaults, the sizes of those defaults, and the accompanying swings in credit spreads, in the history of credit trading. In spite of these traumatic events the market has continued to grow rapidly in percentage terms, although it is still only a small fraction of the size of the interest rate swap market. Investment banks have recently ceded their position as the majority player in the market, and hedge funds have increased their role dramatically, but the key missing player remains the corporate treasurer. Continued development in the size and liquidity of the market, with a consequent reduction in the costs of dealing in credit risk, remains essential to getting the involvement of the corporate treasurer. Further product development to handle the specific nature of the corporate treasurer's risks is also needed.

A combination of investor swings away from equities and government bonds, an asset reallocation in favour of debt by mutual funds, and a change in fund mandates to authorise the use of credit derivatives, all point to a rapidly growing pile of cash looking for a home in structured credit products. Mutual funds and other 'real money accounts' are new and rapidly growing participants in the credit derivatives market, stimulating new and repackaged products, and causing credit derivatives to enter the retail product marketplace in Australia and New Zealand recently.

27.1.2   Methodologies

The recognition of the Normal Copula model for the CDO market as the equivalent of the 'Black–Scholes' model for the equity market, together with the development of the concept of implied correlation, has given all the players in the market a common language for communication. The model and its implementation have problems that will hamper market development until they are resolved.

1. There are a variety of approaches to base correlation, as a means of handling multiple implied correlations for certain CDO tranches.
2. Spread volatility needs to be incorporated in a realistic way, but one that is consistent with the Copula default time model.
3. VaR methodologies generally lag behind the development of pricing models and are usually inconsistent with the latter. For portfolios, use of a correlated transition matrix approach is not widespread, yet can be consistent with market data if the transition matrix is calibrated to that data. In addition, efficient means of handling correlation for large portfolios are not well understood.

27.1.3   Hedging and Risk

1. An understanding of correlation risk is crucial to the development of a secure risk management process. The recognition that not all correlations are the same (F2D and junior CDO tranche, junior and senior CDO tranches), so certain correlation risks cannot be 'hedged' with certain other correlation risks, has led to a bucketing approach to correlation risk. Principal component analysis of correlation is in an early stage of development and primarily requires a longer high-quality history of the correlation 'smile' for progress to be made.
2. Embedded convexity risks – primarily in portfolio products – are also an area where improved data will go hand in hand with theoretical development. Credit risk continues to pose interesting challenges through correlated jump processes.
3. Recovery risks are greater in portfolio products, and more naturally give risk to digital risk when portfolios are embedded in credit-linked notes. A more thoughtful approach to measuring the recovery risk, both its expected level per name and the unexpected recovery risk per name, is needed for portfolio products.

27.2   CONCLUSION

Ten years of rapid growth has seen the credit derivatives market increase greatly in size and mature from a very illiquid and poorly arbitraged market to one where there is an accepted range of standard products, narrow prices and, increasingly, accepted methods for the valuation of these derivatives. Single name default swaps and standardised portfolio credit derivatives have become the core products of the industry and ones where it is often possible to obtain 'choice' prices. The market has matured to the level where volume growth – and particularly expansion of client coverage – should take the market through another 10 years of dramatic growth.

Appendix
iTraxx Indices

The following is quoted from International Index Company's 'General Presentation', June
2004 (www.indexco.com and click 'DJ iTraxx CDS').

PRODUCT DESCRIPTIONS

DJ iTraxx Europe

Portfolio Composition

- A static portfolio of 125 equally weighted credit default swaps on European entities
- Rules based construction based on CDS volumes by Dealer Poll
- Administered by the International Index Company (IIC)
- New series of DJ iTraxx Europe issued every 6 months.

Rationale

- Highly liquid credit tool
- Highly diversified European credit portfolio
- Attractive to investors looking to diversify rather than track
- Attractive to investors looking for European only exposure.

Market Participants

- Bank Portfolio Managers
- Diversify into European credit risk
- Portfolio balancing tool
- Insurance
- Proxy hedge against senior CDO credit portfolio
- Corporate Treasury
- Enhanced access to diversified European credit risk
- Credit Correlation Trading Desks
- Attractive tool for portfolio hedging
- Easy 'ramp-up'.

Terms and Conditions

- Tradable in CDS format or as a note issued by iBond Securities Plc
- Note will be rated by Moody's and S&P
- Standard maturities will be 5 years for the notes and 5 and 10 years for the swaps.

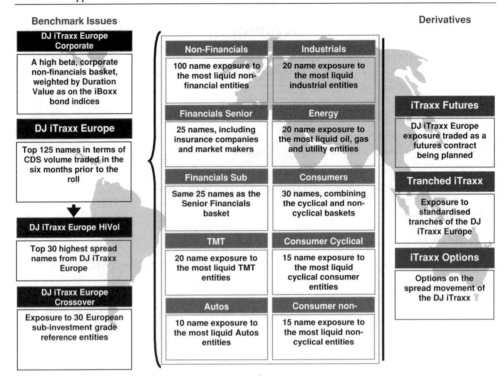

Figure A1   iTraxx product overview

DJ iTraxx Europe – HiVol and Sectors

Portfolio Composition

- DJ iTraxx Europe HiVol – 30 reference entities from the DJ iTraxx Europe with the widest 5-year CDS levels (as determined by Mark-it Partners)
- DJ iTraxx Sectors – baskets of CDS taken from the DJ iTraxx Europe, providing exposure to the following sectors:
  - Non-financials
  - Financials Senior
  - Financials Sub
  - TMT
  - Autos
- Administered by IIC
- New series issued every 6 months.

Rationale

- Highly liquid credit tool
- HiVol provides higher volatility, higher return and higher beta than the iTraxx Europe
- Sector baskets provide for relative value trading opportunities.

Market Participants

- Hedge Funds
  - Relative value trading (name vs sector, sector vs sector, sector vs benchmark)
  - Discreet trading – avoid revealing trading strategies
- Bank Proprietary Desks
- Corporate Treasury
  - Sectors can be appropriate for new issue spread hedging.

Terms and Conditions

- Tradable in CDS format only
- Standard maturities will be 5 and 10 years for the swaps.

DJ iTraxx Europe Crossover

Portfolio Composition

- A static equally weighted portfolio of 30 European crossover credits
- Reference entity ratings will be no better than Baa3/BBB− with negative outlook
- Rules based construction via dealer poll
- Administered by IIC and Mark-it Partners.

Rationale

- Highly liquid crossover credit tool
- Highly volatile corporate credit instrument offering high returns.

Market Participants

- Hedge Funds
- Bank Proprietary Desks
  - With high volatility and liquidity, maximise outright corporate credit views.

Terms and Conditions

- Tradable in CDS format or as a note issued by iBond Securities Plc
- Note will be rated by S&P
- Standard maturities will be 5 years for the notes and 5 and 10 years for the swaps.

RULES OF CONSTRUCTION

A. DJ iTraxx Europe

- Each market maker submits a list of 200 to 250 names, by Bloomberg Corporate Ticker, based on the following criteria:
  - European listed
  - Those names with the highest CDS trading volume, as measured over the previous 6 months

- Volumes for financial names are collated from Subordinated (Lower Tier 2) transactions
- Exclude all internal transactions from the volume statistics, e.g. those with an internal prop desk.
- Volumes for names which fall under the same Bloomberg Corporate Ticker, but trade separately in the CDS market, are summed to arrive at an overall volume for each issuer.
- The list is ranked according to trading volumes, i.e. the issuer with the highest trading volume first, and submitted in the form of Bloomberg Corporate Ticker only.
- The Administrators will collate all submitted lists and remove any names rated Baa3/BBB− and with negative outlook.
- Each issuer is assigned an appropriate Dow Jones sector.
- Each issuer is then mapped to an iTraxx sector and then ranked within its sector by averaging the votes cast by the market-makers.
- The final portfolio will comprise 125 issuers, and will be constructed by selecting the highest ranking issuers in each sector, according to the schedule below:
  - 25 Financials
  - 20 Energy
  - 20 Industrials
  - 20 TMT
  - 15 Consumer Cyclical
  - 15 Consumer Non-cyclical
  - 10 Autos
- For example, the 20 highest ranking Energy issuers, and the 25 highest ranking Financials will be included.
- For each issuer (Bloomberg Corporate Ticker) the most liquid CDS reference entity is assigned
  - e.g. INTNED would be ING Bank NV
  - e.g. FRTEL would be France Telecom.
- Each reference entity in the portfolio will have an equal weighting of 0.8%.

B. DJ iTraxx Europe HiVol

- Select the DJ iTraxx Europe reference portfolio.
- Extract the 30 reference entities with the widest 5-year credit default swap spreads.
- The spreads will be determined by the Administrators from spreads submitted by the market-makers on a specified date.
- Each reference entity in the portfolio will be weighted equally to two decimal places.
- If the sum of these weights does not equal 100%, then the difference will be adjusted as follows:
  - If the total is greater than 100%, then increments of −0.01% will be set.
  - If the total is less than 100%, then increments of +0.01% will be set.
  - The reference entities in the portfolio will be put into alphabetical order.
  - An increment will be added to each name (in alphabetical order) until the total weight of the portfolio is 100%.

C. DJ iTraxx Europe Crossover

- Construction via dealer poll, administered by IIC during the first trading week of the roll month.

- Each market-maker submits a list of at least 30 entities, based on the following criteria:
  - European non-financial entities.
  - Entities which have a rating no better than Baa3/BBB− with negative outlook (one of Moody's or S&P rating).
  - Entities with a minimum spread of twice the DJ iTraxx Europe Non-Financial spread and a maximum of 1250 bp, or up-front of 35%.
  - Entities with more than € 100m publicly traded bonds.
- Affiliates of an entity included in the Index that are already guaranteed by that entity are eliminated.
- Non-guaranteed wholly-owned subsidiaries of an entity are eligible.
- Those entities receiving the greatest number of votes are included in the Index until the Index totals 30 entities.
  - If on the final iteration there are, for example, two places to fill in the portfolio but four possible entities (with the same number of votes) to choose from, each market-maker will give an order of preference for that list of entities to be included in the new Index.
  - Those entities preferred by the greatest number of market-makers are added to the Index until the new Index totals 30.
  - After the poll, each market-maker will submit to the Administrator the fixed rate for the Index. The average of these spreads rounded up to the nearest 5 basis points will be the fixed rate.

References

Altman, E.I. and Kishore, V.M. (Nov./Dec. 1996) 'Almost everything you wanted to know about recoveries on defaulted bonds', *Financial Analysts Journal*, pp. 57–63.

Altman, E.I., Resti, A. and Sironi, A. (2003) *'Default recovery rates in credit risk modeling: A review of the literature and empirical evidence'* (to appear).
Available on www.stern. nyu.edu/salomon/creditdebtmarkets/S-CDM-03-11.pdf

Anderson, N., Breedon, F. and Deacon, M. (1996) *Estimating and Interpreting the Yield Curve.* John Wiley & Sons.

Anderson, L., Sidenius, J. and Basu, S. (Nov. 2003) 'All your hedges in one basket', *Risk*, pp. 67–72.

Andreasen, J. (Jan. 2001) *Credit Explosives.* Bank of America Fixed Income Research Working Paper.
Available on www.ssrn.com/abstract=262682

Baxter, M. and Rennie, A. (1997) *Financial Calculus.* Cambridge University Press.

Bear Stearns (17 May 2004) *Credit Derivatives: Valuing and Hedging Synthetic CDO Tranches Using Base Correlations.*

Billingsley, P. (1995) *Probability and Measure.* John Wiley & Sons.

British Bankers' Association (2003/2004) *Credit Derivatives Report.*
Available on www.bba.org.uk

Chaplin, G.B. (1998) 'A review of term-structure models and their applications, *British Actuarial Journal*, Vol. 4, II, pp. 323–349.

Das, S. (2000) *Credit Derivatives and Credit Linked Notes.* John Wiley & Sons.

Das, S. (2004) *Swaps and Financial Derivatives: Products, Pricing, Applications and Risk Management.* Wiley Eastern.

Finger, C. (Nov. 2000) 'A comparison of stochastic default rate models', *RiskMetrics Journal*, pp. 49–73.

Finger, C. (ed.) (2002) *CreditGrades Technical Document.* RiskMetrics Group, New York.
Available on www.riskmetrics.com/techdoc.html

Fishman, G.S. (1995) *Monte Carlo: Concepts, Algorithms and Applications.* Springer-Verlag.

Flavell, R. (2002) *Swaps and Other Derivatives.* John Wiley & Sons.

Grayling, S. (ed.) (1997) *VAR: Understanding and Applying Value at Risk.* Risk Books.

Gupton, G.M., Finger, C. and Bhatia, M. (1997) *CreditMetrics Technical Document.* Morgan Guaranty Trust Co., New York.
Available on www.riskmetrics.com/techdoc.html

Hardy, G.H. (1999) *A Course of Pure Mathematics.* Cambridge University Press.

Hoskins, R. (1999) *Delta Functions: An Introduction to Generalised Functions.* Horwood Publishing.

Hull, J.C. (2002) *Options, Futures and other Derivatives*, Pearson.

Hunt, P.J. and Kennedy, J.E. (2000) *Financial Derivatives in Theory and Practice.* John Wiley & Sons.

Hyvarinen, A., Karhunen, J. and Oja, E. (2001) *Independent Component Analysis.* John Wiley & Sons.

International Swaps and Derivatives Association, Inc. (2004) *ISDA Market Survey.*
Available on www.isda.org

iTraxx: *Dow Jones iTraxx CDS Indices Europe.*
Available on www.indexco.com (follow 'DJ iTraxx CDS').

Jäckel, P. (2003) *Monte Carlo Methods in Finance*. John Wiley & Sons.

Jae-On, K. and Mueller, C.W. (1978) *Factor Analysis: Statistical Methods and Practical Issues*. Sage Publications.

Jarrow, R. and Turnbull, S. (1996) *Derivative Securities*. International Thomson Publishing, pp. 192ff.

Jarrow, R.A., Lando, D. and Turnbull, S.M. (Summer 1997) 'A Markov model for the term structure of credit risk spreads', *Review of Financial Studies*, **10** (2), 481–523.

Jorion, P. (2000) *Value at Risk: The Benchmark for Controlling Market Risk*. McGraw-Hill Education.

Joshi, M.S. and Kainth, D. (2003) 'Rapid and accurate development of prices and Greeks for Nth to default credit swaps in the Li Model', *Quantitative Finance*, Vol. 4, No. 3, pp. 266 – 275.
Available on www.rebonato.com/

JPMorgan (12 Mar. 2004) *Credit Derivatives Strategy – Credit Correlation: A Guide.*

JPMorgan (6 May 2004) *Credit Derivatives Strategy – A Model for Base Correlation Calculation.*

Khuong-Huu, P. (Dec. 1999) 'JPMorgan Masterclass: The price of credit', *Risk*, pp. 68–71.

Laurent, J.-P. and Gregory, J. (2003) *Basket Default Swaps, CDOs and Factor Copulas*. BNP Paribas working paper.
Available on www.defaultrisk.com/pp_crdrv_26.htm

Li, D.X. (2000) 'On default correlation: A copula approach', *Journal of Fixed Income*, Vol. 9, No. 4, pp. 43–54.

Mark-it Partners (2004) Taken from *Project RED*, and *Credit Pricing* marketing material.
Available on www.mark-it.com

Merton, R.C. (1974) 'On the pricing of corporate debt', *Journal of Finance*, Vol. 29.

Mina, J. and Stern, E. (2003) 'Examples and applications of closed-form CDO pricing', *RiskMetrics Journal*, Fall, pp. 5–33.

Moody's (1996) *The Binomial Expansion Method Applied to CBO/CLO Analysis*. Moody's Investors Service.

Moody's (1999) *Historical Default Rates of Corporate Bond Issuers, 1920–1998* Moody's Investors Service.

Moody's (2002) Moody's Investors Service.

Moody's (2003) *Moody's Approach to Rating Synthetic CDOs*. Moody's Investors Service.

Moody's (Jan. 2004) *Default and Recovery Rates of Corporate Bond Issuers*. Moody's Investors Service.

MoodysKMV: *Expected Default Frequency Methodology, and Implied Asset Volatility* Paper.

Nelsen, R.B. (1998) *An Introduction to Copulas*. Springer-Verlag.

Press, W.H., Teukolsky, S.A., Vetterling, W.T. and Flannery, B.P. (2002) *Numerical Recipes in C++: The Art of Scientific Computing*. Cambridge University Press.

Protter, P. (1995) *Stochastic Integration and Differential Equations: A New Approach*. Springer-Verlag.

Schönbucher, P.J. and Schubert, D. (Dec. 2001) *Copula-Dependent Default Risk in Intensity Models*. Department of Statistics, Bonn University.
Available on www.defaultrisk.com/pp_corr_22.htm (*see also* 24.htm)

S&P (2004) *CDOevaluator* (Credit Ratings – Products and Services; Credit Ratings – Analytical Tools and Software, CDOevaluator).
Available on www.standardandpoors.com

Tavakoli, J.M. (2003) *Collateralised Debt Obligations and Structured Finance*. John Wiley & Sons.

Taylor, S.J. (1986) *Modelling Financial Time Series*. John Wiley & Sons.

Xiao, J.T. (May 2003) *Tag Correlation*. RiskMetrics Group, Research Technical Note.

Index

Index compiled by Annette Musker